W9-ADU-117

BL1485
E38

RELIGIOUS OBSERVANCES IN TIBET: PATTERNS AND FUNCTION

ROBERT B. EKVALL

169335

The University of Chicago Press
Chicago and London

JUN 15 1972

Library of Congress Catalog Card Number: 64-23423

The University of Chicago Press, Chicago & London
The University of Toronto Press, Toronto 5, Canada

Copyright 1964 by The University of Chicago
All rights reserved. Published 1964
Composed and printed by
THE UNIVERSITY OF CHICAGO
PRESS, Chicago, Illinois, U.S.A.
Designed by Donald Kriloff

To the memory of Robert Redfield: scholar,
teacher, and friend. He opened my eyes
to the meaning of culture and urged me
to get to work. I am forever in his debt.

PREFACE

This book is an attempt to bring to life the religion of the Tibetans as a subjective response expressed in a pattern of behavior which makes sense in the context of their world view, as an answer to personal and societal needs, and as a profound influence on many aspects of the culture. The commonplace, everyday comprehension, acceptance, and practice of religion by the people are thus brought into focus and contrasted to the ideological content of that form of Mahayana Buddhism commonly termed Tibetan Buddhism. When so placed in contrast, numerous differences, in emphasis at least, between theory and practice become evident. It is practice, however, which is functional in a culture and thus the subject of this book.

The ideological content of Tibetan Buddhism has long been studied by a considerable number of scholars, and much progress is still being achieved along this line. It is in the shadow of such research, and with due and respectful reference to it whenever it becomes necessary to establish origins and the historical development of doctrines and practices, that this study of the minimal observances of a religion, and their functional role, is presented.

Stress quite naturally falls on current and observable, or verifiable, phenomena in the behavior patterns of a people. Thus, in the tradition of the anthropologist, oral expressions of opinion and viewpoint and descriptions of practices and events are more numerous, as ascribed sources, than citations from texts. Quotations in Tibetan, which are followed by a literal English translation in parenthesis, are in the colloquial—mostly from the regions of Amdo and Khams —the live language of a living people. The translations have at times been kept literal to the point of being solecistic in an attempt to retain and transmit distinctive Tibetan meaning and nuance. This is an experimental device, and quite possibly its value may be minimal.

In keeping with the attention paid to orally expressed source material and literal, if awkward, renderings of meaning, something of an innovation has been introduced in the transliteration of Tibetan into the Latin alphabet. The system corresponds to the one which is currently in use in the Inner Asia Research Project of the University of Washington, with three exceptions: (1) Upper-case letters are used for the consonantal components of those letters or combinations of letters which represent the essential initial consonant of a syllable. This is the letter under which the word is listed in Tibetan dictionaries and, with the exception of combinations involving the Tibetan "l," is the phonetically effective initial consonant. Prefixed letters, superimposed letters, subjoined letters, all finals—including penults when there is a final "s"—and the inherent vowel components of the Tibetan letters continue, however, to be written with lower-case letters. (2) The Tibetan letter called *A CHung* ("little ah") is written upper case, as shown, in those few instances when it appears as an initial, but otherwise, when it occurs as a prefix or final, it is written lower case. (3) The Tibetan letter called *AH CHen* ("big ah"), which occurs exclusively alone or as an initial, is written upper case, as shown. The addition of "h" in the compound accords with the somewhat explosive, or expirate, quality the Tibetans give it. A chart showing the letters of the Tibetan syllabary and the Latin alphabet combinations used to represent them follows on page ix.

Internal capitalization, as a device for identifying the important and phonetically effective consonant in a consonant cluster, has been used by a number of Tibetologists, but in a somewhat erratic and inconsistent manner. Thus it is only in its consistent application—for every initial consonant and for all components of the initial consonant—that this system is in any case an innovation. It has certain advantages of consistency and, by calling attention to the phonetically effective initial consonant, suggests the sound pattern of the syllable more clearly than the somewhat ambiguous form in which the consonant clusters of Tibetan spelling are now presented to the eye for the covert or overt vocalization which each reader makes automatically. By way of illustration, it is suggested that *brGyad* ("eight") has certain advantages—which every speaker of Tibetan will recognize—over *brgyad*.

As all syllables are capitalized, proper nouns are identified by underscoring, in the same manner that proper nouns are identified in Chinese texts. Strict Tibetan spelling has not been adhered to in the writing of well-known place names, such words as lama, and the names and titles of the Tibetan collaborators. In the case of the last, the transcription used in official documents, passports, and so on, will be used.

Some explanation should be given concerning the time context in which the book is written. The book was planned and much of the preliminary draft was prepared prior to the spring of 1959. Ad-

TIBETAN SYLLABARY

| Ka | KHa | Ga
But g when prefix,
final, or before final s | NGa
But ng when final
or before final s | Ca | CHa | Ja |

| NYa | Ta | THa | Da
But d when
prefix or final | Na
But n
when final | Pa | PHa |

| Ba
But b when prefix,
final, or before final s | Ma
But m when prefix,
final, or before final s | TSa | TSHa | DZa |

| Wa
But w when
subjoined | ZHa | Za | A
But a when
prefix or final | Ya
But y when
subjoined |

| Ra
But r when subjoined,
superimposed, or final | La
But l when super-
imposed or final | SHa | Sa
But s when super-
imposed or final |

| Ha | AH | i | u | e | o |

These are superimposed or subjoined to change the vowel that is part of the consonant; e.g., *Ka* with *u* becomes *Ku*, etc.

ditional data recently incorporated into the text have a similar time referent. Thus, throughout the book, the present tense is used in the treatment of the condition and practices current within Tibetan society prior to the destructive Chinese suppression of the Tibetan revolt. The aim of the book is to present a description and analysis of traditional Tibetan society prior to the enforced change which came with the all-out seizure of Tibet by the Chinese Communists. The events of these last four years are too imperfectly known, and the implications of all the changes which have taken place are as yet too dimly apprehended, to admit an accurate description and useful analysis. In any case, the theme of the book—Tibetan religious observance—is placed in the context of a "here and now" which existed prior to 1959, and the resulting analysis should be judged accordingly.

In the planning and writing of this book I am deeply in debt to many. I owe the most to the very large number of Tibetans of all classes and conditions who, during the years I spent among them, discussed and argued religious matters with me at great length. Their contribution, made in volume but all unpremeditated, is the backbone of what has been written. When I first began to think through to the theme of the book, I received stimulation and guidance from Antoinette Gordon, of the Natural History Museum in New York; and shortly thereafter the late Ferdinand Lessing, of the University of California at Berkeley, with unfailing generosity, gave me much valued help and criticism.

Three others who were in Berkeley for varying periods during 1952 to 1953—the Dilowa Huhtuktu, highest ranked living ecclesiastic of Mongolia, who had also spent much time in Tibet; Tokan Tada, the learned Japanese monk and Tibetologist, who had lived for a number of years in Lhasa; and Taktser Rinpoche, the brother of the Dalai Lama—were all variously involved in discussion of the plan of the book. By their comment—both in agreement and sometimes in disagreement—they helped me clarify and sharpen the conceptual framework within which the material has been organized.

And what was of decisive importance, the late Robert Redfield, of the University of Chicago, to whom I had shown the preliminary draft of the first three chapters, urged me on. On February 25, 1953, he wrote, "These pages promise a book of great importance. I like what I read in them very much." That endorsement had for me almost the force of a commission, and being newly placed under the aegis of the University of Chicago as a research associate in the Department of Anthropology, I was all ready to go to work. Then with great suddenness, I was called back on active duty with the armed services and for a number of years was kept very busy doing other things.

In 1958 the invitation to join the Inner Asia Research Project, which George E. Taylor, director of the Far Eastern and Russian Institute of the University of Washington, extended to me, again brought me in touch with scholarly interests, afforded access to an adequate library, and provided the leisure in which to resume work. I am profoundly grateful for the individual and institutional decisions and good will and the funds of the Carnegie Corporation which made this possible. Most of the material in this book was presented to the Inner Asia Colloquium in a series of papers, and I am indebted to those who were members of that seminar from 1958 to 1962 for the benefit derived from their discussion and criticism and for many helpful individual suggestions. I am particularly grateful to Hellmut Wilhelm for his patient willingness to read numerous drafts and for his constant and judicious encouragement. The presence of indigenous Tibetan scholars at the University of Washington since the fall of 1960, which was made possible by a grant from the Rockefeller Foundation, is another circumstance for which I am profoundly grateful. All of the Tibetans have provided valuable information. Those who were particularly involved are identified, and the manner in which their help has been utilized is given in some detail in the following explanation concerning the specific sources of the data for this book and how they are cited.

Reference to and description of current phenomena, and much of the expressed opinion concerning such phenomena, are based primarily on personal observation and experience during the more than eight years (1926–1927, 1929–1935, and 1939–1941) I spent among the Tibetans of Amdo—the northeastern portion of ethnic Tibet. I lived and traveled quite widely among both the nomadic pastoralists and the sedentary agriculturalists and spent several years in residence at a Tibetan monastic center consisting of two large monasteries of the Yellow sect, with twelve- and eight-hundred monks respectively. My work as missionary—which increasingly became involved with medical activity, experimentation with the use of the colloquial as an acceptable literary medium, anthropological research and exploration, and even participation as peacemaker in local wars and conflicts with the Chinese—put me in close contact and communication with all classes of Tibetans.

On-the-spot observations, which at first were limited to local conditions, were extended by travel over a wide area. These observations were supplemented by constant questioning of Tibetans who, as wanderers, refugees, pilgrims, traders, and officials on the move, reported conditions from other regions of Tibet. The officers and officials of the regime of Ma P'u-fang, the war-lord governor of Ch'ing-hai, and the Moslem traders who ranged widely over certain areas of ethnic Tibet were also, in many instances, valuable sources of information.

Most of the subject matter of this book, which was first based on the recording of personal observation, has since been reviewed substantively by being submitted for discussion, emendation, and elaboration to four indigenous Tibetan scholars. All four are qualified to speak with impressive authority on matters of religion, for they have had intensive monastic training, and all four are *sPrul sKu* ("emanation-body") lamas. Taktser, currently better known as T. J. Norbu, brother of the Dalai Lama and former abbot of Kumbum monastery, represents and expresses the viewpoint of the now dominant Yellow sect. The other three belong to the earlier, at one time dominant but now much reduced, Sakya sect. Dachen Rinpoche is the titular religious and secular ruler of that sect and domain; Trinlay Rinpoche, his younger brother, is particularly well qualified concerning matters of Sakya history and doctrine; and Dezhung Rinpoche, the official tutor and man of learning of the Sakya ruling house, is a man of erudition and intellectual brilliance. They have all, in some degree or other, been men of affairs and, among them, represent three widely separated areas of Tibet: Amdo in the northeast, Khams in the east, and the two provinces of Central Tibet in the southwest. Three of them have traveled widely, and two of them have undergone a considerable degree of secularization through a variety of experiences and the roles they have played in national politics.

Their elaboration of the material provided, both in confirmation and in correction of the data from personal observation, much additional detail and precise formulation in Tibetan terminology. As a result, quite a number of changes and corrections were made. On the other hand, much of what they contributed was new, of unexceptional authenticity, and constitutes a most valuable addition to this book.

Thus the final text is based primarily on personal observation and the additional data provided by the Tibetan scholars to whom I owe a very great debt. These two sources will not be cited in footnotes except in the following circumstances: (1) whenever material already published, either my own or original sources cited by the Tibetans, constitutes significant substantiation or supplies important additional detail; (2) whenever there is significant difference of opinion among the Tibetan scholars; (3) whenever descriptions or findings are at variance with what has been recorded and are, therefore, controversial; and (4) whenever specific references or direct quotations in the text have been taken from other writings on Tibet.

Historical and doctrinal material derived from sources outside the two primary ones indicated above will be attributed in the usual manner. Repetitious listing, however, of all who mention well-known phenomena—for example, seeing Tibetans perform circumambulation—will be kept to a minimum to eliminate or reduce "nonsense footnotes" (I am indebted to Fang-kuei Li for this phrase). In any case, sources so slighted will appear in the bibliography.

In all probability this will not be entirely satisfactory to everyone; I am deeply aware of the personal mistakes in judgment which inevitably I have made and, in that awareness, crave the indulgence of all—specialists and others alike—who read the book which I offer to them, as Tibetan politeness requires, from my heart and in my two hands.

CONTENTS

CHAPTER ONE

INTRODUCTION:

ENVIRONMENTAL

AND CULTURAL SETTING

Any study of Tibetan society should be within the frame of reference established by a clear perception of the special nature and characteristics of that society. The state-society of Tibet is unique, in degree if not in kind, in that it is an operating theocracy or, more correctly, to coin a word, a doctrinocracy. *CHos* (religion), administered by a well-organized hierarchy, is the ultimate source of power and the final authority. The result is not a state-church but a church-state. Ecclesiastical rule is, however, combined with secular forms of control, surviving from kingly and tribal systems. Some of these systems are coexistent with the church-state, and in such instances, the control function is shared; but religion retains a preponderance of influence.[1]

It is extremely difficult, if not impossible, to make any investigation of such a society from a strictly secular point of view. Control devices and forms of organization have much of their origin in, and derive their sanctions from, doctrine and religion. Much of this is intentional and planned. But even when not planned, rites and observances (as subjective responses to the requirements and stimuli of religion), although directed solely toward religious purposes, also produce secular effects of far-reaching consequence. These latter are quite apart from the intent of the participants. The efficacy ascribed to such observances by those who engage in them is strictly confined to the religious and moral plane, but the actual observable results are frequently secular and worldly—contributions or accretions to Tibetan culture and forms of social organization.

[1] F. Grenard, *Tibet: The Country and Its Inhabitants* (1904), pp. 342–56; Shen Tsung-lien and Liu Shen-chi, *Tibet and the Tibetans* (1953), pp. 89–115; Spencer Chapman, *Lhasa, The Holy City* (1940), pp. 192–95; P. Carrasco, *Land and Polity in Tibet* (1959), pp. 78–84.

This study is not concerned with the Tibetan religion in its entirety but is focused on the subjective response, as expressed in observances, of the Tibetans to their religion. Objectively, religion is an aspect of culture —a part of the cultural whole—but the subjective response in its functional role becomes a causative agent that, in turn, shapes and modifies the culture. It also may be logically assumed that such response, whenever it is widely current and adhered to with a fair degree of consistency, meets or responds to certain fundamental individual or societal needs. Religious observances, therefore, make a substantial contribution to an individual sense of well-being, to the stability of the social system, and to the overall content of the culture. The underlying purpose of this study is to identify and describe the sources and the varied aspects of those contributions.

Religion, whether as an objective aspect of culture or as a subjective manifestation in observance rites, can never be investigated without some attention to the culture as a whole. The study of Tibetan religion is no exception, for although that religion occupies a position of greater importance in the culture than does religion among most other peoples or societies, it is still only a part of the greater cultural whole. And the cultural whole, in turn, should be viewed against the background of history and cultural relations. Due consideration must also be given to geography, climate, and race; for in cause and effect, these are linked with many aspects of the culture. Before we focus our attention on the here and now of Tibetan religion and seek to evaluate the functional role of the common, or universally practiced, religious observances in the whole of the culture complex, a brief summary of the factors of environment, race, and cultural history is in order.

ENVIRONMENT

Taking environment into account and seeking to assess the extent of its influence does not mean acceptance of environmental factors as decisive in shaping the cultural development of Tibet. That culture, however, even the non-material or subjective aspects such as religion, art, and drama, does exist, not only in time but in space. The mountains, plains, pastures, fields, and forests, however, are the setting wherein the people live and renew themselves generation after generation as they create and perpetuate their culture. Proofs of the close relationship between environment and the material aspects of culture are easily adduced and are obvious. Scarcity or inaccessibility of forests affects building techniques and the development of woodworking crafts. The characteristics of the steppe further the establishment of a pastoral mode of living based on livestock raising and emphasizing mobility. This manner of life determines types of dwellings, clothing styles, and all the material equipment of a pack-and-saddle existence. Again, the lack of large bodies of water, or the presence of specially unfavorable conditions where such bodies of water exist, precludes extensive development of boating techniques and the material equipment that goes with that activity. These and many more similar examples of a cause and effect relationship between environment and cultural development are obvious and need not be belabored.

The relationship between geography and climate and the non-material aspects of culture is less obvious, more elusive of exact delineation, and yet nonetheless real. Environment has a certain degree of influence on forms of social organization and on the development of institutions and the resultant attitudes vis-à-vis these organizations and institutions. The environmental influence appears at times to operate more or less indirectly, but it does operate and is potent. For example, the division of the population, mainly because of topographical and climatic conditions, into two separate segments with different but complementary subsistence techniques—a nomadic herding one and a sedentary farming one—results in extensive and almost universal trading. The dependence of the two groups on trading has fostered the development of trade routes, determined the seasonal movement of trade, created systems of value, and set patterns of behavior in trade associations, which, in turn, are linked with the assignment of status and accompanying prestige attitudes.[2]

The exact topographical or climatic factor which is the effective agent in the differentiation of these two subsistence economies may vary, with a resulting difference in attitudes and behavior patterns in the interrelationship of these two segments of the population. If, as in parts of Mongolia and other areas of Central Asia, the limiting factor is the availability of water, conditions of intense competition and stress may develop, for the expanding economy of the farmers will seek to appropriate, in stages, available water—and thus land—thereby putting increasing pressure on the herders. Such agricultural encroachment on the pastures may take the form of marginal farming, which eventually will ruin the land for both groups. Under such conditions, hostile attitudes may become intense and conflict may develop. Then the symbiotic relationship and ex-

[2] J. Bacot, *La vie de Marpa* (1937), pp. 21–22; R. Ekvall, *Cultural Relations on the Kansu-Tibetan Border* (1939), pp. 77, 80, 82, 83. The three Tibetan scholars listed as collaborators all have sedentary agricultural backgrounds; yet they speak of the nomads in a manner which is close to adulation, assigning to them virtues and superior status in terms such as "excellent," "the best," "the real brave ones," and so on.

change of produce between the two groups, which normally is advantageous to both, may break down or, at best, continue under very adverse circumstances.

Where the limiting factor is altitude, as in most of Tibet, little or no conflict develops. The farmer cultivates the land as far up the mountain slopes as crops will ripen, and from that limit upward the nomadic herdsman exploits the mountain pastures, confident that no attempt can be made to plow and plant the upper slopes and steppes. If, as most frequently is the case, the sedentary population is an expanding one, it does not menace the nomadic way of life as an institution. Encroachment is not cultural, but results from population pressure. Surplus population moves from the sedentary to the nomadic; and in the process of becoming nomadic, it thereby strengthens that way of life and its distinctive culture.

It is with regard to the subjective, or non-material, aspects of culture —the arts, drama, and religion—that it becomes more difficult to trace and evaluate the influence of environment. Yet a chain of causes and effects does exist, and the influence of environment is a real one. It may operate, however, through factors that are not once but a number of times removed. Occasionally, as in the following instance, the origin of a complex of non-material cultural traits can be traced directly back to environmental or topographical factors.

In extremely mountainous regions two high points may be separated by a relatively short distance in space, but they can be linked only, if at all, by long circuitous descent and ascent involving the expenditure of much time and strength. To overcome this environmental factor, special techniques of voice projection have been developed, to attract attention and so to identify location, to control herds and flocks, and to transmit messages. The need for voice projection is met by combining powers and tricks of breathing that have been acquired from mountain climbing with the special acoustic conditions that result from mountain-slope wind currents and echo-producing formations. The techniques of voice projection have been carried over into varieties of yodeling and distinctive styles of singing.

A specific climatic factor may change or neutralize religious dogma. Thus the extreme weather of the Tibetan plateau, which makes agriculture impossible over large areas and necessitates the use of meat for food and the employment of skins and furs for clothing, has almost nullified, or at least greatly compromised, the observance of one of the accepted practices of Mahayana Buddhism: the preference for a vegetarian diet, which is linked with the prohibition against the killing of animals. Weather may be used to circumvent this prohibition in another way, as when garments are hung out overnight in subzero temperatures to get rid of the vermin that should not be killed. So the entire pattern of religious behavior should be studied against the background and over-all influence of environment. Such influence may be direct and obvious or indirect and hidden, operating through a long sequence of causes and effects.

Finally, we must ask, What is the influence of environment on the subjective quality of the Tibetan mind and spirit; what are the nature and intensity of the fears, hopes, desires, predispositions, and aversions which condition his reaction to the exigencies of life and the requirements of religion? Why are the Tibetans, in their religion, so power conscious, as evidenced by their receptiveness to Tantric Buddhism with its alleged demonstrations of magic and supranormal powers? In China, Korea, and Japan, Mahayana Buddhism developed along different lines; only in Tibet, or as taught by the Tibetans to the Mongolians, is it so concerned with thaumaturgic power[3] to such an extent that it dominates personal and communal activity. In the present poverty-stricken state of firsthand scientific investigation in Tibet, it is difficult to trace accurately the exact influence of environment on the temperament and character of the Tibetan; yet in linked cause and effect that influence does operate. What then are the characteristics of that environment?

The land is vast—not vast with human beings packed close in a mass one next to the other, but vast and empty, with only a sprinkling of humanity spread thinly over the high plateau and a trickle of human activity along the valley bottoms. It is more than fifteen hundred miles from the farthest Tibetan village in the east on the borders of China to the last Tibetan temple or tower in the west on the borders of Kashmir, and from north to south the width varies from six to eight hundred miles. In actuality this distance is multiplied by two factors: topography and primitive means of travel. Much of the country is high plateau—sixteen thousand feet and upward—where only those strong of heart may go, and in the far northwest this plateau becomes so high that even the hardiest Tibetans leave it to the herds of wild yak and kiang. Mountain passes, deep gorges, great unbridged rivers, and plains, which are either waterless deserts or vast bogs, multiply the actual geographic distances. Until the takeover by the Chinese Communists, no wheels rolled in the traffic of Tibet and, ex-

[3] H. Hoffmann, *The Religions of Tibet* (1961), pp. 54–65; M. Lalou, *Les religions du Tibet* (1957), pp. 26–34; G.-Ch. Toussaint, *Le dict de Padma* (1933), pp. 242–320; G. Tucci, *The Tombs of the Tibetan Kings* (1950), p. 65.

cept for a few rafts and skin boats on some of the rivers, all travel was on foot—either human or animal. Only in case of emergency, and then for no more than a day or two, would one ride on horseback forty or fifty miles a day. Most travel is paced by the slow movement of yak and sheep caravans, which average eight to twelve miles a day.

Not only do distances, difficult terrain, and the slowness of movement separate the people into small isolated communities, but individuals, too, are separated from each other and are much alone on the mountains and the steppe as they go about their concerns. In both India and China, millions nudge one another daily and never lose the sound of human voices as, in closely knit social institutions, they are held in a beehive sort of activity. But the Tibetan is much on his own and knows much of solitude, for he and his fellows are spread so thinly across the bleak, austere landscape.

Although Tibet is placed in latitudes which, were it not for the altitude, would make for a temperate or even warm climate, the Tibetan climate is extreme—a combination of many extremes of temperature, precipitation, and wind. Temperature variations of 80° and up to 95° F. have been recorded within the same twenty-four hours. Over much of the plateau an average diurnal range of 50°–60° F. is general throughout the year. In summer this will be from near or below freezing at night to 80°–90° F. in the middle of the day, and in winter from —20° F. or lower to 40° F.[4] It may be assumed that such constant and extreme variations must have a considerable effect on the human organism.

In the temperate zones a similar range of temperature change between the seasons, instead of within each day, is often cited as a factor favoring activity, and a correlation has been advanced linking the stimulating effects of such changes with the energies and capabilities of a people and thus the civilization they create. In rapid succession the Tibetan experiences extremes of frost, burning sunshine, storms of rain, pelting hail, and driving snow. What does this do to him? The question as yet has no categorical answers, but at least the question may be raised and this aspect of his environment noted.

The variation in precipitation, due to both geographical and seasonal causes, is also extreme. The northeastern and eastern areas receive more rain and snow than the southern and western portions of the country. In the extreme south, there is a very great difference within a comparatively

---

4 Sir Ch. Bell, *The People of Tibet* (1928), p. 7; G. Sandberg, *The Exploration of Tibet* (1904), p. 121; F. Grenard, *op. cit.*, p. 36; G. N. Roerich, *Trails to Innermost Asia* (1931), pp. 327-28, 436; H. Harrer, *Seven Years in Tibet* (1953), p. 65.

normal control devices and the exercise of thaumaturgic power. It may also be suggested that the extremes of temperature, constantly experienced, have a very special stimulating effect, which may be one of the reasons for the intensive, often compulsive, aspects of Tibetan endeavor once that endeavor has been channeled into religious observance.

All these factors result in living conditions which make great demands on the individual, for life is hard and hardship is universal. Even the possession of wealth does little to ameliorate the rigors of existence. There is no apathy in the Tibetan's response to the demands which his land, its climate, and his way of living place upon him. He values hardihood as a basic virtue and is consistently cheerful to an amazing degree. In any eventuality his primal and strongest impulse is to act, or react, effectively and fast. Anyone who has traveled in a mixed caravan composed of a number of Asiatic peoples will always have a clear memory picture of how much faster the Tibetans spring into effective action than the others.

RACE

Whatever effect geography and climate may have directly and indirectly on Tibetan culture, in its manifold aspects, the fact also remains that the bearers or possessors of a culture belong to a particular race, and to some degree the fact of race will also have its influence upon the culture. But this does not mean that we must yield completely to racial determinism. The Tibetans are Mongoloids, but from that point on much is controversial. Indeed even that statement has been challenged by those who saw in the mGo Log tribes a branch of the Goths lost in the heart of Asia;[11] and the Hor have been identified as Turkic.[12] As Mongoloids, however, they have many physical characteristics and some interesting similarities or parallelisms in material culture which point to a link with the Mongoloids of North America. Unquestionably, there has been some intermixture with Chinese, Mongol, and Turanian peoples; yet on the whole the Tibetan is a fairly distinct type, considering all the adulteration which has taken place by reason of the movements, migrations, invasions, and conflicts which have swirled around this high center of Asia.

Recorded anthropometric studies of the Tibetans are limited to a few observations, and there are only meager data concerning variation in

[11] N. K. Roerich, *Altai-Himalaya* (1929), p. 374.

[12] G. N. Roerich, *op. cit.*, p. 335; R. A. Stein, *Recherches sur l'épopée et le barde au Tibet* (1959), pp. 188, 189, 571; J. F. Rock, *The Amnye Ma-Chhen Range and Adjacent Regions* (1956), p. 93.

height, cephalic index, hair and eye color, hair structure, and facial characteristics. Such records as do exist[13] strengthen the impression gained
from personal observation of the Tibetans that they exhibit a very considerable variation in regard to all these characteristics. Because of this
range in type, the hypothesis that the Tibetans are a composite people
made up of many racial substrains, which, as refugee groups, were pushed
by stronger peoples into the mountains and tableland of Tibet, appears
to be a reasonable one.

CULTURAL DIFFUSION AND CHANGE

Considering the difficulties of travel, the great distances, the sparse
population, and the divergence in physical type indicated above, the culture of the Tibetans is strikingly homogeneous. But in the distinctive configuration of the culture we identify as Tibetan, we find unmistakable
traces of the influences, impacts, and pressures which, within historic
time, have molded and changed that culture. Tibet is uniquely the region
where the two great and competitive cultures of Asia—of China and of
India—have met and been syncretized. In other areas in Asia the line between the two sharply divides two ways of life, and there is comparatively little cultural exchange; but in the natural buffer region of Tibet
there has been an extensive mixing of the two. The mixture has been absorbed and contained, however, by the Tibetan way of life, which, with
great persistency, has retained its own distinctive culture pattern.

In mythology and legend, the Tibetans link the origin of their first
rulers and early forms of government with India[14]—an ascription that
should be accepted with considerable reserve. It may be that at some
point in history, or prehistory, there was an actual importation and acceptance of strong and gifted leadership from India. Moreover, since most
of Tibetan history was written within a religious frame of reference, there
was a pious impulse to ascribe to the "sublime land of India"[15] the origin
of all that was good and true. The rulers themselves probably welcomed
and fostered this impulse. Such ascriptions also served to buttress assumption and exercise of political power by a religious hierarchy.

The impressive borrowings from India in philosophy and religion are

[13] F. Grenard, *op. cit.*, pp. 223–25.

[14] E. Obermiller, *History of Buddhism* (1931), Part II ("Bu-sTon"), pp. 181, 182;
G. N. Roerich, *Blue Annals* (1949), p. 36; S. C. Das, "Contributions on Tibet," *Journal
of the Asiatic Society of Bengal* [hereinafter cited as *JASB*], 1881, pp. 211–12; *Kun
dGaa rDo rJe, Deb THer dMar Po* (1961 ed.), f. 15 *b*.

[15] *dPal lDan Bla Ma Dam Pa rJe bTSun Blo bZang Ye SHes Kyi gSung Las gSang
Bai rNam THar bZHugs So*, f. 2 *b*.

a much less disputable fact. And a very great cultural penetration took place when an adapted system of writing was introduced, along with religion, from India. Yet even with regard to religion, there was strong and competitive Chinese influence at work.[16] Topography had a rather distinctive role in this instance. The protective barrier of the Himalayas precluded any threat of military pressure to Tibet from India. This fact may have reassured the Tibetans and predisposed them to seek and accept freely from India what they acknowledged but grudgingly from China. Yet whatever was received from India was modified by the Tibetans themselves. The movement of trade, however, which follows the eastward tilt of the Tibetan plateau, and the ebb and flow of several centuries of warfare and struggle between Tibet and China, alternating with periods of precarious peace and feigned close relationship, brought to Tibet Chinese patterns of political control and massive borrowings of material culture.[17] "India," the Tibetans say, "is the land of religion; China the land of law."[18]

There was also impact and pressure from a number of other sources. The Mongols and the Dzungars from the north invaded the region and at different periods maintained direct or indirect control.[19] The Nepalese made their military might felt from the south.[20] Successive Chinese invasions led to long-term, but periodically fluctuating, Chinese political control,[21] which was mostly indirect and permitted a large degree of autonomy. But there was always, on the eastern borders, the unchanging pressure of the Chinese race-culture mass, from which the Tibetans had withdrawn both in territory and in culture.

In art forms, which by their very nature best exemplify combination and syncretism, Tibetans reveal both Chinese and Indian influences. As is

[16] G.-Ch. Toussaint, op. cit., pp. 235, 317, 333, 336, 337; S. C. Das, op. cit., JASB, 1881, pp. 221, 223, 227, 228; Das, op. cit., JASB, 1882, p. 3; P. Demieville, Le concile de Lhasa (1952), p. 22 et seq.; E. Obermiller, op. cit., pp. 185, 188, 192, 196; H. Hoffmann, op. cit., pp. 74–78.

[17] W. W. Rockhill, The Life of the Buddha (1907), pp. 209, 215, 217, 221; Sir Ch. Bell, Tibet: Past and Present (1924), pp. 24, 25; S. W. Bushell, "The Early History of Tibet," Journal of the Royal Asiatic Society [hereinafter cited as JRAS], 1880, pp. 445, 446, 467, 468; P. Pelliot, Histoire ancienne du Tibet (1961), pp. 5, 6, 21, 22.

[18] R. A. Stein, L'épopée tibétaine de Gésar (1956), p. 42, n. 4.

[19] L. Petech, China and Tibet in the Early Eighteenth Century (1950), pp. 8–54; T-ts. Li, Tibet: Today and Yesterday (1960), pp. 18–22, 31, 39, 40, 45; I. Desideri, An Account of Tibet (1931), pp. 146–65.

[20] T-ts. Li, op. cit., pp. 51, 52, 61; Sir Ch. Bell, op. cit., pp. 41–47.

[21] T-ts. Li, op. cit.; L. Petech, op. cit., pp. 55 et seq.

to be expected, art in western and southern Tibet shows more Indian influence, and art in eastern Tibet more Chinese influence. In some instances Central Asian influence is also apparent. But there is no slavish adoption from any of the sources, and Tibetan art has its own distinctive character.[22]

The linguistic aspect of Tibetan culture is complicated—but of great interest—and reflects the interaction of disparate sources and influences. On the basis of a generally held assumption that Tibetan is related to Chinese, the majority of linguists place it within the Sino-Tibetan family of languages. In common with those languages it appears to be basically monosyllabic,[23] in the commonly accepted dictionary meaning of the term. In the existence of a considerable number of homophones or words in process of becoming homophones; in idiom and some aspects of sentence structure; in certain principles of combination, whereby synonyms are joined for effects of nuance and emphasis and antonyms are put together to express abstract concepts; and in the appearance of a relatively simple tonal system in the dialect of metropolitan Tibet, where linguistic change has presumably been most rapid, the Tibetan language also exhibits numerous similarities to Chinese. It appears to have undergone change at a somewhat slower rate than the latter and in its current form seems to have phonetic characteristics once possessed, and since lost, by that language. Both eastern and western Tibetan dialects retain some vocalization of the prefixed and superimposed consonants of initial consonant clusters and of very many of the final consonants, either with much of their phonetic value or as glottal stops.

The language of the Tibetans was subjected to strong Sanskrit and somewhat weaker, though long-term, Chinese influences. Under these lin-

[22] M. Palis, *Peaks and Lamas* (1939), pp. 345, 346; G. Tucci, *Tibetan Painted Scrolls* (1949), pp. 271, 280, 290, 323–25; S. Hummel, *Elements der Tibetischen Kunst* (1949), pp. 5–51; A. Gordon, *Tibetan Religious Art* (1952), p. viii; C. Pascalis, *La collection tibétaine* (1935), pp. 8–45.

[23] W. Simon, *Tibetisch-Chinesisch Wortgleichungen* (1930), p. 1 *et seq.*; J. H. Greenberg, "Historical Linguistics and Unwritten Languages," in *Anthropology Today* (1953), ed. A. L. Kroeber, pp. 281–83; H. N. von Koerber, *Morphology of the Tibetan Language* (1935), p. 3; J. Bacot, *Les slokas grammaticaux de Thonmi Sambhota* (1928), pp. i–iv, 180–83; *Grammaire du tibétain littéraire* (1946), p. 7; M. Pallis, *op. cit.*, p. 221; R. A. Stein, *La civilization tibétaine* (1962), p. 211.

Although a familial relationship between the Chinese and Tibetan languages is sometimes questioned, and termed speculative, this assumption is in accord with my own experience of learning Tibetan by the oral method, which I approached from Chinese—for me a natal tongue. In the frame of reference of Chinese structural and semantic patterns, the Tibetan ones seemed like old friends and invited progress.

guistic pressures, a noteworthy characteristic of the Tibetan language is clearly in evidence. It is strongly resistant to, or inhospitable toward, loan words, showing a marked preference for translation, involving the creation of new terms, rather than transliteration. The results of this avoidance and bias appear very clearly in the effort of conceptualization and lexicographical improvisation which characterized the Tibetan response to the very great impact of Sanskrit, which took place when a system of writing, a grammar, and a religion, with its own vocabulary, were accepted simultaneously, or in close sequence.[24]

EFFECTS ON RELIGIOUS OBSERVANCE

From this very brief survey of the salient features of the environmental, racial, and cultural influences which affect Tibetan culture, the following propositions are suggested: (1) The demands made upon the Tibetan by the extreme and peculiar characteristics of his environment have instilled in him attitudes expressive of endurance, hardihood, and even cheerfulness and have forced him to act energetically and effectively. Yet he also has a sense of aloneness in immense solitude; he feels the threat of nature on the rampage; he has a sense of powers and conflicts in the supernatural realm and, as a result, has certain psychological predispositions toward the adoption of supranormal solutions for the problems of existence. To some extent, it could be said that his environment prepared him for the acceptance of the power-conscious and thaumaturgic forms of Buddhism which came to him in the Tantric school. (2) His acceptance and practice of this religion have been shaped by habits of energetic action and application to which he has been conditioned by the harshness of his environment. (3) The manner in which he observes and lives the Buddhism he accepted also reflects the influence of the two great cultural contacts of his history. In one of those contacts, the philosophy and mysticism of an Indian cult was accepted and its esoteric practices faithfully retained. The other cultural contact, which put him in close touch with the organizing genius of the Chinese people, placed its stamp on the *manner* in which he practiced that religion and modified it. He organized its philosophic teachings and mild contemplative practices into disciplined activity, and he created a system of very impressive solidarity: the great hierarchical power structure of Tibetan Buddhism, with all its drive toward assumption of monolithic control.

[24] S. C. Das, *JASB*, 1881, pp. 218–22 and *JASB*, 1882, p. 2; A. Csoma de Koros, *Alexander de Koros Memorial Volume* (1912), pp. 35–39; E. Obermiller, *op. cit.*, p. 183; Kun dGaa rDo rJe, *op. cit.*, ff. 16–17 a.

CHAPTER TWO

RELIGIOUS BACKGROUND:

PRE-BUDDHIST BELIEF

AND PRACTICE

The religion which an individual accepts and practices at a given point in time does not constitute his religious background. His religious background is the sum of the experiences and influences of the past which, in the present, condition his religious thinking and his responses. It is made up of both his own previous religious experiences as an individual—the personal history of his particular religious background—and the religious influences and religious climate of the cultural heritage into which he was born. He may have a more or less clear perception of his personal religious history, for such history is subject to conscious recall, but he is frequently unaware of the religious climate of his cultural heritage. He lives in it but is unconscious of its nature or its significance.

The Mahayana form of Buddhism, sometimes called Lamaism, which is the present-day religion of Tibet, does not constitute the religious background of the Tibetan people. It is now the religion of the land and bulks large in the foreground of activity; but it is not native to Tibet. It is an importation the circumstances and history of which are reasonably well known, for its coming coincided with—in fact, was the occasion for—the adaptation and adoption of a system of writing, and the keeping of records soon followed.

The period of the seventh through the ninth centuries was also a time of intensive and varied contact with China, and some information concerning the content of that importation and the manner of its coming may be found in Chinese historical writings.[1] Much more is recorded in

---

[1] Kun Chang, "Chinese Records of the Early History of Tibet" (unpublished manuscript using as sources: *T'ung Chien, Ts'e Fu Yüan Kuei, Hsin T'ang Shu, Chiu T'ang Shu, T'ung Tien,* and *T'ang Hui Yao*); S. W. Bushell, "The Early History of Tibet," *JRAS,* Vol. XII (1880); P. Pelliot, *Histoire ancienne du Tibet* (1962).

Tibetan religious history.[2] The importation occurred in stages, and at each stage the content varied, the emphasis shifting from doctrine and ethics to thaumaturgic power. The beliefs and practices which were accepted at successive stages in national history were also modified to meet the preferences of the people and the exigencies arising from Tibetan internal and external polity. By a series of involvements in the function of government, the religious organization which had developed, then achieved and extended control so successfully that, until the Tibetan revolt and its suppression by the Chinese in 1959, it functioned as the *sDe Pa gZHung* ("authority center"), or government, over a large part of ethnic Tibet and had vast political power and influence over those other parts of ethnic Tibet where indigenous or imposed secular governments existed.[3]

These numerous developments and changes, the record of which makes up ecclesiastical and national history, are subject to recall and examination and as religious history constitute the consciously recognized background of religion in Tibet. The influences, and that religious climate, however, which have survived in the thinking and practices of the people from the pre-Buddhist religion—or religions—of Tibet are much more difficult to describe and evaluate. Yet they form a background which has withstood time and change and persisted into the present, modifying the forms and practices of Tibetan Buddhism itself. It is difficult to state categorically, in a series of causal propositions, exactly how, or to what extent, this background overshadows current Tibetan religious observance. Yet it should not be ignored, and some appreciation of its nature is an aid to an understanding of Tibetan religious practices. Only by going back and seeking to reconstruct the religion which antedated Buddhism in Tibet may we apprehend somewhat the nature of a religious climate that has persisted from early times down to the present.

Little definite information concerning the pre-Buddhist religion of

[2] E. Obermiller, *The History of Buddhism in Tibet* (1931; a translation of *CHos aByung*, by Bu sTon); G-Ch. Toussaint, *Le dict de Padma* (1933; a translation of *Padma bKaa Yi THang Yig*, by SHes Rabs Od Zer). G. N. Roerich, *The Blue Annals* (1949; a translation of *Deb THer sNGon Po*, by gZHon Nu dPal); Kun dGaa rDo rJe, *Deb THer dMar Po* (1346); Sum Pa mKHan Po, *dPag bSam lJon bZang* (1748); Blo bZang rGya mTSHo [fifth Dalai Lama], *Bod Kyi Deb THer dPyid Kyi rGyal Moi Glu dByangs* (1663); bSod Nams rGyal mTSHan, *rGyal Rabs gSal Bai Me Long* (1508).

[3] Sir Ch. Bell, *Tibet: Past and Present* (1924), pp. 22–58; Shen Tsung-lien and Liu Shen-chi, *Tibet and the Tibetans* (1953), pp. 89–121; H. E. Richardson, *A Short History of Tibet* (1962), pp. 18–27; P. Carrasco, *Land and Polity in Tibet* (1959), pp. 78–206.

Tibet has been transmitted directly to us. No writing is known to have existed in the land at that time, and no indigenous records have been found. Such direct evidence as has been passed along to us, moreover, is fragmentary and blurred by the passage of much time and the shift in focus that results from cultural change. The specific statements about it, which occur in the Chinese annals or in Tibetan Buddhist writings of a later date, suffer a certain amount of distortion by reason of the alien—cultural or religious—nature of the sources. Thus the true outlines of that religious system are fogged by myth and legend.

It was, and is, called the Bon religion. However, the word "Bon" is a name, and therefore, since its meanings and origin are not known, it is not a definition nor is it descriptive. The word appears to stand alone in the Tibetan language, having no identifiable cognates and only two terms manifestly derived from it: (1) the compound word *Bon-Pa* ("Bon-ing"), for which a Tibetan–Tibetan-Chinese dictionary gives *bZlas Pa* ("to murmur spells");[4] and (2) the compound word *Bon Po* ("the Bon one"). It is, however, combined with other words to form compounds such as *Bon bsKor* ("Bon circumambulation") and *Bon CHos* ("Bon religion"). The latter is often placed in antithesis, as, for example, in the phrase *Bon CHos lHa CHos* ("Bon religion—god religion"), which may be shortened to *Bon CHos,* having the meaning "Bonism and Buddhism." *Bon* and *CHos* in this contrasting or antithetical sense occur in descriptions of the strife of doctrinal systems in the eighth century.[5] The substitution of *Bon* for *CHos* ("law") as the second entity in a *Bon* formulation of a triad suggests that originally *Bon* was the term for a doctrine.

It is possible that *Bon* ("Bon") and *Bod* ("Tibetan") derive from an original common source, for in Tibetan the final "n" and "d" are sometimes interchangeable. Indeed the Tibetan–Tibetan-Chinese dictionary cited above suggests, hypothetically, a certain interchangeability of the two terms, and Tibetan scholars agree that this may be so. On the other hand, in the somewhat archaic dialect of Amdo, the initial letter of *Bon* is pronounced as "b," but the initial letter of *Bod* is pronounced as "w." It may be, too, that the word *Bon* is a loan word from the ancient, but long extinct, *ZHang ZHung* language. In a Tibetan account of the work and problems of translation in the eighth century, there is an indication that Bon doctrine was formulated and recorded in that language.[6]

[4] dGe bSHes CHos Kyi Grags Pa, *brTSams Pai brDa Dag Ming TSHig gSal Ba bZHugs So* (1957), p. 565.

[5] G.-Ch. Toussaint, *op. cit.,* pp. 318–19.

[6] *Ibid.,* p. 311; H. Hoffmann, *The Religions of Tibet* (1961)., pp. 70–71, 108.

The religion called Bon which persisted down to modern times and which still exists supplies much evidence concerning the nature and practices of the ancient religion of Tibet, although the fact that the name tag Bon has been attached to both should not lead to the assumption that the two are identical. It is certain that the beliefs and practices of the current Bon religion are different from those religious beliefs and practices which existed before Buddhism was introduced into Tibet. Moreover, it is not certain that the word "Bon" referred to one unified religion, for there is some evidence (from sources which will be examined later) which suggests the possibility that the early religion of Tibet was not one unified system, or at least was unified and organized at a relatively late date, and originally consisted of a loose aggregate of regional or tribal cults which were sufficiently non-antagonistic to coexist and, when complementary, to lend themselves to combination and syncretism. Whatever the case may have been, it is the sum of religious traits which may be discerned in the early pre-Buddhist cults and the long past of religious belief and experience that make up an important part of the Tibetan religious background.

CATEGORIES OF SOURCE MATERIAL

The principal sources for data and evidence concerning the early pre-Buddhist religion of Tibet are (1) the Bon religion of the present; (2) Tibetan Buddhism, with special reference to those traits and practices which are manifestly foreign to Buddhism; (3) Tibetan religious writings; (4) Tibetan historical writings and fragments together with folklore and epic works; (5) Chinese historical records which deal with Tibet; (6) religious practices of neighboring peoples such as Mongols, Chinese, and Ch'iang, which are of particular importance whenever links of affinity or association seem probable; and (7) usage and change in the Tibetan language. These sources, in the order above, will be explored for whatever positive information or inferential evidence they may yield concerning the beliefs and practices which characterized the pre-Buddhist religion of Tibet.

Bonism, Buddhism, and Religious History as Sources

The Bon religion of the present day, in its typical aspect, is found in certain parts of Tibet, particularly in what may be called cultural backwaters, or areas of relatively greater isolation, where there are communities which consciously and purposely call themselves *Bon Po* ("the Bon"). They support a religious organization, complete with temples or idol houses, monasteries of a sort, a priestly hierarchy with grades and orders, and a vast ritual. Their monasteries, as centers for religious gatherings, are organized to administer religion to the communities in which they are located. In their internal structure, they are communes of those who are seeking to learn from their leaders and teachers how to achieve magical powers and to gain proficiency in the performance of magical rites.

The members of these religious communes have no interest in amassing *dGe Ba* ("virtue"), and in advancing along the path of the Buddhist eightfold way. Instead of the blue cloaks[7] which historically, and in modern usage, characterize the *Bon Po*, they may even wear the red robes of Buddhist monks. The vows they take are not Buddhist vows; but much of their ritual and even belief consists of obvious borrowings from Buddhism. It is equally obvious, moreover, that many of the original Bon doctrines and practices have been thickly encrusted with Buddhist characteristics. On the other hand, Buddhism itself has been so interpenetrated by Bon beliefs and practices that it is difficult to identify and extract with precision all the specific traits of the earlier system and label them as Bon and not Buddhist. It is equally difficult to identify original Bon beliefs and practices in modern Bonism.

When the two, Bonism and Tibetan Buddhism, are carefully compared, data concerning three kinds of beliefs and practices emerge: (1) those concepts or beliefs which manifestly are exclusively Bon in character, (2) those observable phenomena of religious observance in which Bon ritualistic practice appears to be a reversal or a contradictory perversion of Buddhist ritual, and (3) those practices which are shared by both, yet which in each religion have a difference in emphasis or frequency of occurrence and thus may be characterized as belonging, comparatively, to one or the other.

Of those concepts or beliefs which manifestly belong exclusively to the *Bon Po* and are a part of the system, as known historically and now practiced, three are of basic importance: (1) a dualistic conceptualization of existence and religion, (2) the significance of heaven in relation to the afterlife, and (3) the nature and role of gSHen Rabs Mi Bo ("gSHen-lineage man one"), or man of gSHen lineage, who is the reputed founder of the Bon religion.

A dualistic concept of existence is implicit in the bipartite classifica-

---

[7] *rJe bTSun Mi La Ras Pai rNam THar rGyas Par PHye Ba mGur aBum bZHugs So* (compiled in thirteenth century); R. A. Stein, *Recherches sur l'épopée et le barde au Tibet* (1959), p. 350; S. C. Das, "Contributions on Tibet," *JASB*, 1881, p. 211.

tion of spirit beings as *lHa nDre* ("god-goblin"); in the conflict between malice and good will that is revealed in the propitiation and coercion of spirit beings; and in the philosophical concepts of *Yod Pa* ("having/being") and *Med Pa* ("not having/not being") as aspects of existence.[8] These two last terms have been variously defined by Tibetans who, although not themselves Bonists, have discussed these matters with Bonist acquaintances, as the all-good and excellent versus the all-bad and evil, the observable or physical versus the metaphysical, or the real versus the void. Such definitions are themselves none too clear and reflect some admixture of Buddhist concepts; but they avoid the ubiquitous triads of orthodox Buddhist thinking and do make clear that *Yod Pa* ("having/being") and *Med Pa* ("not having/not being") are antithetical and that their formulation reflects a kind of dualism.

The significance of heaven, in relation to the afterlife and its goals, is much more clear and is both doctrinal and historical. In a cosmos filled with enduring conflict, escape is not by rebirth and eventual nirvana but, through the use of magic and the aid of the gods, in a sudden passage to the heavens and a very real bliss. The idea of a rope or passage device by which this escape is effected has persisted down to the present as the "seizing rope of the sky," which is one of the "heads" under which a horoscope is organized.[9] A Tibetan historian says of the Bon, "They desire to obtain a body in a happy heaven."[10] Another says, "There was a tendency among certain classes of the Bon to emphasize *gNam* ("heaven"), which once so prevailed that these Bon were called *gNam Bon*."[11] And Nel-pa Pandit says, "Because the Bon-pos adored heaven it was said that these books had fallen from heaven."[12] Other aspects of this preoccupation with heaven, or the heavens, appear in the historical and linguistic evidence that is examined in later portions of this chapter.

The third concept is that relating to *gSHen Rabs* ("*gSHen* lineage"),[13] the traditionally reputed founder of the Bon religion. The fact

---

[8] G. Tucci, *Preliminary Report of the Scientific Expeditions into Nepal* (1956), p. 25; H. Hoffmann, *op. cit.*, p. 104; R. A. Stein, *La civilisation tibétaine* (1962), pp. 209, 210.

[9] L. A. Waddell, *Buddhism of Tibet* (1895), p. 59.

[10] G. Tucci, *Tibetan Painted Scrolls* (1949), p. 715.

[11] *Ibid.*, p. 719.

[12] G. N. Roerich, *op. cit.*, p. 38.

[13] Helmut Hoffmann (in *The Religions of Tibet*, p. 25) has translated *Rabs* as "pre-eminent," probably assuming that the final "s" was a mistake in spelling. My

that in Bon iconography he occupies a place analogous to the one held by Padma Sambhava in the older, or Red sect, Buddhist representations, or the one held by *TSong KHa Pa* in the reformed, or Yellow sect, representations, does not mean that, like them, he is part of the system of emanations and manifestations of the timeless Buddhahood, but only that the *Bon Po*, in a defensive and competitive response to the practices of Buddhism, place him in that position as their patron saint or founder. That he is clothed in blue graphically indicates that he and his representatives and successors, like the *Bon Po* who contended against *Mi La Ras Pa*, have no place in the red-yellow fraternity. It is stated that he was born in *Ol Mo Lung Ring* in *ZHang ZHung* (southwestern Tibet).[14] He is variously called *gSHen Rabs Mi Bo* ("the man of *gSHen* lineage"), *Bon sKu* ("Bon body"), and *Bon gSHen Rabs gYung Drung* ("Bon *gSHen*-lineage swastika"). There is considerable evidence that the word *gSHen* may best be translated as "shaman."[15] Thus the founder of the Bon religion becomes "the man of the lineage of the Bon shaman"—a man uncompromisingly human, making no claim to be a bodhisattva but sure of his *aPHrul* ("divine magic"). Some Tibetans even claim that *Mi Bo* is a contraction of *Mi dPon* ("man-ruler"), which would link the office of shaman with the exercise of rulership.

He is the archetype and leader of all those lesser Bon shamans who in the past were said to come from faraway places such as Kashmir, Burma, the eastern end of the Tien Shan, the Koko Nor region, southwestern Tibet, and Gilgit.[16] In slightly cavalier fashion, they were characterized by the Buddhists as *Dur* ("burial") *Bon, rDol* ("breaking-out," or manifestation) *Bon, rTSing* ("mixed") *Bon, Hang Ral Gyi CHos* ("matted-queue religion"), and *gNam* ("heaven") *Bon*. And in still another context, they were divided into the following categories: (1) the *aPHrul* ("magic-manifesting") shamans who were god-possessed and manifested divinity and had the function of planting the rope which linked earth with heaven; (2) the *PHya* ("lots") shamans who forecast and read signs; (3) the *Dur* ("cemetery") shamans who officiated at funerals; and (4) the *sNang*

Tibetan collaborators insist, however, that the word is indeed *Rabs* and thus refers to lineage. This is in agreement with the meanings given in the previously cited Tibetan–Tibetan-Chinese dictionary (note 4 in this chapter), pp. 819, 821.

[14] H. Hoffmann, *op. cit.*, p. 86; S. C. Das, *op. cit.*, p. 195.

[15] H. Hoffmann, *op. cit.*, p. 25.

[16] F. W. Thomas, *Tibetan Literary Texts and Documents Concerning Chinese Turkestan* (1935), Part I, pp. 268, 293–94.

("enlightened") shamans who chanted and sang. The number of the latter divisions matches the four original clans of Tibet, suggesting that each of the clans may have had a special ancestral god or group of gods and differing rituals.[17]

One of the Tibetan religious historians states that there were three periods in the history of the Bon: the early, sometimes called *rGyu Bon Chab Nag* ("original black-dominion Bon"), the middle, called *aKHyar* ("erroneous"), and the late, called *bsGyur* ("turned"), which itself was marked by three stages. In the first period, the shamans were skilled in witchcraft and knew how to use magic to overcome evil spirits and flesh-eating goblins below, to worship the gods above, and in the middle region, to appease the *Sa bDag* ("earth owners") whenever the hearths were defiled. In the second period, one shaman was described as being able to travel in the sky mounted on a tambourine and in that way to discover mines by reason of his propitiation of the gods *dGe God KHyung* ("virtue-destroying Garuda-eagle") and *Me lHa* ("fire god"). He could also cut iron with feathers. Another could divine by using colored strings or by reading the marks on a "red" (human) shoulder bone. Still another was famed for his skill in conducting the funerals of those killed with knives or swords. The third period is described as the time of a progressive plagiarizing occurring in three stages: Buddhist doctrines were appropriated and restated to become the Bon religion of the present, or Bon doctrines were disguised in Buddhist terminology. Thus Bonism was considered "turned"[18]—one more bit of evidence that what it is today is not what it once was.

The blue-robed founder of Bonism, whether a historical figure or a composite archetype of shaman leaders who sought to maintain the ancient beliefs and practices against encroachment by aggressive missionary Buddhism, carried a sword or dagger as the symbol of his primary function, which was to kill selected victims, not only animals but also human beings, in propitiatory, burial, and divination rites. He was the *sKu gSHen* ("body shaman") or *Bon gSHen* ("Bon shaman") or simply *Bon sKu* ("body of the Bon"), distinguished from all the other shamans by the fact that he seized the victim and used the knife.[19] His unique

---

[17] G. Tucci, *Tibetan Painted Scrolls* (1949), pp. 713–19.

[18] S. C. Das, *op. cit.*, pp. 196–99.

[19] F. W. Thomas, *op. cit.*, Part II, p. 395; M. Lalou, "Rituel Bon-po des funerailles royales," *Journal Asiatique*, T–CCXL–3 (1952), 350.

power was derived from the fact that he was spirit-possessed and -guided: an oracle through whom a god spoke.[20] His mission and work are summarized in Tibetan religious writings in the following terms:

> He pronounced the nine-vehicle doctrine:
> To open the heavenly gate for the living,
> To abolish the gate of destruction for the dead,
> And to lead life to the path of gYung Drung (swastika).[21]

The second category of data concerning Bonism is the form of religious observance which is patently a wilful distortion or perversion of Buddhist ritual. The eight-syllable formula *OHm Ma Tri Sa Le Mu Ye aDu* has been substituted for the six-syllable mantra *OHm Ma Ni Padme Hum*. The meaning of the former, which is allegedly in the ancient, now extinct, ZHang ZHung language, has been lost. When the prayer wheel is used, it is spun to the left, or counterclockwise, instead of clockwise; and circumambulation is performed in the same perversely contradictory manner. The *Bon Po* have appropriated the *gYung Drung* ("swastika") as something distinctively their own; they use it in place of the *rDo rJe* ("thunderbolt") in their symbolism. This swastika is also a reverse one: the "fly-foot" ends of the crossed lines point counterclockwise, to distinguish it from the Buddhist swastika. In a similar perversity, they represent the *KHyung* ("Garuda-eagle") with wings inverted.[22]

This somewhat consciously antagonistic attitude, with its wilful perversions and distortions, toward Buddhism (which brings to mind the Black Mass of Satanic cults) suggests that these religious traits are a comparatively late development or reaction, resulting from the pressure brought to bear on the adherents of the more ancient cults when Buddhism became the religion favored by rulers and gained an influence on policy and rule.[23] To submit by accepting trait complexes and then to

[20] H. Hoffmann, *Quellen zur Geschichte der tibetischen Bon-Religion* (1950), p. 211.

[21] An-che Li, "Bon Magico-Religious Belief of the Tibetan Speaking Peoples," *Southwestern Journal of Anthropology*, Vol. IV (1948), No. 1, pp. 31–32.

[22] G. Sandberg, *Tibet and the Tibetans* (1906), p. 151.

[23] Helmut Hoffmann (in *The Religions of Tibet*, p. 98), after reviewing all presently available sources, sums up this process and the attitude which accompanied it as follows: "But all this developed in an atmosphere of hostility to Buddhism. Just as the mediaeval Satanist desecrated the Host, so the Bon-po turn their sacred objects not in a dextral but in a sinister fashion. . . . The Bon religion had become ossified as a heresy, and its essence lay largely in contradiction and negation." This accords exactly with my impression of present-day attitudes of the numerous *Bon Po* I met in eastern Tibet, with whom I discussed their religion and its relationship with Buddhism.

reaffirm individuality by reversing components of those complexes are somewhat instinctive reflexes of weaker cultures when fighting against aggressive stronger cultures; and much the same thing occurs when an older and less effectively organized religion is being pushed toward limbo by a new and stronger one. Thus the presumption is strong that the swastika, the six-syllable formula, the prayer wheel, and circumambulation had no place in the pre-Buddhist religious observances of Tibet.

Considering the differences in basic concepts, the historical record of intense strife between the two systems, and all the deep antagonism which finds expression in reversal and contradiction, the relationship of the two religions in present-day Tibet presents a peculiar anomaly. The *Bon Po,* by being "turned," accepting so many Buddhist forms and observances, and having so many of their own practices incorporated into Tibetan Buddhism, have achieved the status of *Nang Ba* ("within one[s]"). They, or at least the large majority of them known as "white" *Bon Po,* are accepted by the Tibetan Buddhists, although with a bit of the self-conscious distaste that accompanies the acknowledgment of an illegitimate member of the family.

This interrelationship is aptly illustrated in the way the circumambulation rite is performed by Buddhists and the *Bon Po.* When the latter are at Buddhist monasteries or shrines, they perform the rite, as an act of worship, counterclockwise and thus counter to the manner in which Buddhists are performing the rite. They meet, however, on the path without prejudice and without remark. In the same way, Buddhists, when they are at Bon monasteries, perform the rite counter to the performance of the *Bon Po* but feel no constraint or embarrassment.

The acceptance of the *Bon Po* as "within ones" and thus as fellow Buddhists can be ascribed to the manner in which they have formulated the Triad. For *dKon mCHog gSum* ("Rare-Perfect Three"), they have substituted the concept *gYung Drung gSum* ("Swastika Three"). Their swastika, however, is only a symbol; the concept is defined as the unchangeable and the permanent—the everlasting. For *dKon mCHog dGe aDun* ("Rare-Perfect Virtuous Assembly"), or the community, they have substituted *gYung Drung Sems dPaa* ("Swastika Hero Mind"); and for *dKon mCHog CHos* ("Rare-Perfect Law"), they have substituted *gYung Drung Bon* ("Swastika Bon"). But in their formulation of the Triad, they have accepted *Sangs rGyas* ("Buddhahood") as the first entity, linked, however, to the swastika concept—expressed as *gYung Drung Sangs rGyas* ("Swastika Buddhahood")—and by that acceptance are admitted to be fellow Buddhists. This formulation, moreover, is a good example of both the changes imposed by Buddhist concepts and the tenacity of the original conceptualizations of the _Bon Po_.

The third category of data concerning the pre-Buddhist religion is much more equivocal and difficult to describe. It is neither positive nor antithetic but comparative. It derives from concepts, rites, and observances which are common to both religions but which, because they show differences of intent, aspect, or emphasis, may becomes indexes of the differences between the Bon religion of today and Tibetan Buddhism. These differences are clues which point to the nature of the earlier religion of the land. They can only be studied comparatively, and are found in the following fields: (1) pantheon, (2) magic, (3) prayers, and (4) offerings.

The pantheon, most of which is shared by the two religions, is comprehensively summed up in the Tibetan bipartite term _lHa aDre_ ("god-goblin"), which clearly reflects a dualistic concept of existence. But a tripartite view of the cosmos is suggested in the existence of another system having three categories: (1) those above, the _lHa_ ("gods"), (2) those of the middle region, the _Sa bDag_ ("earth lords") and/or the _gNYan_ ("argali"), or strong ones, and (3) those of the underworld, the _Klu_ ("serpent spirits"), or Nagas.

Of these two systems, the bipartite one is probably Bon in origin and the tripartite one is probably Buddhist. Cutting across these two basic systems of classification are divisions of spirit beings into congeries of three, five, eight, nine, ten, twelve, thirteen, sixteen, eighteen, and so on, up to three hundred sixty. It is not clear, even in regard to the two basic classifications, which gods and demons belong in which category, for the categories overlap and contain duplicates or differing aspects of the same beings. As more Tibetan texts become available, it becomes increasingly evident, as both Guiseppi Tucci and the late René Nebesky-Wojkowitz admit, that the Tibetans themselves are unable to agree as to which gods and demons belong in which class. Tucci makes reference to a classification in an understatement which is almost Britannic—"one of the many attempts of Tibetan learned circles at classifying the extremely rich pantheon of their people."[24]

This uncertainty is particularly evident with regard to the indigenous demons, which, since the time of Padma Sambhava, have been undergoing conversion to, or subjugation by, Buddhism and have been changed from the implacable enemies of that religion into the _CHos sKyong_ ("protect religion"), or guardians of religion. The process is still going on with-

[24] R. Nebesky-Wojkowitz, _Oracles and Demons of Tibet_ (1956); G. Tucci, _Tibetan Painted Scrolls_ (1949), p. 717.

in the respective congeries, and individual spirit beings are being moved within congeries or promoted to higher ones as they make progress in the changes that are a part of the Buddhist theory of existence. The confusion as to which demons are converted and which are still unconverted is further compounded by the fact that there is much evidence to show that conversion to Buddhism is not regarded as necessarily final or enduring: *CHos sKyong* may perhaps backslide. In the prologue to the Gesar epic, Padma Sambhava is shown as concerned and greatly grieved because, although in time past he had bound the gods of the land by an exercise of magic repeated twice—here the Bon number appears—that subjugation was losing its force. Because the thaumaturgic tour de force had not been repeated thrice—here the Buddhist number appears—the native gods were stirring anew in rebellion, and someone was needed to reconvert or reconquer the demons of the Land of Snows.

The gods and demons which are most clearly holdovers from the pantheon of the pre-Buddhist religion—or religions—and thus which are most pertinent to this study, appear in great numbers and in intense activity. The most important of these are the *bDud* ("demons—black and personified evil"), the *gNYan* ("argali"), or strong ones, the *bTSan* ("fierce ones"), *aDra lHa* ("enemy gods"), *Wer Ma* ("furious ones"), *Sa bDag* ("earth lords"), *gZHi bDag* ("place owners"), *Klu* ("serpent spirits [of the water sources]"), or "Nagas," *AH Mes* ("hail ancient"), or mountain gods, *THab lHa* ("hearth gods"), and *PHo lHa* ("personal or tutelary gods").[25]

The Bon version of the shared pantheon is more populous—a vast swarm of primitive gods and demons. In general they have darker and more vengeful dispositions, for they exist within the context of a Bon dualism of unending conflict, a sense of struggle that is all pervading. Thus, as Bon deities filling the *lHa KHang* ("god houses") or *mGon KHang* ("lord houses") of the Bon temples, their basic savagery—draping themselves with human skins and bones, drinking blood, and tearing and crunching human flesh and bones—has been little softened by the ascription of benign Buddhist characteristics and "mild aspects." They and many other little-known sprites of cliffs, caves, groves, and mountain passes; gods of the storm, mountain top, or dark forest; or animals that have grown more powerful than man and boast wild strength are still outside the pale of Buddhism and are feared by the *Bon Po* and worshipped by propitiation and sacrifice.

As they face existence and all its problems, and the vast pantheon of

[25] R. A. Stein, *L'épopée tibétaine de Gésar* (1956), pp. 19 ff., 717.

spirit beings who are either beneficent or malignant but more inclined to wrath, and who swarm above, in mid-space, and in the depths, both Tibetan Buddhism and the Bon religion of today accept magic as an essential dimension of religion. This does not mean that Buddhism has been interpenetrated altogether by magic borrowed from the Bon religion. Magic is common to both. The Buddhism that Padma Sambhava introduced from the valley of Swat into Tibet was quite different from the Buddhism that has survived in south and southeast Asia or from the other forms which developed in China and Japan. Its Tantric school had already accepted magic and was greatly preoccupied with the problem of controlling and manipulating power by the use of ritualistic posturing, incantations, and systems of realization. The ascription of power to the spoken and written word and the use of appropriate thaumaturgic gestures and formulas—written, spoken, mechanically repeated, or represented visually—to achieve religious ends, coerce gods and demons, and control the elements are both intrinsic parts of the Tantric importation.[26]

Magic is thus an important part of the services both religions offer to the Tibetan community. But there are differences in the manner in which such services are offered and the uses to which these services are put. Though the monks and lamas of even the *dGe Lugs Pa* ("ones of the virtue-system"), or reformed sect, practice magic upon request, there is always present, unuttered, an excuse or deprecation of the need for using magic instead of relying on pure doctrine. Those of the *rNYing Ma* ("old ones") are more at ease about the use of magic—less apologetic—than those of the *dGe Lugs Pa* (reformed sect), but it is the <u>Bon Po</u> who are unabashed, uninhibited, and even exultant in the exercise of magic—they are the specialists. The orthodox monks and lamas bless individuals and communities (the benedictions are assumed to have magical power), pronounce protective spells against evil and disaster, combine magic with the use of herbs in healing, and foretell the future for those who ask. It is the <u>Bon Po</u>, however, who are preferred for such services.

There are long-haired wizards, variously called *Bon Po* ("Bon one"), *sNGags Pa* ("spell one"), or *AH Mes* ("hail ancient"), who specialize in trances, farsight into the future, exorcism, and especially, the power, known as "black," of casting curses upon individuals and communities to cause disaster, sickness, and death. These last are described with a wealth of anatomical and malevolent detail that is a specialty of the black <u>Bon Po</u>; violence, torture, and exuberant killing are reflected in the phraseology employed.

26 H. Hoffmann, *The Religions of Tibet* (1961), pp. 59–65.

The practice or incidence of states of frenzy, known to Tibetans as *lHa Babs* ("god–fallen-on"), *lHa aDZin* ("god-seized"), *aDre aDZin* ("goblin-seized"), *lHa Pa* ("god-one"), or *lHa SHon* ("god-ridden"), though common to both, is admittedly a Bon specialty and occurs most often in ceremonies of healing or divination. Those who make a business of it as mediums induce the seizures by a ritual featuring the use of spells, offerings, and special postures, costumes, and regalia. When in this state of possession, the medium shows signs of great physical strain: sweating, moaning, and having convulsions. He may also give astonishing exhibitions of abnormal strength by twisting sword blades into spirals and performing great leaps while weighed down by a heavy harness and helmet. He speaks in a different voice from his normal one, and his utterances are accepted as those of the god or demon by whom he is allegedly possessed. Whenever he is possessed by a goblin (*aDre aDZin*), he is thought to be held by and in communication with the ghosts of those who have died. Some individuals are subject to similar seizures without seeking them—and indeed, with great fear of them—so the practice has a compulsive or non-volitional aspect.[27]

Prayer is equally a part of both religions. Much of the verbal expression of religion by both Bon priests and orthodox Buddhist monks and lamas has in it so many two-way borrowings from both religions that it constitutes the undifferentiated mean and, when only heard or witnessed, could be taken as belonging to either system. The rhythmic repetition of the syllables in cadence and in a special tone, accompanied by percussion and wind instruments—among which a flute made from a human thighbone may be found—belongs to both. But there are specific manifestations of religious utterance which, when heard, can be instantly recognized as belonging, in intention and content, to one or the other of the two religions. Such manifestations are the extremes, the details of which emphasize the basic differences between the two and show no signs of having been influenced by borrowings. The writer has heard both, of a sort and in circumstances which admit of no misunderstanding.

When in a *aDu KHang* ("assembly hall") the *dKyil aKHor* ("mandala") offerings are displayed upon an altar, the *mDo* ("sutra") are being solemnly declaimed by the *THSogs aDu* ("assembly"), or monastery choir, and the sacred words are being reproduced both by being sounded

[27] E. Schafer, *Fest der weissen Schleier* (1949), pp. 149–65; N. Nebesky-Wojkowitz, *op. cit.*, pp. 417–43. The descriptions given by these observers, and a number of others cited by them, correspond in general, although details differ, with instances I have seen and with what my Tibetan collaborators have told me about these phenomena.

and by being scanned as the leaves of the books are turned, the Buddhist observance of *CHos aDon* ("express verbalized religion") is being perfectly fulfilled. The members of the *dGe aDun* ("ones of the virtue-assembly"), or community, are uttering *CHos* ("the law") as first enunciated by *Sangs rGyas* ("Buddha"), and in accordance with the premises of Buddhist doctrine, merit is being built up and the good of all sentient beings is being advanced. In origin, form, and purpose, such a ceremony is all Buddhist beyond mistaking—impeccably orthodox. The Rare Perfect Triad is having its threefold part in fulfilment. By comparison, when, on a windy hilltop before the arrow-filled shrine of an *AH Mes* ("hail ancient"), or mountain god, a long-haired wizard—also called *AH Mes*—throws mutilated and wound-marked effigies into a fire of juniper boughs and calls in tones of urgency and command to the god of the mountain to carry death and mutilation to the enemy against whom armed men will ride, the prayers of the ancient religion of the land are being performed. The wizard promises offerings of blood and entrails to the god, and all the while, mounted men circle the fire counterclockwise, yelling fierce assent and firing their guns to punctuate the incantation. Such offerings and actions are unmistakably part of the pre-Buddhist religion of a Tibet that was turbulent and warlike with unabashed savagery.

In the system of offerings, much of it shared by Buddhism and Bonism, some offerings obviously belong to Buddhism and others retain the characteristics of pre-Buddhist sacrifices. Typical Buddhist offerings range from the symbolism of incense, flowers, grain, pure water, lights, and music to the extensive use of the mandala. The *gTor Ma* ("broken-up") offerings, although used by Buddhists as well as by Bonists, point back to earlier forms of sacrifice. They consist of images or emblems shaped from dough, butter, or similar substances, most frequently dyed red, which, by the performance of the required ritual and the utterance of incantations, become the containers or bearers of retribution or bad luck. Depending upon the nature of the ceremony, they are either burned or broken up and thrown away. In some of the more dramatic ceremonies, the *gTor Ma* is ritualistically attacked with such symbolic weapons as the dagger or ax and cut to pieces before being disposed of. Tibetan legend ascribes the origin of the *gTor Ma* to the prohibition against killing and sacrificing men and animals that was placed upon the *Bon Po* at the instigation of Padma Sambhava, after which he taught them to make substitute effigies of the victims.[28] This legend certainly strengthens

---

[28] H. Hoffmann, *The Religions of Tibet* (1961), pp. 72–73. Hoffmann has assembled data from a number of sources concerning the conversion of the *Bon Po*

the assumption, which seems reasonably certain from aspects of the ceremony today, that the *gTor Ma* is a vestigial survival of earlier forms of bloody sacrifice.

Additional confirmation of the existence of the earlier practice of a selective killing of individuals for the benefit of the community as a whole is given by the curse-bearer ceremony, a specialized form of the *Glud* ("ransom") ritual, which is a part of the New Year festival at Lhasa and which, in various forms, takes place in many other lamaseries all over Tibet. In the *Glud* ceremony an individual is selected to act as a sort of demon scapegoat and dressed for the part. He is appropriately burdened with the communal ill luck of the year, is given a sporting chance to get away from what are sometimes bona fide attempts to kill him, and does his best to escape. It is reported that occasionally—even in Buddhistic Tibet—he does not get away, or at least does not survive the treatment he receives. In such instances, vestigial human sacrifice has persisted with final realism down to the present.

The *Bon Po* specialize in the use of many forms of *gTor Ma* ("broken-up") offerings, even going so far at times as to use parts of slain animals and blood, though as far as is known no sacrificial killings now take place.

A considerable amount of religious paraphernalia is also shared by Bonism and Buddhism. Images and painted scrolls now belong to both. Both use drums and wind instruments, ritual weapons, human bones and skeletons, masks—of both demons and animals—scarves, staves, tridents, bows and arrows, and ancient armor in ritual and display. Both religions hang the stuffed skins of animals, particularly those of animals of the land, such as wild yak, kiang, stag, bear, boar and tiger, in the shrine of the guardian deity of a monastery as *sPyan gZigs* ("eye-viewed") offerings. Sometimes human skins are included in such displays. Among all these items, there is no difficulty in identifying those which are part of a heritage from the shamanistic ceremonies and practices of the pre-Buddhist religion of Tibet.

The difference between the two religions is epitomized in the relative emphasis placed on the goals they have in common. Both seek some assurance concerning existence or condition in the afterlife, and both seek some protection and aid to success in this world. But the goals of Buddhist religious observance are more concerned with otherworldly matters: with deliverance from the sufferings of the wheel of life, from the bond-

---

from the making of bloody sacrifices to the use of substitute effigies. Moreover, the Tibetans known to me insist that the making of the *gTor Ma* offerings derives solely from this changeover.

age of ignorance and desire, and from the evils of existence. In the context of this overwhelming preoccupation with progress toward bodhisattva-ship or *THar Ba* ("liberation") happiness and health in the world are of relatively slight consequence. The *Bon Po,* on the other hand, seek success, health, and protection in this life primarily, with only a secondary or belated interest in some sort of a final escape into heaven. It seems probable that the same emphasis with regard to primary goals existed in the earlier religion.

Tibetan History and Folklore as Sources

In the few fragments of secular Tibetan history that have survived, religious matters are mentioned only in the context of royal genealogies, in characteristics ascribed to the early kings, and as steps in the extension of royal control over somewhat unwilling vassals. The first king is said to have come from heaven, and "this son of the gods ruled over the land of men after which he returned bodily to the *dGung* ("zenith")." The first seven kings, honorifically called *gNam Kyi KHri* ("thrones of heaven"), are said to have succeeded each other in the following manner. "The first kings acted so: when the son was able to ride a horse the father went to heaven." Progressively, the kings extended their control, for it is said that the minor princes, "bewitched by the magic of the king," were mastered.[29]

Another one of the fragments gives in considerable detail the prescribed ritual for the funeral of a king. Many shamans, who are identified according to their differing roles, officiate. There are those who hold the animals, those who strike them down with lances and weapons, those who slaughter—using the knife—those who collect and offer blood, those who cut up the victims and those who make various offerings of grain, foodstuffs, and libations (the exact nature of which is not clearly identified). The animals—yak, horses, sheep, and cow-yak hybrids—are killed in great numbers. Special attention is given to the permissible quality, color, and markings of animals selected for sacrifice. And there are veiled but unmistakable references to human sacrifices.[30]

Although the epic of Gesar is not history in the strict sense, as a source of information it is truly of historical value, for throughout its various versions and mutations it mirrors with considerable fidelity the beliefs, mores, and folkways of the Tibetans of an earlier time. Some

[29] J. Bacot *et al., Documents de Touen Houang* (1940–46), pp. 85–87.

[30] M. Lalou, *op. cit.,* p. 355.

Tibetan opinion maintains that Gesar Norbu—the hero of the epic—lived during the reign of _lHa THo THo Ri_ in the fifth century,[31] which would be approximately two centuries before the official introduction of Buddhism. The epic unquestionably originated before the Tibetans had a system of writing and was preserved and transmitted orally until, at a relatively late date, it was written down. As thus recorded, it now appears embellished by pious interpretations and interpolations which are manifestly Buddhistic in origin and reflect Buddhist ethics. With little difficulty, however, these may be subtracted, even as one reads, and what remains is the story of a refugee bastard who, as an ambitiously rebellious tribal chief, epitomizes in his wars and forays in search of larger lands and broader modes of living the manners and beliefs of the warlike Red-Faced people of pre-Buddhist times. Two excerpts are here presented which, by their contrasts, will shed light on the early religion. In the first short passage, two kinds of invocation—Buddhist and Bon—are placed in apt juxtaposition, and the contrast is sharp and meaningful.

> _OHm Ma Ni Padme Hum._ Song to the eternal religion-gift.
> Hail teacher sublime, Supreme Buddha.
> Holy doctrine, peaceful and separated from passion:
> Community refulgent with talent;
> Hail Union of the Sublime Three.

Immediately after this Buddhist formula, the Bon invocation follows:

> Today from the abode of the gods of war, come three hundred and sixty mouth-terrible ones and give advice to this song of the world. As to this place, if you do not know it, this is the land of _rMa_ ("peacock") the basin of the Yellow River. The two fair ones—sun, moon are joined. High ones, chiefs—sun, moon are joined. Fathers, uncles—eagle, dragon are joined. The six tribes—peace, felicity are joined. If I am not known, I, the descendant on the stem of the trumpet of my ancestors, am the beautiful flower of gold. Pleasant speech circles the turquoise bird—the cuckoo. Speech becomes meaningful with the saying of a single word. If this song is not known, it is the lead part of the poem of the God-region.[32]

Of these two, it is easy to distinguish which one is a mystical formula created and transmitted for repetition and which one is direct discourse packed with folklore and poetic imagery.

The second excerpt characterizes a _gSHen_ ("shaman"). The attribu-

[31] Sir Ch. Bell, _The Religion of Tibet_ (1931), pp. 12–14.

[32] R. A. Stein, _L'épopée tibétaine de Gésar_ (1956), p. 192 (f. 32 _b_ of Tibetan work).

tive uncle of the young Gesar finds the child a threat to his own position and privilege and, having attempted unsuccessfully to do away with him, seeks a Bon shaman for help. A description of the wizard follows:

> In *lCi PHy Nag Lung mDo* there was a *ZHang ZHung* Bon magician called *AH Mes* ("hail ancient") *sGam Pa Ra DZa,* who because of the power of his magic disobeyed even the pre-cepts of the teacher *gSHen Rabs* and viewed blasphemously the religion of Padma. He stubbornly persisted in the practice of evil spells, and during the day, with those evil ones who came to him from the eight classes of spirits, he cut the vital arteries of the religious, both Buddhist and Bon, and, at night, with evil women and she devils, he stole the spirits from out of living creatures.

The uncle then begins his speech with an invocation:

> Take notice, Body of the Bon, teacher *gSHen Rabs;* take notice, Bon of *AH* (mystic syllable) of *CHos sKu* ("religion body, the primal cause"), *sTag lHa Me Bar* ("fire-burning tiger god"); take notice, the one mother, *Srid Pai rGyal Mo* ("queen of the world"); come aid in the song of *sTag Rong* ("tiger valley").

After this, with many elaborations, he promises the Bon magician fabu-lous wealth if he will use his magical power to kill the nephew. The magician agrees and makes the attempt. The contest which results be-tween the magician and young Gesar is thaumaturgic drama at its wildest —two shamans in a life-and-death struggle.[33]

Chinese Records as Sources

In Chinese historical records and particularly those of the T'ang dy-nasty, there are some very clear and concise statements about the pre-Buddhist religious beliefs and practices of the Tibetans. Of the T'ang Hsiang, a proto-Tibetan people later incorporated into the Tibetan em-pire, it is said that they "sacrificed oxen and sheep to worship heaven." At another point, it is stated flatly that "they (the Tibetans) worship the *Yuan-ti* god and believe in seers and witches. They are fond of the doc-trine of Buddha and no important affairs are settled without consulting the Buddhist monks." This appears to be a description of a transitional state when the new religion had already gained high favor at court but the old forms of worship were still practiced. The *Yuan-ti* is the Chinese name for the ram of the Asiatic bighorn sheep, or argali, and corresponds

---

[33] *Ibid.*, pp. 57, 58–60.

to the Tibetan word *gNYan* ("argali"). From the appearance, in most lists, of the word in the names of four successive Tibetan kings, it would seem that the cult of the argali was at its height during the fifth and sixth centuries. As a designation for a god, however, *gNYan* ("argali") has survived down to modern times and appears in the names of many mountain gods.

Other practices are described in Chinese records. In the making of treaties, animals were sacrificed, and blood was smeared on the lips of the parties. Animals and human beings were sacrificed both at the funerals of Tibetan kings and at ceremonies marking the swearing of fealty to the king. Invocations were made to the gods of the heaven, the earth, the mountains, and the rivers, and the sun, moon, stars, and planets. In the burial of a king, his accoutrements and weapons, horses, and so on, are buried with him, suggesting belief in an afterlife; and there is also a statement that ancestor worship was carried on.[34]

Neighboring Religions as Sources

The pre-Buddhist or non-Buddhist religions of neighboring peoples and of those who, in all probability, had contact with the Tibetans in very early times also furnish us with suggestions as to what religious practices may have had a place in the pre-Buddhist religious observances of the Tibetans. On both the eastern and southern borders of Tibet, there are many fragmentary groupings of primitive peoples who have resisted Buddhism and who worship the heavenly bodies, sacred trees, and stones, and practice a sort of shamanism marked by exorcism and the propitiation of spirit beings.

The Ch'iang are a somewhat representative example, and for a number of reasons answer most aptly the requirements of this investigation. They were once a strong people in control of much territory between the Tibetans and the Chinese. Some of them were incorporated into the nascent Tibetan empire early in the fifth century.[35] Though now reduced, by Chinese domination and assimilation, to a mere fragment, they have retained much of their ethnic identity and have also resisted, quite successfully, Buddhism and its influence. Their religious beliefs and practices have been studied and described. They worship many gods, which are divided into two categories: the five greater and the twelve lesser ones. One among the greater gods is called the sky god. The twelve lesser gods have somewhat the same functional roles and status as the thirteen

[34] S. W. Bushell, "The Early History of Tibet," *JRAS*, 1880, pp. 441–43, 527–28.
[35] *Ibid.*, p. 440.

Bon gods of Tibet—god of wealth, protectress of women, god of trade, and so on. Several of the greater gods, however, are described as ancestors—male and female. Thus, it would appear that ancestor worship has projected representative ancestors into the pantheon or community of tribal gods. There is a priesthood which is non-celibate and whose function is typically shamanist. Admission to the priesthood is by initiation after long training in the rites connected with exorcism and sacrifice. The most important part of the training is exact memorization of the entire body of the "sacred books," that is, the prayers and incantations, which have not been written down, since the Ch'iang have no indigenous system of writing. Veneration of trees and white stones is also part of Ch'iang religious belief and practice. Staves, drums, and other paraphernalia figure prominently in ceremonies and are the prized possessions of the priests or shamans.[36]

In the context of its occurrence—a society and culture which are in the final stages of retreat from the pressures exerted against them by a stronger society—this religion of the Ch'iang people may be but a pale ghost of the pre-Buddhist religion of Tibet, which had a much different context—the rapid military and political expansion that marked the Tibetan empire of the fifth through eighth centuries. The Tibetan religion of that time was a robust part of the empire; in content it was undoubtedly much richer than the present-day religion, and in spirit stronger and more violent, but there are probably many points of resemblance.

The pre-Buddhist religion of Tibet has also been likened to Taoism by a number of writers. Even before the eventful period of the T'ang dynasty, China and Tibet were closely involved with each other in conflicts and cross-cultural borrowing. In China the now unknown primitive rites of prehistory had developed into Taoism and Confucianism. Certain aspects of the latter system probably had some influence on the religious practices of the Tibetans. Veneration of heaven and rudimentary ancestor worship may have been borrowings from the official Confucianism of China, but it is Taoism that the Tibetans themselves have identified as the Chinese equivalent of the Bon religion.

Lao-tse has been identified with gSHen Rabs, and Taoism has been described as follows:

> The supreme being is immaterial, shapeless and invisible. He is self-created and matchless and most noble—many other gods possessing shape are mentioned [as] being the presiding deities of the five great mountains of China, of the four great rivers, and

[36] D. C. Graham, *The Customs and Religion of the Ch'iang* (1958), pp. 43–66.

of wind, rain and lightning: beside many powerful demons for whom several ceremonies are prescribed—there are also accounts of many who acquire superhuman powers such as that of performing miracles and illusions. Witchcraft, rites, and ceremonies of mysticism and concatenation of time and circumstance, beside those which are used by gods and sages in the way of Tantricism, are numerous among the To-u-se (Taoists).[37]

The religion of the Mongols prior to their acceptance of Buddhism also suggests, by way of analogy, the distinguishing aspects of the pre-Buddhist religion of the Tibetans. There is a close cultural affinity between the two peoples stemming from the similarities of their cultural past and their historical experiences. One was a predominantly, and the other a strongly, nomadic people, both exemplifying the horse culture in its most typical aspects—living and warring on horseback, following their herds, and seeking ever wider pastures. To both peoples, agriculture was a secondary and less highly regarded way of living. Their tribal organizations had many similarities, and both, in the contest for territorial control and empire, had been in violent competition with the neighboring Chinese. The natural affinity between the two peoples is exemplified by the willingness with which the Mongols accepted Buddhism, special religious linguistic forms and vocabularies, and even, for a time, a new form of writing from the Tibetans, who, in the period from the thirteenth century down to modern times, came to them as religious teachers and guides.

Although historically verifiable contact between the two peoples dates only from the thirteenth century, there are indications that a much earlier—possibly prehistoric—contact or channel for the transmission of religious traits and concepts did exist. One of these indications is the coincidence of thirteen as a number of symbolic religious significance in both cultures. This number appears with great frequency in religious concepts and classificatory systems among the Tibetans and has also survived, with striking resemblances, in some aspects of the shamanism that has persisted among the Buriats.[38]

Both because of the possibility of very early cultural borrowing and because of natural affinity there is considerable, justification for taking the early pre-Buddhist religion of the Mongols as a pattern in the attempt to reconstruct the pre-Buddhist religion of the Tibetans. Fortunately, much is known about the content and practice of the pre-Buddhist reli-

[37] S. C. Das, "Contributions on Tibet," *JASB*, 1882, pp. 112–13.

[38] R. Ekvall, "Significance of Thirteen as a Symbolic Number in Tibetan and Mongolian Cultures," *Journal of the American Oriental Society*, LXXIX (1959), No. 3, 186–92.

gion of the Mongols. During the period it was held and practiced, the Mongols already had a known history of their own and a significant part in world history. They had their own forms of writing and were also under the observation of the Chinese and all those civilized and literate peoples whom they conquered or menaced, including witnesses from the West who reported their observations in Latin. Their religion was a combination of the worship and veneration of a high god related to or identified with the "Blue Sky" and a shamanism that had a very wide distribution among Siberian peoples. The worship of heaven, either *Küke Tengri* ("blue heaven") or *Mungke Tengri* ("eternal heaven"), was the central religious concept of the Mongol empire builders. Their edicts begin with the phrase, "By the providence of the eternal sky."[39] Some have suggested that the difference between "blue heaven" and "eternal heaven" is analogous to the difference between the Chinese cults of *T'ien* ("heaven") and *Shang Ti* ("supreme lord").[40] But whether the high god was personal or impersonal, its characteristics were as stated by Carpini, and agreed to by both Rubruquis and Marco Polo: "The Mongols believe in one god whom they regard as the creator of all things." The shamanism they practiced was characterized by the existence of a class of seers or shamans who performed rites of sacrifice and propitiation, practiced magic in divination and healing, were subject to trances or states of possession by, or identification with, spirit beings, and used an elaborate ritual and distinctive regalia.[41]

An outline of the religious beliefs and practices of the Mongols becomes a relatively reliable guide or pattern for the reconstruction of the pre-Buddhist religion of the Tibetans whenever other evidence, much of which has already been summarized, points to similar religious traits in the early religion of Tibet and confirms their existence.

Linguistic Usages as Sources

Certain Tibetan linguistic usages and examples of linguistic change also furnish clues or information concerning the early religious ideas and concepts of the Tibetans. An adequate coverage of all aspects of this very rich source is far beyond the scope of this study. But as examples of what might be uncovered, the following particularly pertinent items are of

[39] G. Tucci, *Tibetan Painted Scrolls* (1949), pp. 715–16.

[40] H. Hoffmann, *Quellen zur Geschichte der tibetischen Bon Religion* (1950), p. 159.

[41] C. H. Dawson, *The Mongol Mission* (1955), pp. 8–9, 12, 83, 85, 86, 195, 197–201.

interest. In everyday life the pattern of swearing in Tibetan and the taking of oaths, as distinguished from abuse and obscenity, supplies evidence concerning the concept of the Blue Sky as a deity. Oaths are attestations or appeals to concepts of great or supreme sanctity. Thus among the Tibetans we find in common everyday use a considerable number of oaths such as *dKon mCHog gSum* ("Rare-Perfect Three"), *Yum bTum Pa gCig gNYis* ("mother of the twelve wrapped books"–the metaphysical portion of the Buddhist scriptures), *dGon Pa* ("lamasery"), *sKu bZHugs* ("body seated"), and *sKu gDung* ("remains of the body"–of Buddha), and so on, which manifestly make reference to the highest and holiest concepts or objects of Buddhist veneration. There is also another very common oath, *aPHrul Rin Po CHe* ("great precious magic"), which undoubtedly antedates Buddhism and refers to the great manifestation of Bon magic which F. W. Thomas calls "theophany" and which was the attribute of the earliest Tibetan kings.[42] Throughout Tibet, but particularly in Amdo and Khams, one oath, *gNam* ("sky"), or more impressively, *gNam sNGon Po* ("the blue sky"), or sometimes, *gNam rTag Pa* ("sky eternal"), outranks all others as being the most frequently used and most binding. This is not a Buddhist oath and certainly points back to the heavens or sky as the central, or at least, an important, concept of pre-Buddhistic Tibetan religion.

The emergence in Amdo and Khams of the word often spelled *Amnye* (which, for reasons given below, I write *AH Mes*), applied as a title equally to mountain gods—for example, *Amnye Machen*—and to the *sNGags Pa* ("sorcerers"), is an example of a linguistic clue which suggests ancestor worship. R. A. Stein has suggested—and I feel certain—that the term comes from the word *Mes* ("ancestor"), preceded by *AH* (either meaning "hail" or as a prefix commonly used in terms referring to grandparents)—thus *AH Mes*.[43] Throughout Khams and Amdo and other parts of Tibet, the letter "m" is frequently pronounced and, when transcribed by the ignorant, written "ny" in such words as *Mi* ("man"), *Mig* ("eye"), *Me* ("fire"), and so on. Thus *AH Mes*, when pronounced and transcribed, becomes *Amnye*. That mountain gods and wizards should be hailed as ancestors indicates a time when the elders, while living, were family priests who dealt with the spirit world and, when dead, could haunt localities, acquire proprietary power, and command service from the living.

This accords with what may be inferred from one use of the word

[42] F. W. Thomas, *op. cit.*, Part II, pp. 9, 11, 21; R. A. Stein, *L'épopée tibétaine de Gésar* (1956), p. 78 (1).

[43] R. A. Stein, *L'épopée tibétaine de Gésar* (1956), p. 390.

aDre ("goblin"), which has been shown to be a basic classificatory term for the malignant portion of the spirit world. In the detailed description of the elaborate ritual concerning *Bar Do* ("between state") in the so-called Tibetan Book of the Dead, much is made of the lingering attachment of the soul of the dead person to the body and the familiar locality and of the stages necessary before that soul ceases to be, in effect, a ghost, and finally moves on to future cycles of reincarnation.[44] Such spirits do not properly belong to the class of evil spirits called *aDre* ("goblins"), but in common parlance, the souls of the dead who are passing through an uneasy and unhappy time in *Bar Do* are called *SHi aDre* ("dead goblins") and are awarded a somewhat fearful service as real ghosts who have power and spitefulness. So, in the primitive religion of the Tibetans, before the Buddhist doctrine of reincarnation moved these spirits on to other circuits, they must have been believed to be ancestors who were to be feared and worshipped.

CHARACTERISTICS OF THE PRE-BUDDHIST RELIGION OF TIBET

From this very condensed presentation of the material available, it can be suggested with a fair degree of assurance that the pre-Buddhist religion of the Tibetans was characterized by the following beliefs and practices:

1. The belief in the existence of a supreme or high god who transcended all other spirit beings and was closely associated, or identified, with the blue sky.

2. The acceptance of a vast pantheon of swarming spirit beings who, in consonance with a basic concept of the dualism of good and evil, negative and positive, and the continuing conflict between the two, were characterized as *lHa* ("god"), good, and *aDre* ("goblins"), bad. Many of these spirits were of a jealous or spiteful disposition and had to be propitiated by worship and sacrifice or coerced by the exercise of thaumaturgic power.

3. The practice of offering bloody sacrifices of animals and also human beings. The *gSHen* ("shaman"), who carried the knife, was the killer. Some of the sacrifices were imputative, but others were made in connection with burial rites or divination.

4. The practice of magic to control gods and demons, provide ghosts with guidance in the hereafter, heal the sick, control the elements, foretell the future, and by malediction, injure or destroy enemies.

[44] W. Y. E. Wents, *The Tibetan Book of the Dead* (1937), pp. 18–20, 28–30.

5. The occurrence of states of frenzy, or trance, which were ascribed to possession or guidance by either the *lHa* ("god[s]") or the *aDre* ("goblin[s]") of a dualistic spirit world. The individuals subject to such seizures, or purposely seeking them, were regarded as possessors of extraordinary powers essential to the function of the shaman.

6. The existence of a class of wizards—both male and female—possessing the powers mentioned in No. 4, who resembled the shamans of the Mongols and other northern Asiatic peoples and who functioned severally: as priests officiating at funerals; as sacrificers, healers, and diviners; and as those able to use the black magic of malediction.

7. The practice of a ritual in which incantations and special regalia —including drums, weapons, staves of power, masks, headdresses, and special costumes—were used.

8. The ascription of supernatural powers to certain beasts, birds, and reptiles—such as eagles, argali, yak, bears, wolves, tigers, waterfowl, and snakes—thus making them objects of veneration and accessories in the practice of magic.

9. The belief in an afterlife wherein ghosts were recognized and feared. This belief was probably linked with rudimentary forms of ancestor worship. It was also believed that the dead might attain directly to an existence of bliss in the heavens. Certain individuals—the early kings, for example—were believed to have reached heaven directly as visitors from this life. A similar achievement was not considered beyond the range of possibility for great magicians. This belief was linked to the concept of a rope, or passage device, that connected earth and heaven and to the achievement of "opening the heavenly gate" ascribed to *gSHen Rabs.*

This is the outline; these were the probable characteristics of that most ancient far-distant religion that is the continuing pervasive religious background of Tibetan belief and practice. Much of it has persisted into the present, and the influences that emanate from it are still powerful. As we examine the Tibetan universal religious observances of the present, we shall recognize again and again the pressure and compelling force of these background influences.

CHAPTER THREE

THE RELIGION OF

THE TIBETANS AND

THEIR SUBJECTIVE RESPONSE

For many reasons, much interest has been focused on the religion of Tibet. About this land, long hidden behind the snow peaks of the Himalayas or made relatively inaccessible or forbidden by the overt or tacit agreement of China, Great Britain, India, and the Tibetan authorities, there developed the lure of what was cheaply called mystery. Attracted by it, both competent observers and sensation-seekers took great risks and underwent much hardship to view the Tibetan scene. What they saw made good telling. Much of it had to do with religion, for religion dominated life and was expressed in symbols and rituals which were strange and eye-catching. Architecture, art, ceremony, even drama, all had a part in the expression of religion.

AS A SOURCE OF STORY AND FANTASY

The great red cliff of the Potala—part building and part mountain—is, without doubt, one of the wonders of Asia; but every lamasery, and even each small hermitage, reveals some of the same beauty of line and proportion that is characteristically Tibetan. The stupa, originally borrowed from India and called *mCHod rTen* ("offering base"), has been modified into a distinctly Tibetan form; and wherever it is found, from Kashmir to Peking, it testifies by line and concept to the architectural bent, or even genius, of the Tibetans: a dedication to the service of religion. Art equally found religious expression in images of gods and demons, in painted scrolls of great beauty, in silken image banners which cover an entire hillside when unrolled with the many forms and faces of the timeless Buddha, in the color and magnificence of the robes and regalia of officiating ecclesiastics; and in the personal-god shrines made of precious metals encrusted with lapis lazuli, coral, turquoise, and amber, which are worn like jewelry by laymen and ecclesiastics alike. Prayer and benediction are impressively visual in the prayer flags that fly from trees, flag poles, grain racks, housetops, tent ropes, and lances; in the prayer wheels of every size turned by hand or by water and even smoke; and in the silken scarves of blessing and good luck that are worn by every one. The paraphernalia of religious ceremonies—twelve-foot trumpets, painted drums, costumes, masks, ritual weapons, and the thunderbolt and bell—are all recognizable expressions of Tibetan art.

Religious ceremonies and ritual have also had a prominent place in all that has been seen and reported about the Land of Snows. They could not be missed, for they are colorful and impressive and often dramatic in their impact. Thousands of red-robed monks meet in the assembly halls or lamasery squares to chant in organ tones, bending to the rhythm of their praying. The great processions, the torchlight display of the butter images, the throwing out or burning of the *gTor Ma,* or substitute effigy offerings, often accompanied by gunfire or the concerted cheering of the spectators, the *Glud,* or "scape-goat," ceremony, and the great religious spectacles—called *aCHam* ("dance") by the Tibetans, *T'iao Shen* ("dance god") by the Chinese, and "devil dance" by many Western writers—are all staged in a masterful way by a people who have a true dramatic instinct and a very great sense of "good theater."

The spectacles, or "dances," represent a synthesis of ritual and drama, for, though their function is to overcome evil and bad luck and provide blessing and assurance, their form is dramatic—miracle or mystery plays of both historical and allegorical significance. Their purpose is the dramatic portrayal of the power of religion in victorious action, and they are vastly impressive even to the most sophisticated observers. As spectacle, they have attracted much interest and, together with other colorful externals of Tibetan religion, have been ably described and also well recorded in still and motion picture photography.

On an entirely different level, a persistent curiosity has focused on another aspect of Tibetan religion with some strange results. For some, the religion of Tibet has become identified with psychic phenomena. Some sympathetic speculation has considered the possibility that Tibetan mystics, or saintly scholars, under special conditions characterized by asceticism, retirement, and concentrated meditation, have learned and put into operation the control of psychic forces, and thus are able to produce such psychic phenomena as thought-transference, the generation of internal heat, the projection of the astral body, and even levitation. Other speculation or reporting, naïve or avidly sensational, has considered the occurrence of such phenomena as probable or even certain.[1] Thus Tibet and the Tibetan religion have become associated with the wildest fantasies, and from that point on, the tellers of tall tales have taken over, relaying to the Western world stories of the marvelous, until it would seem that the hallmark of authenticity in a book about Tibet is the inclusion of at least one such tale, well told.

It is oddly unpopular to challenge the myth. Thus such a palpable and outrageous hoax as *The Third Eye* can appear in print because, as the publishers state, "The manuscript was submitted to a great many authorities on Tibet and no one would commit himself." Other equally fictitious but less monumental hoaxes have even appeared in the sober company of bibliographies used and compiled by renowned Tibetologists.

The Tibetans themselves tell tales of these marvels in a matter-of-fact way. To them they are completely real. But for the conscientious seeker of facts, the reliable eyewitness is difficult to come by, and a firsthand demonstration is completely elusive. Belief in these marvels, however, and a zestful telling of them are almost universal. They are a part of an existence which itself is believed to be revealed on three planes: the absolute, the relative, and the imaginary. In such a world and such an atmosphere, the doubter—even some Tibetans are doubters—feels impious and crass. His doubts seem out of place. The psychological and social climate is one of faith or credulity. In such a social and psychological milieu, the greatly sympathetic observer is led, by his own desires and the power of suggestion, to accept hearsay and general credence as conclusive evidence. So the legend grows, and the tale becomes reported fact.

AS A SOURCE OF BUDDHIST TRADITION AND DOCTRINE

For more solid reasons a great deal of serious research has also been focused on the religion of Tibet. Preserved in the Tibetan religious writings is a very extensive, possibly the largest known, compilation or record of Buddhist lore and doctrine. The most important part of this collection consists of the Buddhist scriptures and commentaries: the one hundred eight volumes of the *bKaa aGyur,* or scriptures, and the two hundred twenty-five volumes of the *bsTan aGyur,* or commentaries.

[1] Of those to whom respectful credence is due, Madame David-Neel, in her many writings about Tibet and in particular in the books *Mystiques et magiciens du Thibet* (1930) and *Initiations lamaïques* (1947), has gone the farthest in imputing unusual psychic powers to the Tibetan adepts. Her firsthand personal experience and knowledge are unexceptionable, and I have no intention of placing her among "the tellers of tall tales."

Three developments of considerable importance marked or accompanied the introduction of Buddhism into Tibet, and each of these three developments played an important role in favoring the creation and preservation of a record of Buddhist doctrine and history in the Tibetan language. One of these developments was the purposeful creation of a form of writing. This was done by the importation and adaptation of a system of transcription somewhat closely based on a form of Sanskrit and answering very well the phonetic requirements of the Tibetan language. As will be noted later, there are many indications of a certain amount of sophistication in Tibetan appreciation of linguistic problems.

In the Tibetan historical account of the work of the Tibetan scholar *THon Mi Sambhota* and his associates, who are traditionally credited with making this adaptation, there is considerable discussion of problems of phonetics. And the system of transcription itself, with its prefixes and superimposed and subjoined consonants, is sufficiently refined and accurate to provide us with valuable and trustworthy indexes of the pronunciation of the Tibetan language more than thirteen centuries ago. Accounts of this system, when compared with the living language of the present, give us a basis for measurement of the rate and distribution of linguistic change to a degree that is somewhat rare in Asian languages.

The second of the important developments was the creation of *CHos sKad* ("religion-speech")—a special form of the Tibetan language which is known to Western scholars as classical Tibetan to distinguish it from *KHa sKad* ("mouth-speech"), also called *PHal sKad* ("common speech"), or the colloquial. The forms and rules of Sanskrit grammar unquestionably had a great fascination for the Tibetan scholars who were at once borrowing a system of writing and accepting a system of religion from the same source.

The structural simplicity of Tibetan, which has been classified as an analytical language, was made to conform to rules of grammar borrowed from Sanskrit, for example, as when the same suffix appears under the different headings of accusative, determinative, dative, and locative. This forcing of the language into a somewhat alien mold was, moreover, not only a kind of deformation but to a degree an arrestation, at a given point, of a process of change. For classical Tibetan, this process was halted with the imposition of Sanskrit grammar; but for colloquial Tibetan the process of change continued.

Thus *KHa sKad* and *CHos sKad*, although possessing to a considerable extent the same vocabulary, are sufficiently different in structure to be placed by the linguist, Edward Sapir, in two separate categories of language classification.[2] Yet classical Tibetan is more intelligible to an unlettered speaker of modern colloquial Tibetan than, for example, is classical Chinese, *wen-li*, to a Chinese unskilled in the ancient literary tradition.

Chos sKad was an artificial form created for a special purpose. J. Bacot sums up its character in these words. "Par ses textes traduit du sanscrit, le tibétain classique n'est pas un langue morte, car il n'avait jamais vécu. Mais il a eu cette fortune exceptionnelle de devenir dans la suite langue vivante. . . ."[3] And Susumu Yamaguchi, in his introduction to the Tokyo-Kyoto printing of *The Tibetan Tripitaka*, says, "The classical Tibetan language, which is used in the Tibetan Tripitaka, is an artificial language which was constructed on the basis of Sanskrit grammar by Tibetan scholars. . . ."[4] The primary importance of this creation derives from the fact that it is the language in which the Tibetan Buddhist scriptures and most of the associated literature have been written. It also has had considerable influence on the *dPon sKad* ("official speech") and on general secular linguistic usage. But the distinction and difference both for the Western scholar and for the native Tibetan remain: for one it is the difference between classical Tibetan and colloquial Tibetan, and for the other it is the difference between *CHos sKad*, a mode of speech consecrated to the uses of religion, and *KHa sKad*, or *PHal sKad*, the living language of everyday concerns.

The third development was concerned with semantics. The Tibetans of that and later times appear to have had a rather sophisticated realization of the basic semantic problems involved in interpretation and translation. Indeed, there are some indications in Tibetan traditional history (which will be discussed at some length in a later chapter) that an initial Buddhist missionary effort in Tibet, some time in the fifth century, failed because of language difficulty and the confusion arising from the free—or non-standardized—translation into Tibetan of some of the basic concepts of Buddhist doctrine. Possibly because of this experience, Tibetan awareness of the semantic problem involved arose. Very early, Tibetan scholars compiled extensive glossaries in which the basic monosyllables of the living speech were combined into new compounds to which metasemantic meanings were assigned as the equivalents of Sanskrit terms. Thus, standardized and conventional terms for Buddhist concepts—most of which

---

[2] E. Sapir, *Language* (1949; Harvest Books Edition), p. 142.

[3] J. Bacot, *Les slokas grammaticaux de Thonmi Sambhota* (1928), p. 1.

[4] D. Suzuki (ed.), *The Tibetan Tripitaka* (1957), Vol. CLXV, p. iii.

came to the Tibetans in Sanskrit—were established in Tibetan and were widely used. In the eighth and ninth centuries this system of terminology was extensively revised, and later finally fixed, so that little was left to individual choice. As a consequence, there are few of the free variables in terminology which appear, for example, in Chinese texts of the same Buddhist writings.

Such an assignment of equivalency may, however, derive more from the predilection of Sanskrit scholars who work with Tibetan texts, and see all meanings in the context of Sanskrit, than from the Tibetans themselves. The basic Tibetan words used in the construction of these compounds cannot be emptied of their original meanings. Most of them, in a variety of contexts, remain a part of the living speech of everyday concerns. The Tibetan translators certainly had such meanings and such contexts in mind when they selected them to represent the Sanskrit terminology of Buddhist doctrine, *as they then understood it.* Those original meanings persist to influence and color comprehension despite any arbitrary assignment of strict equivalency with Sanskrit. The Tibetan term *dKon mCHog gSum* ("Rare-Perfect Three") for the so-called Jewel Triad is a good case in point. The two words *dKon* ("rare") and *mCHog* ("perfect") are still widely used in colloquial speech in many mundane contexts as "rare" and "perfect" or "most excellent." They are abstractions or attributions of quality but have no concrete referent, such as a "jewel," which is a thing; the Tibetan scholars consulted indignantly rejected any such semantic linkage. Thus the Tibetan etymology of doctrinal terms remains a promising but largely unexplored field in which to discover new doctrinal nuances in, or at least significant commentaries on, the "word of the Buddhahood."

The terms themselves became an intrinsic part of *CHos sKad,* substantially strengthening the special sacrosanct character which set it apart from secular use and influences. This isolation also served to protect it, to a certain extent, from the processes of linguistic change, and this, in turn, reinforced its usefulness as a preservative of original meaning and concept. The case of Latin as the language of religious and philosophical expression in medieval times is a somewhat close analogy and calls to mind the statement "I propose to embalm in Latin my philosophies," poetically but apocryphally attributed to Bacon.[5] *CHos sKad* has proved, indeed, to be a good embalming agent.

As a result of these three developments, the Tibetan and Indian scholars and translators found themselves possessed of the first—or at

[5] A. Noyes, *Tales of the Mermaid Tavern* (1913), p. 47.

least a new—system of writing for Tibetan; a new specially constructed language; and a new vocabulary designed for, and consecrated exclusively to, the expression of all the concepts of Buddhist doctrine and philosophy. They then set themselves, with great industry, to the work of translating and annotating the Buddhist scriptures. With equal industry and scholarship, the Tibetan pandits followed up this work of translation with a great volume of original religious writings in the Tibetan language: prayers, doctrinal dissertations, the life histories of saints and mystics, and what were in effect encyclopedias of Tibetan history and general knowledge. In this period the great Tibetan treasury of the record and teachings of Buddhism was at its full flowering.

The use of paper and ink became known to the Tibetans from the Chinese, and later the art of making these materials was also gained from their neighbors to the east. All indications are that still later the technique of wood-block printing was imported from China. Thus the material aids and techniques for writing and printing the word all came from the Chinese; with those materials, it would seem, the Tibetans acquired some of the special veneration for the written and printed letter as such, which features so largely in traditional Chinese culture. This was combined with that sanctity of the spoken word that is part of the oral tradition of Buddhism and Indian culture.

The art of printing made possible the production of a great number of xylograph editions to supplement or take the place of the manuscript editions already in existence. Large printing establishments, mostly attached to the larger monasteries, came into being; and the increased supply of books resulted in the creation of large libraries. Books came to have an intrinsic value, and the possession of them in great number—massive Tibetan volumes stacked in quantity—became a matter equally of social prestige and of religious reputation and sanctity. Finally, in addition to all these factors which stimulated or aided the creation, in volume, of a great religious literature, the dry, cold climate, ruling out both rot and worms, favored the preservation for centuries, with minimal deterioration, of these libraries.

To effect an entrance into this great storehouse of meticulous record and annotation and to recover lost teachings and doctrines of Buddhism, Western scholars have intensively studied both the language in which it was written and the record itself. The effort made to study and learn the language has been quite out of proportion to the importance of that language in itself, as the speech of but a few million out of the many hundred millions of Asia. The study of the language was, however, the means to a number of ends, chief of which were the recovery of a more complete record of Buddhism, the comparison of Sanskrit and Tibetan texts, and in some instances the reconstruction of Sanskrit texts from existing Tibetan versions. To quote a very pertinent quip: "Tibetan has been learned because of its usefulness as a pony to Sanskrit."[6]

The Tibetan libraries have been found to contain source material of immense value, and serious research has delved deeply into the tradition and doctrine of Buddhism as found in the Tibetan religious writings. The dogma and doctrinal elaboration of the religion of Tibet, as a form of Mahayana Buddhism, have been studied for their differences from the Hinayana, or more correctly Theravada, doctrine of the southern Buddhists. It has also been compared with other forms of Mahayana Buddhism, such as the Chinese or the Japanese. As a result of this comparison, the general outlines of Tibetan Buddhism have been defined with reasonable clarity, and the distinctive doctrines and practices which distinguish it from all other forms of Buddhism have been noted and described.

One distinctive doctrine is that of the recurrent, continuing manifestations of the Buddhahood in the bodhisattvas, which are the bases for the existence of the *sPrul sKu* ("emanation body") hierarchies. The existence of these hierarchies and their function set Tibetan Buddhism apart from all other forms of Buddhism and account for the use of the term "Lamaism" as a name applied to it. In Lamaism a system has been perpetuated of multiple, vicarious, constantly renewed, living manifestations of saviorhood in the persons and function of these *sPrul sKu* lamas. It should be noted that a *sPrul sKu* lama is quite different in origin and status from a monk. The many thousands of monks who outnumber the lamas many times over are, strictly speaking, not lamas, though *Bla Ma* ("superior one") is sometimes applied as an honorific to high-ranking or especially learned monks.

The hierarchy is headed by the *rGyal Ba Rin Po CHe* ("Great, Precious, Victorious One"), commonly known as the Dalai Lama, and the *Pan CHen Rin Po CHe* ("Great, Precious, Great Pandit"), or Panchen Lama. Under them the other *sPrul sKu* lamas—great and small—are a part of the system, having, however, in their persons and positions independence and separate identity. Each one is a savior in himself by reason of birth and discovery, not because, as a result of study, he has received ordination from above. The ecclesiastical organization is centered around these manifestations of the Buddhahood: an administrative structure

---

[6] T. V. Wylie, Oral communication in course of seminar discussion on Tibetan language.

composed of the regents, managers, and business agents of the lamas, and the abbots and members of the lamasery councils.

The only essential and irreplaceable function of the lamas is to assure, through the process of reincarnation, a stable and orderly succession, which, by reason of the rules of celibacy, could not be hereditary. A lama, however, can, and frequently does, assume direction of official matters by taking the exercise of power into his own hands. This has occurred in the case of both the previous Dalai Lama and the present one. The power structure which stemmed from the system of *sPrul sKu* lamas, with the Dalai Lama at the peak, and which first took shape in the administration of religious concerns, functioned effectively, prior to the Chinese takeover, as the government of a part of ethnic Tibet; and in that context, it must be studied both as a religious and as a political phenomenon.

AS SUBJECTIVELY EXPRESSED IN OBSERVANCES

The knowledge of the doctrine and organization of the religion of Tibet which have resulted from serious study and research have, however, like the interest in the Tibetan language, been to some extent a by-product of effort that was motivated more by the desire to recover lost doctrines of Buddhism and reconstruct the past of that system than by any great desire to know the present actuality of the religion of Tibet. In addition to the stories of pageantry and marvels, most of what has become known is centered on the theory of the Tibetan religion. Yet neither the hierarchy of the *sPrul sKu* lamas, the abstruse dogma of the Tibetan version of the noble eightfold way, the marvel of the magical generation of internal heat, nor the picturesque drama of the dance of gods makes up the reality of religion in Tibet. These seek control of and lay demands upon the Tibetan. They astonish and charm him; but only in his subjective response to the doctrine, the magic, and the drama of his faith does his religion become a reality and assume a functional role in his culture. His response finds expression in attitudes and observances; in them dogma is translated into action. Thus and thus only is religion interwoven in the varied web of both behavior patterns and social structure, and only in that way does it mark distinctively the configuration of his culture.

No complete breakdown into categories of the essential elements that make up the total of attitudes maintained and observances performed by all Tibetans is to be found in Tibetan religious writings. The rules and regulations that are found in the scriptures are primarily for the clergy. Most of them are not binding on the laity. Precepts and moral guidance abound in sermons and preachments, and certain prohibitions, intended originally to be binding on the clergy, extend also to the laity; but there is no formal code telling the Tibetan just what the observances are by which he should express his response to religion. As we shall see later, he does many things with great diligence, but he does them because they are a comprehensive pattern of an accepted way of life—which can only be religious—and not because there is a fixed schedule or list of things to be done. He has not been told, as the Moslem has been told, that he must pray five times a day or make the offering of a tithe of what he possesses. In the end, however, he prays many more than five times a day and offers what amounts to several tithes.

Nor, in the thinking of any Tibetan, is there an accurate summary of just what his responses to religion are, for the same reason that a person cannot accurately see himself and know with clarity the image of himself which he projects to others. But a partial consciousness of the difference between the theory of religion and the actuality of religion is reflected in the difference in meaning and application between the terms *CHos* ("religion") and *CHos Kyi* ("religion its"). *CHos* is the dogma, the theory, and the word, to be studied and worshipped. But *Kyi,* one form of the genitive particle, when added, applies religion to man and makes him religion-possessed. The genitive case is a strong one in Tibetan, with a wide range of application and usage. The genitive particle, when added to an adjective, either puts it in the emphatic atypical position before the noun, for example, *dKar Gi rTa* ("white its horse"), or as a copulative verb attributes the quality of the adjective to a noun, for example, *rTa bZang Gi* ("horse good is"). In most dialects when this particle is added to the present verb root it forms the active present, for example, *NGa aGro Gi* ("I go")—either as a statement of fact or intention. Thus "possessed by religion," "religion attributed to," and "religion *activated*" become, in our terminology, "pious," but in Tibetan terminology, much more. The term is used to characterize a king—*CHos Kyi rGyal Po* ("religion its king")—or a man—*CHos Kyi Mi* ("religion its man").

Criteria for Determination of Observances

The subjective responses of the Tibetan to the great compelling whole of religion, as expressed in attitudes and observances, may only be determined by a careful survey of the entire gamut of Tibetan life and activity. A number of criteria, however, are of prime importance in guiding this search for the indexes of religious allegiance. The basic, universally held and practiced religious attitudes and observances, which have strong functional roles in the culture, should conform to the following criteria: (1) Each one, within the context of Tibetan behavior patterns, should be universal: something which is accepted and observed by every Tibetan. (2) Each one should be an observable or verifiable phenomenon; therein is its reality. (3) Each one, as defined by the Tibetans, should be religious in nature or purpose. (4) Each one should have conceptual unity: it should be, in itself, a single simplistic act and not a composite.

The key word of the first and most basic of these criteria is "universal." This concept appears within many frames of reference and in many contexts. Only in a narrowly restricted sense, as qualified by the words "Tibetan" and "religious," is its use permissible in this survey; yet there is no other word to do semantic duty and represent what is intended. Qualified and delimited in this way, "universal" is the key word of the first of the criteria which are used in determining which attitudes and observances characterize the Tibetan's response to his religion.

To the degree that each practice exemplifies a human response more general than Tibetan, and to the extent that at least some of their beginnings antedate Buddhism, they transcend both the Tibetan religion and culture, and are thus, in a larger sense, universal. Yet, for the purpose of this study, "universal" is defined within the context of the Tibetan cultural pattern and is so used.

Such use is based, however, on the assumption that all Tibetans are lamaist and therefore eligible to participate in the observances of that religion. This assumption encounters two difficulties: first, that the Bon religion in its present form persists in many areas of Tibet and has many adherents, and second, that there are some individual Tibetans and a few small communities—mostly on the periphery—which have become Moslem, Christian, or Hindu. Both of these difficulties are more apparent than real. In a previous chapter it has already been shown that the Bon religion, by the adoption of Buddhist forms and practices and by the adaptation of Buddhist doctrines, has taken on protective coloration and has become only slightly more different from the older forms of Tibetan Buddhism than those sects are different from the Yellow or orthodox sect. In the Tibetan formula which cites CHos gCig ("religion one" or "oneness of religion") as one of the criteria for determining the characteristics of a Tibetan, that criterion is stretched with great tolerance to include the Bon Po as Nang Pa ("within ones"). They are felt to be following the practices of Buddhism in a left-handed way. As for those individuals or small communities that have become Moslem, Christian, or Hindu, although it is felt that in a very vital sense they are no longer truly Tibetan, they constitute minor and relatively insignificant exceptions to the rule that the typical Tibetan can be nothing but lamaist in religion. This self-recognition underlies the present central political organization. Much of the culture of Tibet is based on this unity of belief.

Within this unity, only that which applies to all Tibetans is truly universal religious observance. There are many obligations which do not apply to all. Those basic obligations pertaining to monkhood are assumed by only an estimated one-sixth of the population. Even among the members of the order there are differences—individual or organizational—in degrees of observance or attainment. The clergy exercise themselves in the apprehension of knowledge to vanquish ignorance, but this apprehension belongs to only a few. Degrees of enlightenment or attainment of religious power are graduated. None is universal. Only initiates or adepts exercise the extraordinary power attributed to them, and such adepts are few in number. Special roles in ritual are assigned to those specially qualified. Special vows are taken, in connection with special consecration to a course of study or the practice of meditation, by some but not by all. For the laity, vows of silence, vows regulating diet, and vows of elective solitude or other forms of renunciation are taken by some, or a few, but not by all. None of these vows is binding on all Tibetans.

These special observances are called *sDom Pai CHos Las* ("the vow's religion-work") and are designed to result in *sDom Pai dGe Ba* ("the vow's virtue"), in contrast to the universals of Tibetan religious observance, which are called *CHos Las* ("religion-work"). As to their purpose, the Tibetans define them as *dGe Bai Las* ("virtue's work") and, in terms of effect produced, *Bar Ma dGe Ba* ("median virtue"), in contrast to *sDom Pa dGe Ba* ("the vow's virtue"). This median result and its cause, median effort, constitute what may be called the least common denominator, or the mean of religious observance, and belong to all Tibetans. The effort expressed in these observances is shared by all. None is so high or sacrosanct that he is exempt; none is so lowly or reprobate that he is debarred from participation.

Conformity with the second of the established criteria requires that an observance, characterized as universal in the Tibetan context, should also be an observable or verifiable phenomenon. This wording is in itself a confession that the category has a sort of split personality. The necessity for using both "observable" and "verifiable" as defining terms arises from the fact that in the survey of essential religious observances we are dealing with aspects of being as well as aspects of doing. Attitudes are to being what activities are to doing, and attitudes, if not strictly observable, are yet verifiable by patient inquiry.

The third criterion requires that each recognizable phenomenon, which is universal in the Tibetan context, shall be, as defined by the Tibetans, religious in nature or purpose. The words "nature or purpose" constitute an admission that, as in the case of the second criterion, this category also has a split personality. Yet within the comprehensive pattern of Tibetan individual and societal activity, recognition of the religious nature of many phenomena is perception of the obvious. This is particularly true of the many aspects of *CHos aDon*, the observance which is based on the verbalization of religion. Some activities, however, do not submit easily to unequivocal determination. The same activity, according to varying circumstances, may be either religious or nonreligious in nature; or an observance that is religious in nature by Tibetan definition may be directed toward secular purposes. A more detailed elaboration of these problems will be given in the chapters devoted to analysis of each separate observance, but the issues are raised here to show the need for the phrase "nature or purpose" in the formulation of this criterion.

For the purposes of this study, the fourth criterion requires that each of the Tibetan universal religious observances shall have conceptual unity: though an observance may have many aspects, it should yet be simplistic, not complex; a unit in itself, not a compound. Thus it will be an element in the elaborate ritual, a unitary thread (undifferentiated within itself), woven into the patterned fabric of all Tibetan religious observance, which contributes to the texture and color of the whole but which may also be isolated and identified. The many combinations of these simple, basic activities constitute a great part of ritual, ceremony, and the whole of religious observance; but their function in relation to society and a cultural configuration is best studied when they are viewed as the separate, unitary, component parts of the over-all pattern.

The List of Observances

With these four criteria as a frame of reference, a careful and extensive survey of Tibetan behavior patterns and activity, whether societal or individual, yields six—and only six—basic, unitary attitudes and activities which can accurately be called Tibetan universal religious observances. The survey has consisted of a review of much that has been written about the Tibetans by observers who have visited and written about the land; a sampling of the writings of Tibetans about their own life and religion; a meticulous effort to recall facts observed and impressions gained in more than eight years of personal firsthand experience while traveling and living among the Tibetans of Amdo and Khams; and finally, a referral of the entire problem with its many ramifications to very competent Tibetan authority.

The Tibetan scholars identified in the Preface as sources were consulted at length, and their dissent, assent, emendation, or amplification invited. This involved hours of wide-ranging discussion and vivid recall of scenes and activities known to all of us. Their interest was intense, and in the course of final and general endorsement, they advanced much in the way of constructive criticism and reformulated much, using a strict Tibetan terminology. This Tibetan reformulation will be given in the explanations which follow the list.

As thus selected, the six Tibetan universals of religious observance, in the order of their religious importance, are the following:

1. The attitude of *Dad Pa* ("faith")
2. The practice of *CHos aDon* ("religion express," or verbalization of religion)
3. The making of *mCHod Pa* ("offerings")
4. The performance of *PHyag* ("salutations")
5. The performance of *bsKor Ba* ("circumambulation")
6. The recourse to *Mo* ("divination").

There is general agreement that all six observances are practiced by all Tibetans, clergy and laity alike, and therefore that they are universals in the Tibetan context. There was similar agreement that all six are obvious—subject to being seen or heard, or, as in the case of faith, evidenced. There was some uncertainty concerning the undifferentiated unity of each of the observances, but all agreed that they could be combined and therefore were often found as component parts of complicated religious activity. There was complete agreement that the first five are *CHos Las* ("religion-work"), but about the sixth there was considerable divergence of opinion. Thubten Norbu insists that *Mo* is not a part of *CHos*. In such insistence, he is speaking, of course, as a member of the *dGe Lugs Pa* ("ones of the virtue-system") hierarchy and as a religious purist. He believes that if religion is what it should be, then *Mo* is religious neither in nature nor in purpose and cannot be one of the Tibetan universals of religious observance. The Sakya lamas are more inclined to straddle the ideological fence. In their opinion, divination is not exactly religious; yet it is closely involved in religion since the rites of divination are mostly performed by the clergy.

Involved in this discussion is a semantic difficulty concerning the word *CHos* of which all the Tibetan lamas are aware. One of the specific meanings of this word as it appears in the Rare-Perfect Three is—following Chinese usage—customarily "law." In such a context, *CHos* is less comprehensive and has a more narrowly restricted denotation than the English word "religion." This would favor the purist's contention that divination is not within religion. The word has, however, so many meanings that the sum of them comprehends much more than the English word "religion." In its widest context it could certainly take in such matters as divination.

It is also claimed that whenever recourse to divination results in increased works of virtue and intensified religious observance, as very frequently is the case, it then becomes a work of virtue in its own right and, as a contributing factor, should be counted as *CHos Las* ("religion-work"). Thus, religious practice being what it is in Tibet, recourse to *Mo* although equivocal in nature and in theory allowed only on sufferance, is included within the roster of Tibetan religious observances and will be examined in that context. This may not only reveal the functional role of divination in Tibetan culture but contribute to additional understanding of the interrelationship of religion and magic.

In addition to conforming to the criteria used in their selection, these Tibetan universals of religious observance have other characteristics in common. They have roots in the past of the religion of which they are a manifestation; and they have histories within the history of that religion. In some instances their beginnings antedate that history and are a part of the first responses of early man to religion as he conceived it. The universals link the philosophy of Tibetan Buddhism with the behavior pattern of the peoples of Tibet. As the subjective responses of a Tibetan—every Tibetan—they bridge the gulf between theory and action; they transmute dogma into everyday reality. Through them, dogma becomes behavior, and attitudes and activities in turn become religion.

The characteristics these observances have in common, and their conformity in whole or in part to the criteria set up to determine their selection, make them all seem very much alike. It is easy to assume that their differences are trivial and their similarities dominant, but in fact they are clearly and somewhat sharply differentiated. The system of categories used by the Tibetans to classify and explain them points up some of these differences very clearly.

Characterization of the Observances

The first observance, the attitude of *Dad Pa* ("faith"), is the most important. It stands apart from all the others in that it is an attitude rather than an activity. Because of this, it is important in the formulation of a philosophy and a world view. It plays a part in setting ethical ideals; it influences interpersonal and intergroup relationships; and it is a determinant in establishing social, political, and even international attitudes. By the Tibetans, it is classified as *dGe Bai Las* ("virtue's work"), pertaining to, or a function of, the *Sems* ("mind") aspect of existence.

The second, the practice of *CHos aDon* ("express verbalized religion") is an activity linked with speech. It is the verbalization of religion by utterance, writing, reading, and multiplication or amplification by every possible device, from printing blocks to prayer wheels powered by wind and water. Its influence affects forms of speech, oratorical standards, education—both in content and demographic spread—language distribution, and linguistic change. The cultural experience it has entailed has made the Tibetan aware of the problems of semantics, of word or idea borrowing, and of the factors at work in linguistic acculturation. The Tibetans classify it as *dGe Bai Las* ("virtue's work"), pertaining to the *NGag* ("speech") aspect of existence.

The third in the list, the making of *mCHod Pa* ("offerings"), is concerned, as an activity, with the possessions of the Tibetan. It is based, moreover, on ideals of sacrifice and devotion—abnegation of the self and its interests in favor of *CHos* and its maintenance and glorification by worship. Concepts of the responsibility of ownership and possession are involved in its practice. It affects standards of living, per capita income, consumer preferences, distribution and movement of wealth, accumulation of capital, utilization of capital, and behavior patterns of conspicuous consumption and prestige expenditure. The Tibetans classify it as *dGe Bai Las* ("virtue's work"), pertaining to the *Lus* ("body") aspect of existence.

The fourth and fifth observances are alike in many respects. As performances, *PHyag* ("salutation") and *bsKor Ba* ("circumambulation") are the physical expressions of reverence and worship. Both activities are manifestations of bodily effort, some of which may be quite prolonged and taxing. As forms of exercise that rate high in prestige value and social acceptance, they not only contribute to health and a sense of well-being but are psychologically effective for the release of tensions. Both activities have definite focuses in space and play a part in fixing and maintaining meeting points, which, by intent, are religious in nature but become of importance culturally and have societal and economic significance. They strongly influence the movement and meeting of individuals or segments of the population and make a substantial contribution to social cohesiveness and a sense of group solidarity. The Tibetans classify them both as *dGe Bai Las* ("virtue's work"), pertaining to the *Lus* ("body") aspect of existence. They differ in one important respect. *PHyag* ("salutation"), as a means of communication, is a formalization of the trait of making gestures, which is universal in human—and to some degree, animal—societies. *bsKor Ba* ("circumambulation"), however, does not have the same universality in origin but appears to be limited to cultures which have links of descent, or some degree of cultural inheritance, from very early Aryan sources.

The sixth—and in relation to the criteria, the most controversial—of the observances, recourse to *Mo* ("divination"), is primitive science applied to the problem of telescoping time and space for the purpose of forecasting events. In the context of Tibetan notions concerning the continuity of time and the nature of space, it is both within reason and logical. Its function within Tibetan society is extremely complex. The Tibetans classify it as being neither *dGe Bai Las* ("virtue's work") nor *Mi dGe Bai Las* ("not virtue's work") but *Lung bsTan Bai Las* ("the work of prophecy"), which is essentially ambivalent with regard to virtue. It does not pertain exclusively to either the *Sems* ("mind"), *NGag* ("speech"), or *Lus* ("body") aspects of existence.

In succeeding chapters each of these Tibetan universals of religious observance will be examined with care to establish its doctrinal origins—whether enjoined or permissive—its history, its manifestation as a phenomenon, and its functional role in shaping or determining the distinctive configuration of the culture called Tibetan. When all this has been accomplished, it will also become evident that these items, in the aggregate and in their collective functional role in Tibetan society, have a value which is greater than the mere sum of their separate respective roles.

CHAPTER FOUR

THE ATTITUDE

OF *DAD PA:*

FAITH

The attitude of *Dad Pa* ("faith") is rightly the first of the Tibetan universals of religious observance—first in order of treatment and first, too, in the context of causality. Without it, the existence of the other observances is inconceivable, since they are based upon it. Its value is a primary one, and its relationship to the others is that of existence to manifestation —of the function of being to the function of doing. As stated in a previous chapter, *Dad Pa* ("faith") is conceived to be the function, or *Las* ("work"), of the *Sems* ("mind"). But Tibetans formulate that function in the following terms, *Sems rGyal Po Yin* ("mind is king"), and then *Sems KHong Rang Gi Las rNam aGyur Dang sPyod Yin Mod* ("Manner-change and action are indeed mind's own particular work"). Thus it is first *rNam aGyur* ("manner-change"), that is, attitude; but as a succession of attitudes or changes, assumed and constantly renewed in a derived and complementary sense, it is also an activity, *sPyod,* based on motivation and producing end results.

It is both significant and a testimony to the perceptiveness of Tibetan thinking in the coining of compound verbal symbols to express important concepts that the compound *rNam aGyur,* as the Tibetan word for attitude, is very similar to the following modern social-science definition: "The attitude is originally a trial response . . . to control subsequent adjustment behavior."[1] For the Tibetan, an attitude is not simply a fixed pose but a change of manner in response to stimuli.

This dual aspect of *Dad Pa*—as a once-and-for-all attitude and as a continuing activity—characterizes it, in all its manifestations, as a religious observance of the Tibetans; and as a twofold subjective response,

---

[1] L. L. Bernard, in *Encyclopaedia of the Social Sciences* (1950), Vol. II, pp. 305–6.

with all the phenomenal activities which stem from it, it constitutes the religion of the Tibetans. It is primarily an attitude; yet in its conscious renewal and function, it exhibits many of the aspects of an activity. Conversely, the other observances, which are patently and overwhelmingly activities, are not altogether dissimilar from *Dad Pa*. Each one of them, too, has aspects of duality; though they are called activities, they are based on conscious and unconscious mental and emotional predispositions which are truly attitudes. *PHyag* ("salutation"), for example, is a phenomenal activity, strenuous and observable; yet it is so based on value, status judgments, and conditioned responses, that it could well be called the attitude of salutation. In terms of attitude and activity, the true difference between the first of the universals and the other five is the relative proportion of attitude and activity in each.

CONFORMITY TO CRITERIA

As thus defined, the attitude of *Dad Pa* conforms to the four criteria formulated in the preceding chapter. Within the context of Tibetan life, it is universal: it characterizes every Tibetan. Such exceptions as do exist go far toward proving the rule. Tibetan communities which have changed their religion (there have been some in peripheral areas) are regarded by the other Tibetans as having renounced something so distinctly Tibetan that, by the change, they are no longer Tibetan and are truncated from the Tibetan social and political structure. Adherence to present-day Bonism does not have the same effect, for that religion has become so overlaid with Buddhism, and restated in Buddhist terms and doctrinal concepts, that it is now included within the whole of the belief and practice that Tibetans regard as Tibetan religion. There remains the problem of the individual who is a rebel in whole or in part. Such do exist in Tibet, and expressions of skepticism do occur and are even found in writings which are closely related to religion. This sort of skepticism never leads, however, to the final steps of separation or exclusion from the category of the *Nang Ba* ("within ones"), which designation, in Tibetan thinking, includes all who are Buddhist. For a Tibetan, being a *Nang Ba* is one of the distinguishing characteristics of being a Tibetan.

The *rNam aGyur* ("manner-change") of *Dad Pa* also conforms to the requirement that the religious observances that are selected for study shall be observable or verifiable phenomena. Faith, although it may elude direct observation, has reality; and through its many observable manifestations, its existence, strength, and distinguishing characteristics are solidly verifiable.

It is primarily religious in nature and purpose; it underlies all religious activity. As the frame of reference within which acceptance operates and motivation is generated, it also involves the Tibetan in an aggregate of ideas and concepts concerning existence, world view, the nature and structure of the cosmos, and the nature of history. In its widest extension, it specifically includes cosmology, geography, physiology, and the structure of matter, and thus is linked with astronomy, the practice of medicine, and the arts. Thus, though it is religious in nature and purpose, it does exert influence on secular matters.

Dad Pa is not an aggregate of attitudes and activities; it is a basic concept which has conceptual unity and produces attitudes and activities. In Tibetan thinking, *Dad Pa* is sometimes seen as the other face of desire; it is closely related to concepts of credence, trust, and confidence; and it is often compounded in words and phrases that vividly reflect the importance of its functional role in Tibetan life. But by itself, it has undifferentiated unity.

TERMINOLOGY OF FAITH

Since this face toward existence is both an attitude that was (or is) assumed at some point in ecclesiastical, national, or personal history or experience and a succession of "manner-changes" that exhibit the functional role of adjustment behavior (or activities), an examination of its verbal symbol, *Dad Pa*, and of an entire cluster of related terms, among which it is the central and key word, is in order. The circle which delimits the semantic content of *Dad Pa* is a much larger one than the circle which delimits the semantic content of the English word "faith." The terms which cluster around *Dad Pa* express aspects of faith, belief, trust, confidence, acceptance, devotion, reverence, and adoration. Used alone, the word subsumes many if not all of these meanings. *Dad Pa*, moreover, belongs exclusively in a religious context: it cannot be used in reference to any secular concept or to a person. Some of the other related words are linked with it to form compounds which suggest special nuances or indicate directional emphasis. Others are synonyms, of subordinate value, which may be substituted for it on lower planes of meaning in personal or secular contexts.

The word *Dad Pa* is both a substantive and a verb and, therefore, is used with greater flexibility and in more varied contexts than the English word "faith." *Pa* is either the nominal particle or the sign of the infinitive. *Dad Pa* functions as an adjective when the possessive *i* is added to *Pa*. It then precedes the noun in the atypical emphatic form as *Dad Pai Sems* ("faith's mind"). When the adverbial ending *r* is added to *Pa* it has an adverbial function, as in the phrase *Dad Par aDug Gi Yod* (or something like "continuing to be in the manner of faith").

With one exception, it stands alone among Tibetan words, having no cognates. It is a homonym, however, even to the extent of the same spelling, with *Dad Pa*, a secondary form of *aDod Pa* ("to desire"). This ambiguity of form, and possibly also of meaning, which could very easily lead to doctrinal error, is probably the reason why *Mi La Ras Pa,* theologian and gifted writer of the *Hundred Thousand Songs*, indicates an awareness of a close relationship between *aDod Pa* and *Dad Pa*. He attempts to clarify the two in the exhortation, "As it is to be feared that *Dad Pa* may be mistaken for *aDod Pa* it is important that they are not confounded. The first is what may be called divine love and the second love of the family and the matters of this world."[2] This statement, in effect, admits that the two words have a basic similarity of meaning; and consequently, any difference between the two is not one of semantics but one of context and application. Thus the mind's outreach toward the world and its concerns is manifested in desire and toward religion and its concerns in faith.[3]

There appears to be much semantic common ground in the two words. It is possible that both words, now listed separately in dictionaries, derive from an original basic concept that can only be subsumed in the compound desire-faith. They may be related, in Tibetan reasoning and logic, as two sides of the same coin, exhibiting the dual aspects of aspiration and realization, desire realized in faith. Such incorporation of paired meanings within the same word—subjective and objective, causal and resultant—is an interesting and not infrequent phenomenon in Tibetan speech. *Slob Pa* means both "to teach" and "to learn"; *PHebs Pa,* "to go" and "to come"; *gYar Ba,* "to borrow" and "to lend"; *sDig Pa,* "sin" and "suffering"; and *dGe Ba,* "virtue" and "merit."

According to one school of Tibetan doctrinal theory and exegesis, the origin and nature of *Dad Pa* have the following ordered sequence. There are three aspects of conscious being: *Sems* ("mind"), *NGag* ("speech") and *Lus* ("body"). Of the three, mind is king; the other two are servants.

[2] S. C. Das, *A Tibetan-English Dictionary* (1902), p. 617. The interconnection and yet distinctions between *aDod Pa* ("desire") and *Dad Pa* ("faith") are also treated at some length in one of the songs of Mi La, *rJe bTSun Mi La Ras Pai mGur aBum ZHes Bya Ba bZHugs So* (Section *ka*, f. 286 *a*).

[3] This statement represents the consensus of the Tibetan scholars with whom the interconnection and distinctions between desire and faith have been discussed at great length.

Dad Pa ("faith") is the *Las* ("work") of mind; and this work is in turn explained as *rNam rGyur* ("manner-change") and *sPyod* ("activity"). But *Dad Pa* itself is defined as of two kinds: *Jig rTen Pai Dad Pai* ("faith of the earth"), which is for all ordinary men—laity and clergy alike—and *aJig rTen Las aDas Pai Dad Pa* ("faith surpassing the earth"), which is only possible for the *Byang CHub Sems dPaa* ("Purged, Permeated Hero Mind[s]"). In its quality and degree of intensity, faith may be *Dwangs Bai Dad Pa* ("lymph's faith"), which is glandular, like procreative affection, and is of relatively low or medium quality; it may be *aDod Pai Dad Pa* ("desire's faith"), which is "like the thirst for water" and is also of medium quality; and it may be *Yid CHes Kyi Dad Pa* ("enlarged mind's faith"), which, like *Ma-Bu* ("mother-son") affection, is of superior quality. *Yid CHes Kyi Dad Pa* is also known as *PHyir Mi Log Pai Dad Pa* ("not-backward-falling faith").

With an almost evangelical fervor and flavor, it is also stated of *Dad Pa* that it is *dGe Bai sGo* ("virtue's door"), *rGe Bai rTen* ("virtue's base"), *dGe Bai Lam* ("virtue's way"), *dGe Bai Sa Bon* ("virtue's seed"), and *dGe Bai rTSa Ba* ("virtue's root"). This last definition also appears as a lexicographer's definition in the latest Tibetan–Tibetan–Chinese dictionary.[4]

With the particle *Pa* attached, *Dad Pa* is often combined with auxiliary verbs of possession, action, and obligation:

Dad Pa Yod ("having faith")
Dad Pa Med ("not having faith")
Dad Pa Byed ("faith act"), or form faith
Dad Pa Bya ("faith do"), or produce faith
Dad Pa dGos ("faith need")

In its stem or root form *Dad*, it does not appear alone but is used in compounds.

Dad Can ("faith-possessing")
Dad lDan ("faith-filled")
Dad Yod ("having faith")
Dad Med ("not having faith")
Dad Mos ("faith-devotion")
Dad aDun ("faith-supplication")
Dad Gus ("faith-reverence")
Dad bTSun ("faith-reverend," or monk, as distinguished from a drafted monk)

[4] dGe bSHes CHos Grags, *brDa Dag Ming TSHig gSal Ba bZHugs So* (1957), p. 390.

Of these words that are often linked with *Dad,* only three, *Mos* ("adoration"), *aDun* ("supplication"), and *Gus* ("reverence"), have semantic nearness. Adoration is often cited as a synonym of faith. Supplication is very similar to adoration but is defined as having a somewhat narrower and more intensive connotation. Reverence is explained as the expression in mental approach and words of what *PHyag* ("salutation") expresses in action. All three may be, and mostly are, used in religious contexts, but unlike *Dad Pa,* they may also be used with reference to persons and secular concepts.

There is another group of words which are used as substitutes for *Dad Pa* but which never appear in combination with it. They have a somewhat restricted or downgraded use, in the sense that secular and person-to-person use, as distinguished from religious use, may be considered downgraded. They are particularizations of meaning within the over-all or general concept of belief. Of this group, the most widely used phrase is *Yid CHes Pa* ("enlarged mind"), meaning "to believe." With *Yid* ("mind"), *CHes* may be considered either *CHe* ("large"), with the instrumental case ending *s* added, or the perfect form of the verb *CHe Ba* ("to be great"). In a sense it stands antithetically to *Sems CHung* ("small heart"), which means "caution" and contains the idea of uncertainty and lack of assurance. As an expression of assurance, or confidence, *Yid CHes Pa* is much used, mostly with reference to persons. It is never employed in reference to *CHos* ("religion"). Its use in reference to <u>Sangs rGyas</u> ("Buddhahood") would be an impertinence, for it represents a less sublime concept than *Dad Pa.* On the other hand, it is used to express trust in high ecclesiastics as well as in other individuals. A Tibetan affirms *Dad Pa* in the doctrines which underlie the existence of the *sPrul sKu* ("emanation-body") lamas, but as a result of a value judgment, he will also affirm *Yid CHes Pa,* or trust, in the person or the comparative excellence or sanctity of a particular lama. *Blo gTod Pa* ("understanding-leaning") also indicates a function of the understanding with reference to trust and confidence. It is frequently used in describing attitudes of trust or the evaluations on which trust is based. The figure of speech is an obvious one: The mind rests against, or leans on, the object—hence trust. Two other words are frequently used to express certain degrees or aspects of trust: *rTon Pa* ("to rely on") and *Rlom Ba* ("have pride in"). The latter, while primarily meaning to "have pride in" or "be attached to," is often the equivalent of the American idiom, "I bet on him."

FAITH AND BUDDHISM

The origin of faith, as attitude and activity, quite obviously antedates the origins of Buddhism. Long before the Buddha "turned the wheel of the law" and preached to the ascetics, his contemporaries and compatriots held and practiced their religion in the attitude of faith; and before that, still earlier cults were held in the same attitude. There is no need to examine Buddhism for evidence concerning the origin of this universal attitude. Its beginnings are lost in the very beginnings of human experience and in the ancient universal need of mankind to say "I believe." As Durkheim says, "The first article in every creed is the belief in salvation by faith."[5]

But it is pertinent to ask how the Buddha, who in a spirit of basic agnosticism preached that the vanquishing of ignorance and attainment of knowledge would result in the ultimate enlightenment, came to make this compromise with the then current practice and fundamental need of some attitude of faith? In his personal and spiritual experience and history, the Buddha had little to serve as a guide in evaluating the attitude of faith and assigning to it a place of importance within his system. His own experience had consisted of a succession of denials and mental rejections. He had rejected wealth and power; he also rejected, after some experience, the extremes of asceticism. He took nothing for granted and, in a relentless fulfilment of the urge to know and thus vanquish ignorance, formulated the doctrine of the four truths and traced the outlines of the noble eightfold way. Nowhere is there a trace of the attitude of faith, unless in the inference that he believed in the functioning of his mind and thus in himself. But when he preached the truths he had found and the spiritual equilibrium of the middle way to the five ascetics, he found himself confronted with the dilemma that without faith in the teacher or belief in his word the doctrine could not be communicated profitably to others.[6]

The attitude of faith was crucial, both in the personal experience of the disciples and in the history of the rise of Buddhism. The Buddha himself fought a battle, as well as taught a system of meditative, agnostic search for truth and an uncompromising self-discipline. There was no possibility of a truce or negotiated peace between the teaching of the four truths and the noble eightfold way and the Brahma-centered system of belief and sacrifice which was the traditional religion of the land. To

[5] É. Durkheim, "Religion and Society," in *Theories of Society* (1961), Vol. I, p. 677.
[6] W. W. Rockhill, *Life of the Buddha* (1907), pp. 107, 114, 121, 159.

64

displace Brahmanism, it was essential that those to whom the Buddha spoke transfer the faith they had in that system and make the person of Buddha and his word the new object of their faith.

Faith in the teacher was a prime necessity. E. J. Thomas quotes Buddhist teaching: "Hears the doctrine of a Buddha and acquires faith in him."[7] The Tibetan historian and theological writer *Bu sTon* describes the first step in conversion as "faith in the word of Buddha having arisen . . . ,"[8] and says, "Oh, friends, *Dad Pa* ("faith") is a means for the perception of the truth."[9] But this admittance or incorporation of the attitude of faith is judged by some students of Buddhism as being at variance with its essence. J. Bacot writes, "Ce n'est pas un dogme auquel le fidèle soit tenue de croire . . ."; and again, "Les caractères essentials du bouddhism du Bouddha sont le rejet de toute foi préalable."[10] And Madame David-Neel states, "He (the Buddha) never appealed to faith."[11]

Bu sTon, however, makes faith one of the four basic opportunities of the present: "At present the Buddha has appeared, and the favourable state of existence, faith, and the possibility to study the doctrine are all of them secured. Therefore, do away with distraction."[12] Faith is made a prime necessity in the hearing of the word, and even when that hearing leads to little or no comprehension, it is held that the presence of faith makes it productive. "Even those, that do not understand the words they hear, must listen devotedly to the word of Buddha. Indeed, if one but only listens full of faith, one becomes possessed of great virtues and gives increase to the element of Highest Wisdom."[13]

After this first step, the further development of the doctrine of faith in Buddhist teaching was inevitable. With the admission that faith was essential to conversion and acceptance of the doctrine came the listing of its negative aspect, doubt, as one of the hindrances; and there exists an entire series of admonitions designed to eliminate doubt from the mind of the disciple. Faith is defined as "the first universal level, even for one who is only a lay disciple."[14]

[7] H. E. Thomas, *A History of Buddhist Thought* (1933), p. 44.

[8] E. Obermiller, *History of Buddhism* (1931; a translation of *CHos aByung,* by Bu sTon), Part I, p. 10.

[9] *Ibid.,* Part II, p. 8.

[10] J. Bacot, *Le Bouddha* (1947), pp. 33, 40.

[11] A. David-Neel, *Buddhism: Its Doctrines and Its Methods* (n.d.), p. 21.

[12] E. Obermiller, *op. cit.,* Part I, p. 85.

[13] *Ibid.,* p. 81.

[14] H. E. Thomas, *op. cit.,* p. 207.

One further aspect of the doctrinal development of faith makes it somewhat akin to the "faith in God" of the believer in God, for faith in the Triad is made the means of gaining nirvana. "The Arhat develops faith in the Triad." "Must have faith in the Triad." "Faith in the Three Jewels is essential."[15]

In consonance with this, there also developed in Tibet an extensive complex of acceptance and practice centering around faith in *dKon mCHog gSum* ("Rare-Perfect Three") as a means of salvation. The first king of Tibet, unequivocally identified as a Buddhist, placed "To have faith in *dKon mCHog* ("god")" as the first of the sixteen moral virtues enjoined upon his subjects.[16] *THar Ba* ("liberation") becomes possible if one has faith in *dKon mCHog* ("Rare-Perfect"), and such liberation may be either attainment of the bodhisattva stage in the next rebirth or direct passage into *Nub bDe Ba CHen* ("western great bliss"). Faith becomes the base, root, seed, and so on, of virtue and the way in which the teachings of the Buddha are accepted. *Bu sTon* says, "He who hears a single word and through this comes to faith—attains merit greater than an offering of pure morality or deepest meditation."[17] The works which tell of the work of the teachers of Buddhism in Tibet are replete with the phrase *Dad Pa aGyur Ro* ("faith was changed") as descriptive of the attitude and reaction of the hearers and disciples.

Thus step by step, faith came to have a position of great importance within the dogma, and achieved a place in popular acceptance in Tibet greatly resembling that occupied by faith in Christian theology, especially in Catholicism. The definitions previously cited are expressions of the pervasive and satisfying quality of faith so held. It does not accord with the stripped, severe agnosticism of theoretical Buddhism, but it constitutes at once the attitude and the activity of the mind seeking liberation. *Dad Pa Yod Na THar Ba THub rGyu Red* ("if one has faith, liberation will be possible") is the commonest phrasing of this pervasive belief. And negatively, the Tibetan says, *Dad Pa Med Na Rang Red* ("if one does not have faith, no avail").

Certain qualifications or reservations do exist, however, with regard to this attitude. Even as the Buddha, after allowing a place in the doctrine for faith, was then confronted with the existence and problem of doubt, so we find in the universal attitude of faith among the Tibetans the simultaneous existence of a considerable amount of doubt expressed

[15] N. Dutt, *Early Monastic Buddhism* (1960), Vol. II, pp. 20, 87, 227, 306.

[16] S. C. Das, "Contributions on Tibet," *JASB*, 1881, p. 219.

[17] E. Obermiller, *op. cit.*, Part I, pp. 16–17.

in various ways. The very intensity and comprehensiveness of his faith make some occasional denial a necessity: irreverence is the rebound from reverence that has grown overwhelming and well-nigh insupportable. The Tibetan believes completely, for example, in the *sPrul sKu* ("emanation-body") lamas, who are the continuously renewed saviors of his religious system, and, therefore, in all their pronouncements and sayings. Yet, in the same breath with which—hand raised in solemn attestation—he protests his faith, he will mock the lamas and liken their teachings to the variables of linguistic diffusion and change and to the vagaries of justice at the hands of capricious officialdom. The balanced three-line jeer,

> *Lung Ba Re Re sKad Lugs Yod* ("Each valley has its own speech system")
> *dPon Po Re Re KHrims Lugs Yod* ("Each official has his own law system")
> *Bla Ma Re Re CHos Lugs Yod* ("Each lama has his own religion system"),

is a very good example of Tibetan folklore.[18] Or the Tibetan may wise-crack concerning the hereafter: *Za rGyu aTHung rGyu Da Da Red* ("Eating and drinking is now"), or *TSHe PHyi Ma Ni Gang Gi Sa Red* ("Where is the afterlife?"). In such words and their echo, skepticism and non-conformity haunt widely accepted belief.

The Tibetan story of the dog's tooth that became a relic aptly illustrates this dichotomy of response, with faith, however, in final ascendance. The aged mother of a merchant who made frequent trips to India begged him repeatedly to bring her a holy relic of the Buddha and repeatedly he forgot. Finally she added to her request the threat that if he did not bring the relic she would commit suicide on his arrival. Again he forgot, but when he was almost home he remembered the threat and looked around in desperation, wondering what he could do. Seeing the skeleton of a dog by the roadside, he took a tooth, cleaned it, carefully wrapped it in a satin covering, and presented it to his mother as a tooth of the Buddha. With great joy and full of faith, she worshipped it with prayers, offerings, salutations, and circumambulations for many years. Finally she died—but faith had made the dog's tooth a true and holy relic —and amid such signs as signalize the passing of a saint, she went on to the land of the gods.[19]

---

[18] It has been argued that this well-known proverb is merely a factual statement of inevitable differences. But the Tibetan scholars all agree that derision is intended and thus that it is a "jibe."

[19] This story was told by Dezhung Rinpoche with a wealth of detail and in a manner oddly reflecting compassion, faith, and cynicism, which illustrates the attitude in question.

TENETS OF FAITH

From a fundamental attitude of faith toward the supreme concepts of religion, of which *dKon mCHog gSum* ("Rare-Perfect Three") is the primary one in popular acceptance, there stems a widely inclusive accept-ance—faith in a large number of peripheral concepts that have somehow become attached to the concept of religion. To understand how this can happen requires an examination and explanation of what the word *CHos* ("religion") comprehends in the context of Tibetan conceptualization and thought. It is a word which at times may be used to particularize in an extremely narrow and restricted sense, as when it is employed to des-ignate the form of Tibetan letters on paper, without reference to the meaning of the words the letters represent. A scrap of paper with a few letters of the Tibetan alphabet on it is sometimes referred to as *CHos* simply because those same letters of the alphabet were used to write the word of the Buddha and the scrap of paper, because of this association, has become holy to some extent. At the other extreme, *CHos* becomes a term of such generalization, comprehending so great a field of meaning, that it subsumes the whole of human—or rather, Tibetan—knowledge, systems of thought, linguistic usage, and even forms of social organiza-tion. Used in this way, it comprehends more of the whole of Tibetan thought and culture and occupies a position of even greater importance than the word *Tao* occupies in the context of Chinese thought and culture.

In a later chapter there will be occasion to analyze the different doc-trinal denotations of *CHos* found between these two extremes, but it is *CHos* in its widest, most generalized connotation that is of immediate importance in the attempt to define the limits of what is involved when the Tibetan makes *CHos* the object of his acceptance-faith. A quotation from the charter of the Sikkim Research Institute of Tibetology, repre-senting the modern Tibetan viewpoint, summarizes most aptly all that *CHos* comprehends. The objects and functions of the institute are stated in these terms: "To sponsor and promote research in *CHos* and associated subjects like iconography, linguistics, medicine, astrology, history, geog-raphy, etc." Then, in a footnote, Tibetology as the *raison d'être* of the in-stitute is defined as follows: "The word Tibetology is used as a convenient and conventional term meaning the study of *CHos* and the culture and all arts associated with *CHos*."[20] By such conceptualization, basic axioms of the philosophy of existence, propositions in the field of ethics, quite detailed statements concerning cosmology, geography, medicine, rhetoric, rules of grammar, versification, and so on, not only have a certain reli-

[20] *Debar Gazette*, No. 1 (Gangtok, Sikkim), February 2, 1958, p. 2.

gious complexion but are a part of the great whole of *CHos* toward which the Tibetan maintains the attitude of faith.

Subject to the qualifications inherent in whatever doubt, skepticism, and even rebellion may lurk within him, the Tibetan, by this attitude of faith, accepts a number of propositions. Some of these are basic, and others are extensions, by deduction or implication, of basic propositions. Some of his acceptance is conscious and some possibly unconscious in that it is not known until challenged. The propositions which are thus accepted may be postulated as follows:

1. In the Tibetan world view, the reality of existence is debatable; by the terms of the debate, it is relative. In any case, existence, which results from desire based on ignorance, is of no worth; and thus the solution for the problems of existence is to be found in the subtraction of desire.

2. Ethical concepts, which strongly influence behavior patterns, are related to the need to accumulate merit and the ideal of a comprehensive compassion toward all living beings.

3. The universe consists of many worlds, their inhabitants, their heavens, and their gods. Within that universe, our world is described in some detail in terms of the four quarters—their form and characteristics.

4. Material existence is based on a number of elements, which are intricately combined in the components of the body and are linked with the practice of medicine.

5. Within the context of an existence to which he is linked by desire, the individual is the most important of the social units. The family, as a biological unit, is permitted but not truly sanctioned with the highest blessing and, in theory, should be discarded as soon as possible in the individual's progress toward liberation. The larger societal groupings are correspondingly weakened and considered of secondary importance, because withdrawal from the world leads to the supreme good.

6. History, and in particular the history of Tibet, with all its record of changes, makes sense and, indeed, has a real existence only within the frame of reference established by the cycles of religion: past, present, and future.

7. Within such a view of history, self-identification as a society and allegiance to that identification, or patriotism, rest in the main on religious considerations. Religious considerations and evaluations function as determinants affecting international relations and create conditioned responses on the part of the Tibetans as they face toward the modern world.

It will be seen from these postulates that the attitude of faith toward *CHos* entails in one way or another belief in, or adherence to, many matters which to the Western mind are far removed from religion. But in the thinking of the Tibetan, they, too, form a part of religion and stem from his faith. These postulates summarize what the Tibetan believes with reference to the enlarged whole that constitutes his religion. They will be examined in some detail to establish their validity and to trace their function in determining or influencing the world view of the Tibetan, his ethical concepts and behavior, his customs and sanctions, his practice of what might be called the indigenous sciences, his social relationships and the structure of his society, the organization and effectiveness of his political-control system, and finally his feeling and expression of patriotism. As the modern world breaks in upon him, his reactions toward this impact are determined largely by what his attitude of faith has conditioned him to accept or reject.

The Tibetan World View

The world view of the Tibetan is not firmly founded on a clear-cut concept of the reality of existence. Rather, such reality is considered debatable: existence is an illusion. The real versus the ideal as an explanation of existence is, in the Western world, the preoccupation of philosophers, but the Buddhist vacuum, *sTong Pa NYid* ("voidness"), is a part of the common speech of every Tibetan and is the explanation advanced for life and all its riddles. In such a world, the clear-cut interaction of cause and effect is blurred. There is no real first cause, and the so-called chain of causality is more a series of adventitious changes than a succession of results each dependent on the previous one.

Tibetan thinking postulates three *KHams* ("realm[s]"): *aDod Pai KHams* ("desire's realm"), *gZugs Kyi KHams* ("form's realm"), and *Mi gZugs Kyi KHams* ("non-form's realm"). But it is only the realm of desire that has relevancy in this discussion, for the six classes of sentient beings—one of which is human—exist in that realm. Existence, however, is on three planes, or has three aspects, which have been called the absolute, the relative, and the imaginary. These terms are Western apprehensions of, or attempts to summarize, concepts which gain meaning when approached through Tibetan terminology. The so-called absolute is the *NGo Ma* ("the fundamental") or *rTen Pa Bo* ("the basic")—sometimes also defined as the *dNGos Po* ("the real" or "true")—which is only realized upon attainment of liberation. The relative, or the phenomenal—that which is seen, heard, and felt—is the *aKHor Ba* ("the round"), symbolized by the wheel of existence. In relation to the fundamental, this plane of existence partakes of the nature of illusion, for it all vanishes upon the attainment of liberation; but in itself, it has a certain aspect of the real. It is *mNGon Sum* ("perception-whole"): the world of the senses. The imaginary, on the other hand, is *aKHrul* ("delusion"). Dreams are a part of this plane of existence, and so, too, are all forms of magical transformations, manifestations, and even *sGyu Ma* ("impostures"). Tibetan tales and epics are full of such unexpected and baffling appearances wherein things are not what they seem.

All three, however, have validity as aspects of existence, and in the multiple and shifting possibilities and explanations they suggest, they constitute a continuing challenge to the testimony of the senses. In everyday living, the senses are adequate and even acute; behavior is generally based on their testimony. But they and their testimony are not entirely trusted, for relativity, a sense of illusion, and fancy press hard on consciousness; the vague never-never land where anything can happen is very near in Tibetan thinking. Whenever dogma or commonly accepted mystical existence is at variance with the phenomenal world, what is seen, heard, or felt is easily discounted as delusion.

This sort of make-believe, in entirely good faith, is carried to surprising lengths. An extreme instance of this can be found in the explanation of the current, and by no means infrequent, love affairs of emanation lamas. The lama is a *sPrul sKu* ("emanation body") of strange illusory manifestations. Even by those most intimately involved, it will be asserted that all details of the affair, including the sex act itself, are an illusion: phantom activities of a phantom body in which the true body is not involved. The explanation that denies the reality of the act is not so much cynical casuistry as it is the reflection of a world view wherein everything this side of the absolute, which is realized only in liberation, is illusion.

Once I shared a campfire with a group of Tibetan hunters. Their activities and their hopes were strictly down-to-earth and centered on the possibility of killing a big stag with antlers in the velvet, which would bring a good price when sold to the Chinese traders. Yet even on such an expedition, the world of the marvelous was very close. We watched a thunderstorm over a distant lake: clouds, rain, and the surface of the lake seemed joined as if by a water spout. In a most matter-of-fact way, attention was called to the drinking of lake water by a dragon. The dragon was completely real to all the hunters. His voice had sounded in the sky, and now he was drinking. When, to test their credence, an offer of five hundred ounces of silver for the skin and bones of the dragon was made, the conversation turned seriously, as a matter concerning the technique of hunting, to the possibility of shooting a dragon—whether a modern rifle was powerful enough, whether the bullet would have to be silver or specially blessed by a powerful lama, and just how much real danger would threaten the hunter himself. There was no facetiousness; they were seriously considering game of much greater value than a stag, even one with antlers in the velvet.

This universal and unaffected attitude is probably one reason why Tibet has become the source of tales of the marvelous. It is not a matter of the Tibetans' imposing on credulity and baldly telling tall tales: it is a reflection of a basic world view and concept of existence. In every incident, a legend—a true tale of the incredible—is very close to being born. When existence is illusory, how may one draw a sharp line of factual delineation between illusions?

Whether real or an illusion, none of it, in any case, is desirable. Desire itself approaches most closely to being the basic cause of existence. Desire seizes on existence; so the problem of existence may only be solved by subtraction of desire until zero is reached. Not every Tibetan consciously formulates such a statement of the basic concepts which underlie the Tibetan world view. But a surprisingly large number have a reasonably clear perception of the implications inherent in such a view, and others, who have not thought it through, still have a feeling that existence is basically illusory and undesirable.

This sense of the undesirability of existence is the second distinctive quality of the Tibetan world view. The zest for living is ever challenged, and subtraction of its functions enjoined or threatened. Though contrary to instinctive Tibetan reactions, passivism and negativism are widespread and are reflected in attitudes and forms of social behavior.

The schedule of a Tibetan's life is marked by a series of withdrawals of increasing scope and degree. They are not the result of, or in proportion to, failing powers but are purposeful and planned. In early maturity, the life of the lay Tibetan is filled with an activity amply concerned with biological and material success. But very soon the subtractions begin. More and more time is taken out of the daily round for prayers, participation in ritual, vows of silence, and other such steps of withdrawal, which take an increased amount of time and energy as they encroach on productive activity and social participation. Raiding, hunting, and roistering are dropped early, and familial and communal affairs and interests take second place, in order of importance, as more and more time is spent in religious observances at home or at the monasteries.

Such a pattern, of course, is not a completely universal one—doubt, rebellion, many forms of rivalry, and economic pressure combine to produce frequent and even significant exceptions—but it is the general trend. Usually, the management of family wealth and concerns is turned over to the younger members long before the waning of the natural powers or the onset of decrepitude warrant. Thus, loss to the individual, to the family, and to the community as a whole is the inevitable result produced by a world view that characterizes existence as undesirable and the subtraction of desire as the religion-sanctioned rule of life.

The giving of at least one son out of three to the monastic system is an extension of this rule that affects the succeeding generation. The child is given by the family; he has no personal choice in the matter. Later, if he implements his own refusal by rebellion, he becomes a renegade, and a certain degree of disability and stigma follows him for life. Once the son has been given, much of the wealth and material support of the family follow him to the monastery and are subtracted from family and communal development. The cumulative effects of this continuing subtraction on familial and communal activity are enormous and profoundly affect the society as a whole.

Tibetan Ethics

Positive ideals of conduct, as distinguished from the prohibition of such as antisocial acts as thieving, lying, killing, and so on, are largely based on two religious considerations: the attainment and laying-up of virtue, *dGe Ba gSog* ("amassing virtue"), and the equally religious ideal of *sNYing rJe* ("lord-heart"), or compassion, toward all sentient beings. Much of Tibetan behavior is motivated by these two considerations.

The accumulation of virtue by the doing of good deeds is fundamental in any society that is Buddhistic. It is enjoined and accepted as a reason for the performance of social charity, the abstention from taking any life, the building and maintenance of religious structures and even public works such as roads and bridges, and the intensive performance of the minutiae of religious observance. In Tibet the ideal of doing good deeds to accumulate virtue has particular influence on patterns of behavior toward all living creatures. In theory, the six classes of sentient beings are categorized as the superhuman, the human, and the subhuman. But in actual practice, behavior is concerned with the human and the subhuman. In the "common sense world" of societal interrelationships, the difference between men and animals is valid to a certain degree among the Tibetans, yet, in doctrine and in much of Tibetan thinking and practice, animals and men are equally entitled to life and its preservation, to be recipients of meritorious deeds, and to be objects of the manifestation of compassion.

In common with all forms of Buddhism, Tibetan treatment of and attitude toward sentient beings are solidly based on doing good for merit's sake; yet Tibetan behavior toward sentient beings is tinged and even permeated by a very distinctive and marked tenderness that is accompanied by constant reference to *sNYing rJe* ("lord-heart"), or compassion. In doctrine, compassion is an attribute of the bodhisattva alone and, as such, is known as *sNYing rJe CHen Po* ("the great lord-heart"). But the ideal thus created and inculcated has taken hold of the Tibetan heart, and *sNYing rJe CHung Bo* ("the small lord-heart") belongs to all—clergy and laity alike—and is reflected in the use of the words *sNYing rJe* ("lord-heart"), or compassion, in a wide variety of situations, such as acts of charity, deeds of mercy, and a rude but real gentleness in the treatment of animals, to mean "pitiful," "appealing," "adorable," "deserving of mercy," and so on. Compassion thus becomes coequal with amassing virtue as a motivation in Tibetan behavior patterns toward their immediate fellows—human beings, in general, and animals. Accumulation of virtue and a "feeling" of compassion which conforms to or reflects the ideal of compassion of the bodhisattva, rather than acceptance of any hard and fast abstract code of right and wrong, constitute the ethical basis of much of Tibetan behavior.

The dominance of the ideal of compassion in Tibetan motivation is exemplified by Tibetan burial practices. At the presence of death and when faced with the insistent question, "What, if anything, after death?" men instinctively react in accordance with the motivations, ideals, and rites of whatever they hold, as individuals or as members of a culture, to be religion. The preferred form of disposal of the body among Tibetans of all classes is by dismemberment and exposure of the corpse so that the vultures may feed and be nourished. From the testimony of the tombs of Tibetan kings and the records that treat of pre-Buddhistic practice, it is well established that the Tibetans of those times practiced interment of the corpse with a meticulous ritual of sacrifice and commemoration strongly reminiscent of the practices that have persisted in China from earliest times.[21] Compassion for all living creatures is the reason given for the change in funeral custom. The ideal must be strong, indeed, that can

---

[21] G. Tucci, *The Tombs of the Tibetan Kings* (1950), pp. 1 ff.; M. Lalou, "Rituel Bon-po des funerailles royales," *Journal Asiatique*, T–CCXL–3 (1953), 339–63; P. Pelliot, *Histoire Ancienne du Tibet* (1962), pp. 3, 81–82.

change a careful burial practice and respect for the body into a ritualistic dismemberment and exposure of the body to the vultures.

Some aspects of the compassion of the Tibetans have a peculiar subjective quality and an almost masochistic emphasis on suffering for suffering's sake. Stress is placed on intent more than on the conferring of benefit. For example, medical aid will be sought, and the plea will be *Sems bZang Bo bsTan dGos Gi* ("good mind show is necessary"), when there is hope of neither alleviation of suffering nor cure. There is also emphasis on a subjective will to sacrifice one's self, which appears in the numerous tales wherein scenes or acts of vicarious suffering have great prominence. The Tibetans display deep emotion when witnessing dramatic presentations of these scenes or when listening to accounts of such happenings by minstrels and storytellers. In the story of *Dri Med Kun lDan* ("The Visvantara Jataka"), for example, there is little real need that he give his eyes away, but he does so, after having disposed of wife and children, and Tibetans weep openly as they listen to the story or watch the play.

Faith in Buddhism has without doubt softened the cruelty and savage ruthlessness which existed in the earlier Tibetan society and state. From the information which may be salvaged from historical fragments and by deduction from the episodes recorded in various versions of the *Ge Sar Gling* epic, Tibetan society of the pre-Buddhist period was much more cruel and bloodthirsty than at present.[22] Torture and killing still occur but much less wantonly and exuberantly than in those savage times. Religion is on the side of mercy, and the preachments of the faith are all against the infliction of suffering and the taking of life. There are many indications that the religious leaders had a large part in bringing about the substitution of the payment of life-money for the revenge killing of the blood-feud tradition, which has such a large place in savage cultures. According to some Tibetans, this was formally prescribed near the end of the eighth century by *KHri Srong lDeu bTsan,* as part of the suppression of the Bon practice of making bloody sacrifices. Others place this reform in the fourteenth century, ascribing it to *Byan CHub rGyal mTSHan.* In any case, it is the religious authorities who now hasten to intervene in every outbreak of violence, seeking to make peace and prevent the chain reaction of successive killing that characterizes the fully developed feud. They come into each case as mediators, and the function of mediation is

---

[22] A. David-Neel, *The Superhuman Life of Gesar of Ling* (1933), pp. 183, 238, 246, 248, 270; Sir Ch. Bell, *The Religion of Tibet* (1931), p. 13.

strengthened by all the persuasions and sanctions of religion, which is always on the side of peace.

The doctrinal ban on killing has left its mark on many aspects of Tibetan life, although often it would seem to be more honored in the breach than in the observance. It is not, of course, completely effective, for the Tibetans must eat. A large segment of the Tibetan population is nomadic and engaged in animal husbandry. Their subsistence depends on livestock raising. The local production of grain is small; there is a lack of vegetable fibers and textile production is limited; and the harsh climate dictates the use of sheepskins and furs for clothing. Of necessity, the Tibetan must kill to live, and against that necessity, explicitly or implicitly, his creed says he should not kill. The conflict and the compromises or subterfuges that result affect much of Tibetan life.

The use of the knife in the actual killing and the shedding of blood are abhorred. This may stem from the doctrinal rejection of the knife-wielding sacrificer-shamans of the pre-Buddhist religion of Tibet. In general the knife is used only after the animal is dead. Beeves, sheep, goats, and pigs are strangled or smothered. In the latter method, which is only practicable for sheep, goats, and pigs, the nostrils are stuffed with clay and the mouth is held or tied shut until the animal dies. The remark frequently made, "Oh, it is dead," would seem to be an oblique effort to disclaim responsibility and imply that death was accidental. In any case, blood has not flowed, although immediately after the animal is dead a long knife is thrust through the throat into the chest cavity to drain the blood, which is collected and used for sausages. Indeed, in some of the areas where there are Moslems who can be persuaded to do the butchering, the meat they kill and sell is preferred by some, for it has been more effectively drained of blood. In general, only large animals are killed for food. The principle that there is less sin in killing one animal which will furnish a large amount of meat than in killing a large number of smaller animals to secure the same amount of meat is widely but not universally accepted. Widespread avoidance of both fowl and fish as food is said to be related also to ideas concerned with the Tibetan disposal of the dead, for of the three common practices—exposure to the vultures, cremation, and throwing into rivers—exposure to the vultures involves birds' claws, and water burial is assumed to involve fish.

When animals are killed for food and for their pelts, no amount of subterfuge entirely removes a sense of guilt from the Tibetan. In the seasonal fall butchering for the family, the older members, who are beginning their withdrawal from the activities of life for religious reasons, pass on to the younger members the responsibility and consequent guilt for taking life. In large centers, where certain individuals or families set themselves up as butchers to serve the needs of the community, they live under a great weight of social and religious opprobrium, being considered great sinners. A definite guilt complex accompanies even the eating of meat—great meat eaters though the Tibetans are—and extends to the consumption of such delicacies as honey, for the dead bodies of the bees are mute evidence of the double crime of robbery and murder. What effect the consumption of food, constantly accompanied by a conscious sense of guilt, may have on the health of the Tibetans has not been investigated.

The ban on killing also imposes considerable restraint on the practice—widespread nevertheless—of hunting. In general, in accordance with the principle cited previously, only large game is hunted. When going on pilgrimage, the most habitual hunters forego hunting even though they may be on short rations as the pilgrim caravan passes through territory where game abounds. Hunting is prohibited throughout large areas in central Tibet—notably around Lhasa itself—in the immediate vicinity of any monastery, and in numerous other locations hallowed by one association or another of a religious nature. Thus many areas have become extensive wildlife preserves, and the game animals are both numerous and tame. In one monastery I visited, the monks were greatly bothered by the blue sheep which came down from the hills and raided the stores of hay kept in clapboard sheds on the housetops. The sheds were torn to pieces in the process, and though the monks shouted and threw stones in an effort to protect their property, the sheep were little disturbed, being quite aware of their privileged status.

Because of these scruples, pest control, whether of rodents or insects, is quite unacceptable. In the monasteries, as in private homes, rats and mice are bold and voracious, raiding foodstuffs and inflicting much damage by chewing up leather gear and clothing. Any suggestion, however, that something drastic be done about it is rejected with horror. The utmost the younger monks will do is trap the rodents alive and, taking them far from the monastery, release them. Similarly, the search for vermin in clothing is carried on with great care that the bugs are not injured but merely thrown as far away as possible. Garments are, however, put out on very cold nights and then well shaken. The results are quite as desired, but no killing, though some dying, is involved. But even this practice merits punishment in one of the eight cold hells. Such matters as germs and antiseptics and antibiotics pose problems that are very real to the

Tibetans.[23] In my own medical work in Amdo, to avoid much argument, I never went farther back than toxins to explain infection and the action of iodine as an antiseptic.

Unquestionably, the ideal of compassion toward all *Sems Can* ("mind-possessing") or sentient beings has some part in inducing the Tibetan to treat his livestock and beasts of burden in a noticeably more humane manner than the callous brutality exhibited by some of his Asian neighbors. It is natural to think that a pastoral people have more interest and skill in the care of their animals; thus the care shown by the Tibetan nomad may be based partly on value attitudes inherent in the subsistence techniques of his mode of life. But a similar gentleness is characteristic of the Tibetan farmer, and in Tibetan legend and song, kindness to animals is prominently featured as a much lauded religious virtue.

The ideal of compassion reinforces the urge to gain virtue, and the two find expression in a code of sharing the basic necessities of life. The beggar who begs for what he is sure to receive, using the many gracious and honorific expressions for asking and thanking—which abound in the Tibetan language—is not really begging; he is only reminding the donor of his duty, a gracious and virtue-producing duty which also manifests compassion. And the donor gives generously, and with no thought of refusal, less to relieve distress than to gain virtue and to express compassion. The economic result is a partial redistribution of wealth and unemployment and old-age insurance, for no one starves. It also makes the Tibetan surprisingly foot-loose: he is sure of being able to beg his way, with honor and independence, whenever he decides to go on pilgrimage to far places.

The Tibetan Cosmos, Gods, and Geography

For the Tibetan, the composition of the cosmos and, within that framework, details concerning geography, physics, anatomical science, and physiopsychology are laid down and defined in religious contexts. His attitude of faith entails or implies acceptance of these indigenously stated systems of science. According to the cosmology of Tibetan Buddhism, the universe consists of millions of worlds, each having its inhabitants, its heavens, and its hells. Such a cosmic structure is a part of religious dogma, for in these worlds the gods, the titans, and spirit beings meet with the eternally renewed Buddhahood in its successive manifestations, make war, rebel, and are converted in an existence outside of time. Within this vast aggregate of worlds, our world has its own complement

[23] A. Winnington, *Tibet* (1957), pp. 181–84.

of heavens and hells and also the observable phenomena of the sun, moon, planets, and stars, which all have their places in Tibetan science and mythology.

The dogma of Tibetan Buddhism divides the space of our world into three regions: the heavens, middle space, and the nether regions. All three are thickly populated by spirit beings who have different spheres of influence and power. Some of these beings are by nature beneficent, but the greater number are more inclined to malice, and a few are implacably unfriendly. In a previous chapter which dealt mostly with the pre-Buddhist gods of Tibet, reference has been made to those spirit beings which seem to belong alike to the pre-Buddhist cults and to the Buddhism of the present time. In addition to them, there are others, such as the goddesses *dPal lDan lHa Mo* ("Kali") and the two *aGrol Ma* ("Tara"), the fairies *mKHaa aGro Ma* ("dakini"), *gSHin rJe CHos rGyal* ("Yama"), the *gNod sByin* ("yakshas"), and the *Yi Dwags* ("pretas"), which were introduced along with Buddhism. The purpose here, however, is not to attempt a complete list of all the spirit beings which exist in Tibetan cosmology but rather to identify and briefly describe those that are most constantly present and most active in the cosmos, as conceived and accepted through faith.

The following are the spirit beings with whom the Tibetan most frequently has dealings as he seeks to influence or placate them. Above are the *lHa* ("gods and goddesses") who live in the western heavens—somewhat far away and generally beneficent. Of closer everyday concern are the spirits of middle space, including the surface of the earth, and those who are under the earth. Among the gods of middle space are those who dominate a region, have special functions, or have special characteristics. The *AH Mes* ("mountain gods") from the mountain tops, with which they are associated by name, guard localities or have an interest in what takes place in those localities. The *gNYan* ("argali gods"), *mGul lHa* ("gods of the hunt"), and the *bTSan* ("fierce gods") are jealous and powerful and must be placated; the *Wer Ma* ("protectors") act in consonance with their name; and the *THab lHa* ("hearth gods") are concerned with family matters. Individual Tibetans look to their own personal *Yi Dam lHa* ("tutelary god") or *PHo lHa* ("personal god") for special protection and help.

But it is the gods of the earth, *Sa bDag* ("soil-owners"), and the spirits of the nether world, the *Klu* ("serpent spirits"), that are most constantly in the minds and consciousness of the Tibetans. There is at times considerable confusion as to which spirit beings belong in each of these categories. This confusion, as well as the influence these beings have on Tibetan life, is aptly described by G. Tucci: "Civilization, as related in the *Klu aBum* ("ten thousand Nagas"), is nothing but a continuous offense to the *Sa bDag* ("soil-owners") and *gNYan* ("argali")." He then quotes from that book: "'When the hair of the wild yaks was cut in order to make tents, there was strife against the *Sa bDag* who are the four guardians of the door. When upon the earth the pure surface was delimited wherein to erect sacred buildings, or when the earth was bled there was enmity. When temples and tombs were built there was enmity with the *Klu* ("Nagas"), the *gNYan* ("argali") and the *Sa bDag* ("soil-owners"). When the earth is bled—a pond is dug up in order to draw water—enmity is caused; when water is collected in a ditch and led into canals for irrigation enmity is caused with the same spirits. . . .'"[24]

The *Klu* have a special, jealous proprietary interest in water springs, streams, and lakes. Because of their ubiquitous presence, whatever fishing is done in Tibet is carried out surreptitiously and with fear and foreboding; and in all boating activity and rafting of timber, a conscious and strong effort is made to placate these spirits by worship and offerings. Possibly, the strongest influence these spirits have on the Tibetans is to make them meticulously careful to avoid polluting springs and streams in contrast to the conspicuously unsanitary practices of Tibetan life in general.

It is, however, the *Sa bDag* ("soil-owners") who exercise the most tyrannical control over the activities of the average Tibetan. Their attitudes and reactions are likened to the attitudes and reactions of jealous, irritable, and even unreasonable proprietors and lords of domain. Indeed, as lords of domain, they are called *sNang Bai Sa bDag* ("visible soil-owners"), and must be satisfied with offerings, flattery, and adequate returns. In the same way, the *Mi sNang Bai Sa bDag* ("invisible soil-owners") must be placated with prayers, *sTor Ma* ("broken-up") offerings, and requisite worship. Only when these procedures have been fulfilled may one till the soil, dig a ditch, build a wall, make a road, build a bridge, or even cut a tree out of the forest without fear. Even with such precautions, some *Sa bDag* refuse to be mollified and may bring misfortune and sickness on those involved.

Mining is doubly heinous, and no amount of placation makes it safe, because it combines both disturbance and robbery and the *Sa bDag* are malicious misers with regard to wealth. Because of the Tibetan's attitude of acceptance-faith toward religion, he has, in a sense, placed himself

---

[24] G. Tucci, *Tibetan Painted Scrolls* (1949), p. 725.

under the constant, jealous, irritated scrutiny of these *Sa bDag;* however, religion has also given him some guidance concerning the rites and offerings whereby they may be appeased.

In Amdo I know of one village where there is a broad, fallow meadow beside the communal fields that are now far too narrow to support the increased population of the community. But although forced to increase their efforts in the forests in order to exploit timber resources to make up the economic gap, and although such effort also carries its own risk, none of the villagers dares break the fallow ground and add it to the land under cultivation because the particular *Sa bDag* of that piece of ground is thought to be especially fierce and unwilling to allow trespassing on his property.

In eastern and northeastern Tibet, leprosy is widespread in a rather significant pattern of distribution. It is found, in a heavy ratio of incidence, almost exclusively among the sedentary population—those who dwell in houses and dig in the soil, that is, those who break the sensitive skin of the soil. It is not found—or only rarely—among the pastoral nomads who live in tents and seldom disturb the surface of the ground. For the Tibetan, who knows much about contagious diseases and factors of transmission and who knows that leprosy exhibits certain aspects of a contagious disease and yet seemingly depends on other, not easily identified, factors for its spread, this is conclusive evidence that leprosy results from the curses of *Sa bDag* who have become angry because the surface of the soil has been broken and trespass has been committed.

Physical geography is defined within the context of dogma, for the formulation of the basic principles of the science are *Sangs rGyas Gi gSung Ba* ("the utterance of the Buddhahood") and therefore not to be questioned. Later and more detailed formulations such as guide books and descriptive geographies are written in this frame of reference and take on, to some degree, the authority of religion.

The earth's surface is a plane: oval or round in outline. But by the very nature of physical phenomena, there is sufficient latitude to admit of variations, and I have heard Tibetans, both clergy and laymen, who have wandered in their foot-loose manner from Peking and the borders of Siberia to Calcutta, with, for just a few, a trip to London thrown in, accept the roundness of the earth as a phenomenal aspect of geography. It was very clear, however, that they felt doctrine was sufficiently elastic to admit of the world's being a sphere.

The four quarters, or *PHyogs* ("direction[s]"), of the earth are characterized as to shape and nature. The eastern one is *Lus aPHags* ("body sublime"), semicircular in shape and characteristically *ZHi Ba* ("mild"). The southern one is *aDZam Bu Gling* ("area of *aDZam Bu*"–identical with the Hindu *Jambu*), triangular in shape—or like the shoulder blade of a sheep—and characteristically *rGyas Po* ("rich"). The western one is *Ba Glang sPyod* ("cattle use"), circular in shape and characteristically *dBang lDan* ("strength-filled"). The northern one is *sGra Mi sNYan* ("sound not listened to"), or disagreeable, square in shape and characteristically *Drag Po* ("fierce").

The description of the eastern quarter as semicircular may derive from a vague knowledge of the curve of the east coast of Asia, and the characteristic of mildness may have reference to the pacific nature—in theory at least—of the culture of China and its devotion to letters.

The characteristics of the western quarter, circular and possessing strength, may possibly derive from some vague knowledge of a circlet of world powers grouped around a sea at the earth's center, together with a historic recollection which still persists, though faint as the memory of a memory, of the impact of the conquests of Alexander on the heartland of Asia.

The characterization of the northern quarter as *sGra Mi sNYan*, or disagreeable, while derived from the Indian concept of the north being the region of harsh, phonetically disagreeable languages, is also linked with the idea that the fabled realm of Shambala, from whence come the successive *Rigs lDan rGyal Po* ("wisdom-filled king[s]"), is in the north. Also located in the north is the mass of snow and ice that is *Byang Ri Rab* ("excellent north mountain"), also called the *Ri Rab rGyal Po* ("excellent king-mountain"), which has much mystic significance for the Tibetans. They recognize that Indian cosmology has identified Kailas as Meru, the mountain center of the universe; they mystically accept the identification, ascribing to Kailas a special degree of sacredness; yet they also look beyond to the north and the other *Ri Rab rGyal Po* ("excellent king-mountain") with wonder and expectation, for in the north will arise the successive manifestations of the *Rigs lDan rGyal Po* ("wisdom-filled kings").

Within this geographic concept of the world, which is linked to reality, mysticism, and possible changes in world order, the Tibetan makes his own realistic adjustments, for he has a good sense of direction, distance, and topography. In his own foot-loose manner, as pilgrim and trader, he visits many places and asks questions about many others. There are a number of quite accurate travel guides written by Tibetans. The Tibetan has a persistent geographic curiosity, for he wants to know how far it is to the lands beyond the vast outer sea and whether in those lands there truly live headless monsters, all-female populations, and men with ears so large that they are used for sleeping mats and covers. His primary geographic curiosity, however, is focused on the mystic mountain of the north, for that is linked with history, prophesied and yet to be, and cosmic change.[25]

Structure of Matter and the Sciences and Arts

The world of matter is based on, or composed of, five or six *KHams* ("elements"). There are two different lists of elements. One, which is borrowed from Chinese culture and is associated with the calendar and theories of physiology and medicine, lists five: *Sa* ("earth"), *lCags* ("iron"), *CHu* ("water"), *SHing* ("wood"), and *Me* ("fire"). The other list, brought in with Buddhism from India, initially gave four—*Me* ("fire"), *CHu* ("water"), *Rlung* ("wind"), and *Sa* ("earth"), to which *mKHaa* ("ether") and *rNam SHes* ("manner known"), or consciousness, were later added. The elements of the second list also appear in medical theory in connection with the secretions and humors of the body.

The existence of two such lists—not identical, yet of equal standing—points up the fact that a basic view of existence that is precariously based on illusion makes possible the acceptance of differing if not entirely contradictory explanations of the composition of matter. The two lists are also a reminder of the degree to which the culture of Tibet has received borrowings from the cultures of China and India, accepting aspects from both with wide tolerance even when unable to completely syncretize all that was received. Such differences, for the Tibetan, are but another aspect of illusion.

The Tibetan science of anatomy includes some empirical knowledge of the structure and organs of the body and of their functions derived both from a general knowledge gained from dressing butchered animals and from the dismemberment practiced in preparing corpses for the "burial of the sky." This knowledge is mixed with yoga concepts, particularly with reference to the veins and arteries and their functions. As arter-

[25] The marked interest in geography on the part of the Tibetan is a recurrent theme throughout much of Tibetan conversation. To a considerable degree, it stems from the awareness of topography resulting from the mobile habits of the nomad, the requirements of long-distance trade, and the overriding importance of pilgrimage in Tibetan patterns of religious behavior. *Mk'yen Brtse's Guide to the Holy Places of Central Tibet,* by Alfonsa Ferrari, edited by Luciano Petech, and *The Geography of Tibet According to the 'Dzam-ling rgyas-bshad,* by T. V. Wylie, now make available in English translations two examples of the many Tibetan guidebooks.

ies and nerves are not differentiated, it is thought possible, in certain states of meditation or trance, to direct either breath or secretions to the heart or the brain and to achieve physiopsychic reactions.

The seven constituent elements of the body, *Dwangs Ma* ("lymph"), *KHrag* ("blood"), *THSil* ("fat"), *SHa* ("muscle"), *Rus Pa* ("bone"), *rKang* ("marrow"), and *KHu Ba* ("semen") are known as the *Lus gZungs* ("body power") or *Lus SHed* ("body strength"). The body is also thought to be pervaded by the *NYes Pa gSum* ("three humors"): *Rlung* ("wind"), *mKHris Pa* ("bile"), and *Bad Kan* ("phlegm"). In contrast to the strengths of the body, the humors exercise an unfavorable influence and are associated with the origin and course of numerous diseases. Wind, which is also one of the elements of matter, has a special place in diagnosis and is believed to be associated with mental and nervous disorders and all forms of paralysis.

The practice of medicine is marked by a dichotomy similar to that which appears in all the indigenous sciences. The science of medicine is included within the over-all concept of religion and therefore has a primarily religious basis in theory and in practice. This basis, however, is combined with an empirical and common-sense use of herbs and other substances to produce assured results. The practitioners are, in general, lamas or monks, whose knowledge is believed to stem primarily from their knowledge of religion and the science of medicine as sanctioned by religion. In diagnosis, first consideration is given to the horoscope of an individual and then to whatever spirit beings may be involved—the ones which may have been offended and must be placated. This is combined with an empirically useful examination of pulse, tongue, eyeballs, urine, and excreta. Treatment has a similarly dual character: offerings to spirit beings and the performance of rituals of prayer, salutation, and circumambulation are prescribed; charms are applied or eaten along with pills and powders having magical properties; and concurrently, very effective febrifuges, purges, and digestive stimulants are administered. Acupuncture and moxibustion are also extensively practiced. Thus it is very difficult to distinguish between the results of the autosuggestive power of an incantation, the counterirritant of raising a blister, and the administration of a purge. Some of the lama doctors have a wide herbal lore and select, prepare, and administer herbal preparations with much skill. Except for amputations, surgery is not attempted, although considerable skill is shown in treating bone fractures and dislocations.

The arts have an equally close or even more intimate involvement with religion. Reading and writing came into existence in the process of accepting religion, and the religious establishments became the centers of learning and the repositories or guardians of knowledge. Thus grammar, logic, rhetoric, and versification, because they are functional in religious teaching and ritual, take on a sacrosanct status and are regarded as being included within the greater whole of religion. The arts, such as music, painting, and sculpture find their chief manifestation in religious activity and are governed by rules and considerations derived from doctrine. The subjective intellectual powers that are brought to bear on the several fields of learning and abstract thinking are a part of religion. The powers of memory, gifts of eloquence, the faculty of ratiocination, and excellence in debate are devoted to the service of religion. Equally, their possession and their degree of excellence are considered as the concomitants of sanctity or are attributed to religious achievement or enlightenment. The attitude of faith accepts all these classifications, which place most, if not quite all, of the aspects of culture within the great whole of religion.

Social Structure: Status of the Individual

The attitude of faith has influenced or modified the character of each of the units that make up the structure of Tibetan society, and the view of existence that stems from that attitude of faith has had a decisive effect on social attitudes, groupings, and structure. As a generalization, it may be stated that the doctrinal emphasis on impermanence seems to have weakened the will to create societal units of enduring strength. If we begin with the individual, it is immediately apparent that he is more important and occupies a position characterized by greater individual freedom in relation to the groups of which he is a part than the individuals of many of the peoples of Asia. Religion, by placing a premium upon withdrawal, has weakened the hold of such units as the family and the immediate community upon the individual, and by reason of this, the importance and status of the individual who has the power to choose such withdrawal have been enhanced. Without doubt, there are other factors, such as mobility, the prerogatives of flight, and the inviolability of refuge, which also operate on behalf of the individual, but consideration of these factors is not within the scope of this investigation.

Thus abetted and sanctioned by religion, the individual has much freedom to withdraw and subtract his normal contribution and efforts from the family endeavor. No reproach fastens on him; indeed, the religious view of existence dictates approval of his course of action if he concentrates all his efforts on his personal progress toward liberation. The attitude of faith toward religion encourages each Tibetan to take time out —the more time, the greater piety and efficacy—for religious observance. This is well illustrated by the general attitude toward participation in pilgrimages by all members of the family. Daughters, for example, who are valuable for the hard work they perform, who are subject to the greatest degree of control by the family, and who would not be spared for any other reason, may take off on pilgrimages of a year's duration with complete assurance. The family cannot easily stop them; no family responsibility is allowed to interfere with any of the acts of withdrawal sanctioned by religion.

Buddhist doctrines of reincarnation effectively rule out any form of ancestor worship or even any long-time remembrance of ancestors, with the related emphasis on descendants and the maintenance of continuity in the family line. Little account is taken of the ancestors, and little or nothing is expected from the descendants; thus the urge to make sure of the succession is weakened. Tibetan burial customs are a significant index of the weakness of the link between generations. For the general populace there are no family graveyards, no graves of ancestors or monuments of remembrance. The highest form of burial is disposal of the body in accordance with the precept of compassion toward all sentient beings, that is, the flesh is fed to the vultures and even the bones are broken up so that this manifestation of charity may be complete. In some instances a king or a chief may have a special mountain top reserved for him and for the members of his family for the "burial of the sky," but there are no monuments and no graves, although there were in ancient times and their ruins have survived.

The low or secondary doctrinal status of the *KHyim Ba* ("house-one"), or householder, and the value systems and attitudes which have developed as a result also adversely affect the strength of the family as a societal unit. The barely tolerated status—permitted but not blessed—of the procreative function within the family has weakened the latter as a biological unit; thus, although economic considerations give it a degree of cohesiveness, the breakup of the family, either by formal divorce or by persistent absenteeism, is more easily and completely effected than in either of the neighboring cultures of India or China. The relative fragility of the Tibetan family is significantly reflected in the fact that *Rus Ming* ("bone name[s]"), or surnames, are somewhat of a rarity among the Tibetans and, even among families having noble status or long histories, are used sparingly. *TSHang Ming* ("house name[s]"), which are somewhat more numerous and have often been mistaken for surnames, are frequently based on personal names, which change from generation to generation.

The Tibetan family is either monogamous, polygynous, or polyandrous in character; in structure it may be either nuclear or extended. There is a general tendency for the extended family to fragment into nuclear families at an early stage, for the older generation has, or retains, little dominance over the younger generation. This may be because of the frequent, early relinquishment of control mentioned previously; but it is also attributable to the relatively low status assigned to the function of fatherhood and to the scant regard for forebears.

Clan or linear-relationship groupings have persisted from ancient times but at present are not sharply defined. They appear to be in a state of decline and seem to have no great, or only residual, strength. Thus, next to the family, the immediate community, whether encampment or village, has the closest claim upon, and exercises the greatest degree of control over, the individual. This power of the immediate community to bring pressure to bear upon the individual is often shared with the next larger social unit, the district or tribal organization.

The individual's final responsibility toward the community and the obedience owed to the will of that community are, however, even weaker than toward the family. He withdraws easily from the family to link himself with pilgrimages or attach himself to monastic existence and to engage in religious observances; with even greater ease, he may withdraw from the community. It cannot hold him if he decides to devote time and wealth to religion. This weakness of the community is exemplified by the ease with which an individual or a family may move from one community to another, from one tribe or political division to another, or from one region of Tibet, across its entire breadth, to another region.

The distinctive societal grouping of Tibetan society and the one which really dominates all other groups is the monastic organization which is centered and housed in the monastery, also known as the lamasery. An estimated one-sixth of the population is found within monasteries and nunneries. The monasteries greatly outnumber the nunneries and are of greater size and importance. The inmates, in good and regular standing, are of two categories: those who are *sPrul sKu* ("emanation-body") lamas and those who, strictly speaking, are not lamas but monks or nuns. The true lamas, who number approximately 1 per cent of the monastic population, are *sPrul sKu* lamas by reason of birth, like the two highest members of their class, the Dalai Lama and the Panchen Lama, and can never be anything other than lamas. Even if they break the monastic rules—as the sixth Dalai Lama is reputed to have done—they continue as lamas until death. The monks and nuns, on the other hand, are such by reason of choice and a vow—familial as well as personal. If the choice is made for the child by the family, it is later confirmed by the individual.

If monks and nuns break the basic rules, they are said to have fallen, and are unfrocked and revert to lay status. However, many of the monks who have fallen and may no longer participate in the lamasery religious services continue to wear the robes of the clergy, although they are actually laymen, retain houses within the monastery, and are addressed by courtesy as *AH KHu* ("hail uncle")—the common courtesy title given to monks. They also frequently occupy managerial or administrative positions in the monastery organization.

The clergy who are members in good standing of this special unit within the social structure, a unit that owes its existence and continuance to religion, also have a persistent and surprising degree of personal freedom. The freedom to fall from religion is a dubious, yet a real, freedom. The freedom of the individual who remains a monk is the freedom to go on pilgrimages and to move to another monastery when he so desires. He may attach himself temporarily, for the purpose of pursuing special studies, to a number of monasteries in succession. In no sense is he irrevocably tied to any one of them. If he wishes, he may also withdraw for special meditation and become a hermit. Thus even the monastery, which is the most tightly structured unit in Tibetan society, does not dominate the individual with finality.[26]

The Tibetan View of History

The attitude of faith toward an all-inclusive religion furnishes the Tibetan with a distinctive and very special view of history. It also determines the philosophy of history that influences or directs Tibetan participation in the making of history. The concepts which stem from such a view underlie, to a considerable degree, the political systems which have developed in Tibet; they also determine the kind and degree of the Tibetan's allegiance and the strength of his patriotism.

Tibetan history, as seen and told by the Tibetans, is the history of the progress and development of religion, specifically, of Buddhism among the inhabitants of *Bod Yul* ("Tibet-home"). It begins in myth and legend with the story of a Tibetan ape who fathered the children of a female

---

[26] R. Ekvall, "Three Categories of Inmates within Tibetan Monasteries: Status and Function," *Central Asiatic Journal*, Vol. V, No. 3, pp. 206–20.

rock demon and, later, taking pity on his offspring, fed them grain, where-upon their tails fell off and they came down from the trees and began to live as the Tibetan people. At this point in the myth, religion intervenes and there is a moralistic discussion of the various and contradictory char-acteristics inherited by the Tibetans from a demon and an ape. In Bud-dhist history, the ape became a convert, whereupon it was revealed that he, too, was a manifestation—one among many—of the timeless Buddha-hood.

The myths of creation become legendary history with the story of the first king (who apparently claimed divine origin) to achieve control over the tribes and petty kings. His coming was later given a religious gloss, with the ascription of his origin to India in accordance with the pious Buddhist tendency to make the holy land of India, from which religion would finally come, the source of all that was good or worthwhile. Leg-endary history becomes to some degree history with the reign of *lHa THo THo Ri gNYan bTSan* around the fifth century A.D. Again it is a religious consideration that spotlights his reign, for in the story of a miraculous fall from heaven during his reign of a number of objects associated with Bud-dhist worship, which became known as the "beginning of the holy doc-trine," there is a clear indication of an early abortive effort to introduce Buddhism into Tibet. The influence of that introduction appears again, somewhat as a determinant, in the reign of his great-grandson, who was said to have been healed of blindness and who took a special name sig-nalizing that healing, because he worshipped the "mysterious helper" which had fallen from heaven.

With the reign of the latter's grandson *Srong bTSan sGam Po,* in the early part of the seventh century, legendary history becomes history, for he fell heir to an expanding empire, Tibet acquired a system of writing, laws were promulgated, tribute was exacted from neighboring countries, and formal diplomatic relations—interspersed with wars—were established with China. Tibetan historians, however, write of him as a zealous con-vert to Buddhism who, encouraged by two of his wives—a Chinese princess and a Nepalese princess, who were both Buddhists—pressed Buddhism upon his people and was eventually hailed by the theologians as an incarnation of Avalokitesvara. His successors are celebrated pri-marily for their piety: *KHri Srong lDeu bTSan* was the protector of religion and invited Padma Sambhava to effect a second and more suc-cessful introduction of Buddhism. *Ral Pa Can,* selected by the Buddhist ministers, patronized the religious orders to such an extent that he per-mitted religious teachers to sit on his long hair—hence his name, which means "the one having long hair or braids." He was killed by his brother _Glang Dar Ma_, who, although he reigned only a short time, so perse-cuted the Buddhists that the progress of religion was set back for a period of from seventy to one hundred twenty years. _Glang Dar Ma_ is execrated by the Tibetans as the great apostate. His assassination by a Buddhist monk is celebrated yearly in miracle plays and dances throughout Tibet as a great religious victory.

The subsequent breakdown and final end of centralized authority are told in terms of the rise of the great ecclesiastical hierarchies. Nothing is considered important but the competition between different schools of doctrine which eventually culminated in the emergence of the _dGe Lugs Pa_ ("merit-system one[s]"), also known as the Yellow Hat sect, and the maneuverings which finally brought into being the theocratic rule of the Dalai Lama.[27]

In accordance with such a philosophy of history, international rela-tions are seen as the associations, circumstances, and events which made possible, for example, the importation of religious teachers or writings from China or India, the conversion of the Mongols to Buddhism, the winning of imperial favor and patronage from a convert such as Kublai Khan, and the final attainment of a favored status as a religious system subsidized by the Chinese emperors and recognized as a church state as well as a state church. Consolidation of kingly control, centralization of power, political and military organization, economic and cultural devel-opments that make for power, conquest and achievement of a balance of power with the great Chinese empire of the T'ang dynasty—these and similar developments, which are the real materials of history, are ignored, or only mentioned incidentally, by the religious historians. Also scarcely noted, is the long decline of Tibetan power from the eighth century down to the present. The loss of territory, the absorption of population by the Chinese on the east, the accumulative effects of Mongol, Dzungar, and Chinese invasions, the shrinking economic and military might of Tibet itself, the pressure from Nepal, the dwindling population, the encroach-

[27] Sir Ch. Bell, _Tibet: Past and Present_ (1924), pp. 21–58; E. Obermiller, _op. cit._, pp. 181–224; G. N. Roerich, _The Blue Annals_ (1949–53), pp. 35 ff.; Kun dGaa rDo rJe, _Deb THer dMar Po_ (1961), ff. 15 _b et seq._ Details incorporated in my text are to be found in one or another of the histories listed above, but the general tenor of what has been written owes much to my reading of the first part of a history of Tibet which is being prepared by Dachen Rinpoche. In its general content and original slant, it represents what constitutes Tibetan history in the opinion of a Tibetan ruler who is knowledgeable in his own culture but who is not a historian. He voices the cultural concept of Tibet's history, not a historian's careful findings.

ment of Chinese authority in Tibetan affairs, and the manipulation of Lamaism itself to further Chinese imperial policy in Tibet and Mongolia are only touched on by historians who view and write about all history—past, present, and, indeed, future—in the context of religion.

Such a philosophy of history not only explains the past but provides a frame of reference for evaluating current historical developments. The end of the Manchu dynasty broke, for the Tibetans, a special tie that existed between the emperor, as imperial secular ruler, and his religious chaplain, the Dalai Lama, and the religious system of which he was the head. The Manchu emperors were held to be *sPrul sKu* ("emanation bodies") of *aJam dByangs* ("mild melody"), or Manjusri, and thus, in a strictly religious context, co-bodhisattvas with the Dalai Lama and, as such, part of the religious system. Nothing the Republic of China, as a secular government, could ever promise or urge could quite rejoin the broken religious and secular ties of that relationship, although the religious adulation lavished upon the Panchen Lama by the Chinese authorities in the late 1920's and early 1930's made a great impression. During the Second World War there was widespread hope among the Tibetans that the Japanese would win, because, among a number of other reasons, the Japanese were considered *Nang Ba* ("within ones"), that is, Buddhist. Even another religion, especially if devoutly practiced as in the case of the Moslems, is regarded as preferable to a secularized philosophy of personal and national existence.

The same philosophy of history also provides the Tibetan with a predetermined outline of the history of the future. Of all the happenings in contemporaneous history, he wonders whether one or another may not be the curtain raiser to the coming of *Byams Pa* ("Loving One"): the Maitreya of the future. The many prophecies extant are sufficiently vague and contradictory as to signs and dates that it could happen at any time from now to a thousand years hence.

Until the spring of 1959, the structure of government was patterned after forms of organization that had been employed by the great sectarians of Tibetan history. Government positions were so divided between the clergy and lay personnel that the clergy retained a preponderance of policy and administrative control and the complexion of government was clearly religious. The function of government was backed and reinforced by the sanctions of religion. Yet, one of the enduring realities of Tibetan history is the continuing struggle between conservative hereditary and communal secular systems of control and the aggressive encroachment of a religious system and hierarchy that seeks to gain complete political power. The apostasy of *Glang Dar Ma,* the persistent existence of a central Tibetan nobility with meticulously kept records of descent from past Tibetan kings, the paired exercise of authority by ecclesiastics and laymen in the organization of the Lhasa government itself, the very real political power of kinglets and chieftains throughout Tibet, and the continued existence of tribal and communal councils constitute strong evidence of this—by no means ended—struggle. Tibet is a vast laboratory of case histories for the study of the relationships between rival systems of religious and secular control. These histories exhibit all degrees of conflict and interlocking adjustment, compromise, and synthesis. That secular power of any sort has continued to exist is testimony to its intrinsic strength and the depth of its roots in the history and experience of society.

In their dealings with Tibet in the past, the Chinese have tampered with both systems. They have given titles and grants of authority to kinglets and chiefs, thereby helping them preserve their power against the encroachment of ecclesiastical control. However, from the history of the past and present, it would seem that the Chinese count most on manipulating or exerting influence on the religious control system. In the time of the Yuan dynasty, Tibetan religious leaders were granted political power. Later, the Dalai Lama's bid for supreme power in Tibet was confirmed by imperial edict. The Chinese have intervened in the selection of Dalai Lamas; they have established procedures whereby they could influence that selection or exercise a form of veto; and they have exploited with considerable success the cleavage in the Tibetan power structure that results from the existence of a Dalai Lama and a Panchen Lama. This exploitation of a very complicated religious and political rivalry extends back in history, through the lifetimes of not one but several Panchen Lamas.

It is significant that in spite of the extreme secular and antireligious philosophy of the present Chinese Communist government it first felt constrained to approach the problem of controlling the Tibetans through their religious system and sought to rule Tibet through the only religious leader left in the land. It also sought to exploit to its own advantage the difference between the manifestation of *sPyan Ras gZigs* ("Avalokitesvara"), who as Dalai Lama is supposed to concern himself with terrestrial matters, and the manifestation of *Od dPag Med* ("Amitabha"), who as Panchen Lama, and by tradition the onetime teacher of the former, is the final authority on celestial matters. For many years the Chinese government, whether Nationalist or Communist, worked to transform the doctrinal difference in roles into an effective intervention into Tibetan politics. Even after the revolt of the Tibetans in 1959, the Chinese still tried to operate through the Panchen Lama, using him as a puppet.

When, in the summer of 1951, the Dalai Lama returned to Lhasa from the Indian border, where he had taken refuge earlier in the year, and again shouldered the real leadership of the Tibetan people, the Chinese Communists brought the Panchen Lama from Ch'ing-hai to central Tibet and smoothly effected a reconciliation between the two. Then, by placing both of them in the new supreme Tibetan committee, as chairman and vice-chairman respectively, the Chinese sought to make sure that the historic rivalry would continue to weaken the Tibetan position and further Chinese designs. When the Dalai Lama fled from Tibet in the spring of 1959, the Chinese pushed this arrangement to its logical conclusion, claiming that the Panchen Lama, as vice-chairman, was merely functioning in the enforced and, by implication, temporary absence of the Dalai Lama, who in theory continued to be the chairman. Such maneuvering and apparent temporizing with a system that is at complete variance with Communist political philosophy are ample proof that the Chinese, with hardheaded realism, know that the Tibetans, by reason of their attitude of faith toward religion and the philosophy of history resulting from that attitude, are strongly predisposed to adopt religious solutions to problems of control and are resistant and hostile toward any move that would tamper with the religious character of the traditional control structure.

The Tibetan philosophy of history has had a very great influence on the basis and entire course of Tibetan-Mongolian relations. Much in the culture of the two peoples would seem to predispose them to become natural associates and allies, or, indeed, component parts of one political and cultural whole. Nomadism as a way of life belongs in whole or in part to both cultures. At the time of the rise of the Mongol dynasty, there was considerable contact between the two peoples. Later, for a time, a Mongol khan and his heirs held Lhasa and exercised control over Tibet, and the Dzungars, or western Mongols, made their bid for control of Tibet on a religious issue in order to create a Mongolian-Tibetan united front against China. By the fifteenth century, when the two peoples would most naturally have coalesced, both had had similar historical experiences: a sudden rise to imperial status and dominance or equality with China, followed by an almost equally sudden collapse before, and subjugation by, the enduring strength of the Chinese race-culture mass. Certainly the possibility of a jointure of Mongol and Tibetan strength, which would have threatened the entire Chinese position in Central Asia, was one that

Chinese strategists clearly perceived and countered with persistence, as shown by the care with which they maintained at all costs their position in the corridor between Mongolia and Tibet. A religious philosophy of history, however, determined the character of the association between Tibetans and the Mongols, and the Tibetans, adroitly abetted by the Chinese, preached Buddhism and its inherent pacificism to the Mongols and were content to be religious teachers, preaching a renunciation of force instead of becoming allies in an effort to resist Chinese pressure by force.

Tibetan Self-identification and Patriotism

Tibetan patriotism, to the extent that it is based on something more than loyalty to the fellow members of a small community, or consciousness of attachment to a locality, is founded on a sense of "oneness" in a number of characteristics. As enunciated by the Tibetans, these characteristics are

> *CHos Lugs gCig* ("religion-system one")—religion
> *KHa Lugs gCig* ("mouth- or part-system one")—culture
> *sKad Lugs gCig* ("speech-system one")—language
> *Mi Rigs gCig* ("man-lineage one")—race
> *Sa CHa gCig* ("soil-extent one")—territory.

With the exception of the first one, these criteria for determining "oneness"—these characteristics whereby the Tibetan recognizes his fellows, toward whom he maintains certain attitudes and from whom he expects reciprocal treatment—are valid criteria of the social sciences. The characterizations he formulates relate to cultural self-consciousness, *KHa Lugs gCig* ("mouth- or part-system one"); a common language, *sKad Lugs gCig* ("speech-system one"); a degree of racial self-recognition, *Mi Rigs gCig* ("man-lineage one"); and location in space ("soil-extent one"). Common culture, language, race, and territory are recognized as reasons for a sense of "oneness." Reference to political organization is conspicuously lacking.

The first two characterizations which are used by the Tibetan in his self-identification, *KHa Lugs gCig* and *sKad Lugs gCig*, are closely linked. Indeed, if we accept without elaboration or analysis the literal renderings given, *sKad Lugs gCig* ("speech-system one") could be assumed to be only a particularization within the somewhat more generalized category of *KHa Lugs gCig* ("mouth-system one"). This latter term requires, however, careful analysis. It is not speech alone that is meant. The primary meaning of *KHa* is "mouth." By association, as in the English use of the word "tongue," it means speech or language. *KHa Mang Gi* ("mouth is much") designates one who is talkative or "mouthy." It also has reference to manner of speech in such terms as *KHa aJam Gi* ("mouth is soft"), used to describe a mild manner of speaking, and *KHa gSHaa Gi* ("mouth is suitable"), to designate an orator. *KHa* has a still different meaning when it refers to eating habits or food avoidances. In this sense a Tibetan will say that the Chinese have the same *KHa* as Tibetans because they will eat what Tibetans eat but that the Moslems do not have the same *KHa* because they cannot eat the meat the Tibetans have killed or the food they have prepared. They are said to be *KHa KHa KHa Red* ("mouth part-part are," or mouth apart).

As illustrated by this phrase, the word *KHa* is also used to mean "the constituent part of," the "characteristic aspect of," or "that which pertains to." In these meanings, it appears in a very ancient term for Tibetans, *Bod KHa Ba* ("Tibetan-part ones"). The same term has at present very wide usage as the most comprehensive term for Tibetans. *Bod Pa* ("Tibet one"), which would appear to be the more logical and definitive term, has, for many Tibetans, become particularized into meaning the inhabitants of *dBus,* the province in which Lhasa is located; and *Bod KHa Ba* ("Tibet-part ones") is used for all Tibetans. If *KHa,* in its meaning "pertaining to" is joined to *Lugs* ("system," or "practice of"), the resulting term, *KHa Lugs* becomes a folkloric term for "culture," and *KHa Lugs gCig,* "culture one."

Within this generalization, the Tibetan particularizes oneness of speech, *sKad Lugs gCig,* as an important characteristic by which he recognizes his fellows. It is of considerable significance that from the linguistic border in the east, where the Tibetan language maintains itself against the pressure of terms from the Chinese language and where communities that still identify themselves as Mongol have become Tibetan in speech, to the extreme west, where the Tibetan language is known to have supplanted at least one language—*ZHang ZHung*—and remains the speech of a people like the Balti, who have lost other aspects of Tibetan culture, one language, *Bod sKad* ("Tibetan speech"), mutually intelligible to all to a marked degree, is in current use. The *Sa sKya* abbot who staved off a Mongol invasion under Genghis Khan's grandson, in writing the account of his mission and labors, says all was done "for the benefit of the Tibetan speaking population,"[28] thus using language as the criterion by which to define the Tibetan people.

Conforming to ethnocentric tradition, the Tibetan identifies his own

[28] G. Tucci, *Tibetan Painted Scrolls* (1944), p. 10.

people as having racial distinctiveness. Legend takes the racial origin back to what might be considered the beginnings of the human race—the great apes fathering the children of a female demon. For the Tibetan, that event is the beginning of a lineage that accounts for all Tibetan populations: the people of *Mi Rigs gCig* ("man-lineage one"). Distinctive racial identity as a basis for self-conscious "oneness" is, however, the least clearly defined and admittedly the least important of the characterizations listed above.

Sa CHa gCig ("soil-extent one") designates the contiguous territory in which those dwell who by religion, language, culture, and race are self-recognizably Tibetan. Topographic factors determine the limits of this territory, which is all high plateau, but the demographic aspects match them closely, for in general the people who live on that high plateau are Tibetan in culture and language. It is not a politically-drawn area of predetermined size within whose limits all are arbitrarily assumed or forced to be Tibetan. Ladakh in the far west is included, although historically it was a separate kingdom and part of it, passed on by the British, is now under Indian control and administration. In the east, Khams and Amdo are also included, despite the fact that both areas have been politically fractured, though remaining independent under chiefs and kinglets, and more recently have been under pressure from the Chinese. These areas have been diminished by the encroachment of Chinese populations, and military and political penetration has placed them under varying degrees of direct Chinese political control. No Tibetan thinks of land not now occupied by Tibetans as *Bod Yul* ("Tibet-home"); *Bod Yul*, for him, is that large plateau-land where Tibetan communities, no matter how differently ruled, are linked one to another by a sense of oneness.

The four characterizations which are used by the Tibetan to define or state a sense of oneness are of considerable importance, and his loyalty is stimulated and his patriotism will respond whenever any of them is challenged or menaced. But when compared to the primary one, *CHos Lugs gCig* ("religion-system one"), they are of secondary importance. The Tibetan's deepest loyalty is brought into play and his patriotic response is most fervent whenever this first and most important of the characterizations of oneness is threatened. For him *CHos Lugs gCig* is the true and final criterion for determining who his real fellows are—those to whom he is conscious of owing his utmost in co-operation and loyalty and from whom he expects a reciprocal fulfilment of responsibility. This characteristic largely takes the place of any sense of political unity, which, as we have seen, is notaby lacking. And whatever is of true worth in the other characterizations is assumed, in the final analysis, to derive from *CHos.*

The sense of oneness based on *CHos Lugs gCig* ("religion-system one") is a sublimation of nationhood; it points to and outlines a structure that exists in different times—past, present, and future—in this and other worlds. The Tibetan values cultural, linguistic, racial, and territorial unity; but by reason of faith, religious unity is the one value of prime importance. *CHos* is the true focus of patriotism.

TIBETAN REACTIONS AND ATTITUDES AS FUNCTIONS OF FAITH

The seven propositions defining the distinctive Tibetan view of existence given earlier (p. 68) have thus been elaborated at some length. Data have been cited and evidence adduced to buttress their validity as the results or products of the attitude of faith. The next step is to show the degree to which, as functions of this attitude, they determine or influence the Tibetan response to modernism: ideologies, science, technology, and the problems and choices of international relations. Such a formulation becomes a matter of opinion, and the degree to which such opinion is justified can be determined by the evidence adduced and the argument presented. In such a frame of reference, the following conclusions are presented as general answers, in order and substance, to the postulates already stated.

1. The world view of the Tibetan little disposes him to accept with eagerness or subservience a new cultural impact. In a world of illusions, he is not overwhelmed by the illusory wonders of Western civilization; untroubled by awe, he is open to persuasion, even conviction, but is always predisposed to "take new developments in his stride."

2. Because in ethics the ideal of compassion influences his behavior, he is likely to find much that is admirable in modern goals, and means, of alleviating pain and suffering. But ruthless subordination of the interests of the animal and insect world to benefit humans would be a shock. The idea that germs cause disease would introduce for the Tibetan the paradoxical dilemma of having to kill life in uncounted numbers in order to save life.

3. The adjustment of his own cosmology and geography to Western cosmology and the more precise particularizations of Western geography would not involve very great strain. Even now he adjusts the geography he is taught to that which he learns on his travels. He already concedes that doctrine may admit of the earth's being round, and new explanations

of the sun and moon interest but do not bother him. What final difference does it make? All is illusory in any case.

4. The difference between the indigenous explanation of the structure of matter and quantum physics poses no great problem. Two different explanations of matter are already accepted and held with no sense of dilemma. In medicine the Tibetan has made so many adjustments between theory and pragmatism that he now asks only whether or not a remedy works.

5. The democratic ideal has an instant attraction for the Tibetan. The importance of the individual and the ideal of human dignity are in accord with his deepest instincts, with the relative freedom of the individual in his society, and with his relationships to the units that make up the structure of his society. In managing communal matters he already knows much of a rudimentary, but very basic, democracy. He will question, however, any system of values that appears to be entirely secular or based solely on material and societal considerations.

6. The same religious considerations apply to his view of history and his acceptance of history in the making. History, all of history, is only incidental in the cycles and progress of religion. But within those cycles, there are prophecies of great change and renewal. That sanctioned factor of change helps him, therefore, to make shrewd adjustments to the exigencies of the historical here and now, while reserving judgment on its final value.

Political change as an internal aspect of history bulks large in his experience. The conflict between secular and religious control systems has conditioned the Tibetan to accept many adjustments and accommodations, provided that religion, organized in a hierarchy fashioned from the human and material resources he himself has given, and headed by those who signify the possibility of liberation, endures as the symbol of all toward which his attitude of faith remains constant. What will favor the preservation of religion in its accustomed manifestations is the basic consideration that will determine his attitude toward, and association with, other societies and ideologies.

7. His patriotism is deep and strong. Its highest present expression is a function of the attitude of faith. Even extensive secularization will not take that consciousness from him. He is, however, realistically aware of those other and, in his view, lesser considerations which make him one with his fellows in their love of their culture, speech, and land.

CHAPTER FIVE

THE PRACTICE OF

CHOS ADON:

EXPRESS VERBALIZED RELIGION

CHos aDon ("express verbalized religion") is the second of the Tibetan universals of religious observance. Quite logically, however, it is the first of those that may be characterized as activity observances: doing as the function of being. Contemplation and meditation, exercises of the mind permeated with faith, are not enough. Overt activity must follow, and quite naturally the Tibetan moves from attitude to action—the exercise of the power of speech in the verbalization of religion. From faith he goes on to the manifold expression of that faith in *CHos aDon* which he defines as *NGag Las* ("speech work"). This is his first response, powered with utterance and amplified by many devices, to the demands and compulsions of his belief.

THE IMPORTANCE OF SPEECH AND ITS RELATION TO RELIGION

Of all the religious observances, only this one is primarily an exercise of speech—that distinctive faculty or attainment which first differentiated the human from the animal. As Benjamin Whorf has written, "Speech is the best show man puts on."[1] Man, "the talking animal," by reason of his primal need to communicate with his fellows, or as some believe, with his God, became the possessor of speech. It was magic, for with it there dawned a consciousness of the possession of power hitherto unknown: power to transmit the lessons of personal experience, with the sum of those experiences becoming the stored wisdom of mankind—great for good or evil. And magic, of one sort or another, has characterized the use of words ever since. The Tibetan shares this faculty with all men; he is burdened by the same urgent need to communicate; he accepts without

[1] B. L. Whorf, *Language, Thought and Reality* (1956), p. 249.

reservation all the magic ever ascribed to the function of speech; and he, too, is dominated by the verbal symbols of his conceptual world.

In Tibetan metaphysics, which owe much to Indic influence, speech is held to be one of the essential aspects of personal existence, which is a threefold manifestation on two planes. On the plane of being, the threefold manifestation is *sKu* ("body"), *gSung* ("speech"), and *THugs* ("mind"). On the plane of doing, existence becomes manifest in *mDZad Pa* ("deeds"), *bKaa* ("words"), and *dGongs Pa* ("thoughts"). The overriding importance of language is also evidenced in the Tibetan listing of the *Rig gNas* ("knowledge"), or the compartments of learning. Of the five major ones, two, *sGra* ("sound"), or phonetics, and *gTan TSHigs* ("ordered jointure"), or dialectics, are directly related to communication; and another, *bZo Ba* ("to construct"), or the mechanical arts, renders service to discourse in the forming of letters in writing and printing. Of the five minor sciences, three, *sNYan NGag* ("agreeable speech"), or composition, *mNGon brJod* ("evident word"), or lexicography, and *sDeb sByor* ("put together"), or metrics, have to do with the use of words.

Thus, the concept of personal existence postulates speech as coequal with body and spirit as the components of being, or the functions of being. The concept of general existence postulates the *dNGos Po* ("real"), or absolute, the *aKHor Ba* ("the wheel of transmigration"), or relative, and *aKHrul* ("delusion"), or the imaginary, as equally valid, though each is of differing value.[2] Together they predispose the Tibetan to identify the word with the concept or object of which it is the verbal symbol. This transference of identification from concept or object to symbol is the basis of much of word magic. In such a frame of reference the word is no longer the mere symbol of something: it becomes identified with that something. Manipulation or activation of the word thus becomes manipulation or activation of that something for which the word stands.[3] E. J. Thomas, commenting on one aspect of this phenomenon in his chapter on spells, in the Lotus of the True Doctrine, says, "This is a form of sympathetic magic which consists of asserting that a certain wished-for event is

[2] In addition to stating the lexical definitions, Dezhung Rinpoche, in a long discourse, pointed out that the *dNGos Po* ("the real") is also *NGo Ma* ("the original"), which in turn can be *rTen Pa Bo* ("the basic"). *rTen Pa Bo*, which is the absolute, is only realized after *THar Ba* ("liberation"). The *aKHor Ba* ("cycle") aspect is the phenomenal—that which is seen, heard, felt, and so on. This aspect, the world of the senses is somewhat illusory since it vanishes with liberation. The third aspect is that of *aKHrul* ("delusion"), which is "like a dream." The magical transformations, which appear again and again in the Gesar epic and other Tibetan stories to deceive and hoax antagonists, belong in this aspect of existence.

[3] G. Tucci, *To Lhasa and Beyond* (1956), pp. 98–100.

taking place, and by the *power* of the *word* it is supposed that, if every detail is properly performed, the event does take place."[4]

The fundamental importance accruing to speech because of such theories of personal and cosmological existence is in accord with current everyday practice. It is recognized that the mind and thinking of a man are chiefly made known through speech—a recognition aptly contained in the common aphorism, *Sems Gi sGo NGag Yin* ("The door of the mind is speech"). Through that door, communication is achieved, and the affairs of life are regulated and become orderly. The spoken word is thus powerful in ordering the pattern of daily living, and certain characteristics of the language help to make it so.

The Tibetan language appears to be basically monosyllabic and is generally so characterized.[5] It has the sharpness of definition—unblurred by inflexional changes—characteristic of such speech, but it is also, through the free employment of compounds and a copious use of auxiliary verbs, flexible and rich in possibilities of nuance.[6] Somewhat like French or Japanese, the Tibetan language has no strong fixed stress on syllables, and thus stress may be freely and effectively used for emphasis alone or to accentuate language melody. It lends itself to eloquent oratory and generous use of the balanced aphorism and epigram. The Tibetans are habitual and often magnificent orators who argue freely and effectively in the living speech and also construct masterpieces of dialectic discourse, richly interlarded with epigrams and proverbs. The events or circumstances leading up to any situation are ceremoniously told in conversation that frequently has in it the recognizable beginnings of epic narrative.

This characterization of the oratory and orators of Tibet is largely based on the eloquent oral discourse I have heard from quite a number of Tibetan *bSHad mKHan* ("professional speakers"), or spokesmen. Specifically, the following were masters of that art: *gDug dKar sKyabs,* the illiterate but shrewd, logical, and very articulate headman of an encamp-

---

4 E. J. Thomas, *The History of Buddhist Thought* (1933), p. 189.

5 This personal, somewhat impressionistic characterization of the Tibetan language is based on extensive usage of Tibetan contrasted against a background knowledge of Chinese. In such a frame of reference, Tibetan does not appear to be as fundamentally monosyllabic as Chinese; yet the basic monosyllabic structure is recognizable. In the following citations, one from a great linguist (E. Sapir, *Language* [1949], pp. 135, 142, 196), one from a speaker of Tibetan whose command of the language is known to be superb (M. Pallis, *Peaks and Lamas* [1939], pp. 221, 366), and one from a scholar of stature in both Chinese and Tibetan studies (R. A. Stein, *La civilisation tibétaine* [1962], p. 211), I find echoes and confirmation of my statement.

6 P. Pelliot, *Histoire ancienne du Tibet* (1961), pp. 1–2.

ment near the source of the Klu river in Amdo. His advocacy of my cause before the chief of his own tribe and before the authorities of the _sTag TSHang lHa Mo_ monastery in 1929 and 1930, his part in arbitrating the differences between his and another tribe in 1932, and his daily management of his own concerns throughout the months I spent at his tent door gave me ample opportunity to hear and note the effectiveness of his eloquence. _bKraa SHis Don aGrub,_ official spokesman for the chief of the _TSHo Ba bCu gNYis_ tribe in Amdo, who, though also illiterate, had wide fame as an orator and negotiator. He was the principal speaker at an intertribal council which I attended as participant and mediator in the summer of 1934. _Mei rGyal Po,_ the king of _lNGa Ba_ in Khams, to whom, as a guest in his palace in the summer of 1940, I listened for hours as he met delegations, passed down judgments, and bargained tenaciously for his rights and prerogatives with representatives of the Chinese government—an eloquent, sophisticated, and highly literate orator. _AH KHu dKon mCHog,_ ex-monk and man of affairs, who was equally at home in doctrinal debate, in extravagant flights of persiflage, and in hardheaded political argument. The last time I heard him make one of his justly famous speeches was at a council on New Year's Day, 1948, when the Tibetan leaders of Amdo were pledging support to the governor of Ch'ing-hai, Ma Pu-fang, in his resistance against the Communists. And last but by no means least, one of the four Tibetan scholars already cited in the preface, Dezhung Rinpoche, who has answered many of my questions with homilies which were masterpieces compounded of learned doctrinal formulations mixed with the common, and even racy, proverbs of Khams.

A common colloquial proverb points up the importance of the spoken word, summarizes most aptly the linguistic difference between the culture of the Tibetans and the culture of their great neighbor to the east, and is also a good example of parallelism in the structure of the epigram. _rGya Yin Ni THe Red: Bod Yin Ni KHa Red_ ("The seal, indeed, for Chinese; the mouth, indeed, for Tibetans"). Even the aspirates _THe_ ("seal") and _KHa_ ("mouth") ring like counterpoint.

Before it had a system of writing—when covenants were crudely recorded by the use of notched sticks and knotted strings—Tibet was already expanding into an empire which challenged the might of China—the great Asiatic empire. Armies were assembled and directed by smoke signals, and verbal orders were authenticated by symbolic arrows. In such circumstances the spoken word acquires enhanced importance: powerful as an order, weighty as an oath, or solemn as a treaty. Comprehensive planning and far-flung operations become effective when the powers of memory and the spoken word are joined. Even among those Tibetans of the present time who are highly literate, dependence on the sureness and clarity of the spoken word has persisted. Sir Charles Bell notes that in official communications there was always a spoken message that accompanied the written message, and invariably this word of mouth portion was the most important part, frequently modifying the terms of the letter.[7]

The tradition of the word-of-mouth message, begun in the time when there was no system of writing, has retained its primal importance. To maintain maximum efficiency, its form has become carefully stylized as shown in the following example of current practice. A wishes to send a message to C by B. B meets C and states, "A has sent you a message." As a direct quotation, he then recites the message, concisely and carefully as though he were reading it from a telegram form. When he has finished quoting the message he asks C, "Have you understood?" When C says he has understood, he then repeats the message in its original form back to B as evidence of his precise comprehension. If the repetition is not sufficiently accurate to satisfy B, the latter quotes the message again and asks for a repetition. When the repetition by C is sufficiently exact to satisfy B that the message has been truly understood, the latter then says, "Now it is on your head, no longer on mine," and talks of other matters or goes about his business. Such precision is far removed from the vagueness of hearsay and makes for very effective and accurate communication.

In the frame of reference established by the importance of the spoken word, verbalization of religion takes on added and varied significance. And in the context of Tibetan religious thinking, this significance is explicitly stated. *CHos aDon* ("express verbalized religion") is *CHos Las* ("religion-work"), but in purpose, it is a *dGe Bai Las KHa* ("merit's work part"). It is also *NGag Las* ("speech work"). The last category differentiates it from the observances of *mCHod Pa* ("offering"), *bsKor Ba* ("circumambulation"), and *PHyag* ("salutation"), which are *Lus Las* ("body work"). The various *CHos Las* ("religion-work[s]") are separated into categories of *NGag Las* ("speech work") and *Lus Las* ("body work") both by reference to instrumentality—the mouth and the body—and by the causal necessity of achieving accordance between offenses and the expiation for such offenses. As stated in a Tibetan sermon, "The place at which you fall to earth is the point at which you must get up."[8] The expression of verbalized religion is thus matched, as cure or atonement, to

[7] Sir Ch. Bell, *Tibet: Past and Present* (1924), p. 89.

[8] This is a direct quotation from one of Dezhung Rinpoche's homilies.

the sins of utterance, for offenses of speech are expiated by works of speech, as offenses of the body are expiated by works of the body.

Since there are more offenses of the body than of speech, *CHos aDon* is less important than the sum of the three other observances, which are all body works, but it is much more important than any one of the three. There is general agreement, however, that verbalization of religion is observed to a much greater degree than the others—possibly because it is more easily carried out. Some Tibetans would voice the suspicion, at this point, that it is possible that *CHos aDon* is observed to a greater degree because offenses of the mouth, being more easily perpetrated, constitute a greater total than all other offenses. The part speech itself plays in preparing and aiding sundry offenses of the body—such as, for example, adultery—is amply appreciated and fulsomely expounded in any Tibetan discussion of the problem.

The phrase *CHos aDon,* which summarizes this verbalization, is equally a part of *KHa sKad* ("mouth speech"), or the colloquial, and *CHos sKad* ("religion speech"), or classical Tibetan. It is the term most commonly used to comprehend the entire range of formal chanting, the pronouncing of incantations, the proffering of prayers, and the endlessly muttered repetition of the six-syllable formula *OHm Ma Ni Padme Hum.* It is central among a cluster of concepts that embrace all of religious utterance and the representations linked with it. More than any other term, it comprehends the semantic content of the activity which, in this study, is treated as the second of the Tibetan universals of religious observance.

CONFORMITY TO CRITERIA

As thus subsumed, the activity of *CHos aDon* conforms to each of the four criteria formulated in chapter iii. Within the context of Tibetan life, it is universal. Everyone who considers himself a *Bod KHa Ba* ("Tibetan-part one"), that is, characterized by the sense of "oneness" explained in the preceding chapter, participates personally in this activity. Such personal participation may be limited to a single syllable, ejaculatory in nature, or it may be a most extensive repetition or reading of an enormous mass of doctrinal preachments and formulas. Participation is not, however, limited to strictly personal participation. It may take the form of sponsorship participation, in which thousands of monks are engaged to read and chant the scriptures, prayer wheels are bought and erected, and extensive printings of prayers and charms, or rock carvings of them, are ordered and supported. Within the context of Tibetan life, the universality of the observance is without question.

It is an observable phenomenon in all its aspects. Indeed, in the Tibetan scene the performance of *CHos aDon* is so constantly heard and viewed—for it has its visual aspects—that in a short time the more common or all pervasive manifestations are no longer noticed. They become accepted background and as such cease to have impact as phenomena. Eventually, the constant rumble of muttered prayer, which is a sort of background music to conversation—whether it be commercial, casual, or even amorous—the steady movement of the rosary through the fingers, and the spinning of the prayer wheels register on the senses, paradoxically, only when they are interrupted or missing.

The observance is religious in nature and intent. In fact, it is the only one of the Tibetan universals of religious observance that by its name is self-defined as religious. Although in its strict denotation the term *CHos* means, as we shall see, that portion of the Buddhist Triad called the law, the extended meaning of *CHos,* as the whole of religion, is imposed whenever the term is used. Thus *CHos aDon* leads all the activity observances as the consciously accepted, supremely effective activation of religion. More than in any of the other observances, religion is made to function in this verbalization.

Finally, it has conceptual unity. The limits of the concept are broad but are also sharply defined. Original sermonizing, imprecation, and the recital of stories are clearly excluded. The activity of which *CHos aDon* is the most widely accepted verbal symbol has many facets and aspects, but it is not a composite. In itself it is simplistic and, as such, is a clearly distinguishable element of the many composite rituals and observances of which it constitutes a part. It frequently occurs in combination with other Tibetan universals of religious observance but never loses its own identity.

TERMINOLOGY AND SEMANTIC IMPLICATIONS

As the most comprehensive verbal symbol used to denote the expression of verbalized religion, but one frequently supplemented by other verbal symbols, the phrase *CHos aDon* requires some analysis. *CHos,* the first word of the phrase, has an entire series of meanings. In its most comprehensive aspect, it represents the universal norm of existence; and if that norm is broken down into natural and moral law, it embraces both. *CHos NYid* ("intrinsic religion-self"), for example, is defined as natural law and the basic principle of existence.[9] As the word for religion in its

---

[9] This definition of *CHos* emerged from long and intensive discussion with the Tibetan scholars—but especially out of argument and exposition by Norbu and Dezhung Rinpoche. The former, making reference to Chinese terminology, characterized it, in that language, as being much like *tsu-jan* ("natural").

widest sense, it may be applied to each and every religion, that is, the religion of the Moslems, of the Christians, or of the Hindus, and so on. In Tibetan usage, when it is employed alone without any qualification, it means the Buddhist religion, although, as mentioned in a previous chapter, it may be extended to mean all that is wrapped up in the word "Tibetology."

In its narrow, more sharply defined sense, *CHos* means "law": the second entity of *dKon mCHog gSum* ("Rare-Perfect Three")—the Jewel Triad of Buddhism.[10] In this context it refers primarily to the *bKaa* ("words"), or utterances, of the Buddha to which the explanations, annotations, and elaborations compiled by Buddhist saints and scholars have been added. These scriptures constitute an enormous mass of written material and contain prayers, sermons, stories, commentaries, and tantric incantations.

By a strange working of the law of association, the written or printed letters themselves on any paper, even when the meaning is unknown, are also sometimes called *CHos* by the illiterate and accorded worshipful care and treatment by all. A devout Tibetan scholar will reverently touch his head with a Tibetan book, even when he knows it is secular in subject matter, because the letters in themselves retain something of religion.

Comprehension of the three principal semantic aspects of the Tibetan word *CHos* is aided by a comparison with the Chinese terms employed as equivalents in the same context of Buddhist practice. The Chinese word for *CHos,* as religion, in its widest sense, is *chiao;* the Chinese word for *CHos* as the second entity of the Triad—an exclusively Buddhist concept—is *fa;* and the Chinese word for *CHos* as a reference to sacred writings is *ching. CHos aDon* ("express verbalized religion") in Chinese is *nien ching* ("to chant a liturgy").[11] Thus *CHos* subsumes all and more of the meanings of the three Chinese terms.

[10] "Rare-Perfect" is here suggested as the closely literal and semantically valid rendering for the Tibetan compound *dKon mCHog,* which designates the highest point of Buddhist aspiration and adoration, commonly called—following the Sanskrit—"The Jewel." The Tibetan scholars argued strongly against the use of any English term that would have any material object or substance as referent. A "thing" such as a jewel was completely unacceptable to them, and to guide me in framing a term in English, they elaborated at length the basic and everyday meanings of *dKon* ("rare," "scarce," "hard to find," and so on) and of *mCHog* ("perfect," "best," "most excellent," "exactly right," and so on). See also I. Desideri, *An Account of Tibet* (1712–27), pp. 251–54, for a somewhat similar analysis.

[11] R. H. Mathews, *Chinese-English Dictionary* (1931; new American ed., 1960), p. 657.

The second word of the phrase, *aDon* ("express," or "intone"), is one of those Tibetan words which have paired meanings, which because they are antithetical or because they are expressions of cause and effect have a logical but often paradoxical relationship. *aDon* means "to put out and to draw forth"; "to put in and to extract" (as gold from the earth in mining), "to recite and to read silently," "to elevate and to arrive at," and "to ejaculate and to taste."[12] Here again reference to the Chinese word used in the same context is helpful. *Nien,* which means "to read aloud," also means to cogitate or mull over in the mind reflections and ideas, and semantically, it has a link with such paradoxical renderings of *aDon* as "to recite and to read silently."

In the third of the paired meanings, thus listed, the paradoxical juxtaposition of "to ejaculate and to taste" suggests another esoteric aspect of *CHos aDon:* a mystical sacramental tasting or partaking of religion by the very act of intoning and, by enunciation, liberating the magic power of the syllables. This indication is strengthened by common linguistic usages. Acceptance of religion or the subjective individual response to the process of conversion is called *KHas Len Pa* ("to take by mouth" [instrumental case]). The writer has also heard Tibetans speak of a Tibetan who has become a Moslem as one who *Hui Hui CHos Za Yod Gi* ("has eaten Hui Hui religion"). To take a vow is to *Dam bCaa Ba* ("chew a vow"), and when an oath is violated or broken, it is said that *mNaa Za Yod* ("the oath is eaten").[13] Thus when a Tibetan intones religion, he tastes *CHos* by that ejaculation and ingests its power in the same way that vows are chewed or oaths, when violated, are eaten.

Another word frequently used to indicate verbalization of religion is *aDebs* ("sow" or "cast"). It is combined with *sMon Lam* ("wish-way"), or wish-prayer, *gSol Ba* ("request"), and *mTHu* ("force") to mean, in the first two cases, the saying of prayers and, in the last, the bringing into play of supernatural forces on one's behalf. Even when used with *gSol Ba,* it does not connote the idea of praying to any being, possibly not even for anything, but rather the idea that prayers, whether wish-prayers or appeals to magic, are, by purposeful intent, broadcast or sown in utterance and, according to the laws of causality and by reason of intrinsic efficacy, bring a harvest of fulfilment.

[12] H. A. Jaschke, *A Tibetan-English Dictionary* (1949), p. 281; dGe bSHes CHos Grags, *brTSams Pai brDa Dag Ming TSHig gSal Ba bZHugs So* (1957), p. 390.

[13] These meanings were carefully established by discussion with Norbu and Dezhung Rinpoche, especially that of "chew" for the Tibetan word *bCaa.* Dezhung Rinpoche even clicked his teeth to make clear the meaning.

The *sNGags* ("charm[s]"), rhythmic, short, and often consisting of syllables from the Sanskrit that have no retained meaning for the Tibetan, constitute a specialized class of religious utterance. They are categorized as *gZungs* ("power"), *Rig* ("wisdom"), and *gSang* ("secret") *sNGags*. All are forms of persuasion, sometimes extending to coercion, of spirit beings. The word *sNGags* is identical, phonetically and in orthography, with one form of the verb *sNGag Pa* ("to praise"). Thus a semantic link, if not complete equivalency, is highly probable. The words charm and spell in English usage have an ambivalence that illustrates something of the nature of this link. The verbs *sGrub Ba* ("to realize"), *aDebs Pa* ("to sow"), *sPel Ba* ("to propagate for increase"), and *Zlo Ba* ("to murmur") are used to express the activation of charms.

Within the musical form of verbal religious expression, there is the closest approach to a recognized distinction between secular or profane forms of any of the categories of religious utterance, for *mGur*, or *mGur Ma* ("hymn"), is the honorific of *Glu* ("song"). *mGur*, in common usage, distinguishes the sacred from the profane, but the songs of Milaraspa are called both *mGur* and *Glu*. They are equally secular and religious, with a wide popular appeal, and as such a part of religion. The verbs used with *mGur* are *gSung Ba* ("to speak" [honorific]), *Len Pa* ("to take up"), and *aTHen Pa* ("to draw out"). Though freely interchangeable they make unmistakable reference to different aspects of psalmody: the first stresses speech, the second suggests the raising of the voice, and the third, by reference to drawing on the strings of a musical instrument, concentrates on melody.

The original injunction by the Buddha that religious utterance should be practiced in a solemn manner has been elaborated in Tibet through pitch, rhythm, musical prolongation of sound, and melody, which have become standard and impressive parts of religious utterance. The musical accompaniment to such utterance has been developed to the degree that musical scores indicating the exact part of each instrument have been written.

This list of the general categories of verbal religious expression is representative rather than exhaustive, but it does summarize the principal aspects. Verbal expression of all the prayers, charms, and formulas is thus most noticeably vocal; yet visual representation of that same verbal expression is rich and varied. Both vocal and visual forms may be subsumed in the term *CHos aDon*. This is the central and most inclusive concept on which to focus attention in the study of the history, doctrinal position, and functional role of religious expression in Tibetan society.

HISTORY OF THE OBSERVANCE

This observance antedates Buddhism. Long prior to the introduction of Buddhism, prayers were said and invocations were made by the Tibetans. This may safely be assumed as a general proposition because of the nature of man and the nature of religion—any man and any religion. Such an assumption is strengthened by reference, for purposes of analogy, to Mongolian shamanism and Taoism in China prior to the introduction of Buddhism among those peoples and to the religious practices still existing among neighboring peoples such as the Ch'iang,[14] who to this day have refused to accept Buddhism. The general aspects of pre-Buddhist religion among the Tibetans have been discussed in an earlier chapter, and samples of non-Buddhist prayers have been given.

All these non-Buddhist, and therefore, presumably pre-Buddhist, prayers have certain characteristics in common: a definite but free directness and intensity quite different from formulas and stereotyped utterance. They summon, invite, harangue, supplicate, flatter, and inform the spirit beings to whom they are addressed, giving, often in great detail and with no false modesty, the identity, status, and location of the speaker. There is very little exact repetition or emphasis on getting the prescribed syllables said correctly the greatest number of times but considerable repetitious free appeal. These prayers are, in form and intent, direct speech to somebody for something. They ring with the urgency of tribal alarms; they are punctuated with syllables from the war cries of a raider; and they shout harsh appeals to powerful beings for intervention and help.

Though in some instances influenced by the spirit and form of this religious utterance of an earlier time, the Buddhist prayers and formulas which are the present-day verbal expression of religion are radically and unmistakably different. Compared with the earlier prayers of primitive asking and naïveté, these latter have lost the urgency of appeal and the specifics of request are blurred by conceptual generalities. No one identifies himself or tells where he is and what he wants. Instead he repeats, seeking by multiplication to give the syllables an intrinsic mechanical strength, the words and phrases called *CHos*.

Through translation, most of the actual words and phrases, and certainly the emphasis on repetition, came to the Tibetans with the introduction of Buddhism. In Buddhism four practices combined to make recitation and repetitious utterance an important part of religious observance. One derived from the injunction that monks and laymen practice,

[14] D. C. Graham, *The Customs and Religion of the Ch'iang* (1958), pp. 69–79, 86.

as necessary ritual, the threefold repetition of the formula of taking refuge in the Buddha, in the Doctrine, and in the Order.[15] The second was the practice of reciting the twelve classes of the sacred texts for the sake of bringing about the happiness and welfare of the fourfold congregation.[16]

The third practice developed from the fact that, for at least three centuries after the passing of the Buddha, there was no written record of either the rules or the teachings. All records and communication were oral, and the need to guard against errors, omissions, and additions in this transmission of the doctrine resulted in the office and function of the reciters. According to tradition, shortly after the funeral of the Buddha, the first council was held for "reciting and collecting the Doctrine." Twice a month the members of the Order assembled to recite the rules and, by intricate cross-questioning, to check and insure that the recitation was correct. By the time a written record was made of the doctrine, the observance ritual of reciting had been invested with very great importance, which came to have doctrinal significance. "Those who *hear* only a single verse of the suttra (recited) are sure of enlightenment"; and again in reference to the spells of the Lotus sutra, they "will bring blessing to any who *hear* them, who *read* or *write* them, or *cause them to be written* [emphasis added]."[17]

The fourth of these practices was the outgrowth of the Buddha's acceptance, with some reservations and a degree of reluctance, of the use of spells. This practice was widespread in India and had existed in Vedic, and even pre-Vedic, times. The permissive incorporation of this practice into Buddhism is recorded in the sutra that tells how the Buddha, having received from the Four Kings a spell in verse that was a charm against evil spirits, repeated it to the monks. Many of the spirit beings, however, were thought to be well-disposed toward Buddhism. If monks, nuns, laymen, or laywomen would repeat the spells, such beings would protect them. Nor was it necessary to understand the spell. "The belief in the magic power of the word led to the view that the words need not be intelligible."[18]

[15] E. J. Thomas, *The Life of the Buddha* (1931), p. 272.

[16] E. Obermiller, *History of Buddhism* (1933; a translation of *CHos aByung*, by Bu sTon), Part II, p. 60.

[17] E. J. Thomas, *The History of Buddhist Thought* (1933), pp. 8, 16, 27, 28, 183, 186–88.

[18] *Ibid.*, pp. 186, 188; A. L. Basham, "Jainism and Buddhism," in *Sources of Indian Tradition* (1958), ed. W. T. De Bary, pp. 188–89.

In the Buddhism of a later period—specifically, in the Buddhism of the seventh century, when it was first effectively introduced into Tibet—the doctrine and practices of the Tantric school, founded on the use of spells combined with yoga practices, were apparent. The intensified introduction of Buddhism into Tibet in the time of Padma Sambhava in the middle of the eighth century brought with it the fully developed Tantric system; and the emphasis on spells and their repetition inherent in that system was transferred into the distinctive form of Mahayana Buddhism that was taking shape in Tibet. Thus all these factors and developments, both before and with the introduction of Buddhism, combined to set the form and prescribe the pattern of the verbalization of religion in Tibetan Buddhism. It is along the way of such practices and such a tradition that the six-syllable formula *OHm Ma Ni Padme Hum* probably made its appearance in doctrine, ritual, and personal observance.

The introduction of Buddhism into Tibet occurred in several stages, which may be summarized as follows: an early abortive introduction some time in the fifth century; the first effective introduction in the middle of the seventh century; an intensive introduction, with Padma Sambhava as the victorious apostle, in the middle of the eighth century; and a final introduction by Atisha, with large elements of vigorous reformation, in the middle of the eleventh century. The second of these stages, which by tradition has been acclaimed as the official introduction of Buddhism into Tibet, has been appropriately embellished with stories and a halo of religious glory and achievement. From differing viewpoints, this event could be characterized as the result of the palace intrigues of the two foreign wives of a Tibetan king; as the victories and defeats of contending systems of magic; as the conflict between radical foreign innovation and the conservatism of native culture patterns; or as a very interesting example of competition between the cultures of India and China, meeting in a buffer zone, which resulted in a syncretism of the two.

Tibetan historians, however, present this and the other stages in such a manner that they appear, in some degree, as examples of semantic problems in communication. In the first stage, during the reign of *lHa THo THo Ri*, this aspect is very clearly indicated. One Tibetan version states that a golden casket fell from the sky, and when it was opened, two books and a golden stupa fell out. The king was promised that in the fifth generation from him the *meaning* of these books would be known.[19] Another Tibetan historian states more simply that the books were brought to the king by *Pandita Blo Sems mTHso* and the translator *Li THe Se* but that

---

[19] E. Obermiller, *op. cit.*, pp. 182, 183.

since the king could not read and understand the meaning the pandita and translator went away. The situation is summarized in the words, "In the beginning of the Doctrine, in the reign of *lHa THo THo Ri gNYan bTSan*, though religious books had become available, there was no one to write, read or explain their meaning." There is also a suggestion that the initial introduction of Buddhism was abortive partly because of mistakes in interpretation or translation of the key concept of *Bodhi*.[20] There are other references to the finding, in the time of *Srong bTsan sGam Po*, of images and inscriptions—including those of the six-syllable formula— which had been hidden in the hills and caves;[21] and there is a fair degree of agreement as to the contents of the books in the casket which fell from heaven. All these bits and hints, admittedly traditional rather than strictly historical, suggest that some time, prior to the official introduction of Buddhism into Tibet in the middle of the seventh century, writings containing spells and rules of worship, descriptions of the form and significance of the stupa as a structure for containing the relics of the Buddha, images of Avalokitesvara, and the specific connection of the six-syllable formula with his worship had entered the Land of Snows. The religion of which these were aspects and symbols—though misunderstood and handicapped because of unresolved problems in translation—would seem to have gained a degree of acceptance. For at least three reigns after that of *lHa THo THo Ri gNYan bTSan*, this acceptance, although confused and abortive rather than actual, had its influence at court, and some sort of an undercurrent or intermittent adherence to the cult persisted down to the time of the second, and linguistically effective, stage in the introduction of Buddhism.[22]

The development of Buddhism in Tibet follows a pattern of which these items constitute a prophetic outline. A sense of the importance of writings per se, revealed in the traditional stories, stimulated the creation, through sophisticated adoption and adaptation, of a system of writing. The problems posed by the first awareness of non-comprehension were later met by the careful construction of a standard and official vocabulary of Tibetan terms to which semantic equivalencies with concepts expressed in Sanskrit were arbitrarily assigned. In the vast labor of translation which followed, strict adherence to this vocabulary was the rule. Spells were recognized as important, and their use was furthered by their

[20] G. N. Roerich, *The Blue Annals* (1949), pp. 38–39.

[21] S. C. Das, "Contributions on Tibet," *JASB*, 1881, p. 218.

[22] *Ibid.*, p. 217; E. Obermiller, *op. cit.*, p. 183; G.-Ch. Toussaint, *Le dict de Padma* (1933), p. 232; Kun dGaa rDo rJe, *Deb THer dMar Po* (1961), f. 16 *a-b*.

reproduction, first in writing and later by wood-block printing, and their wide dissemination. The pattern of the stupa foreshadowed the emphasis that was later placed upon the building of religious structures and monuments. The images and instructions were the beginnings of the extensive flowering of Tibetan religious art that was to come, in which *sPyan Ras gZigs* ("Avalokitesvara") is revealed as the central figure of the orthodox Tibetan pantheon and as the guardian saint of the land. The six-syllable prayer, whose beginnings are ascribed to that period, also became the ubiquitous and representative form of *CHos aDon*—the Tibetan verbalization of religion.

THE DEVELOPMENT OF WRITING AND ITS EFFECT ON THE OBSERVANCE

In the Tibetan cultural development, the marriage of speech to a system of writing was the result of a purposeful and calculated effort on the part of the Tibetans, although it did not develop entirely from within the culture, nor was it a complex of cultural traits imposed by aggressive missionary pressure from without. *THon Mi*, the Tibetan wise man, and his staff were sent to India to bring back a system of writing. In dedicating the results of his work—a system of spelling and grammar—to *aJam dPal* ("Manjusri"), the mighty one of language, he expressed the wish that all men of Tibet may come to a like designation.[23]

The initiative taken by the Tibetans had as its *raison d'être* a number of considerations. Contact with religious writings and the recognition of linguistic insufficiency and non-comprehension postulated above had created, to some degree, a sense of need. Although the Tibetan account of the effort made to meet this need places it largely in a religious context— this distinctively Tibetan view of history has already been touched upon in a previous chapter—there is good reason to assume that political and administrative reasons of state as well as factors of cultural competition[24] may also have had a part in Tibetan recourse to India for a system of writing and linguistic guidance. But according to tradition—and as a consequence, in all popular regard—the marriage of speech and a system of writing was consecrated to the service of religion, the religion of the Buddha, and hallowed beyond all mundane associations. This union produced a set of three equally hallowed practices—the reciting, the writing, and the reading of *CHos*—a threefold verbalization.

Initially, this verbalization constituted the major part of a calculated

---

[23] J. Bacot, *Les slokas grammaticaux de Thonmi Sambhota* (1928), p. 164.

[24] S. C. Das, *op. cit.*, p. 218; "Ancient China," *JASB*, 1882, pp. 99–100.

propaganda and missionary effort which had as its objective the establishment and spread of Buddhism among the Tibetans. As a means to an
end, it served the practical purpose of announcing the doctrines of the
Buddha, making a permanent record of those doctrines available to the
Tibetans, and fostering study of, and reference to, that record. The prag-
matic usefulness of this method was well appreciated by the Tibetans, who
realized that the knowledge and use of writing was indeed of pivotal importance in the propaganda verbalization of religion.

The gap between that initial propaganda verbalization of religion
and the verbalization of religion that now exists in Tibetan society is more
than a hiatus of thirteen centuries of time or a long pause in a continuum
of purpose. It is the sort of break that occurs when purpose, or meaning,
is raised or lowered to a new level. Verbalization of religion in the earlier
time was largely a means to an end in a missionary and propaganda effort;
it aimed at a result which would have existence in time and space—the
immediate establishment of Buddhism as the religion of the people of
Tibet. In the context of present religious practice and observance, verbalization of religion is largely an end in itself, and its practice is measured
in terms of its own intrinsic value, though it also contributes to the mystical accumulation of virtue and thus to eventual liberation.

To some degree the seeds of this change were no doubt present in
some of the values and potency ascribed to verbalization of religion at
the time Buddhism was introduced into Tibet. Primitive Buddhism had
emphasized the intrinsic value of reciting, writing and reading, the doctrine; and imported tantric schools fostered verbalization. The importance
of language in the culture and the general linguistic awareness of the Tibetans, which was touched on in the first part of this chapter, may have
aided the change from a means-to-an-end verbalization into a reflexive
end-in-itself verbalization. Other factors not now known may also have
contributed to this change. In any case, when we examine contemporary
verbalization of religion in Tibet, we arrive at the certainty that such a
change has occurred.

Of the three activities, reciting, writing—or printing—and reading,
that of writing would seem to have the closest connection with objective
and material reality as an effort in long-term communication. The paper
on which meaningful marks or impressions are made is preserved indef-
initely in the favorable conditions of the Tibetan climate; the record made
is therefore available for a long period of time. If read it communicates;
yet this method of verbalization also furnishes the clearest example of an
act that is an end in itself rather than a means to an end. In the context of

contemporary verbalization of religion and the values ascribed to it, it is not the record and what it communicates that is of prime importance but the act and effort of making the record. The page so made and the hundreds of books so made are valued as the record of pious effort—fossil remains testifying to a religious observance. Thus books may be used to line the tomb of a grand lama that is destined never to be opened or may be carried, but not read, in procession around communal fields in blessing.

The ultimate exemplification of this can be found in the practice of printing on water. The monks who sit along the rivers and streams all over Tibet printing pages of charms and formulas on the surface of the water have no thought of making a record, they only strive to make as many impressions as possible as they slap the woodcut blocks on the water. This practice, too, is an expression of verbalized religion, for the impress has been made and gravity and the winds combine to move the water and vibrate or activate the blessing inherent in the act of printing, which is performed as an end in itself. It is in this practice that a rather close link between the drawing or printing of the likenesses of all the manifestations of the Buddhahood and the drawing or printing of the letters of Tibetan writing appears, for often what is printed on the water is a picture. But the specific pre-eminence of the written word over images is stoutly maintained. As one Tibetan scholar stated it, "One letter formed is of greater value than a likeness of Buddha formed, for the letter aids knowledge."[25] This statement, and the attitudes and behavior pattern of which it is the expression, suggests that, among the Tibetans, grapholatry is more real than idolatry.

FORMS OF PARTICIPATION AND THEIR DISTRIBUTION

A survey and description of the contemporary manifestations of the observance of CHos aDon must take into account two qualifying considerations of basic importance. One is the universality of the observance within the Tibetan frame of reference, and the other is the distinction between personal participation and sponsorship participation.

As a category of activity, CHos aDon is a Tibetan universal of religious observance, that is, every Tibetan has practiced some degree of personal participation. But not every Tibetan personally participates in all of the varied forms of the observance. Indeed, in the more intricate forms of verbalization, personal participation is confined to a great extent to selected groups and individuals who are specialists. Universal personal participation is limited to the employment of a few of the simplest forms.

[25] Personal communication from T. J. Norbu.

Sponsorship participation, however, is universal. It makes possible all of the extremely varied and often elaborate manifestations of the verbalization of religion found in the Tibetan scene. Sponsorship support, in its farthest extension and widest base, comes from every Tibetan. Everyone engaged in productive activity recognizes and agrees passively or actively that some percentage of what he produces will be devoted to the support of this observance whenever, in its most intricate and elaborate forms, it is ministered by any of the specialists—from the Dalai Lama down to the lowliest serving monk or itinerant sorcerer.

As a result of the interaction of these two factors, the observable manifestations fall naturally into three categories: (1) those minimal observances in which all Tibetans have a part through personal participation; (2) those more varied and elaborate observances in which many or —in inverse proportion to their complexity—some Tibetans have a part through personal participation; and (3) all the mass-organized observances performed by the religious specialists in which some Tibetans directly, and all Tibetans indirectly, participate as sponsors.

Personal Participation

Because of the present scarcity of detailed scientific data on Tibet, determination of the number and description of the character of those observances in which Tibetans have a part through personal participation cannot be done with statistical finality. Inescapably, enumeration and description are matters of informed opinion—in this case the writer's own, based on many years of immersion in Tibetan life and much firsthand observation. In a series of lengthy discussions, however, my observations have been submitted to the collaborating Tibetan scholars for confirmation, rejection, or emendation.

There is agreement that the minimal manifestations of the verbalization of religion that are observed by every Tibetan and, thus, that are universal within the Tibetan context are limited to the following: (1) the enunciation of a few one-syllable charms, a few short phrases, and the basic six-syllable prayer formula; (2) the use of the aPhreng Ba ("rosary"); and (3) the manipulation of the Mani CHos aKHor ("mani religion wheel"), or commonly, "prayer wheel" or "prayer mill."

The enunciation of sacred syllables, phrases, and the six-syllable formula is mixed with, and shades into, such mundane vocalization as the taking of oaths, exclamations expressing assorted emotions, and the use of mere epithets. Of OHm, AH, and Hum, the three one-syllable charms,

AH, although a "mystical exclamation" and "symbol of the deity"[26] possibly borrowed from Sanskrit, has a wide mundane use both as a simple exclamation alone or in compounds and as a salutation meaning "hail" when combined with terms of relationship. It only becomes recognizably religious when linked with a religious phrase, when accompanied by ritual gestures, or when murmured over one of the three keeper beads attached to a rosary. When these three beads are fingered, they are named *OHm, AH,* and *Hum* in turn.

OHm and *Hum* are strictly religious in connotation and, when joined to common ejaculations, raise them to a level of religious significance. The phrases *dKon mCHog gSum* ("Rare-Perfect Three"), *dKon mCHog mKHyen* ("Rare-Perfect knows"), *Bla Ma mKHyen* ("the lama knows"), and similar ejaculations are used as exclamations of wonder and amazement or as asseverations of solemn import. They become unmistakable verbalizations of religion when prefixed by the mystic Sanskrit syllable *OHm* and accompanied by ritual gestures of salutation. The many oaths found in the Tibetan language, which cite or appeal to religious concepts, also become unmistakably religious in nature and intent whenever they are preceded by the syllable *OHm.* Similarly, whenever oaths are followed by the Sanskrit syllable *Hum,* they become religious. Since *OHm* is the first syllable and *Hum* the last syllable of the six-syllable mantra *OHm Ma Ni Padme Hum,* it is evident that much, if not all, ejaculatory *CHos aDon* is linked with the formula, and repetition of it constitutes the basic verbalization of religion.

It may safely be stated that there is no Tibetan—excluding the completely witless and speechless—who does not personally participate in this enunciation and not one who is completely certain just what the phrase means. The traditional explanation is that it is a vocative, an address to *sPyan Ras gZigs* ("Avalokitesvara"), hailing the jewel in the lotus and thus referring to the incarnation of the Buddhahood. Esoteric explanations abound, and much has been written to show that the six syllables have special reference to the six classes of sentient beings, or that they have deeper and deeper meanings.[27] There has also been some erudite speculation that *mani* ("the jewel") and *padme* ("the lotus flower") are symbols of the male and female principles, joined in the formula, and thus that the formula is based on the Indian veneration of the linga and

26 H. A. Jaschke, *op. cit.,* p. 607.

27 M. Pallis, *Peaks and Lamas* (1939), pp. 178–86; A. David-Neel, *Magic and Mystery in Tibet* (1932), pp. 258–63; W. W. Rockhill, *Land of the Lamas* (1891), pp. 326–34.

the yoni as representing the male and female organs.[28] Modern linguistic research seems to establish the fact that the form of the Sanskrit original makes it a vocative addressed to a female deity.[29]

The Tibetan Everyman, however, does not bother his head about any of these explanations. In the context of the mystical metalinguistic power ascribed to the syllables, meaning is of secondary importance. What is important is the number of times the syllables are repeated. The requirement of speed and as much repetition as possible frequently reduces the entire phrase to a vocal blur something like *OHm-m-m–Hum*. The initial and final syllables alone survive this phonetic erosion, but their survival helps confirm the separate and doctrinal existence which *OHm* and *Hum* already have.

Two other syllables of the mantra have also acquired a special meaning. *Ma Ni* very often does duty for that portion of the mantra that follows the initial syllable *OHm*. The mantra thus becomes *OHm Mani–m*. The mantra has also come to have a substantive meaning as representing or subsuming the entire scope of the doctrine that hails *sPyan Ras gZig* as the guardian saint of Tibet and his incarnation, *Srong bTSan sGam Po*, in his traditional role as royal patron of Buddhism in that land. The mantra, in this special context, called *sPyan Ras gZigs Yi Ge Drug Ma* ("Avalokitesvara's six letters"), is also ascribed to this first of the religious kings of Tibet,[30] and the intoning of it is sometimes called *KHa Ma Ni* ("mouth *mani*"). The syllables *Ma Ni*, representing both tradition and doctrine, appear in the title of the book *Ma Ni bKaa aBum* ("one hundred thousand *mani* words"), which treats of these matters. They also appear in the terms *Ma Ni CHos aKHor* ("*mani* religion wheel"), or prayer wheel, and *Ma Ni gDong* ("*mani*-faced"), the stone walls or heaps made of slabs which have the mantra engraved upon them and which are objects of both salutation and circumambulation rites.

In the borderland between China and Tibet, among Chinese populations having contact with the Tibetans and their religion, *mani* has come to mean the doctrine of Tibetan Buddhism. The Tibetan verbalization of religion is called *Nien ma-ni* ("repeat-aloud *mani*") as an alternate of *nien-foh* ("repeat-aloud Buddha"), and the religion is called *Ma-ni chiao* ("*mani* religion"). This is quite distinct from, and is not to be confused with, the literary and historical Chinese term for Manichaeism.

[28] W. Simpson, *The Buddhist Praying Wheel* (1896), pp. 37–39.

[29] E. J. Thomas, *op. cit.*, p. 187.

[30] S. C. Das, "Contributions on Tibet," *JASB*, 1882, pp. 6–7; E. Schlagingtweit, *Le Bouddhisme au Tibet* (1881), p. 52.

It has been noted that when *OHm* is used to prefix an exclamation of amazement or some form of asseveration—especially when accompanied by the upraised right hand—secular usage has become sacred. This process may also be reversed; when the syllable *AH*, for example, is used in daily greeting, the sacred may be downgraded and by tone and obvious intent become the secular.

When a Tibetan takes a vow of silence for a period of time, the only utterance permitted is the verbalization of religion; therefore, in theory he is bound to the utterance of prayers alone. In such a case the mantra *OHm Ma Ni Padme Hum* may serve many conversational needs. The tent wife who is bound by a vow of silence for the day may shout it in your ear to call attention to the fact that she waits to fill your tea bowl, and I have seen many a trespassing dog rise and depart with speed when told *OHm Ma Ni Padme Hum.*

The minimal, and therefore in the Tibetan context, universally shared, personal participation in the verbalization of religion involves the use of the rosary. This use, though not as universal in its distribution as the verbalization of religion, is not peculiar to Tibetan Buddhism or even to Buddhism. It is common to a great many religions, and its origins are far back in prehistory, if not contemporaneous with the very beginnings of religion itself. The multiple charms of bone that were found on a ring in a Swiss lake-dweller site certainly suggest the beads of a rosary. Thus there is nothing distinctive in the incidence of the rosary in religious observance among the Tibetans, unless it is the universality within the context of Tibetan custom and practice.

Traditionally, the Tibetan rosary is supposed to conform to Buddhist practice and to have 108 beads. The Tibetans themselves accept this number as a norm, but in actual use the number may vary from 100 to 114; anything below the norm of 108 is more a matter of inadvertence than intent. The leaders of the *Sa sKya* sect insist that for their members the number should be 111. They claim that this has been the distinctive practice of the sect for hundreds of years and that by having extra beads there is complete assurance that, even if by inadvertence a prayer is occasionally dropped and a bead missed, the round-number stint of a thousand, ten thousand, or even one hundred thousand will be known to have been achieved.

On the typical rosary, in addition to the beads, two small counter thongs are attached to the main string. One of these thongs has at its end a tiny thunderbolt, the other a bell of similar size, and both have ten little silver rings. The rings, or counters, on the thunderbolt string are for recording the hundreds; those on the bell string are for recording the thousands. In addition to the counter strings, there is a short string of three keeper beads attached to the main rosary string opposite the point where the knot is tied. Frequently, one or more small articles for personal use, such as tweezers for pulling facial hair or a metal toothpick, may be attached to the rosary for convenience. When not in use, the rosaries are either wrapped around the right wrist or worn around the neck.

The beads are used to keep a record of the number of times any prayer or charm has been uttered. In every pause in activity, the beads are a constant reminder to the wearer to stack up an ever larger toll. Without clearing the strings of beads and counters, one can record up to 10,800 prayers, or in the case of the Sa sKya Pa, 11,000. Such a total is a normal one day's stint for some of the clergy. Thus the beads not only prompt the Tibetan to the performance of this observance but tell him the sum resulting from his efforts.

They also help him to suspend *utterance* of the prayer but keep his thoughts at work, that is, he may *think* the syllables of the formula and move a bead. In effect, the movement of the bead becomes a substitute form of verbalization. In the course of conversation, if one of the participants does not happen to have his own rosary with him, whenever he has ceased talking and it is the other person's turn, he will borrow—with the casual social grace with which one borrows a light for a cigarette—the rosary from the other, and later when his own turn to speak comes around, he will then hand the beads back to the one to whom he is speaking so no time will be lost. Many Tibetans are extremely expert at talking and praying simultaneously, and the beads slip steadily through their fingers no matter what the subject matter or pace of the conversation.

Such fragmentary and scrambled practice of the observance, however, does not have a very high rating. It is better than not praying—if the prayers and other subjects are actually kept separate in the thoughts— but the danger of mixing the two and thereby committing sacrilege is very great, as pointed out and lampooned in a stock Tibetan story: A high ecclesiastic had been asked to perform an important religious service for a wealthy family and, setting up the altar and all the props on a beautiful meadow, had carried through the service with great unction. It was an outstanding success, and he had received a very fine horse in payment. The next year he was again asked to perform the same service, but while making all the preparations, he kept thinking of the horse, and wondering whether he would receive one as good or perhaps even better than the one previously given him. Such avaricious thoughts eventually found expression in words which supplanted many of the words of the pages turned, and he was heard to say "Horse . . . horse" to such an extent that there was much uncertainty whether he *rTa aDon Gi Yod* ("was expressing horse") or *CHos aDon Gi Yod* ("was expressing religion"). The Tibetan assessment of the ecclesiastic and such praying is stated simply as *sDig Can CHen Po, NYes Pa Mang Po Mang Po Yod* ("great sinner, having much much guilt").[31]

The use of the *Ma Ni CHos aKHor* ("*mani* religion wheel") is the third form of universally shared personal participation in the verbalization of religion. It is restricted to the Tibetans and to peoples, such as the Mongols, who received Buddhism from the Tibetans. Where it originated is not presently known, but there is nothing to suggest that it came from India. It is based on two value systems: one which assigns special significance and efficacy to the act or process of revolving or putting into revolution anything which may be turned, and the other which credits the written or printed word in itself—whether read or not read—with special power. The first of these value systems is closely linked with both the circumambulation rite and the concepts that gave rise to the metaphor in which preaching—first by the Buddha and later by all the great Buddhist teachers—is characterized as "turning the wheel of the law." Turning the wheel of the law was associated with a deep veneration for the word—first, the spoken word, but later, in India and in other southern Buddhist countries, the written word. This association, however, did not result in the development of the prayer cylinder in those lands. What was lacking in the oral tradition of those cultures was the value system which ascribes special power or sanctity to the written and printed word per se. In those lands there was a certain lack of interest in the reproduction of what had been written, which may be one of the reasons why printing appears so much later in Indian culture than in the Chinese and Tibetan cultures. The Tibetans, however, both by reason of a relatively sophisticated appreciation of the importance of meaning and the exact, recorded word in connection with religious concepts and by reason of stimulation-diffusion, if not outright borrowing, from China, had special regard for the written and printed word. Thus influenced, the Tibetans, driven by their compulsion to act, may have created the prayer wheel.

In its basic form, however, it may have come from China. Leon Hurwitz cites the facts that a revolving library that is hand-turned by worshipers occurs, although somewhat rarely, in Japan, and that Chi-

[31] Dezhung Rinpoche told this story, and the judgment given is in his own words.

nese tradition credits the invention of the *lun tsang* ("revolving store") to Fu Hsi, a Chinese Buddhist of the fifth century, who is said to have invented it to enable illiterates to gain the merit that comes from reading the scriptures although not able to read.[32]

The devotion of the principle of the wheel to the uses and practices of religion appears to have inhibited the Tibetans from using it for mundane purposes. Although much of Tibet is quite well suited to the use of wheeled transportation and although wheeled vehicles were known to the Tibetans from very early times from both the cultures that have pressed their cultural achievements on them, not a wheel has rolled in Tibet up until very recently; one of the reasons given for this is that the wheel and its powers should be exploited only for religious reasons. There are some exceptions, for example, water mills for grinding flour, but the traditional avoidance of the use of wheeled means of transportation is very marked. The idea of a wheel's being rolled on the ground and sat upon by a man has overtones of desecration and is avoided. In the borderland between China and Tibet, where frequently the population on one side of a fordable stream is Chinese and on the other bank Tibetan, the difference is striking. The terrain, crops, and basic subsistence economy on both banks are the same; even the livestock are the same. But on the Chinese side, the *mDZo* (hybrid of yak and cow) or yak pulls two-wheeled wooden carts in all the operations of farming and lumbering, while on the Tibetan side of the stream everything is packed on the backs of the animals, although such a technique is obviously wasteful of both man and ox power.

[32] Personal communication from L. Hurwitz, confirmed by the following note: "My immediate source of information on the revolving bookcase is the article RINZŌ in ODA Tokunō's *Buddhist Dictionary* (BUKKYŌ DAI-JITEN) (reduced photoreprint edition; Tokyo, 1930), pp. 1804c–1805a. There he quotes the *Shih men cheng t'ung* section on stūpas (*t'a miao chih*) as follows: '... as for the building of book depositories in the Buddhist monasteries of the various regions, formerly the bodhisattva Shan-hui (proper name FU Hsi, courtesy name Hsüan-feng) of the Liang Dynasty was moved to pity by the fact that, though laymen are rather appreciative of faith in this Way (Buddhism), yet where the life-ransoming Dharma-treasure (i.e., the scriptural canon) is concerned there are men and women who from birth have never known how to read, or who, if they do know how, are so pressed by their other involvements that they have no time to read. The bodhisattva for this reason especially devised a scheme. He created a revolving bookcase, so that those of believing heart, if they would but push it one revolution, would have the same merit as if they had read it through. Accordingly he took a vow, saying, "If there be any who ascend into the gateway of my bookcase, may he throughout all incarnations never lose human bodily form. Also, if he can turn the case an incalculable number of times, may the merit accumulated by this person be no different than if he had read the Scriptures. ..."' The *Shih men cheng t'ung* not being in our library, I can give you no more than this."

Some Tibetan terminology reflects aspects of this avoidance. *SHing rTa* ("wood horse"), the word for "cart," refers to function rather than structure, for in the latter the wheel would be of prime importance. In modern terminology, however, this avoidance has begun to disappear, as evidenced by the appearance of such secular terms as *Dus THSod aKHor Lo* ("time-measuring wheel") for clock, *Me aKHor* ("fire wheel") for locomotive, and *aKHor Lo Can Po* ("provided with wheels") for machinery. Moreover, bicycles and even scooters have appeared in Lhasa.

Whether invented in Tibet or imported from China, the prayer wheel or prayer cylinder nevertheless became a distinctly Tibetan phenomenon. The use of the small portable and personal prayer cylinder belongs exclusively to the Tibetan and to those to whom he transmitted his religion and its forms of observance. Its universal employment, as one form of the verbalization of religion, is shared with no other religion. Some Tibetans claim that the principle of turning prayers was brought to Tibet by Padma Sambhava at the end of the eighth century, but the earliest known reference to a prayer wheel is said to occur in a biography of Milaraspa in the early part of the eleventh century.[33]

The prayer wheel has thus become one of the identifying marks of a Tibetan. It is in the form of a cylinder and may vary in size from not more than three inches in each dimension to several feet in diameter and many feet in height; it is packed with a tight roll of paper or cloth upon which prayers and formulas—principally, the six-syllable mantra—have been written or printed as closely as possible. The large prayer cylinders are set up along the approaches to shrines, in the galleries which constitute sections of the circumambulation paths around monasteries and holy places, within temples and shrines, and inside the village chapels, which are often called *Ma Ni CHos KHang* ("*mani* religion house"). The prayer wheels that are set along the paths are made with protruding spokelike handles so that passing worshippers may set them spinning by a single push. The very largest ones, which are set singly within shrines and "god houses," are operated by a pull rope, and one may sit all day tugging at this rope to make the *mani* wheel turn. The small, portable ones are mounted on handles which are a prolongation of the pivot, may be less than a foot long, and are meant to be held in one hand; others have somewhat longer handles, which are grasped at mid-length, the lower end resting on the ground. Such prayer wheels have one or two

[33] Dezhung Rinpoche claims that in one of the editions (not presently available) of the "Songs of Mi La" it is said of the nun that "she was neither separated from *KHa Mani* ("mouth *mani*") nor from *Lag aKHor Lo* ("hand wheel")."

short cords that are weighted at the ends and attached to the circumference of the cylinder to function much like flywheels and aid the spin. When held by the handle, a simple twist of the wrist sets the wheel spinning and activates all the prayers written on the rolled paper.

Portable prayer wheels are personal or family property, and are constantly in use either by the owner, by members of his family or immediate circle, or by guests or associates as they sit with him to visit or transact business, for a man may talk and confer earnestly—giving the matters in hand all his attention—and yet keep the prayer wheel spinning. To push on the handles of the large prayer wheels that are placed within shrines or in sections of the circumambulation path at shrines and temples, and thus set them turning, is an invariable part of the performance of circumambulation and is as universally observed as that rite.

Thus *CHos aDon,* as observable phenomena, has a twofold impact: one of sound only, from the steady murmur of charms and prayers which pervades every Tibetan scene and all the activities of Tibetan life; and the other of sight and sound, from beads that move and click through Tibetan fingers to make a record of the number of prayers—and in so doing, to formalize and keep the *thinking* of the spell in order—and from the whirl and whine of the visible spinning prayer wheels that supplement vocalization of religion. Thus sound and sight both testify to the personal participation in this observance of all Tibetans.

It should be noted here that employment of the rosary and prayer wheel is invariably a part not only of the basic, minimal observance of *CHos aDon* which is universal but equally of all the more elaborate and varied forms of the verbalization of religion. The beads and prayer wheel are used by all—from the lowest to the highest.

In addition to this minimal and universal personal participation, more varied and elaborate forms are found in a graduated series, beginning with the verbalization of religion practiced by illiterate laymen and extending in a variety nearly as great as the number of individuals involved, through successive degrees of elaborateness to the extensive and complicated private devotions of the most learned monks and lamas or to the verbal and mental conceptualizations practiced by the tantric adepts. As an indication of their range, a few of these more varied forms of personal participation will be discussed.

The personal participation in verbalization of many illiterate laymen is only slightly more elaborate and varied than the minimal verbalization previously described and characterized as universal. The term "illiterate" is here taken to mean "not able to distinguish and pronounce the letters of the Tibetan alphabet or any of their combinations." There is no way of knowing just what percentage of lay Tibetans are illiterate, according to this definition. Most of the women are illiterate, but literacy of the male lay population varies greatly from district to district and from community to community, as well as according to class or position.

I have found isolated communities, both nomadic and sedentary, in which most of the men, the nobility, the tribal rulers, and the very wealthy—both men and women—could read. I have also found communities quite equal to the former in material well-being in which only a very small minority of the men could read. Thus, stray and sporadic reports by travelers concerning literacy have varied enormously. One Tibetan estimate, based on wide experience and a breakdown into percentages of the lay population in a number of regions, maintains that an overall average of approximately 50 per cent of the Tibetan male lay population can read to the extent of being able to identify the letters of the alphabet and to approximate the sound of the combinations. They are thus able to follow the lines of familiar prayers and even haltingly to learn new ones.[34]

Of those who cannot read, however, there is a large number—particularly of males—who in their observance of CHos aDon go beyond the minimal verbalization of religion practiced by all Tibetans. Moreover, among those whose personal participation in the verbalization of religion is—to a greater or lesser degree—more elaborate and varied than the universal minimum, there exists a great variability in the range of their participation in the observance. Literacy is not necessarily a reliable indicator of either the intelligence brought to bear on the performance of CHos aDon or the inherent interest in it. There are illiterates who have learned only one or two additional prayers of special import, such as prayers or charms for protection or deliverance from demon influences or prayers to personal guardian deities, with which to supplement the saying of Ohm Ma Ni Padme Hum; and there are illiterates who have

---

[34] This estimate was taken partly from one made by Dezhung Rinpoche that was based on the following. In his village of thirty-seven families, there were fifteen males who could read. Among the nomads the percentage of literacy is always higher than among the sedentary farmers (this agrees with my own observation), and of the nomads west of Litang, who were his ecclesiastical subjects, about two-thirds of the males could read. All the nobility of central Tibet—men, women, and children—can read, but the literacy of the farming peasants is lower than among the farmers of Khams. The nomads of the Byang THang ("north plain") have a high rate of literacy—higher than the peasants—and among the nomads of Nagchuka and Kongpo the rate is still higher. In over-all terms he estimates that one-half of the male lay population can read. There are, however, many sharp differences between localities quite close together, and the figure of 50 per cent can only be an estimate.

utilized the full powers of minds and memories, well trained in a habit of life in which there are no notebooks and memorandum pads, in committing to memory a great number of charms and prayers. Many of these are of considerable length and complexity.

There are two essential differences in the praying of the illiterate and the literate. The illiterate must learn each new prayer and charm from someone, whereas the literate, independently of the help of other persons, may learn or use new ones from a book. The illiterate cannot use a book in his praying, except to hold it in his hands and raise it to his forehead to "rub off blessing" as he intones the syllable *OHm*. The literate, on the other hand, derives greater benefit by being able to scan the lines and turn the pages, for such activity is also a part of verbalization. He visualizes the meanings in their written form and holds them in his mind. Such comprehension constitutes an added degree of observance.

The maximum degree of verbalization practiced by illiterates is greater, in volume and elaborateness, than the minimal degree of verbalization practiced by literates, but the over-all average of verbalization by literates is higher than that of illiterates. There are a number of reasons for this. Literacy in itself is prima facie evidence of greater interest and zeal in religion. Even among Tibetan laymen, the principal reason for learning to read is a religious one—the desire to read the many prayers, charms, and sermons of the Buddhist scriptures and religious manuals.

Reading is taught by monks to other monks in the monasteries, to the boys—and occasionally, the girls—of a community whenever they are gathered for periodic schooling sessions, and, by private monk chaplains, to the children of the rulers and the wealthy. If an adult decides he must learn to read, so as to verbalize religion more efficiently and in greater volume, he goes to a monk for instruction. Instructional material is religious in content. Since visualization of the words and their meanings and the appropriate turning of the pages are essential parts of the most effective observance of *CHos aDon*, the immediate rewards, in greater personal satisfaction, assurance, and psychological relief, are greater for the literate than for the illiterate. Literacy also stimulates the acquisition and use of books on the part of the laity. Possession of these books, in turn, makes it possible for those who can read to learn and use an ever increasing number of formulas.

Possession of the books also becomes, in itself, a matter of prestige and something of a status symbol in community regard. The books constitute a communal religious enrichment, an additional portion of religion belonging to the group as a whole. They may be borrowed for communal or individual rites—to be either used in chanting services or carried or displayed in circumambulation rites—with a consequent gain in prestige for the owner. By the very fact of their possession, moreover, as something in which wealth has been invested, they prompt and stimulate their own use and an increased religious observance.

As a form of private religious devotion, personal participation by the great majority of the monks, in average range and volume, resembles to a considerable degree that carried on by literate laymen. Much of the monks' time is taken up in formal chanting services of varying degrees of elaborateness which serve the religious needs, and answer to the demands, of sponsors, both communities and individuals. But, in addition to this activity, they spend much time in private verbalization of religion for personal benefit: the accumulation of virtue and eventual liberation. Among the monks, as among the other members of the community, the intensity and scope of this activity varies greatly, depending on the individual. Since they are specialists and professionals in the repetition of all the formulas, sermons, and invocations and since they also have easier access than do laymen to the written record and thus greater opportunity to learn additional forms, the general average of their personal participation is proportionately higher than the general average of participation by literate laymen, to about the same degree that the participation of literate laymen is higher than that of illiterate laymen.

Of still greater scope and intensity are the private devotions and meditations of the great lamas, the ascetics, and the adepts. It is among these that CHos aDon reaches its apotheosis, not only in the scope of that which is read and verbalized but in the degree of concentration on, and visualization and conceptualization of, symbols, syllables, and formulas. Such concentration is considered to be an important factor in the induction of supranormal states of psychic awareness and in the attainment of the successive stages of realization and enlightenment. From the most simple and lowest forms of observance to the most complicated and difficult, involving the greatest concentration and discipline of the senses, all are part of the great whole of personal participation in the expression of verbalized religion.

Sponsorship Participation

In addition to this enormous and incalculable range and total of personal participation, there is a very great amount of verbalization which is sponsored. There are two varieties of sponsorship: the first is involuntary, yet extends to all Tibetans and, therefore, in the Tibetan frame of reference, has a universal base; the second is voluntary, existing by conscious choice and decision, and is therefore limited and selective. The latter type may be direct or indirect.

Sponsorship is of great importance and appears very early in Buddhism. Blessing is promised to those who write or *cause* to be written, who build or *cause* to be built, and so on.[35] Indeed it was mostly by sponsorship, in its varied forms, that the householder could hope to have a part in the observances and benefits of religion. As a consequence, sponsorship became involved to a considerable degree with the making of offerings. In the context of the vicarious observance of *CHos aDon*, however, we shall not be concerned with the offering itself and the consequent movement of wealth but with the degree to which the burden of involuntary sponsorship is universally spread and the assumed benefits are, in equal universality, enjoyed.

To the same extent that no one in American society is free of the burden of taxes that, as hidden or open levies, are linked to every one of the necessities of life, so every Tibetan helps maintain and participates in involuntary sponsorship of all the most varied forms of *CHos aDon* by the specialist-practitioners of verbalization. On every unit of value produced, a hidden levy is imposed, with or without his consent. Each Tibetan, however, is assured that the benefits of the vicarious observance made possible by the tax will extend in some degree to him, although such benefit is peripheral and not to be compared with that resulting from conscious and pious intention.

Direct and purposeful sponsorship, by individuals, societal groups, and communities, of vicarious formalized *CHos aDon* takes many forms. The most common one is sponsorship of services or rituals in which selected prayers and portions of the Buddhist scriptures are recited or, more preferably, read by members of the clergy. Such observance may vary from the simple saying of a few short prayers by a single monk to the most elaborate and impressive chanting services in which the complete text of the Buddhist scriptures is scanned and chanted by the full membership of a monastic *THSogs aDu* ("gathered assembly") in the great chanting hall. Such a rite is performed with great pomp: trumpets are blown, bells are rung, and drums are beaten; and incense sticks and votive butter lamps are lit. It is additionally hallowed by the presence, if any are available, of *sPrul sKu* ("emanation-body") lamas, who dispense benediction.

Direct and purposeful sponsorship of such rites is motivated both by

[35] See footnote 17 for applicable references.

the compulsions and the sense of need which inspire personal participation in this observance and by a sense of the relative incompleteness
and failure of such personal participation. No matter how many prayers
have been said, there are yet more that should be learned and said. The
total is never complete. To add to it—to multiply it and to increase it by
whatever means are available—is the never satisfied desire of the Tibetan.
The resources of the whole of the Buddhist scriptures are tantalizingly
unavailable to most Tibetans for use in personal participation in the
verbalization of religion. Those resources may only become available
through sponsorship. This amplified, more efficacious observance of CHos
aDon must be hired, thus establishing, by sponsorship, vicarious participation in the effort and assurance of the benefit to be derived.

In the context of such basic and general motivation, the immediate
occasions for the exercise of sponsorship are manifold. Personal or familial uncertainty, worry, or trouble of any kind, all suggest that it would
be well to sponsor some CHos aDon both for the improvement of one's
religious state of being and as an aid in the solution of the immediate
problem. The important events of personal existence such as births, marriages, and deaths require sponsored observance; and it is also an integral
part of the treatment of disease. The monk and lama practitioners of
medicine invariably prescribe prayers along with pills. Even personal
success, the satisfaction of having accumulated a surplus of wealth, is
accompanied by the prompting, from within or from friendly advisors,
that it would be well to devote at least some of the gain to the sponsorship of the verbalization of religion, thereby exchanging a material surplus for spiritual credit.

Individual or familial participation in sponsoring such rites, when
they are celebrated on a somewhat elaborate scale in the home of the
sponsor, takes on the aspect of a festival, for the clergy who chant industriously throughout the day are well fed and the family and invited
neighbors share in the feasting. The head of the family, in his role of
sponsor, has a momentarily enhanced status within the community. The
prestige which is acquired lingers, moreover, for a long time, and some
of it is never entirely lost. If a man is able and willing to sponsor a Mang
Ja ("much tea"), or mass celebration of CHos aDon by the gathered assembly of the nearest monastery, he becomes, on that occasion, a man of
note and an honored guest of the monastery. He is flattered and praised.
For the moment he is supremely conscious of community approbation.
The members of communities—village or tribal—find each communal experience, each great event, an occasion for similar sponsorship of the

observance. War is waged, peace made, victory gained, defeat endured, disaster suffered, and achievement or harvest celebrated to the necessary accompaniment of a community-sponsored verbalization of religion.

Another aspect of direct sponsorship, which is somewhat like endowment investment, relates to the creation of forms, and the setting-up of devices, which function automatically once they have been established, and furnish a continuing amassment of virtue—primarily for those who bore the initial expense. Virtue, however, accrues to many more than the original sponsors. The culture of Tibet is filled with creations which owe their existence to this type of indirect participation.

The ordering of printings of the Buddhist scriptures and prayer manuals is an example of such endowment investment. In addition to the great and famous printing establishments such as those in Narthang, Derge, and Kumbum, where complete impressions of the *bKaa aGyur* and *bsTan aGyur* (a total of over 330 volumes) can be secured, virtually every monastery has some sort of print shop where prayers and charms, much in demand, may be printed on paper or on the cloth of which prayer flags are made. Subsidizing the making of a set of woodcut blocks or ordering an impression made from blocks already in existence is equally a form of *CHos aDon* and has a value in the creation of religious credit that is far removed from a mere commercial transaction.

Irrespective of who orders the printing, the making of the impression verbalizes religion. When in 1927 the Library of Congress ordered a complete printing of the *bKaa aGyur* from the *Co Ni* monastery, it was—and probably remains to this day—quite unaware of the religious credit it gained for itself and the fringe benefits of virtue accruing to all who labored in the transaction. If they had the right thoughts, the ink-daubed workmen were also splashed with virtue, and the artisans who carved the woodcut blocks also created virtue as they shaped the letters. Nor is virtue confined to the original operation, for every time the book is used— even if only carried around the fields as a form of blessing—virtue is gained for those who sponsored and had any part in the printing. The investment is multiplied in the same way whenever an individual or a community sponsors the setting up, or the renewal, of prayer flags that fly from trees, mountain-top shrines, grain racks, tent ropes, or lances. Verbalization is then multiplied by every breeze or the savage wind which eventually whips them to shreds.

As another form of sponsorship, the carving on rock of the six-syllable mantra or the syllable *OHm*, both in the Tibetan or in the Lantsa character, has a special fascination for the Tibetans. The letters appear on rock walls and on slabs piled on mountain tops; they are built into *CHos rTen* ("stupa[s]") and monastery walls and form the *mani*-faced prayer dykes. Each stone so cut becomes a part of religion in its recorded, and therefore verbalized, sense. The phenomenon has been reported from all over Tibet but seems especially in vogue among the Goloks of Amdo. A rather numerous class of stonecutters live in tents with the moving communities of these most-nomadic-of-all nomads and earn a good livelihood by selling their services to the raiding, rebel Goloks who want their prayers carved in stone—to last forever—and who pay well for the work with booty taken by robbing pilgrim caravans.

The setting up of prayer wheels which are powered by water, wind, and even the smoke of chimney tops, is also based on the factor of multiplication. The act of sponsorship and the initial making of the words of magical power on paper are but the beginning. Without further effort on the part of sponsor and craftsman, the wheel spins on, in a process of multiplication of astronomical proportions, as the restless winds blow, the smoke flies upward, or the water flows downhill.

The virtue gained from all these forms of mechanical verbalization is spread wide, but with a nice sense of proportion. The original sponsor—the one who initiated matters and bore the expense—receives most of the benefit. The next largest portion of virtue belongs to the craftsmen who shaped the letters of the woodcut, printed the prayer or charm, or constructed the wheel. Then come, in the case of the water wheel, all sentient beings living in the water which turns the wheel; in the case of the smoke wheel (called "fire wheel," for fire is the source of the energy), all sentient beings smelling the smoke; and in the case of the wind wheel, all who are blown upon by the wind after it has turned the wheel. In addition, as a general principle applicable to all forms of indirect participation, all creatures who see, hear, feel, or by any other sense are aware of any of the forms and devices that have been described receive some benefit as an aid along the way to liberation.

This survey of the phenomenal aspects of *CHos aDon* in the pattern of Tibetan individual and group behavior is necessarily brief. It touches only the salient features of a phenomenon having many aspects, with individual variations of dramatic significance and kaleidoscopic local color; but at least it traces the outlines of personal participation and direct and indirect sponsorship participation. Before proceeding to an analysis of the function of this phenomenon in Tibetan society and culture, something must be said about those individuals and that organization which makes possible sponsorship participation in the observance.

The specialists who purvey this service to the sponsors—the Tibetan people—may be loosely categorized as the clergy of Tibetan Buddhism. Such a classification, however, is not a strict one and requires some explanation and qualification. Most of those who explicitly or implicitly proffer the professional, elaborate, and greatly amplified observance of *CHos aDon* to all takers and prospective sponsors are the *Grwa Pa* ("school one[s]"), or monks, who function either as individuals, in their spare time, or collectively, as members of the gathered assembly of the monastery.

A monk who is visiting his home at vacation time is asked by neighbors to express verbalized religion for a day. (*Nyi Ma sCig Gi CHos aDon dGos Zhu Zhu* ["One day's *CHos aDon* needed, please, please"].) He does so and receives a suitable gift. The members of a travel caravan find there is a monk among their number and ask him to *CHos aDon* in order to hallow the camp which has been made or to create protection for the caravan when it crosses a robber-haunted mountain pass. He brings out the carefully wrapped, worn, and thumb-marked volumes of prayers and charms he may be carrying in his saddle bags and solemnly prays for all as he sits by the campfire, receiving at the close suitable contributions from all the members of the caravan. When families or small communities, conscious either of communal need or of a small surplus of wealth that should be changed into religious credit, are not able or willing to finance a "much-tea" chanting service by the full membership of the monastery assembly, they invite a learned monk and one or two assistants. The monk asks—and generally receives—permission to be absent from monastery routine for such purposes and serves the clientele with an efficacious performance of *CHos aDon*. All such activity supplements the formalized and well-subsidized verbalization of religion rendered by the assembly of the monastery.

There are at least three other classes of individuals who purvey vicarious, specialized performance of *CHos aDon*: (1) the *sPrul sKu* ("emanation-body") lamas, (2) the *sNGags Pa* ("spell one[s]"), or wizards, and (3) the *Ban sDe*, or members of lay orders.

Emanation-body lamas are not monks. In the context of Buddhist doctrine they are not necessarily members of the *dGe aDun* ("virtuous assembly"), or monastic community; the higher ones, at least, are considered manifestations of *Sangs rGyas* ("the Buddhahood"), the first entity of the Triad.[36] In relation to *CHos aDon*, as a religious observance

[36] There is much difference of opinion on this point. Most agree that the Dalai Lama and the Panchen Lama are manifestations of the Buddhahood; but the point

that is an expression of worship, they have a dual role. They are objects of worship—as manifestations of the Buddhahood they receive adoration and dispense benediction—and as such they hallow the chanting services of the assembly of the monastery. But at the same time, they may verbalize religion for sponsors. Observance by the lamas on behalf of sponsors is, of course, more efficacious than that performed by mere monks.

The wizards are neither monks nor lamas, though they may wear the garb of monks. In appearance they are distinguished from other Tibetans by their long hair—often ten to fifteen feet—worn in the shape of a turban. They are adepts in thaumaturgic practices, specialists in pronouncing charms and spells—both those that bind malignant spirits and forces and thus are protective in nature, and those maledictions that are destructive in intent. The verbalization of religion which they proffer for sponsorship is, in the entire spectrum of Tibetan religious observance, included within *CHos aDon*.

In addition to the lamas, monks, and wizards, there is another rather numerous class of purveyors of religious service which, for want of a better term, might be called the "lay brother" clergy. They call themselves *Ban sDe* or *aBan bTSun*, and both the regular clergy and the laity use the same terms when speaking of them. They are said to belong to either one or two of the five classes of *dGe bsNYen* ("merit helpers"), which is the first stage of monkhood. Nevertheless, in many respects they resemble laymen. They live in the encampments and villages, have families, possess and exploit herds and fields, and engage in other secular pursuits. They wear laymen's clothing and have not necessarily lived in monasteries, nor do they have quarters there. They are not under structured religious control but are very much a law unto themselves, operating individually or in voluntary association. They are, however, clearly differentiated from the ordinary laity. They do not wear leopard-skin collars on their cloaks, and the cloth borders of the latter must be red or purple rather than black. They do not wear swords or carry other weapons and abstain from hunting, raiding, and all killing. Having their own wives, they are specifically enjoined from the rather general sexual promiscuity which exists among the lay population.

They are recognized, moreover, as specialists in the celebration of ritual and religious services and are much in demand to perform the vicarious verbalization of religion for which, like the clergy, they receive

---

in the hierarchy of the *sPrul sKu* ("emanation-body") lamas, at which a lama ceases to be a manifestation of the Buddhahood and is only a member of the community occasions much discussion. The viewpoints of both sects and individuals differ.

gifts of appropriate value. They all read, and many of them are quite learned or have received special tantric initiations from lamas and teachers. They are found among all sects and should not be confused with the *Grwa Log* ("School-one rebels") or *Ban Log* ("monk rebels"), who are found in every community and who themselves are specially trained in intoning religion. They are also said to have a status somewhat similar to that reported for the *Ser KHyim Ba* ("yellow house one[s]") in the southern border region of Tibet.

FUNCTIONAL ROLE OF THE OBSERVANCE

The phenomenon of *CHos aDon,* in all its many aspects and forms, has a definite functional role within a culture, a role that also reaches into the field of intercultural relations with determinative effect. It is a role which operates quite apart from the intent of the participants, since in general they are not aware that the observance may result in anything other than the accumulation of virtue to aid progress toward the final goal of liberation. When it is pointed out to the Tibetan that the verbalization of religion may affect in-group and out-group attitudes, linguistic diffusion and change, and education, and may create demands which affect trade and the borrowing of culture traits, he admits, with a sort of amazement, that such results do flow as a by-product from the observance. He is not amazed, however, that such effects do, or do not, result from the verbalization of religion, but rather that such a secular frame of mind and way of thinking should exist to focus on his prayers and their results.

In this frame of reference the observance of *CHos aDon* will be seen to have a threefold function within Tibetan society and culture: (1) it answers basic psychological needs and compulsions of the individual; (2) it creates ties which link the individual with his fellows in a ritualistic association, binding them into a self-conscious in-group; and (3) it strongly influences, possibly in some aspects to a determinative degree, the culture as a whole. In addition, in the context of intercultural relations, it has an important role in determining the status of Tibetan culture within the world family of cultures and the cultural relations and exchanges that follow from the assignment of status.

As Individual Satisfaction

For the individual, *CHos aDon* is an observance answering to the basic, primal need of "man the talking animal" to say something, to verbalize his experiences, his needs, and his aspirations. Equally for the child of three who stubs his toe and for the adult who misses his putt at the eighteenth hole is the almost irresistible need to say something—to talk it out. Helen Keller in her autobiography poignantly describes the unutterable, hopeless rages of the deaf mute, denied the compensating, healing relief of words. In different contexts, the confessional and the psychiatrist's couch testify as well to this deep human need, and many a man has talked himself back from the brink of a suicide's despair.

Such relief is not only permissively allowed to the Tibetan but even urged upon him with all the solemn sanctions and promises of religion, reinforced by the weight of communal approval. He is urged to use it again and again. Even the eternally right words are furnished him, with the assurance that, as a vehicle, they are both apt and potent beyond any he himself could choose or create, for they are religion itself, placed in his mouth to answer every need and compulsion to speak.

The saying of the words also fills time with work well done. In any life there are segments of time, varying in length, that are empty of interest, since boredom is one of the ills of life. For the praying Tibetan, however, those empty spaces may be filled with something effective and thus with something accomplished. There are long moments of waiting—for those who are late at a rendezvous or for those who give audiences—which for others would mean time to be killed; yet for the Tibetan, such time is filled with *CHos aDon* and the benefits—intangible, yet having their own reality—that flow from that observance.

As Communal Tie

The saying of the words links the Tibetan into a fellowship; in a special sense he is made one with all others who say the same words. It is the process of the tower of Babel in reverse, a process having two component parts: one the factor of identification and recognition; the other the state of psychological union or submersion which results from mass verbalization.

As a means of identification, the password, whether formally chosen or merely a matter of accent and pronunciation, goes far back into pre-history. It has always been of crucial importance, often a matter of life or death. Men have died suddenly without recourse or appeal because they sounded a vowel or a consonant incorrectly. "A friend" is an empty claim, more of menace than assurance, until confirmed by the "word" which lets "pass." Similarly, mannerisms of speech enable men to identify their fellows, whether they arise from place, status, craft, age group, calling, or those more formalized associations and orders that have their own passwords or signs.

In the same way, by the shortest syllable or phrase prayer—never long unsaid—the Tibetan identifies others—the ones who say the same thing—as his fellows and members of an in-group with common standards and common behavior patterns. In a subtle sense, at each new encounter, two that were strangers are no longer altogether strange because of the prayer that is never long unuttered; each is a member of the within-ones and so on common ground.

The ritual of saying the same words is not only a means of identification and recognition but, when occurring in unison, creates its own bond and sense of oneness. Creeds, national anthems, slogans, oaths of allegiance, battle cries, even the gibberish of the cheering section at a football game, all operate on a common principle—to merge or submerge the individual in a corporate mass consciousness. The crowd at the baseball game is just a little different after the singing of the national anthem; something more than words has been added. Two words, *Heil Hitler,* contributed to the hypnotizing of a great people and imperiled the rest of the world.

In the winter of 1928 I was captured and held for a few hours by the soldiers of the Moslem rebel Ma Chung-ying, sometimes known as Big Horse, just as they were pinned down in a most disadvantageous position by Chinese government forces, which were more numerous and much better armed. The only possible chance of escape was by some desperate breakthrough against superior forces in the face of machine-gun fire. Then the Moslems began to chant "Allah, hudah! Allah, hudah!" with rising intensity and force. As they chanted they changed, becoming stronger than the maximum total of their individual strength and bravery; and at the final shout of "Allah," that strength naturally flowed into a wildly successful charge, of drawn swords against machine guns, that won them a road of escape and years of time in which to storm through Central Asia with mixed dreams of pillage and empire.

Functioning on the same principle, the verbalization of religion helps bind the individuals of the thinly scattered Tibetan people into a community of interest and a sense of corporate oneness, despite the many divisive factors that stem from distance, primitive means of communication, paucity of media of mass communication, and the fragmentation naturally imposed on a mountain people. With the murmur of *OHm Ma Ni Padme Hum,* the Tibetan is infolded in the comforting assurance that he is not alone. He is reminded that he is a *Nang Ba,* a "within one," and the reminder is both a comfort and a binding tie.

In the world outside Tibet, in that society which does not consist of "within ones" but of ones without—those who are not linked by the same tie and whose world is a greatly different one—the Tibetan finds that *CHos aDon* also gives relief and brings assurance. Under the stress imposed by the unfamiliar—sights, sounds, and activities which could well overwhelm him with astonishment—he resorts to familiar vocables, which are not mere expressions of amazement but are the power of religion made operative at the instant they are uttered. Whether they are inaudible, evidenced only by the movement of the beads of a rosary, or fairly shouted, like a veritable curtain of sound raised for protection, they are the first reaction and response.

I have taken a Tibetan official for his first ride in a jeep at speeds he had never experienced, during which he was assailed by unfamiliar noises and smells. I have walked down Broadway at midnight with the brother of the Dalai Lama on his first event-filled day in America, when he had come, with little pause, directly from the Tibetan plateau. And I have guided a Tibetan scholar and mystic, come directly from his meditations, through the crowds and alien bustle and confusion of a shopping center on a Saturday afternoon. In each instance, the response was the same— *CHos aDon*—in confident recourse to the resources of religion. In the context of those resources, made available by verbalization, what was new and even menacing did not overwhelm; after all it, too, was illusory. Each of the three Tibetans, fortified and reassured, could smile and be at ease, with the distinctive poise and rare nonchalance characteristic of their people.

Influence on the Culture as a Whole

The influence which the observance exerts upon the culture as a whole is not vaguely diffused but operates in definite cause-and-effect sequences, affecting specific facets or aspects of the culture by (1) influencing the utilization of time; (2) establishing an identifiable *quid pro quo* (which is subject to evaluation and even measurement of a sort) in the value received by the Tibetan for his support of the religious hierarchy; (3) influencing language—its character, diffusion, and rate of change; (4) influencing the form and style of oratory; (5) stimulating education; (6) markedly affecting the graphic arts, or techniques, of writing and printing; and (7) creating certain needs or demands which affect trade and the borrowing of cultural traits.

Possibly more than any of the other religious observances, *CHos aDon* places demands on the Tibetan for time and thus, by establishing patterns and habits in the utilization of time, affects the society as a whole. From a secular point of view, time is withdrawn from the normal activities of life: subsistence activities of making a living; biological activities of producing and caring for the young; societal activities of achieving and maintaining position and status; and all those other activities that are done for the sheer joy of doing them. Each is reduced in scope because time has been subtracted; the behavior patterns of the culture are changed because time—much time—is devoted to *CHos aDon* in all its forms.

From another point of view, time that would be lost or wasted is redeemed or saved. Much time would be empty and unused were it not for *CHos aDon,* for example, the period of delay when a rendezvous is off schedule or the long wait for an audience with patrons or officials. There are periods of slack in the diurnal or seasonal routine—when boredom becomes one of the ills of life and time itself needs "killing"; with *CHos aDon* available, however, none of these blank spaces need be wasted, for time can be filled with effort and achievement, with benefit on a high level to follow. The interest vacuum of old age may also be filled with a sense of worthwhile work well done, as the elderly sit in the sun in company with a common purpose, to verbalize religion by the observance of *CHos aDon.*

In his role as sponsor, the Tibetan is linked with the observance both as believer and as client and customer. Even the involuntary sponsor, who has contributed to the support of the monks merely by being a part of the economic system, derives satisfaction in knowing that he partakes of the value created by the many hours of chanting by the clergy. But it is as a direct or purposeful sponsor that he especially senses his prerogatives as customer. Then he exercises the inherent right, even obligation, to inspect or judge that for which he is spending his wealth. Popular acclaim invests him with special status for the occasion. He is not a recipient of charity; he is a *Yon bDag* ("fee master") or *Byin bDag* ("bounty master"), for the one who presents the fee or bounty is the owner or master of it. If verbalization is sonorous and unctious, he comments on it with nice discrimination to his fellows, and eventually the participants hear what has been said.

As the lines are scanned and the pages turned, verbalization is diligently being added into a total. The observance is subject to quantitative as well as qualitative evaluation, and when judged to be adequate and good, the fee master is conscious of the satisfaction that adequate value has been received. The principles of fair exchange and fair trade have not been violated. Verbalization is also being multiplied into a result, and the

important factor in that multiplication consists of the professional participants, whose value may also be measured. The fee master ticks off the
number of participants on his fingers, or the beads of his rosary, for he
feeds and distributes weighed portions of tea and butter to each one. The
result is also fair and easily understood, though multiplication is a more
difficult process on the beads than addition.

In the observance of *CHos aDon,* the establishment of a definite, an
identifiable *quid pro quo* that can be measured and evaluated by the Tibetan layman contributes directly to the stability of the entire religio-
political system of Tibet. As a result of the acceptance of the inherent
worth of *CHos aDon,* financial support of the system derives not only
from gifts offered for the sake of giving and contributions exacted by
various financial devices and the pressures of community opinion but
also from a businesslike fair-trade relationship between client, or customer, and producer. *CHos aDon,* ceremoniously and unctiously performed, is a service to the community that has value, and its purchase
conforms to the trading instincts and traditions of the Tibetan. More than
a mere matter of trade, it generates deep satisfaction in the heart of the
sponsor client. It may seem no bargain, but at least it is a fair exchange.
He receives an immediate value of which he can judge the quality and
measure the quantity. It has *rGyu aBras Yod Gi* ("cause-consequence"),
or "It is fair," he says to himself or to others and adds *OHm Ma Ni Padme
Hum.*

The influence of the observance on language is natural, even inevitable, and affects (1) the character or strength of the language, (2) the
distribution of linguistic forms, and (3) the rate of linguistic change.
That verbalization of religion affects language is readily apparent to the
Tibetan. Much, if not quite all, of the written Tibetan language has been
ceded to religion for its use and is called *CHos sKad* ("religion-speech").
Its forms, by reason of their close association with *CHos* as the "law"
entity of the Triad, have acquired a certain sacrosanct character. Thus
religion's effect on language is for the Tibetan at once natural and acceptable.

Something has already been said concerning the importance of speech
in the Tibetan cultural configuration and concerning certain marked qualities of structure and usage that foster sententious utterance and result
in phonetic and semantic parallelism in both oratory and prosody. What
is pertinent to the present study is a characterization of the Tibetan language in terms of its strength or the factors of resistance that it possesses
in relation to the impact of other languages. Tibetan language usage

may be said to be relatively conservative. It has a marked ability to resist tenaciously linguistic penetration and to reject loan words in favor of indigenous terms to which new meanings are assigned. Translation of the apprehended meaning of foreign words into Tibetan syllables, which are then formed into compounds, is preferred to transliteration of such words, although a phonetically adequate alphabet would make the latter process relatively easy. There are, it is true, a considerable number of loan words in the Tibetan language, many of which have already been identified by linguists. Many more will doubtless be recognized as the study of linguistic diffusion in this region makes progress. But, in the main, there has been reliance on the Tibetan language alone to express all that has come from other languages to Tibetan experience; this is revealed in the work of the translators who rendered into Tibetan the Buddhist works which came to them in Sanskrit and, to a lesser extent, Chinese. A new vocabulary was created—mostly of compounds—but the basic words used were Tibetan.

The conservatism and linguistic independence that played a part in setting the Tibetans of the seventh and eighth centuries to creating strictly Tibetan words for the overwhelming profusion of philosophical and religious conceptualization that came in with Buddhism were not the result of *CHos aDon*, for that did not yet exist. But this conservatism has been strengthened since that time by the universal observance of *CHos aDon*. With every repetition, the Tibetan is reminded that his language was found adequate for the most important task of all—the expression of religion—and therefore, when any need to name something new arises, that it need be neither slighted nor discarded. *CHos aDon* has a part in maintaining, if not a linguistic superiority complex, at least a reassuring sense of linguistic adequacy that sets up defenses against wholesale word-borrowing. In most respects Tibetan culture is relatively primitive in comparison with the cultures from which such borrowings would most naturally be made, but Tibetan linguistic usage has an assurance and quality of resistance out of proportion to the holistic scale of Tibetan culture and the number, or world importance, of the people who speak the language.

This consideration leads quite naturally to the question of linguistic diffusion and change and the influence of the observance on the distribution and maintenance of the Tibetan language. Reference has already been made to the many natural factors which hamper communication and the easy flow of persons, commodities, cultural traits, and ideas among the Tibetans. All the natural factors of terrain and climate that make for isolation and the separation of a people into small communities, with the result of a less and less mutually and widely intelligible speech, are present in Tibet. The classic pattern of the fragmentation of language into dialects among mountain peoples is well known. In the face of this, the Tibetan language has maintained, to a remarkable degree, a common intelligibility for all who use it.

I speak only one of the dialects of Amdo, but I have found that I could understand, and make myself understood to, Tibetans from the far western limits of Tibet—Ladak or Leh—from southeastern Tibet near the borders of Yunnan, from Lhasa, and from Shigatze. The refugees who have poured into India since the spring of 1959 come from every part of Tibet, yet they all communicate with and understand each other.[37]

A number of factors have influenced this wide diffusion of language and maintenance of language intelligibility between remote and naturally isolated communities. Some of these factors are linked with other religious observances or complex combinations of them, which will be discussed later in this study; but *CHos aDon*, as a universal religious observance, has had a very important part in the process. Linguistic norms of phonetics and meaning have been preserved and diffused by the verbalization of religion.

Even in regard to phonetics, where the tendency to change and variation is greatest, a common and corrective point of reference has been established in the alphabet—or more specifically, syllabary—of the Tibetan system of writing. The phonetic *value* of each letter is also the *name* of each letter, and is shouted when the alphabet is learned as the preliminary step in learning to read. The manner in which the alphabet is used in Tibetan spelling also focuses on phonetic value. Not only is each letter named phonetically, but as each one is added, the phonetic total is sounded. Whereas a mathematic representation of English spelling would be $3 + 5 + 2 + 4 + 1 = 15$, a representation of Tibetan spelling would be $3 + 5 = 8 + 2 = 10 + 4 = 14 + 1 = 15$. Even in differing dialects, when somewhat different values are assigned to the letters, the alphabet and the way it is used in spelling establishes a common phonetic point of reference for purposes of recognition or correction.

A similar form of phonetic reference, corrective and strongly conservative, which inhibits change and favors standardization is to be found in the manner in which Tibetans read and, in particular, in the manner in which they read aloud when intoning religion. They speak and read

---

[37] Oral communications from H. E. Richardson, who has visited the camps, and from T. J. Norbu, as well as the testimony of the refugees who are at the University of Washington, uphold this statement.

quite differently. When they read, the phonetic rendition follows much more closely the phonetic value of the letters and the spelling; finals are sounded more carefully and are even exaggerated, and more attention is given to the respective phonetic values of the components of the complicated consonant clusters with which many syllables begin. This process is more marked in some dialects than in others but in a greater or lesser degree exists in all dialects.

The corrective, standardizing influence is operative on every level of proficiency in reading. The beginner who stumblingly spells out the words of his lesson or a new prayer he is learning conforms perforce to a pattern that may be quite different from the way he speaks. The eager, more advanced pupil or young monk shouts the standard sounds, trilling or biting hard on finals, to win his teacher's approval, and the man of letters pays attention to the phonetic niceties of spelling in his enunciation, for that is the way in which education and the knowledge of letters is reasserted each time the leaves of a book are read and turned.

Verbalization of religion also operates to maintain and even spread the use of a common vocabulary—a common semantic core—throughout all the dialects. A surprisingly large proportion of the vocabulary that is intoned as a religious observance—at least the basic components of religious terminology—remains in current use in the vernacular throughout Tibet and constitutes a common semantic frame of reference, with a consequent maintenance of intelligibility for all speakers of the language. Even when phonetic change has occurred in common usage, a knowledge of the more widely diffused phonetic forms in religious phraseology maintains a point of reference for clarification or correction. For example, throughout most of Amdo and in some other districts of Tibet, the word *aGro* ("go"), is pronounced *njo*. But when found in the religious term *mKHaa aGro Ma* ("sky going female"), it is pronounced *kha ndro ma*. Knowledge that *ndro* is a more correct pronunciation than *njo* for the word *aGro* is so widespread that a speaker who had said *njo* and thinks he has not been understood will often correct himself and say *ndro*.

Not only has the Tibetan language maintained itself against the factors that make for isolation and fragmentation, but within historical times, it has replaced the ZHang ZHung language, the language of the Hor (probably a Turanian people), and whatever language was spoken by the many Ch'iang, who were absorbed in the Tibetan empire. It now is in the process of replacing the language of some of the rGya Rong tribes[38]

---

[38] Monks from six different Sino-Tibetan border tribes who called themselves *rGya Rong* but who could not communicate with each other in their own languages

and the language of the Mongols in Amdo. Among the latter, a number of tribes, who are still called _Sog Po_ ("Mongol"), either speak nothing but Tibetan or, in one or two instances, are bilingual.[39] For both _rGya Rong_ and the Mongols of Amdo, Tibetan is the language of the religion they accept, and the observance of _CHos aDon_ in that language unquestionably has aided the process of language replacement.

The problem of the rate of linguistic change is also closely interwoven with that of diffusion and language intelligibility and is equally affected by the universal verbalization of religion. In the wide diffusion of word forms and phonetic renderings through the observance of _CHos aDon_, the linguistic center, which would be the area of most rapid linguistic change, and the fringe areas, with slower rates of change, are interactively and effectively linked. Again, isolated communities are linked with each other as well as with more central areas, and the development of dialecticisms is inhibited to the advantage of more widely understood usages.

That varying rates of linguistic change exist is recognized by some of the Tibetans themselves. In 1935 the brother of the Panchen Lama of that time remarked in answer to my apologies for speaking to the Panchen Lama and him in the fringe-area Amdo dialect, "That is original Tibetan. That is the way Tibetan was spoken when it was first written."

Aside from its influence on the character of the Tibetan language and various aspects of linguistic usage, the observance of _CHos aDon_ has been instrumental in creating a special, and uniquely artificial, style of oratory much favored by the Tibetans. Oratory in quantity pervades the interpersonal and intergroup relationships of the Tibetans, and oratorical skill is highly regarded. There are two different forms or styles of speechmaking. One of them resembles any effective oral discourse in the employment of pauses as spacing between principal ideas or their components. Such pauses, which are in effect punctuation, set phrases apart, are

---

were encountered in the summer of 1940 in the monastery of _AH mCHog mTSHan NYid_, about fifty miles south of the upper knee of the Yellow River. They all spoke Tibetan, which was quite natural as they were in a Tibetan monastery, but they said that in their home communities all who read "books of religion" in Tibetan could also speak some Tibetan. Again, "Bolotzu" tribesmen whom I met south of Sung-p'an in the summer of 1941 read Tibetan and could speak some, although their own language was not recognizably Tibetan.

[39] J. F. Rock, _The Amnye Ma-Chhen Range and Adjacent Regions_ (1956), p. 57. Rock speaks of only one tribe, the A-rig, who were bilingual but says they no longer speak Mongolian. However, I have met a number from other so-called Mongol tribes who spoke both Tibetan and Mongolian.

common to all oral discourse, and play an important part in making meaning clear and precise. This form of oratory is similar the world over.

The other form is fundamentally different. It is extremely stylized, has a prestige rating high above the less artificial form of speech-making, and is very frequently used by acknowledged orators—whether ecclesiastics, chiefs, or men of recognized eloquence. It is quite difficult to acquire and practice and, on first hearing, is hard to understand. This stylized *KHa dPe* ("mouth habit") of the finished Tibetan orator is characterized by a steady, uninterrupted flow of words uttered at a uniform rate, with no pauses to function as natural punctuation. There is, however, punctuation, which is of a quite artificial, but effective, form. Filler words are inserted—the number dependent on whether they are the equivalents of a comma, a semicolon, or a period—which have no meaning or no assignable meaning in the context. The insertion into oral discourse of such words as *dGung, Gang, Ra, Da,* and *Dus mPHro,* many times repeated, is not a matter of inadvertent stuttering or the "uh-uh-uh" of the hesitant speaker but a purposeful, conscious employment of vocal padding between phrases, sentences, and paragraphs. The words function as a form of punctuation, the equivalent of the natural pauses found in ordinary oral discourse.

As explained by the members of the oratorical fraternity themselves, this style is based on the desire to make oratory resemble as closely as possible the observance of *CHos aDon,* the ideal of which is to make the words follow each other at a uniform rate, without any pause or interruption, as smoothly without a break as "the flowing of water." Thus does the manner of the observance itself set the seal of its influence upon the style of oratory most often used when Tibetans meet to talk out their difficulties and come to solutions and agreement.[40]

Oral and manual aspects of the observance also play functional roles of a different kind in the scenes of argument and verbal strife that are the occasion for oratory. Such occasions are many in the behavior patterns of Tibetan society. There are few if any fixed prices; therefore there is much haggling and close bargaining. Few laws are known or uniformly enforced; consequently much is left to mediation and the effecting of compromise between conflicting interests. There are many degrees of independence between social and political units, and as a consequence,

---

[40] R. Ekvall, *Tibetan Skylines* (1952), pp. 11–12. This peculiar style of orating has been known to me for years. I even tried, without much success, to acquire the technique. Its characteristics and *raison d'être* have been discussed at some length with Norbu, who naturally has used it.

there is much intense negotiation. The conflict may be on a small scale, but all aspects of pressure tactics, stalling, and other tricks of international conferences will appear and be employed with effectiveness.

When the Western labor leader, business executive, or statesman is in a tight conference and has said his say, he may seek to relieve tension by endlessly lighting and extinguishing his cigarette or he may set up psychological defenses by doodling or other such device. At considerable cost in nervous effort, he may even steel himself to a semblance of stolid indifference. The Tibetan negotiator under the same strains retires behind the defensive wall of murmured *CHos aDon,* which in no sense can be construed as either a discourtesy or an interruption, and relieves tension by counting the beads of his rosary as he faces his adversary, murmuring with perfect, but faintly mocking, courtesy, *OHm Ma Ni Padme Hum.* He thus finds the observance relaxing and well worthwhile.

The role of *CHos aDon* in stimulating education is obvious and of far-reaching significance. Until the Chinese Communists attempted to introduce communism and enough modern education and literacy to answer to the requirements of effective propaganda, verbalization of religion supplied the motivation for most of whatever education was gained in Tibet. The teachers, the instructional material, and the goal of achievement were largely religious. Final utilization of the skills of reading and writing had, of course, its secular aspects. The nomad who learned to read so that he might scan new and still more effective prayers was not completely oblivious of other uses for letters; and he used writing for recording matters of importance and for sending messages in the same matter-of-fact manner in which he used his rosary for doing sums in arithmetic or counting his herds. The tribal chieftain and the nobleman used their knowledge of these skills, gained primarily by reason of religious motivation, in reading and writing official documents and in transacting secular business. Yet such incidental profit from the knowledge of how to read and write was not in itself sufficient inducement for the time and trouble of learning to read—it opened no doors to the learning of anything but religion. It was for religion's sake that the alphabet was taught and learned, and it was for that reason, too, that the percentage of literacy was much higher—in certain areas, surprisingly higher—than the general subsistence techniques and level of culture of the Tibetans would seem to warrant.

The observance of *CHos aDon* has also had a marked effect on the arts of writing and printing. By increasing the general demand for manuals and religious books, it fostered an industrious devotion to writing and copying, which has continued from early times down to the present. Although paper and ink were unquestionably borrowed from the Chinese, the Tibetan pen is not like the Chinese brush pen but is made of bamboo with a cut nib much like the pen as we know it. It is used to produce some beautiful examples of calligraphy. One variant of writing is the development and refinement of the technique of engraving letters on stone slabs, which is done with a loving care that stems partly from a sense of personal involvement in the blessing that flows from the expression of sacred words.

The Tibetans have possessed and practiced the art of wood-block printing for at least five hundred years and possibly for much longer. In the colophon of the Blue Annals, it is said that they began to carve the *Par SHing* ("wood print") in 1481. Dezhung Rinpoche insists that wood-block printing was practiced in the lifetime (1378–1441) of *TSong KHa Pa;* and the owners of two great printing establishments in Eastern Tibet have said that they have been printing books for more than five hundred years.[41] It would seem that any great use of the prayer wheel would of necessity be dependent on the technique of printing to create the requisite amount of text. If such is the case, reference to a prayer wheel in the lifetime of *Mi Las* (previously mentioned) suggests that printing was practiced by the Tibetans during the eleventh century. We also know that books were being printed in West China as early as the middle of the ninth century,[42] and the eastern Tibetans would have had ample opportunity to borrow the technique from nearby Chinese sources. In modern times every monastery of any importance has a print shop where the needs of the local population for charms and prayer manuals are met. Thus Tibet, although in many respects in a cultural backwater, had the art of printing before it was invented in Europe, and the observance of *CHos aDon,* by the interest and demands that it created, was partly responsible for that development.

The influence of the observance on the arts of writing and printing operates not only to create a large demand for the finished product but also to raise and maintain standards of excellence in the very effort put forth to create the product. The effort, in itself, is believed to be meritorious and has been assigned religious value; the value is greater than the

[41] A. Winnington, *Tibet* (1957), p. 47. The *Co Ni dPon Po* in Kansu also told me, just after the *Co Ni* monastery press had been burned by the Moslem troops of Ma Chung-ying, that the press had been in existence for more than five hundred years.

[42] T. F. Carter, *The Invention of Printing in China* (1956), pp. 56–62; R. Grousset, *Histoire de la Chine* (1942), pp. 254–55.

satisfied pride of the craftsman or the sense of fulfilment that comes to the artist—what is done is done for religion's sake. The careful stroke of the pen that may be writing a text in gold on paper of turquoise blue and the painstaking pressure of the knife that shapes a letter in the wood block, when accompanied by pious thinking, are also prayers, having equal rating with other forms of the verbalization of religion, and that fact and its realization contribute to painstaking care and excellence of craftsmanship.

The many aspects and forms of the verbalization of religion which have been described or touched upon quite naturally result in the creation of a demand for certain goods and products. These are made available by importation, the acquisition of certain techniques to produce similar goods, or the spontaneous development within the culture of techniques and crafts to produce what is needed. The following is a list, by no means exhaustive, of these goods and products, with brief statements of specific uses for each one. It is not claimed that all of these products are in demand only because of needs arising from the verbalization of religion—many of them also have other uses—but *CHos aDon* has an important role in creating the demand for them.

Paper	Used in writing and printing charms, prayer manuals, spells, all religious books, and the rolls of formulas placed within prayer cylinders.
Ink	Used in writing and printing religious works.
Cloth	Special trade cloth—used for making prayer flags. Various other kinds of cloth—used for book wrappings.
Beads	Tree seeds, flower seeds, reptile vertebrae, human bones, semiprecious stones, wood, glass, porcelain, and so on—used for rosaries.
Metals	Silver, brass, or bronze—used for bells, symbolic thunderbolts, ornamented or worked cases for prayer cylinders, and rings for counters on rosaries. Steel—used to make tools for carving printing blocks.
Coloring substances (including powdered gold)	Used for making colored inks and for sizing and coloring specially prepared paper.

Paper is very much in demand and is imported in considerable quantity both from China and from Bhutan. It is also produced in Tibet, from bark, roots, wood, and bamboo. Paper-making techniques probably came from China, for according to one of the provisions in a T'ang Period Sino-Tibetan agreement, workmen were to be sent from China to show the Tibetans how to make paper and ink.[43] There is nothing to indicate whether the importation of methods and techniques from China was the next logical step following the prior importation of the product itself, or whether under stimulation from both China and India, the Tibetans had already begun to make rough paper by primitive methods and wished to refine those methods with the aid of Chinese technicians. It is known, however, that the Tibetans had used both wooden slips and leather prepared as parchment before the first appearance of paper and that they were acquainted, from their extensive use of felt, with the principle of matting fibers.

Ink—both black Chinese, called "India" in trade, and vermilion from cinnabar—is also imported in considerable quantity from China. The special techniques or refinement of techniques used in making ink were, as has been mentioned, also brought from China. But it is reasonably certain that crude ink was made with lampblack and other coloring agents by the Tibetans at the time of the introduction of writing and even before. Certainly, the use of dyes and coloring agents was known, for the earliest Tibetans painted their faces red.

Although weaving as a technique is well known and considerable quantities of yak-hair tent cloth, coarse and fine woolen fabrics, and some heavy handwoven silk are produced in Tibet, the special cotton cloth—largely white but sometimes rust-colored—that is used in making prayer flags is mostly imported from China. This particular variety of cloth, which is narrow—approximately twelve inches wide—very flimsy, and fit only for taking the inked impression of prayers and formulas, is in such general demand that in Eastern Tibet rolls of a standard length have a fixed value of exchange, as a form of currency, with particular weights of barley, butter, and tea. Most of the cloth used to make the square covers with which Tibetan books are wrapped—with the possible exception of handwoven silk produced in Lhasa or southern Tibet— is imported from India and China, although the actual places of origin may be as far away as Japan or England. Cloth for this purpose must be of sufficient width and body, like velour, moleskin, heavy silk, and satin, and preferably red or yellow.

Beads for rosaries are made in Tibet and imported. The imports consist of seeds; beads of glass, porcelain, wood, ivory, and plastic; and beads

[43] P. Pelliot, *op. cit.*, p. 6.

made from semiprecious stones such as amber, coral, lapis lazuli, and turquoise. In Tibet itself, beads from human skulls and some of the wooden beads with special shapes are made by hand. In some areas, local materials are used, such as stones of special color and tree and plant seeds.

Such metal objects as the cases for the small hand-operated prayer wheels, bells, small bronze thunderbolts, and the rings placed on the counter strings of rosaries are imported from India, Nepal, and China and are also produced locally, using imported metals.

The making of blocks for woodcut printing has resulted in a search for suitable woods, some of which are imported. Birch and rhododendron wood are preferred in some areas. Some walnut slabs have been reported. The preparation of wood blocks is an indigenous industry carried on by Tibetan craftsmen, who for the most part use locally available raw materials. Quality steel must be imported to make the tools for cutting the blocks, but local metal workers are well able to shape them.

The use of colored earths and certain minerals to size paper and give it a special texture or tint and the use of vegetable dyes for tinting the edges of the leaves of a book probably grew out of techniques diffused in prehistoric times or discovered by the Tibetans themselves. Unquestionably, many refinements were brought in from either India or China. Lac and suitable oils used for making the heavily lacquered blue and black leaves of special editions no doubt came from those two countries. Powdering gold and silver for use as ink instead of black or red is at present skilfully practiced by Tibetan craftsmen.

Thus both trade and indigenous manufacture play complementary parts in making available to the Tibetan public those products which are in demand because of the observance of *CHos aDon*. This demand is relatively stable. Fluctuations in the quantities required are small, and the taste that determines such matters as quality, form, and color is very much more conservative than the taste that influences personal choice of styles in clothing, decoration, and articles for personal use, such as knives, bowls, girdles, and so on, which, even in Tibet, vary from place to place or change with time. But religious styles are more widely diffused and change much more slowly. This stability of demand, which is based on needs rather than wants, has its influence on all who trade, within or across borders, and on all who work in cloth, ink, paper, and metal to make what is in demand for the verbalization of religion in all its varied forms.

To conclude this discussion of the role of *CHos aDon* within Tibetan society and culture it must be added that the observance has also played a part in giving the Tibetan culture a special place within the world family of cultures and in focusing the attention of a world-wide fraternity of scholars on Tibetan culture and, in particular, on the Tibetan language. The interest of the world of scholarship is out of proportion to the actual importance or stage of development of Tibetan culture itself or to the small number—out of all the many millions of Asians—who speak the language. It appears to have resulted from the many varied forms of the verbalization of religion, which have helped make the Tibetans into translators, writers, book-makers, and librarians of Mahayana Buddhism. They are a poverty-stricken, reduced people, living by primitive subsistence techniques in most inhospitable regions. They are plagued with disunities stemming from fragmented political power and uneven social development. By many criteria, they are a retarded, and, in some respects, primitive people; yet they read and revere books with singular devotion and possess a stored record of the teachings of Buddhism equal if not superior to those possessed by the great literate societies of the Orient. And, as among all peoples who venerate books, there are learned men among them of great scholarly bent and attainment. Thus, because the culture of this people possesses one of the attributes of greatness, an extensive literature and a long and admirable literary tradition, it has attracted the attention of those who study the great cultures of the world.

The same considerations have made the study of the Tibetan language of interest to scholars the world over. This interest is also out of all proportion to the degree to which the Tibetan language is heard in Asian and world affairs. Such languages as Vietnamese, Cambodian, or Indonesian are spoken by many millions of people, and the countries in which they are spoken are now of critical importance in Asian affairs. Yet their importance is not recognized by the study of their languages in universities around the world to the extent of the interest in Tibetan. In the context of research in Buddhism, Tibetan is bracketed with Sanskrit and Chinese—one, the oldest member in the family of Aryan tongues, and the other, the language with the longest literary tradition in the world, which is currently spoken by more than one-quarter of the world's population. Thus the observance of *CHos aDon* has also had a strong functional role in placing the Tibetan culture and language in the somewhat unique position they occupy in comparative ratings of world cultures and languages.

CHAPTER SIX

THE MAKING OF

MCHOD PA:

OFFERING

The third of the Tibetan universals of religious observance, *mCHod Pa* ("offering"), is not only *Las* ("work"), or an observance, in contradistinction to *rNam aGyur* ("manner change"), or attitude, but is formally classified with salutation and circumambulation as *Lus Las* ("body work"), or physical activity. In popular stories and legends, offering is bracketed with salutation and circumambulation as acts of worship engaged in by gods, men, and beasts. But there is also what might be called an attitude of offering. According to this idea, all other activity observances—prayer, salutation, and circumambulation—are forms of offering. The expression of a stated number of verbalizations of religion is an offering of that size. Similarly, the totals of completed salutations or circumambulations are also reckoned as offerings. Whether an attitude or an activity, offering is solidly based on the obedience which arises from the attitude of faith.

It differs in some important aspects, however, from the other activity observances. *CHos aDon* ("express verbalized religion"), *PHyag* ("salutation"), and *bsKor Ba* ("circumambulation") are manifest in speech and movement; they constitute action for action's sake. But *mCHod Pa* ("offering"), though it is also action—doing as a function of being—is not action as an end in itself. It is concerned with the disposal or employment of accumulated resources, material and religious—not with what a man does, but with what a man does with his possessions or accumulations.

UNIVERSAL AND CULTURAL BACKGROUND

The phenomena of possessing property and the conscious utilization of what is possessed are as universal in human experience as the faculty and use of speech. Possession leads to concepts of ownerhip; and utilization is evidence and confirmation of ownership. Ownership, however, may be personal and individual or communal and collective. What is personally owned and what is communally owned vary widely from society to society and from culture to culture. There is no society, however, in which there is not some degree of individual ownership, as there is no society in which there is not some degree of collective ownership.[1]

The allocation for religious purposes of some portion, great or small, of one's possessions is as universal in human experience as the phenomenon of religion. By personal choice, the allocated may come from that which is individually owned. By communal choice or decision, it may come from that which is collectively owned. Or, by a communal decision which limits individual ownership to some extent, it may come from that which is individually owned. In whatever way the decision is arrived at, however, and from whatever form of ownership the allotment is made, the giving of some part of one's possessions for religious purposes is an important aspect of the behavior patterns that are the common heritage of mankind.

Thus merely by being part of the commonality of the human race, the Tibetan is involved in *mCHod Pa:* the act whereby he devotes some of his resources to the needs and uses of religion. But the manner in which this act is performed—its degree of intensity and the rituals employed—reflects not only the concepts and requirements of his religion but also the influences of folkways and traditions. Certainly, it is against the background of Tibetan folkways that the religious observance of offerings must be examined.

Some Tibetan opinion maintains that the original Buddhist concept of offerings has been greatly influenced by *Bod Gi dPe TSHul* ("Tibetan custom") with regard to giving and that the characteristic lavishness of the Tibetan observance derives in part from a distinctively Tibetan pattern of behavior.[2] In deference to such an opinion, it is necessary to take note of three factors that underlie the custom of giving: (1) the Tibetan concept of ownership—its strength and forms; (2) Tibetan value systems connected with commerce, status, and prestige; and (3) the forms and function of gift-giving in Tibetan interpersonal relationships.

[1] M. J. Herskowitz, *The Economic Life of Primitive Peoples* (1940), pp. 271–352; F. M. Keesing, *Cultural Anthropology* (1958), pp. 233–36.

[2] This phrase "Tibetan custom" as an explanation of the characteristic lavishness of Tibetan offerings was given by Dezhung Rinpoche, who was, however, backed up by all the others. He felt that the doctrinal requirements of Buddhism with regard to offerings were much more modest, in value and quantity, than the current pattern of Tibetan offerings "to religion." Thus pre-Buddhist Tibetan habits of lavish giving and expenditure were at least partly responsible for the munificence of Tibetan religious offerings.

The Tibetan conception of the rights and responsibilities of ownership is both strong and extremely complex. The sense of property rights
and the desire for possessions are very intense. Many aspects of contemporary Tibetan behavior bear witness to a widespread and even passion-
ate acquisitiveness. Trading is universal among all classes and carried on
with hardheaded and tightfisted carefulness. Nothing is obtained, except
as a gift, without hard bargaining. Interest rates are high, and close attention is given to the profits that can be made on money, commodities, crop
seed, and the loan or farming out of livestock. The rights of the individual
to his share of a collective enterprise are jealously maintained. In response to a demand or in case of a change in status (resulting, for examples, when a person leaves a family), that share is paid or accounted for
down to the last thread or morsel. There is intense competition, often
culminating in strife, between individuals and communities for possession or control of land rights, grazing rights, water rights, passage rights,
and so on. Villages carry on long involved suits, or go to war, over fields
and forests; transients frequently are required to pay compensation for
water and grass; and caravans often pay, either in gifts or at a fixed rate,
for passage rights. Moreover, such law as does exist, whether religious,
national, tribal, or based on community custom, is most often administered on the general principle that payment—in good and sufficient
amount—takes the place of punishment. Such payment in the form of res-
titution, compensation, fines, largess to mediators, and bribes is considered not only the logical settlement of equity cases but the preferred
solution in criminal and personal injury cases.

Crime itself is mainly concerned with infringement of ownership
rights—filching, petty and grand larceny, robbery, raiding livestock herds,
and trespassing on grass, water, and forest rights, which may range from
that of a single individual or his beast to that of entire communities. Most
of the crimes of violence throughout Tibet consist of those incidents or
accidents that arise in the course of thieving, robbing, or raiding, which
all have booty as their primary objective. Wealth gained by such activity
may be an addition to personal wealth or to communal wealth, either in
whole or in part. If the community as a whole had an active part in the
crime, it quite naturally shares in the profits. If, through loyalty to one of
its members, the community became involved only after the fact or in the
course of settlement, it still receives some of any advantage gained.

This strong, even greedy acquisitiveness operates within a concept of
ownership that is complex and finely nuanced. The complexity derives
from two factors that qualify individual ownership and affect the rights

of possession: (1) the limit of the range of individual ownership by concepts of communal ownership, and (2) the claims and constraints imposed on individual ownership by custom and the pressure of community opinion, even when no question of communal ownership is involved.

The ratio between private ownership and collective ownership varies greatly, and no fixed pattern applies without exception to the whole of Tibetan society. There are a number of reasons for this. First of all, the political structure of Tibet is a collection of dichotomies of schizophrenic complexity. This is manifested in the duality of leadership at the peak of the religious hierarchy in the persons of the Dalai Lama and the Panchen Lama; in the paired religious and secular personnel and functions of the government of Central Tibet; in the political division of Tibet into two areas—Central Tibet and those areas, previously independent, that have tribal systems of administration dominated or menaced by Chinese political encroachment; and in the duality of political control in the formerly independent areas, where tribal governments function under, or in competition with, increasingly direct Chinese rule. Such competitive forms of political organization and control have fostered or imposed many differing concepts of public and private possession and ownership.

Tibetan society is further fragmented into three societal groupings: (1) the religious monastic community, (2) the sedentary agriculturists, and (3) the nomadic pastoralists. All three groupings, by a large number of criteria, are sharply differentiated and distinct from each other.

The religious monastic community, as distinguished from the other two groups, is oriented toward religion and is not self-sustaining by population increase but draws both members and material support from the other two groups. These latter, alike in being secular, are yet so different in subsistence techniques, habits of life, attitudes, and even ideals that they constitute two distinct subcultures within the Tibetan culture.

All three, however, are closely interrelated, held together by a web of common interests—interdependence in trade and the movement of wealth—with relatively free movement of population from one to the other. Their interdependence and the amount of population movement between them necessitates frequent compromise of the differing concepts of possession and ownership customary in each of the groupings.

In each group there is a different idea of just how "to cut the pie" between the varying claims of individual and collective ownership. In general, individual ownership is more limited in range and has a shorter duration in time—to the advantage of the collective ownership—within the monastic societal grouping than in the two secular groupings. And between the latter, the individual's rights are somewhat greater and more secure in the nomadic grouping than in the sedentary grouping. But in all three groupings, collective communal ownership constitutes a larger section of the whole of possible ownership, with a consequent smaller range of individual ownership, than in American society.

Moreover, private ownership, by reason of custom and community consensus, may have claims upon it that the possessor, who is freely admitted to be owner, feels obligated to honor. For example, when a man is in trouble and must pay a fine or indemnity, he has a claim upon the wealth of his acquaintances that is so great that he need make only a minimal overt appeal when he visits them to collect contributions. A somewhat informal hint is all that is needed. The strength of the claim, freely acknowledged by all, does the rest and, a substantial donation is made to the cause as a matter of course.

Other claims on private property that are generally recognized as valid are for two types of commodity—the universally needed and the relatively rare. For example, the claim on fire is so completely a matter of right that the one who takes away a ladle full of coals from a fire that may have taken the owner much time and trouble to build merely says, *Me Cig dGo Gi* ("one [bit of] fire is needed"), which is explanation rather than acknowledgment, although the Tibetan language is extremely rich in finely nuanced words for asking favors, acknowledging obligation, and expressing thanks. Medicines, on the other hand, are relatively hard to come by, and their procurement generally depends on unusual opportunity or the expenditure of considerable wealth. The claim that all members of the community have upon it is so strong, however, that the possessor actually holds it more in trust than in complete ownership. The only defense against requests based on this sense of rightful claim is secrecy concerning the fact of possession, which may be somewhat difficult to maintain. In addition, considerations of status are involved, for the possession of a rare commodity enhances the prestige of the possessor. In any case, with the thinly veiled demand for sharing a much-needed medicine, there will be *PHyag rTags* ("hand token[s]"), or gifts, and fulsome verbal acknowledgment of the obligation incurred and of gratitude. The one who shares the precious medicine, moreover, has made a substantial deposit of mutual-aid credit upon which he can draw and has been raised in communal esteem.

The observance of *mCHod Pa* must also be considered in the context of value concepts related to trade, status, and prestige. Because of the very great sweep and range of trading, both internal and across the borders, and because of its near omnipresence, Tibetans, even those in isolated areas, have a keen and reasonably current sense of market values. Much of the trading is by barter, but even in that type of exchange, values are discussed in terms of currency. The currency may be coinage, bullion by weight, or a fixed number of units of a basic trade commodity, such as a certain weight of butter among the nomads, of barley among the sedentary people, or of tea at tea-trading centers. Commodities exchanged in barter are just as carefully valued in terms of a particular currency as if they were to be paid for in pennies.[3]

On the other hand, a marked feature of Tibetan life is the employment of wealth for the purpose of establishing status symbols rather than for utilitarian purposes or even for the sake of comfort. For example, accumulations of firewood are a status symbol in certain areas in Eastern Tibet. Year after year, additions are made to great walls or dykes of firewood, the lowest layers of which rot into complete uselessness, although actual consumption of firewood may be rather limited. Comfort itself is sacrificed to the more pressing claims of status.

Conspicuous spending to increase prestige appears most clearly in adornment, expenditures for social entertaining, and the exchange of gifts. Embroidery, metal work, and semiprecious stones are used lavishly on everything that can be ornamented. Silver, when earned by work or trade, is often used immediately as ornamentation on swords, knives, pipes, guns, women's headdresses, and personal bowls. The nomad may go half his lifetime without a shirt or jacket to wear under his sheepskin cloak, but when he can afford one, he will make it of silk or satin; and though in his general subsistence level he uses a leather thong or hair rope as a girdle, when he buys a cloth girdle, it will be silk, although, perhaps, very coarse. His expenditures for reasons of ostentation—*THsul KHa* ("appearance part")—are out of all proportion to his scale of living and bear no relation to his normal level of comfort, which is very low but about which he is not greatly concerned.

His expenditures for social entertainment at times approach potlatch proportions. He will have tsamba, tea, butter, cheese, meat, and yoghurt ready for all who come, although the effort may be a severe drain on his

---

[3] I was able to get from Tibetans from different districts and social levels the most detailed information on basic prices and transportation costs and to check the effect of the latter on trade-goods prices. Prices were given either in terms of basic food stuffs—weights of barley or butter—or in units of basic value such as silver or gold bullion. The detail and the consistency of price in relation to transportation costs reveal how lively and precise the sense of trade values is.

supplies and his own family may have to eat sparingly, so that he can boast that in a single day fifty men tied their horses at his door. This is especially common among the nomads, although all Tibetans seem strongly compelled to offer, with the least possible delay, food and drink to all comers.

At festival time, when the population of a region gathers in a central community for the celebration, the local inhabitants scout for and entice guests. There is intense competition as to who will entertain the greatest number of guests, and there is early planning so that special delicacies, such as spiced sauces, honey, and sugar, can be offered as inducements to those prospective guests who can be waylaid and urged to come. At the end of the day, the harried hosts, with resources depleted and cupboards bare, will then boast to all who will listen of the number of guests for whom tea was poured.

The observance of *mCHod Pa* must also be considered in the context of the nature and function of gift-giving in Tibetan society. The concept of giving—or bestowal of bounty or bountifulness—is of very great importance and special significance in Tibetan thinking and Tibetan behavior patterns. It is the essential element in two important and exalted religious concepts: glory, or splendor, and blessing.[4] *Byin* ("glory" or "splendor") is the perfect form of the verb *sByin Pa* ("to give"), which in its substantive form is the word for "gift" or "present." *Byin Can* ("bestowal one") is the word for "glorious one," who is glorious because he gives or bestows. But *Byin Pa* can also be translated "to bless," and is frequently combined with *Rlabs* ("wave")—*Byin Rlabs* ("bestowal wave")—to convey most completely the idea of active, emanating bestowal on a sublimated level. *Byin rTen* ("bestowal base") is a religious monument or structure from which benediction flows whenever activated by appropriate religious observance. The concept is of significance in the relationship between the one performing salutation or circumambulation and the holy bestowal base before or around which he practices these two observances.

Gift-giving in Tibetan society is not primarily a social amenity or an expression of personal liking, though it may be prompted by these motivations as well as others generally assumed to underlie the giving of presents. Basically, it is the key or pivotal act in a succession of moves that establish a web of interlocking claims and obligations between the giver

---

[4] The extremely close conceptual relation between giving and splendor and blessing has been argued exhaustively by Dezhung Rinpoche. "The root of the two," he says, "is one."

and the recipient.[5] This process is initiated by the universally accepted custom that no one should come to a face-to-face meeting—particularly the party who sought the meeting—with *Lag Pa sTong Pa* ("the hand empty"). This principle of behavior underlies the universal use of the so-called scarves of felicity, the *KHa bTags* ("mouth tie")—also called *mJal Dar* ("meeting silk")—which are exchanged with much ceremony at formalized meetings and when new acquaintances are being made. Such an exchange of scarves is, in actuality, a symbolic exchange of gifts. Scarves are also draped over gifts when they are presented so that symbolic and actual giving are combined. Two expressions meaning "gift"—*Lag bTags* ("hand tie") and *mTHSam bTags* ("interval tie")—point up one of the functions of giving, that is, to create a tie between individuals that encourages harmonious interaction and links them in a special relationship with reciprocal responsibilities.

The giver, particularly if he is the initiator of the exchange, signifies by his gift his recognition of the status of the recipient. He also signifies his own need, desire, and willingness, if requested, to honor the responsibilities he has assumed by giving. By accepting the gift, the recipient, for his part, assumes a special relationship with the giver and accepts equal responsibilities toward him. The giver has made a deposit in the bank; in one way or another, the one who has received the gift must honor checks drawn on that deposit. The traveler or the stranger who aspires to membership in a community achieves a certain status by having a gift accepted. He may then call the one to whom he has presented the gift *bDag Po* ("master"), or sponsor, and thus no longer be ownerless or without protection in the society in which he finds himself.

On the occasion of the initial presentation of a gift, an immediate return of items of value may or may not take place. If it does take place, some of the credit to the giver has been expended. The value of the return, however, is always less than the original deposit, and some credit for the intangibles is left. This, in any case, is only the beginning of the exchange. From that point on, the two parties are involved in a never ending trading of gifts and realization of mutual responsibilities by means of patronage, aid, moral support, and loyalty. The calendar festivals, occasions for condolence or congratulation, and all the incidents of meeting,

[5] B. Malinowski, *Argonauts of the Western Pacific* (1922), pp. 177–94; M. Mauss, *The Gift* (1950), trans. Ian Cunnison (1954), pp. xiv, 37–74. Many of the forms and functions of gifts in primitive societies, as described by Malinowski and Mauss, are to be found in Tibetan society. This is particularly true of the idea that the gift itself, in addition to being a manifestation of an attitude, has a continuing power that is, in effect, coercive.

parting, and beginning a journey or pilgrimage are accompanied by a further punctilious exchange of gifts and the extension or strengthening of the ties of the relationship.

Introductions, *Gros gTam* ("advice remark"), in Tibetan usage are a social rite rather than a mere gesture and have a significant role in extending the web of relationships into a multipersonal pattern. They are much more formal and more important than in Occidental usage. Simple identification is a different matter and consists only of pointing out someone and naming him. Introduction, on the other hand, is in practice the recommendation of a friend to whom one is linked by the gift relationship to another friend to whom one is also linked, so that the two who are being introduced may assume the same relationship to each other, in all its ramifications. With such important consequences resting on introductions, they are made selectively, with nice discrimination.

FULFILMENT OF CRITERIA

It is against the background of such a system of values and pattern of behavior that the Tibetan universal religious observance of offerings flourishes. It meets all the criteria previously formulated for selection as a universal observance. Every Tibetan makes offerings of symbolic or real value. Even if the Tibetan, in disbelief or nascent agnosticism, were disposed to ignore the claims of the Buddhahood in all its manifestations, of the Community, or of all the gods and demons inherited from the religious past, organized communal offerings would still involve him in some degree of participation. Thus, in the Tibetan frame of reference, *mCHod Pa* is universal.

It consists of phenomena which may be both observed and verified. At least some aspects of the observance, or indications of its existence, have been noted by most visitors to Tibet and commented on by most students of the Tibetan scene. Flowers and scarves decoratively placed; butter lamps burning by the thousands within darkened shrines; heaps of grain piled before altars; pure and tinted water in gold, silver, and brazen cups; mandalas and friezes of butter and dough; and the scented smoke from burning juniper boughs, fragrant shrubs, and incense—these and other perceptible manifestations could not have been missed.

Other aspects, although they have not been seen, have been verified. Wealth in precious metals, goods, produce, and livestock is often transferred from individual or communal secular ownership to individual or collective monastic ownership, to be devoted to religious uses. Such movement of wealth may be crudely measured, even though exact statistics of the Tibetan economic structure do not exist as yet. Even a cursory review of the history of religious institutions yields extensive evidence concerning the gifts, donations, and endowments made by kings and tribal chieftains that made possible the building of temples and the setting-up of monastic institutions. Land, peasants, labor, and movable wealth were all offered for the purposes of religion. Thus both from practice and from the records of history, the phenomenon of offering may be verified.[6]

The observance is religious both in nature and intent. It exists within the vast interlocking complex of Tibetan cultural traits connected with gift-giving. Unquestionably, it is reinforced by all the sociological ramifications and functions of that practice, in much the same way that the observance of *CHos aDon* draws strength from the importance of oral expression in Tibetan behavior patterns. In Tibetan opinion and evaluation, however, it is marked and set apart as strictly religious in purpose. This is clearly evident in the terminology in which *mCHod Pa* ("offering") or *mCHod* ("offer") appears. In all the combinations in which it is used, it adds a restrictive connotation. It raises giving—or the gift and the place of the gift—to an exclusively religious level and religious significance.

mCHod Pa is thus the verbal symbol for the central concept of the observance—the transference of possessions from secular ownership and utilization to religious ownership and utilization. There are many Tibetan terms that refer to various forms of material support and subsidization of religious activities and institutions, which can only inferentially be linked with *mCHod Pa* and yet which are important phases of the observance. *mCHod Pa*, however, is the center of the observance, and the other aspects are secondary or subsidiary.

Although this observance has many phases, it has a basic conceptual

[6] P. Carrasco, *Land and Polity in Tibet* (1959), pp. 18–19, 21, 24, 33, 69, 104, 106, 116–17, 123–25, 138, 139, 147–50, 156, 172, 175–78; J. F. Rock, *The Amnye Ma-Chhien Range and Adjacent Regions* (1956), pp. 49–50. P. Carrasco has gathered most of the pertinent documentation concerning the historical endowment of the monastaries and the religious hierarchy with lands and people. The citation from J. F. Rock has been listed because it contains information about an endowment that touches on the experience of the writer. Huang-ho Nan Ch'ing Wang, who gave the land and people of the Labrang district to the first head of the Labrang monastery, also gave the grassland of the region of the knee of the Yellow River to the chiefs of the nomadic tribes who now occupy the *PHyi aBrog* ("outer wilderness") country. Those same chiefs then gave land and people to the founder of the *sTag TSHang lHa Mo* monastery, where I lived for about six years. Some of the monastery subjects were known as *lHa sDe* ("god district"), and some were simply called *aBul Ba* ("the given").

unity and identity. It is frequently combined with other observances, but it should not be confused with them. Among the activity observances, it has special significance, for it alone is concerned with the transfer of wealth from secular consumption and right of disposal to religious utilization under hierarchical control. In that transfer, some of the wealth is consumed—in honoring religion and the gods—but the residual portion, although under different control, remains a part of the economic resources of the society.

ETYMOLOGY OF THE TERM

At this stage some consideration of the etymology and semantic relationships of the term *mCHod Pa* is a necessary part of its definition. In its primary sense, it signifies worship and, on a slightly lower level, honor. As a logical extension of this meaning it has come to mean "offering" in general and current use. The logical relationship between this meaning and the primal meaning is embodied in the current phrase for "honor" or "worship," which is *Nang Gi mCHod Pa* ("inner offering"). *mCHod Pa,* like many Tibetan verbal symbols, also has paradoxically paired meanings: "to present" and "to accept." In most of common usage, the latter meaning is implicit, or secondary; yet its existence, even implicitly, suggests the reciprocal aspects of gift-giving in Tibetan society.

In its meaning "to offer," *mCHod Pa* appears in the compounds *mCHod Pa aBul* ("give offering" [from lower to higher]), *mCHod Pa gTor* ("scatter offering"), *mCHod Pa sByin* ("give offering"), *mCHod Pa Srag* ("burn offering"), and *mCHod Pa sTon* ("show offering"). *mCHod* without the particle *Pa* also appears in many combinations, such as *mCHod Me* ("fire offering"), the term used for the lamps that are kept burning in the shrines by the offerings of butter; *mCHod rTen* ("offering base," or receptacle), the widely used term for stupa; *mCHod KHang* ("offering house"); *mCHod gNas* ("offering place," or recipient); and *mCHod bDag* ("offering owner").

PRE-BUDDHIST CONCEPT AND PRACTICE OF OFFERING

The making of offerings as a religious observance did not come first to Tibet with Buddhism. An early Tibetan account of funeral ceremonies, which has little or no trace of Buddhist influence and specifically identifies the officiators as Bon priests, describes various acts of offering, which are called *gSol* ("beseech"), or supplication. There were offerings to the dead of gold, silver, and precious stones, libations of different kinds, show offerings, burnt offerings, and food offerings. Many animals were killed and cut up; blood was used; animals, food, and garments were distributed to the officiating priests, among whom there were many classes, each with numerous assistants. The animals were killed in a variety of ways: by beating, spearing, shooting with arrows, or being slaughtered by the sacerdotal butchers. With each service—the performance of funeral rites, divination, or healing—the shamanlike Bon priests were paid or took a share of what was offered.[7]

From other sources, it can be ascertained that human sacrifices, *dMar mCHod CHen Po* ("the great red offering"), were made in divination, in rites of healing, and in honoring or propitiating royal ancestral spirits.[8] All the early pre-Buddhist Tibetan practices to propitiate spirit beings and solemnize events were more truly sacrifices (in the sense of the word generally accepted in the history of religious observances) than offerings. The red offerings, in particular, were bloody sacrifices involving the taking of life, and were linked with concepts of propitiation, substitution, soothsaying, and the sending of human beings and animals to the world of the dead to serve and comfort them. All such concepts, including those of the world of the dead, are completely foreign to Buddhism.

OFFERINGS IN PRIMITIVE BUDDHISM

When Buddhism was introduced into Tibet, it had its own fully developed system of offerings. The concepts on which the system was based and the history of its development were completely at variance with the background of the sacrifice-offerings that were part of primitive Tibetan religious observance. The Buddhist system had two distinct types of offerings: symbolic offerings—to honor and please—and material offerings—to support the religious community.

Symbolic or "honor" offerings were not instituted by the Buddha, nor were they derived from any doctrine which he enunciated. They were a heritage from the past, from the folkways and the culture within which Buddhism originated, and as such they became a part of primitive Buddhism. Symbolic offerings do appear, however, during the life of the Buddha. He was offered flowers, which he accepted; and by that acceptance, he permitted the incorporation of "honor" offerings into Buddhist practice. After his death, the gods sang and offered him perfume, flowers,

[7] M. Lalou, "Rituel Bon-po des funerailles royales," *Journal Asiatique*, T–CCXL–3 (1952), 348–59; G.-Ch. Toussaint, *Le dict de Padma* (1933), pp. 318–19.

[8] H. Hoffmann, *The Religions of Tibet* (1961), pp. 20–22.

and incense. Incense and music, which had previously been banned as too conducive to sensuous pleasure, were later admitted into Buddhist ritual.[9]

Material support for the members of the community, on the other hand, was an essential and somewhat distinctive part of primitive Buddhist practice. The position of the householder, the symbol of the monk's bowl—known as the begging bowl—and the practice of endowment were factors of prime importance.

According to Buddhist thought the wheel of the law was turned so that individuals might be persuaded to become members of the Community and thus to move along the noble eightfold way. The householder who did not enter that community could only partake of what might be called the "fringe benefits" of religion. This minimal participation consisted of acceptance of the basic ideals of morality embodied in the law and assumption of the responsibility of supplying the subsistence needs of the monks. The function of the householder was thus a housekeeping one; and "householder" became in effect synonymous with "supporter."

The monk's bowl appeared very early; both as a utensil and as a symbol of the monk's right to support from the householder. At the time of the great renunciation, the bowl is listed among the eight requisites of a monk that were miraculously furnished to the Buddha. After undergoing the austerities and before he began his preaching, the first gift the Buddha received from a human being was food offered in a golden bowl, which he kept for a while. Later, when he threw it in a river and it miraculously took its position with the bowls of the previous Buddhas, he established the bowl, by that act and the result, as one of the signs of his own Buddhahood. The gods also gave him bowls (of stone), so he could accept the food offered to him. In his initial approach to the five who were to become his first disciples, he is described as carrying the bowl; and he and they lived on the alms collected in that bowl by one or the other of their number. Tradition ascribes to him the following endorsement of the beggar's bowl, "Give the mendicant's bowl to the Buddha and thou shalt be thyself the vessel of the highest doctrine. He who offers the bowl to such like me shall never be deprived of wisdom and memory."[10]

The practice of endowment also appeared at a very early stage in primitive Buddhism. It was closely linked with almsgiving, which pro-

[9] W. W. Rockhill, *The Life of the Buddha* (1907), pp. 11, 32–33, 143; E. J. Thomas, *The Life of the Buddha* (1931), pp. 151, 154; E. Obermiller, *History of Buddhism* (1932), Part II, pp. 34, 39, 40, 61, 63.

[10] W. W. Rockhill, *op. cit.*, pp. 30, 34, 41, 143; E. J. Thomas, *op. cit.*, pp. 55, 71, 86, 101; E. Obermiller, *op. cit.*, pp. 34, 40.

vided food for the monks and contributed their eight requisites: three robes, bowl, razor, needle, strainer, and girdle. Anything beyond food and these requisites assumed the character of endowment, the first manifestation of which was the gift of grass to the Buddha, with which he produced a mat. Very soon thereafter gifts of value—such as land, a bamboo grove, and religious structures—from men of wealth or power followed. The apotheosis of endowment was reached when royal patronage gave official status to Buddhism, and the resources of the state were placed at the disposal of the order. According to legend, even the gods built a hall for the Buddha.[11]

In the process of being introduced into Tibet, the forms of offering that were practiced in primitive Buddhism underwent considerable change and amplification. As behavior patterns that had become rituals in another culture, they were transplants which had to displace indigenous rituals and undergo adaptation to a new cultural climate and environment. They not only underwent change but were overlaid with many accretions as well.

A TAXONOMIC SYSTEM OF OFFERINGS IN TIBETAN BUDDHISM

As a result of the importance and function of gift-giving in Tibetan behavior patterns, the following changes took place in the primitive Buddhist system of offerings: there were a multiplication of the forms of offering, a great increase in the volume of offerings, and, as an index of enhanced importance, the proliferation of categories within which presentations were to be made. The taxonomic system is a complex one. In the establishment of categories, form, function, motivation, and the dichotomy of the noumenal and phenomenal are all taken into consideration; and there are numerous overlappings.

The categories are (*a*) the *gTor Ma* ("the scattered"), the *Glud THSab* ("ransom-substitute"), and the related *dMar mCHod* ("red offering")—all closely linked with earlier forms of sacrifice; (*b*) the *NYe Bar sPyod Pai mCHod Pa* ("offerings to accomplish drawing-near"), which include all of the simple honor offerings of primitive Buddhism and which are broken down into seven or eight subcategories; (*c*) the *rGyu rDZas bNGos Poi aBul Ba* ("presentations of substance of real value"), which, as the term suggests, are the *bsNYen bKur* ("help-homage") offerings for the support of the religious establishment; (*d*)

---

[11] W. W. Rockhill, *op. cit.*, pp. 31, 34, 43, 48–49, 50, 52, 125; E. J. Thomas, *op. cit.*, pp. 55, 71, 105, 106, 118, 145, 149; E. Obermiller, *op. cit.*, p. 35.

the *bKur sTi* ("homage") offerings, or services consisting of effort output; (*e*) the *sPyan gZigs* ("eye-viewed") offerings, which include many pre-Buddhist forms; (*f*) the *ZHing KHams* ("field-realm") offering, which is the mandala offered as a representation of the universe from the *Sems Can Kyi ZHing* ("field of sentient beings") to the *Sangs rGyas Kyi ZHing* ("field of the Buddhahood"); (*g*) the *aDod Yon lNGa* ("five desire fees") offerings, which in their intent are functionally related to the five senses; (*h*) a three-level evaluation of offerings: *Rab sGrub Pai* ("of excellent realization"), *aBring bKur sTii* ("of median homage"), and *THa rNYed Pai* ("of low profit"); and finally, (*i*) the *Yid Kyis sPrul Pai mCHod Pa* ("offering emanating from the mind") and *dNGos Su aByor Pai mCHod Pa* ("offering adhering to the real"), of which the former is noumenal and the latter phenomenal.

The Scattered, Ransom–Substitute, and Red Offerings

Displacement of the slaughtering of animals and the concept of bloody sacrifice was achieved only through compromise with the earlier forms and concepts. In the terminology of sacrifice, the early idea of *gSol* ("beseech"), or supplication, was replaced by the idea of *mCHod* ("offering"). The animals and their body parts, which were used in the earlier sacrifices, were not completely displaced but were represented by replicas and by symbolic figures made of wood, dough, and butter. These replicas are called *gTor Ma* ("the dismembered-scattered"), and are either molded by the fingers or stamped out of clay and dough. In form, they may be representations of gods, men, beasts of prey, domesticated or game animals, birds, or reptiles. The choice of form depends to a certain degree on the peculiarities or preferences of the deities to whom the offerings are made: some *Sa bDag* ("soil-owners"), for example, like bears; others like birds; and the *Klu* ("serpent spirits") regard fish and snakes with favor. When the effigies are made in the form of human beings, it is felt that *Sangs rGyas La gYog Po PHul Yod Gi* ("servants have been presented to the Buddhahood"). The symbolic figures most often resemble stupas.

The *gTor Ma* class of offerings is divided into three subcategories, each of which has different incantations, ritual, and final disposal. They are the *gTor Ma lHar bsGom Pa* ("the broken-up meditated toward god"), the *gTor Ma mCHod Pa aBul Ba* ("the broken-up offering presentation"), and the *gTor Ma dNGos Grub Tu Za Ba* ("the broken-up toward perfect food"). The first of these is, in effect, the creation of a god —the embodiment of a god within the *gTor Ma*—who is then worshiped.

Contrary to the terminology of the category, the offering is not broken up or disposed of ritually but is worshiped. Since the *gTor Ma* offerings, as a class, are historically related to the pre-Buddhist religion of Tibet, as will be shown, this particular form, dealing with "god-making," presumably derives from some pre-Buddhist practice, which, however, has not yet been clearly identified.

The second form, from which the entire class of *gTor Ma* takes its name, is the most typical and most commonly used. The figures which constitute the offering are broken up by ritual weapons or by hand and are thrown out, or scattered, and sometimes burned. Both the form of the offering—replicas of animals, human figures, and even parts of animals, occasionally dyed red—and Tibetan historical tradition link this category unmistakably with earlier forms of bloody sacrifice. The replicas were the substitution arrived at when the killing of animals for sacrifice was prohibited in the eighth century, under the urging of Padma Sambhava.

The third form, like the first of the three, does not conform to its name, since it, too, is not broken up and thrown away. It is made for the specific purpose of eventually being eaten by the participant and by him alone. It is a kind of ingested sacrament, having esoteric value, and is highly regarded as a remedy for or preventative of sickness. It is not clear to what, if any, pre-Buddhist ritual it is related.

The *Glud THSab* ("ransom-substitute") is closely related to the *gTor Ma* and, as a form of offering, would also seem to have its roots in past forms of bloody sacrifice. It combines the concept of substitution and the concept of an agent who will bear away misfortune and disaster by assuming the guilt for the sin which has caused them. Domesticated animals—particularly yak, sheep, and goats—are symbolically saddled with guilt and sent on their way to be killed by whoever finds them or to become the prey of wild animals. Messengers on horses ride far, carrying substitute figurines and emblems, which they discard in beyond-the-limits places. As a national and annual rite in Lhasa, and occasionally in local communities in response to natural disasters or epidemics, an individual is selected, or is induced to serve, as an actual scapegoat.[12]

In violation of basic Buddhist ideals, the infliction of injury upon one's self as a form of offering has also survived from pre-Buddhist forms of propitiation such as suicidal immolations and self-mutilation. Burns, purposely self-inflicted and often performed on the body or head with lighted incense sticks, are called *dMar mCHod* ("red offering"). The

[12] L. A. Waddell, *The Buddhism of Tibet* (1895), pp. 512–14; A. David-Neel, "Le bouc émissaire des Thibetans," *Mercure*, 1924, pp. 649–60.

burning of one or more fingers is an extreme instance of this kind of self-torture, which, though rare, is not unknown. When a person decides or makes a vow to burn off the first or the first two joints of a finger, the third finger, sometimes on both hands, is the one usually chosen. The stages leading to this form of offering include not only religious exercises inducing a state of exaltation but also very matter-of-fact practical arrangements such as the putting of tourniquets around the arm and, more tightly, around the finger to induce numbness. Wooden splints are then bound on the finger, and the space formed by the splint ends is filled, and the bindings are smeared, with butter. To complete the ritual, the ends of the splints are lighted, and the hand is held aloft, with the finger as a perpendicular flaming torch, and waved back and forth until one or two joints burn off and the bones explode with a crackling noise. Such a sacrifice of the *dMar mCHod* class is specifically called *mDZub Moi Mar Me mCHod Pa* ("finger's butter-fire offering"). It is believed that this kind of offering, if it cancels out defilement, will result in visions of deity. In the instance described by Dezhung Rinpoche, the lama was said to have had a vision, within the day and night following, of the three lords *sPyan Ras gZigs, aJam dByang,* and *PHyag Dor.*

Other close links with bloody sacrifices have persisted in some aberrant, but still sanctioned, rites in which meat, parts of the body—heads, limbs, and internal organs—and blood are employed. In rare instances these offerings are human. Bloody sacrifices are somewhat infrequently observed, but there are some members of the Tibetan Buddhist pantheon who may only be approached through such propitiation. Therefore, when the need is great, rites are performed which, in all but the on-the-spot butchering of the animal, conform to an earlier pattern.

The Offerings To Accomplish Drawing-Near

The symbolic offerings designed to honor deity also underwent change as they were adapted to the Tibetan cultural climate. In Tibetan terminology, they are called *NYe Bar sPyod Pai mCHod Pa* ("offering to accomplish drawing-near"). The one who makes the offering approaches with flattery in his hands. The offering may consist of any of seven or eight specific substances or objects. The members of the Sakya sect list only seven; for them, the symbolic objects representing music are omitted. The other sects list eight, which make up the collective offering ritually displayed upon the altar, and which are also representative of the many variant forms of individual offerings that are made according to need or opportunity. The eight forms are the following: (1) *mCHod Yon* ("offer fee"), (2) *ZHabs bSil* ("cool the feet"), (3) *Me Tog* ("flowers"), (4) *bDug sPos* ("burnt incense"), (5) *Mar Me* ("butter fire"), (6) *Dri CHab* ("scented water"), (7) *ZHal Zas* ("face food"), and (8) *Rol Mo* ("music"). Each of these subcategories requires further definition and description, for each one, which may have numerous components, is intended to satisfy the very personal needs or desires of a particular deity.[13]

The first of these is a drink served to the deity being honored. Common forms are tea, milk, yoghurt, and gruel; but various delicacies such as honey, white sugar, rock candy, molasses, and certain medicines—preferably, the *Ghi dBang* ("bezoars"), which are considered to be tonics and febrifuges—are also offered, as representations of the special beverages in which they are used.

The second is the clean water with which the deity washes and refreshes himself. It must be cool, good tasting, light, mild, pure, odorless, uninjurious to the stomach when imbibed, and uninjurious to the throat when swallowed—eight excellences. Rain water, called *gNam CHu* ("sky water"), is considered the best; next, in order of excellence, comes water from waterfalls or rushing streams. Well, spring, and cistern water are not desirable but may be used if nothing else is available; but salty, brackish, muddy, or polluted water is not acceptable.

The third is closest to the first offerings with which the Buddha was honored. Fresh flowers are preferred, but because of the climate of Tibet they are very often not available. Artificial flowers of paper, wax, various plastics, or even carved from wood may be substituted. The most common substitution is grain or tsamba, which is arranged to represent flowers. Flowers embroidered on cloth or pieces of silk and satin folded to represent a blossom are also acceptable.

The fourth is fragrance created by burning. The primary pattern is the burning of incense. The incense may be either imported from China and India or of indigenous manufacture; in any case, the materials are much the same—aromatic barks and other vegetable products—though not identical. Although there is no preference as to origin of material, another characteristic is of fundamental importance—whether the material is purely vegetable or whether it contains some musk, though in very minute quantities. Many deities, particularly the *Sa bDag* ("soil-owners") and *CHos sKyong* ("religion protectors"), prefer the scent of burning musk, whereas the *Klu* ("serpent spirits"), or Nagas, dislike it intensely.

---

[13] L. A. Waddell, *op. cit.*, pp. 423–26. The "drawing-near offerings" listed by my Tibetan collaborators agree in the main, with slight differences in terminology, with those listed by Waddell, but are described in much greater detail.

Furthermore, other gods have strong individual preferences in the matter. The commonest form of scent (*bSang*) offerings are those made by burning juniper twigs, fragrant herbs, rose petals, and fragrant woods in incense stoves on rooftops, at entrances, on sod altars set up in front of tents, and in auxiliary campfires lighted for the purpose. Other substances that may be burnt or scorched to produce acceptable odors are grain, tsamba, butter, tea leaves, milk, yoghurt, and cheese. Unless in frank reversion to pre-Buddhist forms of offering to deities not yet accepted into the Buddhist pantheon, meat, blood, hides, hair, and so on, are never scorched or burnt, even inadvertently, for fear of angering certain spirit beings—particularly the *Klu*, or Nagas. Fires for making scent offerings may be of wood or argols but never of coal or peat.

The fifth is light to please the sense of sight of the deity. The butter lamp, which is the preferred receptacle, is filled with butter and a cotton wick inserted. Butter made from yak milk is generally considered the best for such an offering. Yak butter is a most typical Tibetan product and represents one of the basic units of value in the Tibetan economy. A mixture of butter and animal fats or vegetable oils may be used; and it is conceded that even a flame of *THang SHing* ("sapwood"), or pine splinters, would be acceptable as an offering if the giver is poor, yet has devout or good *Sems* ("mind").

The sixth is not indigenous to Tibet as a substance or a practice. It is deodorant, offered to the god for use after bathing. Some perfumes are imported for special offerings by very exalted personages, but common Tibetan practice is to add *Gur Gum* ("saffron"), either from Kashmir or—a somewhat less desirable variety—from Nepal, to impart a slight fragrance and an unmistakable yellow tint to water. If saffron is not available, aromatic herbs such as *sPang sPos* ("meadow incense"), which is a variety of valerian, or other native plants may be used.

The seventh is part of the *mDo Lugs* ("sutra rite") and consists of tsamba, grain, vermicelli, various kinds of bread, yoghurt, cheese, and dried fruit or fresh fruit when it can be obtained. Not all foods are admissible in this more completely orthodox rite; meat, mushrooms, onions, and garlic are taboo. Of the various *mCHod aBru* ("grain offerings"), rice, wheat, barley—both white and black—and "coarse barley" may be used in that order of preference and value, but not buckwheat, millet, oats, peas, and beans. Cheese may be substituted for grain—particularly among the nomads who have little of the latter. In general, root or tuber foods are not highly regarded, but *Gro Ma* ("potentilla tubers"), whether alone or made into a paste and mixed with cheese and butter, are often used.

In the somewhat aberrant *sNGags Lugs* ("mantric," or "tantric," rite), meat, mushrooms, onions, and garlic are not only permitted but often prescribed. The meat may even be of such generally taboo varieties as pork, fish, and fowl. In some rare but authentic instances human flesh was made a part of the offering. To certain deities, notably those of the *CHos sKyong* ("religion-protector") class, the fierce original gods of Tibet, who are tamed only superficially to the service of Buddhism, beer and spirits may be offered. Meat and beer are always the appropriate offering when deities in the *Yab Yum* ("father-mother"), or sexual-embrace, manifestation are worshiped, for at that instant they crave stimulants.

If a clerical or a lay specialist officiates on behalf of a person or household when foods are offered, a deviation in the actual use of the offering frequently takes place. The basic food stuffs are provided in considerable quantity, but only a small part is actually prepared and heaped in the offering dishes; the large remainder becomes the property of the person officiating and may constitute part, or maybe all, of his remuneration for his services. In certain instances, the foodstuffs that are offered may later be shared by members of the household, who partake of the "food of the gods" as of something very special.

The eighth is represented in the display of ritual offerings by the *Ting SHags,* a small pair of cymbals. They are omitted from the display by members of the Sakya sect. Music, however, is part of both general and special services within that sect as within all other sects. Such music is either instrumental—percussion, winds, and strings—or vocal. One hundred eight melodies are said to exist; but that number is, unquestionably, symbolic rather than a precise enumeration.

The utensils in which the eight substances or objects are offered may be of two different shapes—bowls or platters and plates. They may be made of many different materials. If nothing else is available, the crudest dishes of wood or pottery may be used, hallowed and ennobled by the pure and sincere thoughts of those making the offering. The dishes are expected to be the best a man has; and within that frame of reference, there is a preferred selection of metals and other materials, based on the nature or aspect of the god to whom the offering is to be made. According to the *sNGags Lugs* ("mantric rite"), the gods may be *ZHi Ba* ("mild"), *rGyas Pa* ("increasing or expansive"), *dBang* ("powerful"), or *Drags Po* ("fierce"). Dishes used for offerings to the mild ones should be either crystal, white gold [perhaps platinum is meant], silver, bell metal, if it is white, or even pewter or tin; for offerings to the increasing or expansive ones, either yellow gold, brass, or bell metal, if it is yellow; for offerings to the powerful ones, copper, bell metal, if it is red or copper-colored, or bronze; and for offerings to the fierce ones, black stone and pottery. For the last group of gods, there must be one bowl made from a human skull.

Presentations of Substances of Real Value

The *rGyu rDZas dNGos Poi aBul Ba* ("presentations of substance of real value") are not broken down into subcategories having functional significance, since a complete listing of them would contain most of the substances and objects of value in the material culture of the Tibetans. They are characterized as *bsNYen bKur* ("help-homage"), that is, presentations rather than offerings, and are designed to support the religious establishment. It is within this category that a very large proportion of the wealth and substance that Tibetans devote to religious purposes is transferred from secular control and utilization, which may be private or communal, to religious control and utilization, which may also be private—under the control of an individual monk—or communal—under the administration of the hierarchy of a religious organization.

Money, precious metals, food stuffs of all varieties, trade goods of every description, grain, livestock, the continuing harvest that is reaped from the herds and flocks of milk products, meat, and skins, and the special products of meadow and forest, hay and timber—all are channeled in quantity in an endless transfer from secular utilization to the higher purposes of religion. The amount involved in each specific presentation may vary from a handful of butter, taken from the churn and placed in the collection bag of the monks who ride from tent to tent, to scores and even hundreds of livestock offered by a wealthy, and perhaps somewhat aged, nomad.

Besides the presentations of movable wealth in an economy that is still to a considerable degree based on barter, there are even more fundamental transfers of value in the *rGyu rDZas bNGos Poi aBul Ba* series. Farming rights, grazing rights, forest and water rights, and even the lives and labor of the people who live on the lands are deeded to the religious organizations—to affiliated monasteries, independent monasteries, or individual *sPrul sKu* ("emanation-body") lamas, whose power and holdings are perpetuated in the *Bla Brang* ("high palace") or *Nang CHen* ("great house") establishments. As a result of such transfers of wealth and rights, the administration of which is, in effect, a governmental function, political sovereignty has, in varying degrees, been transferred to the centers of organized religion.

The great movement of wealth and political power into the hands of the religious hierarchy thus had its beginnings in the begging bowl of the monk, in the duty of householders to supply the four—later changed to eight—basic needs of the monk, and in the principle of endowment, first manifested in the gifts of land and the building of monasteries. In Tibet the begging bowl has acquired symbolic significance as the *lHun bZed* ("mass container") and has largely lost its practical functional value as the monk's personal bowl in which he receives his daily food from the public. The ideal of simple, direct, daily support, to avoid any possibility of accumulating wealth and misusing it, is well known and widely praised, and there are known instances of its observance and practice. They are the exceptions to the rule, however, for in Tibet the begging bowl is most often the bowl of real beggars or, occasionally, the bowl of the monk who is on pilgrimage.

The support of the monastery and all its inmates comes through other and more intricately organized channels, which are, for the most part, analogous to well-known situations in Western society: family support (like that which keeps a favored son in boarding school); the endowment of monasteries (like the endowment of private colleges); the underwriting of religious festivals, including short-term support of all the monks (like the financing of a municipal orchestra or opera); the accumulation of capital in monastery holdings and enterprises that are run for profit (like the growth of a well-managed business enterprise); the largess received by individual and groups of monks for the performance of religious services; the well-run collection of contributions (like a thoroughly planned Community Chest drive). To all of these sources of support are added the devout, expansive, prestige-weighted potlatch impulses of the Tibetan, to whom lavishness in gifts and giving is a kind of creed—the devotion of most of what one has to religion. Through all these channels and from all these motivations, the great sum of the "presentations of substance of real value" is heaped up to support the religious establishment, to build and maintain the monasteries, and to confer upon them, as a consequence, the power that accompanies wealth.

The Homage Offerings Consisting of the Output of Effort

Closely related to the real-wealth presentations are the offerings classified in the somewhat minor category of *bKur sTii mCHod Pa* ("the offering of homage"), which includes all the activities that involve the output of effort in the service of religion. The labor donated to build or repair a monastery or shrine or to build or repair roads and bridges that give access to shrines or are used by a monastic community constitutes an homage offering. Services to religious personages, especially to emanation-body lamas—the effort put out to welcome them with impromptu horse races and fanfare or to escort them and their possessions on their journeys; the loading and unloading of their pack animals; the making of camp, with priority on setting up the tents and yurts of the lama himself; the gathering of fuel and the making of the campfire; the bringing of water; even the privilege of leading the mount or shouldering the palanquin of the lama—are all worthy homage offerings. The loss of flesh by a horse when ridden hard in welcoming ceremonies and the sweat on a man's face as he ropes and reropes the loads of the lama are considered to be visible proof that homage has been offered. Although these services belong within a somewhat minor category of offerings, yet they rank high because there are no price tags on them and because they are an expression of effort. They are frequently the result of communal decision and a collective effort, but the individual's part is neither lost nor forgotten, either in his own remembrance or in the regard of others.

The Viewed Offerings

The category of *sPyan gZigs* ("eye-viewed") offerings includes, as the terminology suggests, forms that are observable. They are displays and are offered, in the vast majority of instances, to the early gods of the land. The specific form from which the category takes its name consists of a collection of objects hung or placed within the *mGon KHang* ("lord house"), which is usually one of the more popular shrines of a monastery and is generally located on the outer edge of the monastery complex but within the circumambulation path that surrounds the whole. Very frequently the *mGon KHang* has its own special circumambulation path, and worshipers often concentrate their efforts in this small circuit, pausing at each round to make salutation at the entrance of the shrine.

The offerings in the *mGon KHang* are made to the original gods and demons of the land, which have been only tenuously subdued to the service of Buddhism and are known as the *CHos sKyong* ("protectors of religion"). Indulging their unconverted tastes and preferences, the displays consist of ancient weapons, coats of mail, and helmets; the heads or stuffed skins of beasts of prey, game animals, and domesticated stock; and occasionally, stretched human skin, with hair attached, as a memento of barbaric and bloodier rituals. Similar displays on a smaller scale—sometimes limited to a single skin or head with horns or antlers—have found their way into the local shrines or at points where local *Sa bDag* ("soil-owners") are honored.

The various flag-marked mountain-top shrines which honor the so-called mountain gods—the *AH Mes* ("hail ancestors"), *Sa bDag* ("soil-owners"), and the *gNYan* ("argali"), the class of gods identified with particular peaks—are manifestations of the *sPyan gZigs* offerings. In Eastern Tibet these shrines are called *La bTSas* ("pass fare"), and in Central Tibet they are known as *lHa THo* ("god-marker"). Primarily dedicated to mountain gods, they may, however, be located by springs and lakes, near corpse-disposal sites, and even on open plains. They are mainly filled with periodically renewed offerings of crudely made, giant wooden arrows and *Dar gDung* ("flag-lances"), which frequently give the impression of untidily put-together sheaves. Occasionally, real weapons, ancient guns or steel-pointed lances, make up part, or in some rare instances, the entire stack, of the *La bTSas*. The replenishment of the symbolic weaponry, which is offered for the pleasure of war-loving gods in order to win favor and protection, may be an individual project; but more frequently, the expedition to the shrine to make an offering is a periodic enterprise undertaken by the community nearest the shrine or by organized groups from greater distances who, when making war, raiding, moving camp, or setting out on important journeys, feel the need to win the favor of a powerful local deity. The latter type of expedition, both by reason of its objective and the warlike inclinations of the participants, is made with great military pomp and fanfare. The best horses are ridden, gala dress is obligatory, and every weapon possessed by the party is ostentatiously displayed. Depending on the available ammunition, there is a great amount of gunfire to the accompaniment of the traditional cry of elation and/or attack during the offering ceremony.

Another manifestation of the "eye-viewed" offerings is the cairns at the top of most mountain passes. They are also found at bridge sites, beside springs, and at entrances to villages. Called by the Tibetans *rDo aBum* ("hundred thousand stones") or *rDo sPungs* ("stone heap"), they consist, as their names indicate, of heaps of stones, none larger than may conveniently be carried by hand. These cairns are frequently decorated with prayer flags, which are tied to nearby bushes and trees or to lances that are set upright in the heap or near it. The offering connected with the cairn is made by carrying a stone to the pass and throwing it on the heap. The act is generally accompanied by the shout *lHa rGyal Lo* ("the gods are victorious"), which signalizes relief and a sense of victory at the fact of safe arrival. It has often been noted by visitors, for it is a significant detail in the routine of travel. In accordance with the general principle that the value of any offering increases in proportion to the amount of effort involved, the carrying of a stone from the foot of the pass or for some distance increases its value as an offering. A greater benefit also accrues to those who were the original builders of the rock and slab foundations of the cairns. The stones that are added to the cairn are graded as to whether they are clean or dirty—the former are those taken from running streams—and as to color—white being much preferred. The great frequency of this particular form of offering is well attested both by the number and size of the cairns and by the relative scarcity of stones of the right size along the trails near them.

The three kinds of "eye-viewed" offerings thus far described unquestionably have their origins in very ancient, and in the case of the stone cairns, very widely distributed, forms of religious observance. By reason of their deep roots in the behavior patterns of the Tibetan people, they resisted displacement by Buddhist offering rituals and, in a sense, forced their way into acceptance and adoption. In the instance of the display offerings placed within the *mGon KHang* ("lord house"), a veneer of Buddhism has been spread over the observance by the fiction of the conversion of the *Drag Po* ("fierce ones") to *CHos sKyong* ("protectors of religion") and by including the *mGon KHang* itself within the monastery complex. In the offerings exuberantly presented at mountain tops and heads of passes, however, the older pre-Buddhist religion of Tibet is undisguised.

A final and widely noted form of display which also comes under the classification of "eye-viewed" offerings and which, moreover, is closely identified with Buddhism and its symbolism is the allegorical dance which takes place on the thirteenth of the First Moon. It is the essential element of the *sMon Lam* ("wish way"), often called the "wishing prayer," or *sMon Lam Chen Mo* ("great wish way"). This colorful ceremony, which is ritual and drama combined, is a spectacle presented to the gods, but it is also of benefit to men. Through it, the old year, with its sins and disasters, is pushed into the background; and the new year is purged —by breaking-up and destroying the *gTor Ma*—and safe-guarded for all who watch and worship. Following this ceremony, on the fifteenth of the First Moon—the night of the full moon—the monasteries of the Yellow sect and their supporting populations throughout Tibet celebrate the *bCo NGai mCHod Pa* ("the offering of the fifteenth") festival. It is a time of special relief and expectancy. The "wishing prayer" presumably has been successful and the new year will be fruitful; all feel free of the guilt of the past and all look forward toward the new year with expectancy. A display of butter images is presented, primarily as an "eye-viewed" offering to the Buddhahood but also, in what is a natural dilution of pious purpose, as a *lTos Mo* ("spectacle") for all who, by a contribution to the display or by the homage of their reverential attendance, have had a part in the *sMon Lam* ("wish way"), or "wishing-prayer" festival.

The festival has indeed become a noteworthy exhibition of current Tibetan art. The butter images—displayed only once and then destroyed before the dawn of the very next day—are planned and executed with great care by carefully trained artists, each with his own particular skill and renown. Months of planning and lavish expenditure go into their creation; and the element of competition that has become a part of the display has helped produce, or maintain, an excellence of execution and beauty of line and coloration. The various organizations within the monastery—the colleges and the establishments of the emanation-body lamas —assume responsibility for different units of the exhibition, and there is intense rivalry among them to put on the best show.

The images, which are shaped of naturally colored and tinted butter, are commonly bas-reliefs and are mounted on board backing; although occasionally, the representation of some saint, Buddha, or god is sculptured as a three-dimensional figure. Scenes from the birth stories of the Buddha; images of Buddhas, deities, and saints; and symbols—the seven jewels, the eight emblems of felicity, and so on—are the main themes of the exhibit. The images are arranged around the principal square of the monastery or the open space at the monastery entrance, which becomes a concourse for passers-by in a festive and, very frequently, gaily mundane mood.

Those who pass, with prayers on their lips and wonder and admiration in their eyes, look on torchlit and moonlit art forms of real beauty— made for a day but representing concepts beyond time. These same passers-by commonly turn the "offering of the fifteenth" into a night of revelry, carousal, and condoned—even socially suggested—license and promiscuity. Thus, this one purely Buddhist form of offering in the "eye-viewed" category may yet be linked with some full-moon bacchanalia of ancient but untraced and unidentified origins.[14]

14 The Butter Images Festival—also called the Feast of Lights—was discussed at considerable length with my Tibetans colleagues, who confirmed and elaborated in great detail what I personally had learned about this celebration. For a Tibetan's version of it, see T. J. Norbu, *Tibet Is My Country* (1961), pp. 136–39; and for the saturnalian aspects of it, see my *Tibetan Skylines* (1952), pp. 79–90.

There is one further display ceremony which may perhaps be linked with, or inferentially included within, the category of the "eye-viewed" offerings. Periodically, at most Tibetan monasteries, images made of satin and silk, resembling great banners or scrolls, are unrolled and stretched on hillsides or hung on cliffs, primarily as representations toward which acts of worship—principally, salutation and circumambulation—may be directed. But in the degree to which the display is an offering of homage to the gods, it, too, may be included within the category of "eye-viewed" offerings.

The Field-Realm Offerings

This category contains only one purely Buddhistic—or rather Indic-transmitted-through-Buddhism—form of offering: the mandala, or in Tibetan, *Man Dal dKyil aKHor* ("mandala–center wheel"), and therefore, the establishment of a special category would appear at first to be unnecessary. The offering is, however, also a reflection of the Buddhist view of existence, as both phenomenal and noumenal: the *Sems Can Kyi ZHing* ("field of sentient beings"), also called the *Ma Dag Bai ZHing* ("impure field"), and the *Sang rGyas Kyi ZHing* ("field of the Buddhahood"), also known as the *Dag Bai ZHing* ("pure field"). In this view of existence, the mandala is an offering of the universe, in symbolic form, from the field of sentient beings to the field of the Buddhahood. The *KHams* ("realm") so offered is composed of the *sNod Kyi aJig rTen* ("world of the vessel"), or inanimate nature, and the *bCud Kyi Sems Can* ("nourishment-essence of sentient beings"), or animate nature, and is held to subsume all offerings regardless of category.

In theory, mandalas may only be offered to the *dKon mCHog gSum* ("Rare-Perfect Three"), but, of the Triad, *Sangs rGyas* ("the Buddhahood") is the logical recipient. According to the strict *mDo Lugs* ("sutra rite"), even the various emanation-body lamas do not qualify to receive the mandala, for they are held to be components only of the *dGe aDun* ("virtuous community"). In the *sNGags Lugs* ("mantra-rite") view, however—and the mandala is a mantric offering—all lamas, from the Dalai and Panchen on down, are proper recipients of the mandala, because (*a*) each lama constitutes in himself a complete *dKon mCHog gSum* ("Rare-Perfect Three"), made up of *sKu* ("body"), *THug* ("mind"), and *gSung* ("speech"), and (*b*) emanation-body lamas are manifestations of *Sang rGyas* ("the Buddhahood").

In form and intrinsic value, the mandala offerings vary greatly. They are symbolic replicas of the universe, as conceived in Buddhist cosmology, complete with *Ri Rabs* ("excellent mountain"), or Mount Meru, in the center, surrounded by the quarters of the earth, the continents, and the seas. They may be made of precious metals encrusted with jewels; some of such mandalas presented to the Dalai and Panchen lamas have been fabulously valuable. Or they may be simple symbols, shaped of dough or outlined with colored sands upon the ground. There is, moreover, considerable variation in the colors and proportions used, for each manifestation of the Buddhahood to whom the offering is made—whether Buddhas in the heavens or emanations on earth—has his own preferences as to detail. The simplest form of the mandala, which is termed a *TSHab* ("substitute") mandala, is realized by interlacing the fingers of the two hands, with the palms turned upward and the two third fingers—back to back—pointing upward to represent Mount Meru. The simplest ascription of function to the mandala offering, which mystically completes and ends all offerings, is expressed in the following explanation: "*KHang Ba* ("a house") has been presented to *Sangs rGyas* ("the Buddhahood")." Such a conceptualization, which sees the universe being offered to the Buddhahood as an abode, answers the basic urge—endlessly manifested in all the temples of the world, yet never entirely realized—to house deity—and gives added meaning to the mystical symbolism of the "realm" offering.

The Five Desire Offerings

The *aDod Yon lNGa* ("five desire fees") category of offerings is a taxonomic device to group the various offerings by their effect on the five senses. This category applies most directly to the drawing-near offerings but is not limited solely to them. All the classes of offerings may be judged by the kind of impact or effect they have on one or more of the senses. By a direct anthropomorphic device, offerings are taken out of doctrinal frames of reference by the Tibetan and redefined or interpreted in terms of universal sensory experience. They are described in terms of *gZugs* ("form") which appeals to the eye; *sGra* ("sound") which appeals to the ear; *Dri* ("scent") which appeals to the nose; *Ro* ("flavor") which appeals to the taste buds; and *Reg Bya* ("touch") which can be enjoyed through the fingers or other parts of the body. Every man senses these qualities emotionally—they are closer to the experience of living than any intellectual understanding—and he is deeply convinced that forms should be pleasing, sounds pleasant or in tune with the mood of the recipient, scent pungent yet sweet to the nostrils, flavor savory to the tongue, and surfaces delightful to the touch, like a caress.

Offerings of Ultimate Value

To the great proliferation of categories of offerings based on function, there may be added one category which is concerned with the ultimate value of the offerings. In this category material and even prestige considerations are dismissed in favor of a judgment of the ultimate religious values of the offerings. They may be rated *Rab sGrub Pai* ("of excellent realization"), *aBring bKur sTii* ("of median homage"), or *THa Ma rNYed Pai* ("of low profit").

The principal religious observances dealt with in this book—the attitude, or "mind work," of faith; the expression, or "body work," of the verbalization of religion; circumambulation; and salutation—are all adjudged "of excellent realization." The offerings "to accomplish drawing-near" are also in the highest class.

Among the offerings that are considered to be unequivocally "of excellent realization" are the *Srog bSlu* ("life-enticed") offerings. This observance, which is characteristically Buddhist, is known among Chinese Buddhists, for example, as *fang sheng* ("set life free") and consists of ransoming or buying animals that are doomed to slaughter and setting them free. Among the Tibetans, the more complete form of this offering consists of setting ransomed animals completely free of forced association with human society and any possibility of exploitation by the members of that society. This is generally done only with large animals—principally, yak and horses. Only perfect animals of outstanding beauty and appearance are devoted to this purpose. They may go off *Ri Dwags aDra Ba* ("to be like game animals"), or they may continue to associate with the herds for protection and company; but they must never be used in any manner. They have become *lHa gYag* ("god yak") or *lHa rTa* ("god horse") and have acquired something more than freedom—the sacrosanct nature and veneration of the gods. These animals, which are basically "substances of real value" and therefore rated on the low plane of *bsNYen bKur aBul Ba* ("help-homage presentation") and "of low profit," are in this case reclassified both as "an offering to accomplish drawing-near" and as an offering "of excellent realization." In a limited form of this observance, in Tibet, sheep, goats, and cattle may be ransomed and marked in order to be safe from slaughter, although their wool, hair, and labor may still be harvested or used.

Effort expended in the cause of religion and all the services rendered to deities, emanation-body lamas, and other ecclesiastics are considered to be "of median homage." Such personal efforts as transporting, meeting, entertaining, and escorting religious dignitaries—even the drudgery of making camp and building campfires or the more exciting activity of riding a horse until it loses flesh on errands for those honored—are offerings "of median homage"—a rather high rating for personal service.

Material offerings, on the other hand, even when in impressive quantity—the subsidization of hundreds of monks, the building of a great structure for the uses of religion, or, in one historic act of lavish endowment, the transfer of wealth, territory, and political power to a religious organization—are rated, in theory at least, at the bottom of the scale. They are "of low profit" and thus of less ultimate religious value than the simplest act of personal effort.

Noumena and Phenomena Offerings

Finally, offerings may be classified as either *Yid Kyis sPrul Pai mCHod Pa* ("offering emanating from the mind") or *gNGos Su aByor Pai mCHod Pa* ("offering adhering to the real"). This breakdown reflects the Buddhist concept of existence as being of two modes: the immaterial and the material, or what may be called the noumenal and the phenomenal. The noumenal offerings emanate from, or are projected by, the mind, or the immaterial mode of existence; and the phenomenal offerings consist, very simply, of objects and substances belonging to the material mode of existence.

"Offerings emanating from the mind" and presented by the mind, when realized by disciplined psychic effort, have greater value than material offerings. And noumenal offerings may also affect phenomenal modes of existence by transmuting substance without changing form. According to traditional examples, a brazen bowl was transmuted into a golden bowl and water was changed into other liquids. There is a Sakya legend that the previous head of the sect, who was the grandfather of the present Sakya emanation-body lama, changed water into beer, on which his retainers became tipsy. It is also believed that the substitute mandala created by the hands may be transformed into a golden mandala having an appropriate jewel for each component part. None of the Tibetans with whom I have talked will say he has seen this done, but none will deny that, when the *Sems* ("mind") is clean of *sDigs Pa* ("sin"), it can be perfectly realized—for it is according to the word of the Buddha.

None of the categories described above is completely and finally definitive. Not only are there overlappings, but there is considerable mobility from category to category. An offering that was originally in a lower classification, when evaluated in the context of the attitudes and actions of *Sems* (which may be understood, in this instance, as motivation or intention) and the complicated Buddhist doctrine of causality, may be redefined into a higher category. The "presentations of substance of real value," for example, when prompted by pure intent, are frequently raised into the class of the "offerings to accomplish drawing-near"; and an offering originally rated "of median homage," if it contributes to exalted and holy effects, may become an offering "of excellent realization."

There is one offering, however, that eludes classification, yet is of very great importance—the giving of sons and daughters to become monks and nuns. Primarily, it is a contribution to the monastic community—one entity of the Triad—and thus to the maintenance of *Sangs rGyas bsTan Pai rTSa Ba* ("the root of the Buddha doctrine"). If the son or daughter becomes a pious monk or nun who accomplishes the purposes of the doctrine for the good of sentient beings, the offering may then be classified, along with the offerings of religious observances, as "of excellent realization." If the son or daughter breaks his vows and accomplishes little for the doctrine, the final excellence of the offering is somewhat in doubt, although the original pious intention—again, much depends on *Sems*—still makes it one of the greatest of offerings.

In theory, this type of offering can only be made as a matter of free will; but in practice, many external pressures—explicit orders from higher authority to maintain a quota, community consensus, and social constraints—tend to enforce the original Buddhist rule that one child, at least, from each household must be given to religion.[15] In some areas the pressures are so formalized that a household having no sons is constrained to "buy" a son for the purpose. Even the price involved in such a transaction has been standardized. To all external pressures are added the inner compulsions that stem from a basic biological urge of existence, reflected in the choice of a man and woman to live together, to give something of life itself to religion and to link the family, by the tie of its best son, with all the sanctity, power, and prestige of the monastic community, which is, indeed, one part of *dKon mCHog gSum* ("Rare-Perfect Three").

ASPECTS AND DEGREE OF PARTICIPATION

This partial but representative listing of the offerings of the Tibetan people, by category, suggests in outline the very great variety of observances whereby the Tibetan transfers thought, intention, attitudes, effort, material wealth—in every form known in his economic system—political power, and finally, the fruit of his body from secular to religious owner-

15 W. W. Rockhill, *op. cit.*, p. 53.

ship and uses. An exhaustive enumeration and detailed descriptions of these observances are not possible within the limitations of this book. However, they range, as we have seen, from the momentary gesture whereby drops of tea or beer or crumbs of food are flipped into the air, through rituals of display and disposal that are overlaid with symbolism and esoteric significance, to the great, matter-of-fact transactions by which a wealthy man meticulously divides all his possessions into two halves and transfers one of the halves to the uses of religion. They include as well the moment when parents leave their son at the monastery to become something new, no longer a member of the family, and the official action whereby a chief or kinglet transfers to religious ownership title and rights to building sites and territory, including fields, pastures, forests, and the people who live in the deeded land. Land and people are known thereafter as *lHa sDe* ("god district") or, by a nickname that has become a recognized identification, *aBul Ba* ("the presentation ones").

Participation in offering is, in the Tibetan context, as universal as participation in the expression of verbalized religion. There is no Tibetan who has not taken some part in the former; but both in gradations of participation and in qualifying factors, it is somewhat less complex than the latter observance. Every individual, in the course of a lifetime, is certain to have had a personal part in the offering of food, drink, scent, and light —from butter lamps—which are offerings that "accomplish drawing-near." Each also has a pervasive, if at times somewhat vague, knowledge that other religious observances, such as the attitude of faith and the activities of prayer, salutation, and circumambulation, constitute offerings "of excellent realization" and that when he has accomplished them he has directly and personally participated in the highest and most acceptable forms of offering. Each, too, has had a personal share, if only a small one, in the "presentations of substance of real value," of which all forms are qualitatively equal, although quantitatively often very different. There is also a strong probability that every Tibetan, in effort put forth in some form or other, has offered the homage of personal service.

The degree of personal participation in the observance is not qualified by any extraneous factor, in the way that literacy effects personal expression of the verbalization of religion. Since ownership of possessions is a universal possibility, everyone starts from the same qualitative base in the making of offerings, and the quantity of the offering is a matter of personal decision. In theory, measurement of quantity is relative to the giver's resources: half of a poor man's possessions is a more acceptable presentation than a tenth of a rich man's possessions, even though the latter may be many times greater in absolute value. In practice, the presentations of impressive size—hundreds of livestock or ostentatious quantities of trade goods—are the ones that win acclaim and become a part of legend and tradition.

Sponsorship of offerings is both direct and indirect, as in the case of the verbalization of religion. Direct sponsorship is the result of a purposeful individual decision and consists in securing the services of technicians to make the most effective display and presentation of material resources possible. Special help is particularly in demand for the proper shaping and ritualistic disposal—whether by scattering, burning, or sharing (as with food)—of the "broken-up offerings" and for correlating the correct verbal formulas with such offerings as the burning of juniper boughs, incense, and so on, for scent and the renewal of the arrow and lance shrines of the mountain gods. Direct sponsorship also finds expression in the support or underwriting of such specialized forms of the "eye-viewed offerings" as the butter-image frescoes of the wish-prayer festival and the great silken images which are periodically displayed. Indirect sponsorship is automatic and inescapable: no unit of value is gained or produced a portion of which is not eventually transmitted, by means of "help-homage" offerings, from secular to religious possession and ownership, thereby swelling and accelerating the movement of wealth into ecclesiastical coffers.

FUNCTIONAL ROLE, OR CONTRIBUTIONS, OF THE OBSERVANCE

When the Tibetans devote (according to various estimates by their own scholars) from one-fifth to one-third of their material resources and approximately one-sixth of their population to the uses of religion, their intended goals are that the gods shall be pleased, that the root and form of Buddhism shall be maintained; and that collective and individual virtue shall be created which shall flow in blessing to all sentient creatures and in particuar to the one who has made the offering. That this religious observance should have any non-religious functional role in relation to the individual and to the society and culture of Tibet seems completely irrelevant to the Tibetan. When, however, that functional role is defined in terms of specific contributions, he will admit the reality of the contributions.

No judgment will be offered as to whether the contribution is good or bad, favorable or unfavorable. It would appear quite certain, however, that no behavior pattern, or complex of cultural traits, will persist within a society unless it answers certain needs of the society, has won some degree of favor and acceptance, or has been of benefit to some members of it; at least, the members of the society must believe that these criteria have been met. The functional role of the observance of offerings will be assessed on the basis of its contributions to the individual Tibetan, his society, and the culture of which he and his society are the bearers.

The Function of Offering and the Individual Tibetan

In common with the other religious observances, that of offering contributes to the satisfaction of the individual, for each time he makes an offering he gains assurance, in a tangible manner, that he and his concerns have been involved in the processes and benefits of religion. As a part of his material, biological, and even religious resources is purposefully spent, or transferred, he believes himself to have established favorable and fruitful relationships with beings of supernatural power. These beings will now regard him with increased beneficence. He finds, on his part, that his affection and faith follow the gift he has bestowed and that both are increased. In consequence, he holds his religion more dear than before.

This very natural sequence of effective causes and results is strengthened by the value systems of his way of life. In accordance with them, he dispenses wealth in trade to gain something of appropriate value and to make a profit; he spends a great amount of his wealth for what are essentially status symbols and to maintain and broaden his social obligations. This system of values leads him to believe that solid value is received for his offering of part of his wealth; that a real—that is, religious—status has been achieved; and that lavish entertainment of anyone—even Buddhas, gods, and demons—implies friendly and potentially advantageous relationships.

The behavior pattern and function of gift-giving in Tibetan society, in which every individual has participated, either as recipient or giver or both, further strengthens the practice of offering by the formation of habits and judgments. In the vast majority of instances, whenever a gift is presented, a return gift of somewhat lesser value comes back to the donor with little or no delay. The giver also has the satisfying consciousness that the difference in value between the two gifts is—in some fashion—held as credit in his account and constitutes a real asset on which he may draw for material aid or the equally or more valuable intangibles of moral backing, sponsorship, and loyalty. Many of the offerings he makes, especially those presented to the emanation-body lamas, conform to this pattern. Following the presentation of the offering, the donor is touched with hands or a blessing wand, and a scarf of benediction, on which a blessing has been breathed by the lama, is placed around his neck—a return has taken place immediately. Something, moreover, has also been left as an intangible credit from which blessing and the accumulation of virtue will flow. These assurances, effective interactions, and the renewal or enhancement of confidence are real contributions to an individual sense of well-being.

The Function of Offering in the Social and Power Structure

The functional role of offering in Tibetan society has several aspects, some of which are shared with other religious observances and some of which are uniquely its own. In common with other religious observances, it establishes behavior patterns by which individuals identify each other as belonging to the same in-group. Such identification facilitates integration of members into the group and strengthens the cohesiveness of the group correspondingly. The functional role of offering that is unique is the creation of a basis for the existence of a special subsociety within the Tibetan social structure. This subsociety gives the Tibetan social structure its special character and Tibetan culture its own distinctive configuration.

The manner in which a Tibetan disposes of his wealth in offerings is a periodically manifested identification signal to those around him that he is a member of an in-group, the members of which have similar value systems and patterns of behavior. It is a trustworthy form of self-identification since, being unself-conscious, it is least likely to be distorted or falsified. Mutual identification very frequently flows, with little pause, into associative action. Strangers light similar butter lamps at the same shrine; bring real wealth in food, grain, and valuables to be mingled in simultaneous presentation; or jostle one another in an uproarious ride to welcome —with an offering of homage—an emanation-body lama arriving at a festival. In each instance, they are then no longer entirely strangers to each other. Every such experience clarifies and strengthens the Tibetan's inner image of his society and of the value systems and behavior patterns that bind him and his fellows.

The secular function of the observance of offering—thoroughly unintentional—is its determinative role in creating the monastic community, the distinctive subsociety within Tibetan society. Although numerically smaller than the other two principal subsocieties, the pastoral nomadic and the agricultural sedentary, it is the most tightly structured of the three. Because it has a monopoly on learning and an organization to facilitate the accumulation of wealth and its manipulation as capital, it possesses all the power that flows from such a combination of resources and skills.

At different periods in the history of Tibet, there has been, by turns, a person or number of persons who has constituted the nucleus of the monastic subsociety: a king suddenly become devout; a Buddhist missionary magician fighting autochthonous systems of magic; "seven selected men called together";[16] the "six men from *dBus* and *gTsang*" on a mission of revival;[17] or a lone hermit in a cave to whom disciples came. In each instance, the observance of offering, by endowments, grants of building sites, lands, and labor, and the assignment of taxes and revenue, brought into existence god-houses, chanting halls, shrines, and cloisters to house the monastic subsociety and its specialized activities. Currently, the same observance takes care of the upkeep of the monasteries, the running expenses of their routine activities, and the support of their personnel. In addition, the continuing gift of sons—and to a lesser degree, daughters—guarantees the replenishment of the subsociety's manpower and ensures its perpetuation. Finally, to complete the circle, the observance has furnished an outlet of remunerative service to the members of the monastic community, for they are the technical specialists who conduct the more complicated rituals of offering—who know how to mold and shape the appropriate forms, make the correct displays, and carry through without mistake those ceremonies in which offering and the expression of verbalized religion are combined.

Another function of the observance of offering is to create an effective link between the family, as the basic unit within society, and the monastic subsociety. Moreover, virtually every family, whether nomadic or agricultural, is affected and drawn into a relationship with the monastic subsociety, since virtually every family gives at least one son or daughter—often more—to the monastery, believing that they have, in a sense, bartered a biological link with the future for a mystical religious link.

Having made such a gift, the family follows with material support, depending to some degree on its resources. Wealth is expended in gifts to teachers of the novice, in securing cloister space and furnishings, in supplying robes and footwear, and in supplementing or subsidizing the supply of food. The monastic subsociety thus becomes an organization in which the family has a double investment—of manpower and of material support—and its interest and loyalty follow. In the social structure, the

[16] E. Obermiller, *op. cit.*, p. 190.
[17] G. N. Roerich, *The Blue Annals* (1949), pp. 62, 67.

monastery then becomes the most important annex of the home, a familial monument, an architectural investment, and a source of pride—also somewhat of a storehouse, safety vault, and place of refuge. In committing a son or daughter to the monastic subsociety to follow a new and higher vocation, the members of the family have thereby reoriented and directed their affections and loyalty toward that new and higher goal and have pledged to support the organizational means whereby it will be attained. It is from such loyal support on every level that the monastic subsociety draws much of its continuing strength.

The practice of offering has not only operated to create the monastic subsociety and ensure its perpetuation but, both directly and indirectly, has been instrumental in facilitating the concentration of political power and administration in the hands of those who constitute the religious hierarchy. Initially, by the grant of lands and their inhabitants or simply by the allocation of taxes, togther with right of collection, for the support of the monasteries, real or potential political power was transferred directly to the monastic subsociety. Such grants were renewed and expanded according to the pious impulses of secular rulers who, from motives of fear, fascination, conviction, or penance sought to meet the demands of religion. In such a way Kublai Khan gave control of Tibet to the Sakya hierarchy in the thirteenth century; and again in the seventeenth century, Gusri Khan gave Central Tibet to the fifth Dalai Lama. Thus, political power and the function of rule was given and is still being given—at least, until the Chinese Communist takeover of Tibet—either to the monasteries, as organizations, or to the emanation-body lamas who reside in them.

Such arbitrary and impulsive acts, even when mixed with other more devious designs, may or may not have any permanency. But through the observance of offering, permanency was indirectly ensured by giving the highest status, capacity, and intellectual and governing skills to the members of the monastic community. In their persons and position, they were in a measure sacrosanct; something similar to the divine right of kings gave legitimacy and weight to their claims and decisions. And because they had been given leisure to become learned and to profit from the discipline of often rigorous training in analysis and logical debate, they brought mental capacity as well as mere clerkish skills to the handling of the affairs of government. Even the law they sought to administer was inextricably mixed with the precepts and sanctions of the creed to which all—rulers and subjects alike—gave adherence. Thus trained and fitted, whenever political power came to them as part of an offering, they knew how to use it well and so retain it.

Even when they did not directly hold political power, their privileged position and status—their persons were generally inviolate from the ordinary dangers of a turbulent society only partially tamed—fitted them well to intervene advantageously, as mediators, counselors, and arbitrators, in the politics of secular rule, to challenge its decisions or influence the course of both war and peace for their own aggrandizement. In contest or competition with secular systems of control, they could operate on two planes—the mystically religious and the pragmatically secular—greatly to the disadvantage of a king, kinglet, or chieftain who could maneuver only on the latter, less exalted plane.

The Function of Offering in Tibetan Culture

Similarly to the functional role of offering in Tibetan society, its functional role in Tibetan culture has some aspects which are shared with the other religious observances and others which are uniquely its own. It shares, for example, the demands on and the degree of control over the Tibetan's utilization of time. It shares with *CHos aDon* ("express verbalized religion") the function of stimulating learning; and although the role of all the other observances in bringing a new value system into Tibetan culture is somewhat restricted, the observance of offering shares this role with them and is the predominant one in the process. Of all the observances, moreover, it has a uniquely strong influence on the development of the fine arts; and it affects economic patterns of behavior with regard to the creation of surpluses, the movement of wealth, and the accumulation of capital and its utilization.

The demands the observance makes on the Tibetan's utilization of time relate both to the actual time spent in the observance, with its sometimes complicated ritual, and the much larger segment of time needed to procure and prepare all the substances and items that are offered. Such time is purposely subtracted from time needed for other activities; never, as is sometimes the case in *CHos aDon*, is it time that, because of idleness, needs to be "killed."

The role of the observance of offering in stimulating and aiding education, which it also shares with *CHos aDon*, is not, like the latter's role, the creation of motivation and the setting of goals, but more the provision of the necessary leisure and facilities for the pursuit of learning. A somewhat carefully selected segment of the population is relieved from the immediate need of spending much time in making a living and is given the housing, the instructors, and even the instructional materials so that they, according to their several abilities and ambitions, may become

188

learned. The monasteries are the repositories, relatively safe and secure, of the accumulated and recorded experience and wisdom of the past, which is the most important part of the Tibetan cultural heritage; the observance of offering operates to place there the brightest sons of the bearers of culture and gives them time to absorb that heritage and, perchance, to make their own contributions to it.

The observance of offering has had a predominant role in enriching Tibetan culture with a value system that is unconnected with those arising from commerce, status, or prestige, which have previously been described. Whether tangible or intangible, the considerations involved in the latter systems are all worldly and morally ambivalent. The value system of commerce is baldly concerned with the *Rin Gong* ("value-price") of what is bought and sold both in internal trade and in export and import. The system of status symbols relates material wealth to considerations of self and community esteem. And prestige is measured in terms of social and interpersonal success and acclaim in the fulfilment of social obligations. The value system implicit in the observance of offering, on the other hand, relates material wealth, from which the price tag has not even been removed, to otherworldly considerations. Offerings become more than status symbols ministering to self and community esteem; they become the earnest of mystical approval and benediction. They are judged by motivation (mind attitude) and effort expended; and thus a value system concerned with moral standards and ethical considerations is added to the Tibetan culture.

Uniquely, or with only slight assistance from other observances, the observance of offering has contributed to the stimulation, guidance, and support of the fine arts. This is specially true of the arts of design—architecture, drawing, painting, and sculpture—but it also extends to the arts of drama, dance, and music.

The very amplitude of the early royal gifts,[18] coupled with the high purposes announced at the building of the first great monasteries and the architectural bent of the Tibetan people, as previously expressed in the building of forts and castles, made it certain that the structures would be impressive and enduring. To the solidity and clifflike silhouette of the great stone forts of earlier and bloodier times were added the grouping of structures in accordance with the imported Indic cosmic pattern and

[18] G.-Ch. Toussaint, *op. cit.*, pp. 256–61. The Tibetan record of royal good will and gifts for building the monastery of *bSam Yas*, contained in Toussaint's work, is a good example of the endowments given by the "religious kings" and other Tibetan rulers for the creation and upkeep of monasteries.

the refinements of Buddhist symbolism embodied in meticulously drawn decorations and murals. These early edifices became models for all successive buildings devoted to the uses of religion throughout Tibet. As a consequence, the land not only has the Potala, which may well be one of the architectural wonders of Asia, but many other monastery complexes which have much the same beauty of design shown in its tapering walls that meet in upward-sweeping curves at the corners. They are all solidly constructed and decorated with careful technical skill inspired by an exuberant, if at times somber, artistic imagination.

Painting and sculpture received an equal impetus and stimulation from the same source. In every building devoted to religious use, there are symbolic decorations, in which every line and shade of coloring has special significance, and murals of allegorical or historical meaning. *THang Ka* ("scroll paintings") of Buddhas, bodhisattvas, and protector deities are made in great quantities to be hung in the *lHa KHang* ("godhouses") of monasteries and in private family chapels. Great numbers of idols—three-dimensional images of the same deities—are placed in the god-houses so that there are a sufficient number of objects of worship, and additional representations of the converted demons stand guard as doorkeepers and sentinels.

Materials used in making these images include precious metals, bronze, brass, iron, stone, papier-mâché, plaster, and clay, some of which are found in Tibet and some of which are imported. Fine silken and cotton fabrics, which must be imported, are required for the scrolls and images of the Buddha; and for all painting and decorating, sizing agents, such as gypsum and glue, and oils, inks, and colors are needed. The latter materials are both imported and produced from Tibetan resources. Cinnabar, for example, is imported in considerable quantity from China but is also mined locally. Fine Chinese ink, too, is imported but is supplemented by a native substitute made from lampblack by using borrowed techniques.

Many techniques are employed in this great volume of artistic activity: draftsmanship, drawing, painting with both water colors and oils, varnishing, casting, carving, hammering, molding and stamping with presses, appliquéing, and embroidering. Initially, most of the techniques and artists were imported from China and the Indic region, in particular, Nepal. Yet a Tibetan artistic tradition did develop, which, though it reflects both Chinese and Indian influence and is, in a sense, a syncretism of the two, is distinctively Tibetan. Tibetan artists, most of whom are monks, working within this tradition, occupy important positions in Tibetan society. In their leisure, in which they may acquire the requisite skills, and in the continuing stimulation to artistic endeavor that is a part of monastic life, they exemplify the contribution made to artistic activity by the functional role of offerings.

Their efforts are not limited to the creation of permanent artistic productions or to the restoration and renewal of them. They also meet the continuing, periodic demand for art forms executed in perishable materials, such as the butter images and friezes of the Butter Images Festival and the great number of symbolic forms—including mandalas—made of dough and butter for the *gTor Ma* ("broken-up") and other offerings. By such constant effort, artistic skills are preserved and refined and the artistic imagination of artists and craftsmen is stimulated.

Metalwork—to fashion various symbolic objects and the utensils used in the display and presentation of offerings—has also been greatly influenced by this observance, which has fostered fine gold- and silver-smithing and the expert casting of brass, bronze, and bell metal.

The arts of the drama, dance, and music have also felt, to a slightly less determinative degree, the influence of the observance of offerings. A symbolic representation of music is one of the eight "drawing-near" offerings; and music is the accompaniment of many offering ceremonies. Religious dramatic productions containing dance routines with musical accompaniment are both spectacles, for the populace and offerings presented to the gods. The actor-dancers and the musicians, all of whom are monks, are indebted to the observance of offering for the leisure in which to acquire musical and dancing skills and to learn and practice their dramatic roles; even their costumes and accoutrements—masks, weapons, and ritual objects—which are made of the most expensive materials and are lavishly adorned, owe their existence to offerings. In fact, the monastic community itself, without which there would be no dramatic expressions of religion, owes its support to the human and material resources made available by the observance.

The Economic Role of the Observance of Offering

The economic role of the observance of offering in Tibetan culture is quantitatively greater, if not qualitatively more important, than its role in influencing learning and the arts. The offerings of particular importance are the massive transfers of wealth involved in "the presentation of substance of real value," or "help-homage" offerings, which, though quantitatively impressive, are considered to be "of low profit." Whatever their rating, it is they that subsidize the entire religious establishment and thus play a significant economic role.

The economic functions of offering in the culture may be summarized as (1) to motivate the members of the group to create adequate economic surpluses; (2) to implement the accumulation of capital; and (3) to establish a workable banking system by which to put accumulated capital to work.

Accumulation of economic surpluses, above and beyond subsistence needs, does not follow automatically from the existence of surplus resources and surplus labor; an incentive must exist or be created. Indications are that, in a country like Tibet, economic surpluses are relatively easy to achieve. Current Chinese Communist complaints about production in that land mainly center around two factors—that there is much unused land and that Tibetans are unwilling to work all the time. The sympathetic observer must also admit that there is unused land and that, though the Tibetans work hard, they do not seem driven by the dilemma of "work or starve," as are the populations of some other Asian countries. The existence of very large stores of grain in Tibet, which are easily preserved for many years in the Tibetan climate, is a positive indication that agricultural surpluses are relatively easy to produce, and the very great numbers of livestock on the Tibetan plateau suggest that there is a comfortable economic surplus among the herders as well.

Although the value systems that have been discussed earlier—of commerce, status, and prestige—suggest and stimulate incentives for the creation of a disposable economic surplus, each one has its own inherent limitations. Luxury expenditure in any great volume is sharply inhibited by the isolation of the Tibetans and the limited availability of luxury goods. Buying tends to focus more on the quality of materials and on objects to satisfy elemental needs than on goods that would raise the standard of living to a new dimension of luxury. An example of the latter type of expenditure would be the acquisition of an insulated quonset hut with an oil stove by a nomadic plutocrat who numbers his cattle in the thousands and sheep in even larger units and heats his drafty tent with a smokey fire of argols. Expenditures to establish status and prestige also have their own built-in limitations, although such limitations are less easy to define. Conspicuous consumption may, indeed, become involved with fictitious values. Thus, in a purely secular frame of reference, the volume of wealth may increase at a good rate, but the satisfactions resulting from its expenditure may increase more slowly and, from the point of view of the effort expended, eventually reach a point of diminishing returns. In the religion-oriented culture of Tibet, however, the observance of offering and the special incentives which it supplies, based on a qualitatively different value system, offer new, supremely worthwhile, and unlimited possibilities of expenditure. Judged by the sublime values of religious achievement, all of one's wealth is not enough, and the greatest surplus may be expended to a real advantage—the reality of the doctrinal absolute.

In the Tibetan economic system, incentives for capital accumulation are weak, and devices to facilitate its formation are few and not very effective. Surpluses may be stored; but otherwise, they are generally put back into whatever activity first produced them: additional cattle are added to the herds or landholdings are increased. There are no formally capitalized industries with large plant and equipment outlays that would require considerable sums of capital. Small handicraft industries are begun on an *ad hoc* basis and are enlarged slowly by using the profits. Trade is mostly a matter of the turnover of surpluses within the economy—often by barter—or the channeling of those surpluses, one by one, into a demanding world market. All these activities require some capital, as do such other small ventures as the establishment of ferries and rudimentary transport facilities; but none has an urgent enough need to bring into existence procedures for capital accumulation or capital-holding devices or pools upon which such ventures might draw.

The observance of offering, however, not only supplies effective incentives for the creation of economic surpluses but fosters and implements their accumulation into capital. Very great amounts of wealth are channeled into what inevitably becomes a capital-holding device or pool. Only a small fraction of what is offered in the observance is immediately consumed; a somewhat larger portion, the size of which may vary greatly according to local conditions, is spent in subsidies and current expenses; the remaining portion is accumulated as potential capital. Most of the last becomes investment capital, since the members of the religious organization that has received it cannot use it directly in gainful enterprises, either because they do not control a sufficient quantity of the material bases of production—land, grazing rights, livestock, and available labor— or because they are enjoined from performing such labor or do not have the requisite leisure. Circumstances thus constrain them to devise procedures whereby wealth will produce wealth—through investment or lending for interest.

As a capital-holding device, the religious organization does not need to seek surplus wealth as capital, though elicitation and even solicitation are not, to say the least, unknown. In the vast total of "presentations of substance of real value," wealth is brought to it—even forced upon it—with a minimum of solicitation.

The accumulated capital in the form of offerings is received, held, and administered at four levels by a number of subdivisions within the monastery: (1) the *Grwa Ba* ("school one"), or individual monk; (2) the *Grwa TSHang* ("school den"), or college, of which there may be several within the monastery; (3) the *Bla Brang* ("superior palace") or *Nang CHen* ("great house"), which are the residences and administrative organizations of the various *sPrul sKu* ("emanation-body") lamas of the monastery; and (4) the *dGon Pa* ("solitary one"), or monastery as a whole.

The individual monk finds himself in the possession of capital whenever the subsidies he receives on a somewhat regular basis and the offerings presented to him as marks of personal esteem or as payment for liturgical services amount to more than his expenditures. Some monks seldom, if ever, have a surplus; others of greater sanctity and renown accumulate considerable amounts of convertible wealth. Theoretically, no monk is supposed to engage in gainful occupation; and in practice, though the rule might be broken, the monk who is in great enough demand to merit offerings in any quantity does not have time for direct participation in such enterprise.

The productive function of wealth is well known to the Tibetans, who, in the common phrase for interest from capital, describe it in biological terms as *Ma Bu* ("mother-son"). To make the "mother" produce "sons," the monk either lends his money at interest directly or through the purchase of shares in small trade ventures or invests it in milch cows (yak or hybrid) or—if the amount is small—ewes. The animals are farmed out with nomadic acquaintances, and the monk receives an agreed-upon payment of butter or, sometimes in the case of sheep, wool. The rate of such payments varies according to the area and circumstances. In the *PHyi aBrog* ("outer wilderness") region of Amdo, the average rate per year for a good *mDZo Mo* ("hybrid milch cow") would be about twenty-five pounds of butter. This is approximately one-fifth the original price of the cow. In return for the trouble and responsibility of caring for the cow, the nomadic family would receive any butter over and above the twenty-five pounds (depending on many factors there might or might not be a surplus), buttermilk for consumption or making cheese; dung for fuel; the calf, which in the case of *mDZo Mo* is usually butchered at birth; and the annual harvest of hair for making cloth and rope. Loss by sickness or robbery is borne by the monk owner if it is part of a general loss in which the nomad, too, suffers a loss of cattle. Disease epidemics, exceptionally severe weather with heavy falls of snow, or a general raid on the cattle of the nomad are possible causes of such loss. If only the monk's animal is lost and if carelessness is suspected, the nomad may have to bear all or some of the cost. The exact rate and schedule of payment, responsibility in case of loss, and conditions for the continuance or termination of the arrangement are all subject to negotiation and bargaining and are usually precisely defined in the contract, which may be oral or written.

Investment in shares for interest conforms in general to current patterns throughout the world. The terms and conditions are precisely defined in great detail. Factors of risk—the possibility of political change, the weather, and so on—and the relation of market values to internal or external trade are considered. Investment in seed grain, for example, is conditioned by such factors as the relative fertility of the land and the known average harvest, the possibility of drought or damaging hailstorms, and whether payment from the shares may be made in other commodities —fuel or timber, for example—than the grain of the harvest. These terms are either all stated in some detail in formal oral or written contracts or are explicitly left open to ex post facto appeal and renegotiation, which may involve mediation and arbitration.

Investment for interest, in particular, is conditioned by the risk of default. Assignment of collateral in substances and objects of value, such as jewelry, valuable weapons, fine garments and furs, and so on, and the furnishing of guarantors or bondsmen are matters which directly affect the rate of interest. Interest rates are high when compared with those in the West, but not, in general, with other Asian practice, at least before some of the drastic reforms now being carried out. "Light" interest is reported to be annual repayment of one unit of value for ten units borrowed (10 per cent); "median" interest is one for six (16 2/3 per cent); and "heavy" interest is one for four (25 per cent). There are, of course, many variations within this over-all pattern, and all such matters as schedule of payments, possibility of renewal, conditions resulting in case of default, and so on, are subject to negotiation at the time the loan is made or to appeal and arbitration at any time thereafter.[19]

[19] Students of Asian economic systems will recognize that the three degrees of interest given here, which were developed by careful cross-questioning of my Tibetan collaborators, are relatively moderate, even when regarded as norms which at various times and circumstances may be exceeded. These rates agree in the main with my personal knowledge, although I did once hear of a 36 per cent yearly rate. Even Win-

The level within the monastery at which the greatest amount of capital is received, held, and invested, and at which the most elaborate organization and procedures have been developed, is the *Grwa TSHang* ("school den"), or, as it is sometimes called, college. (In many of its aspects, it might be most aptly called a monk commune.) In small monasteries, there may be only one *Grwa TSHang;* in which instance, it is somewhat indistinguishable from the monastery as a whole. But usually, there are up to four *Grwa TSHang* within a monastery. This subdivision and grouping of the monastic population, which is characterized by a very specific self-identification, is very powerful in monastery politics, for it commands strong loyalties from its members. There is much rivalry between the different *Grwa TSHang.*

Being of such importance, the *Grwa TSHang* is the level at which the greatest volume of business is transacted. Not only does it draw wealth from offerings, but it also inherits all the wealth of its members upon their deaths, unless there are nephews of the deceased within the membership of the *Grwa TSHang.* The wealth of the group is administered by a formally and tightly structured organization based on the *gZHung* ("central"), or corporate, membership of the *Grwa TSHang* and headed by a *sPyi Ba* ("superintendent"). Frequently, there are two superintendents, who are elected or appointed from the membership of the *Grwa TSHang* for terms of two to four years. The term may be longer, or it may be extended. To help them, they may have one or more *gNYer Ba* ("stewards") and such *sPyi gYog* ("superintendent servants") as needed—frequently totaling a good-sized staff. The wealth in goods and currency is kept in a *sPyi KHang* ("superintendent house"), from which operations are directed. Holdings may also include buildings within the cloisters, fields, grazing rights, livestock, forests, and organized transport caravans.

The *sPyi Ba* serve under a general requirement that they shall so manage the wealth that at the end of their terms of office they may be able to report an increase in holdings and substantial earnings on wealth lent at interest or invested in trade operations. At the time their report is made, or sometimes when a particularly large gift has been received, the two *sPyi Ba,* upon agreement between themselves, may distribute their surplus on a pro rata basis to the membership. To be successful, the *sPyi*

---

nington (A. Winnington, *Tibet* [1957], pp. 54, 146, 167, 180), who favors the figures furnished him by the Chinese Communists, says that rates vary from 5 to 60 per cent. The Chinese Communists themselves (*Jen Min Jih Pao* ["People's Daily" (Peking)], May 15, 1959), in trying to make a case for themselves and their much publicized "interest-free loans," claim that interest rates were as high as 100 per cent.

Ba must combine the talents of good business executives, the acumen of investment bankers, and the special gifts of salesmen. They must be able to plan and manage such business ventures as the dispatch of trade caravans, the management of livestock herding, the cultivation of fields, and various handicraft activities, building projects, and the general upkeep and maintenance of all the projects. They must know how and to whom to lend wealth at interest to the best advantage, avoiding unprofitable enterprises and defaulters. In addition, they must be effective salesmen, advertising and proffering the religious services of the monastery so as to elicit, if not directly solicit, gifts to the *Grwa TSHang*. Salesmanship is also required to induce individuals, families, and communities to accept capital funds as an investment from which the *Grwa TSHang* may be assured of regular income. In Central Tibet, the collection of taxes is one of their principal duties.[20]

Bla Brang ("superior palace") and *Nang CHen* ("great house")—the residence of a *sPrul sKu* ("emanation-body") lama as well as the administrative organization of his establishment—are terms which designate another level of monastic organization at which business is transacted. Generally, the lama leaves all the details and even general oversight of such business to the chief of his staff. The latter is frequently a long-term director—his tenure sometimes extending through the lifetimes of two lamas —although, if he came to office with the lama, he is usually a kinsman of the latter. He is known as *dBon Po* ("manager") or *PHyag mDZod* ("treasurer") and may have a *gNYer Ba* ("steward") or two to assist him, as well as monk servants for menial tasks.

The interrelation of this administrative unit with the other units of the monastery—the individual monk, the college, and the monastery as a whole—is one of some complexity. The sources of wealth—offerings, endowments, and earnings from wealth—of the *Nang CHen* are in general similar to those of the other levels of administration, except that they are subject to greater fluctuations. Much of their volume depends on the personal religious renown of the lama himself. If he is highly regarded, the offerings and gifts may be of spectacular size, but if he is held in low

---

[20] The function of the *sPyi Ba* ("superintendent") and the finances and establishment he administers on behalf of the "college of monks" as described by Tibetans have many points of resemblance to the "jisa," which Robert Miller discusses (R. Miller, *Monasteries and Culture Change in Inner Mongolia* [1959], pp. 87–119). In Tibet, however, the *sPyi Ba* and his work and the *mDZod* ("treasury") over which he presides as administrator are clearly separate. In the process of transplanting the function and its terminology from Tibet to Inner Mongolia, the treasury became known by the name for its manager.

popular esteem, they may dwindle to a trickle. They also fluctuate in proportion to his activity in visiting the communities of the region. The expenses of his great house are generally quite large, and both he and his establishment are more frequently involved in prestige expenditure—for example, the entertainment of guests—than the other units of the monastery.

The *Nang CHen* is not in the direct line of the administrative hierarchy of the monastery; yet its fortunes are very closely linked with those of all parts of the monastery. It is a prestige and propaganda asset and tends to attract support to the monastery as a whole. It, in turn, frequently presents offerings to the colleges or to the *TSHogs aDu* ("gathered assembly") of the monastery. Conversely, when pro rata distributions of wealth are made by the other units, the lama may receive a share, which, in recognition of his special status, is five, nine, or even more times the share of the individual monk.

The management of wealth by the *Nang CHen* of a lama follows much the same lines as that of the other organizational units of the monastery, with, however, a certain shift of emphasis. The *Nang CHen* is dependent to a greater extent on current gifts and is correspondingly less concerned with the manipulation of wealth by investment and participation in business ventures. Greater attention is thus focused on the elicitation and collection of offerings than on investment management.

The *dGon Pa* ("solitary one"), or monastery as a whole, also receives, holds, and administers wealth. The base of its organizational structure is the *Mang TSHogs* ("many gathered") or *TSHogs aDu* ("gathered assembly"), which is the entire monk population of the monastery. At the peak of the hierarchy of this administrative unit is the *KHri Ba* ("seat one"), or abbot, or a lama official called *dGon Bla dPon* ("solitary high official"). The other functionaries within this structure, who concern themselves with instruction, discipline, and ritual, have no significant relationship to the business activities under investigation. The abbot or high official who is the head of the monastery is the one who usually receives gifts and endowments for the monastery as a whole. He has under him stewards and other assistants and occasionally a treasurer. If the monastery is a small one, with only one *Grwa TSHang*, the *sPyi Ba* of the college acts for the monastery. The offerings received are put to use in the extension or repair of monastery buildings and shrines; and if there is a surplus of income, it may be used in investment. Two of the principal functions of the head of the monastery are to seek sponsorship of the *Mang Ja* ("much tea") chanting services and to oversee the distribution of the subsidy received from the services to the members of the monastic assembly.

The principles and the practices followed in participating in business ventures and in lending money at interest are much the same for all the corporate groupings of the monastery membership and, in general, conform to those described in the section concerning the management of wealth by the individual monk. For the larger and higher official units, however, the risk factor is somewhat less than for the individual entrepreneur; because of their greater authority and influence, they can exert greater pressure to ensure prompt payment and compliance with the terms of a contract. This, in turn, affects the terms of contracts and also interest rates, which tend to be slightly lower.

It is the *Grwa TSHang*, or college, however, which, in the office and operations of the *sPyi Ba*, or manager, corresponds most closely to the organization and function of investment banking in other parts of the world. The analogy, though close, does not hold good in every respect. Although it operates like an investment banker, the monastery bank derives its capital from gifts and not from deposits on which it would have to pay interest or from other financial services. Capital accumulation is a by-product of offerings made in the interest of religion; it costs the monasteries nothing in interest or other financial outlay. The self-sacrifice of those who give, in terms of satisfaction derived, has not been ruinously or appallingly great. Nor have the *sPyi Ba* and others imposed altogether unreasonable interest rates or altogether stifled economic development. The sacrifice expressed in offering and the management of wealth together represent an economic contribution to the culture of Tibet. The immensity of the accumulation which has resulted and the uses to which it has been put are a measure of the economic function of the observance of *mCHod Pa* in the culture.

CHAPTER SEVEN

THE PERFORMANCE OF

PHYAG:

SALUTATION

PHyag ("salutation"), the fourth of the Tibetan universals of religious observance, is one of the activity observances, based, however, on a mental attitude. It is the phenomenal manifestation of the mental attitude of reverence. When, as an action, it is arrested in time and fixed in space, it becomes, quite obviously, the physical attitude of salutation. When the worshiper prostrates himself, he acts; when he remains prostrate, his action becomes an attitude.

The making of gestures and assumption of postures, indeed, have a far wider universality than as Tibetan phenomena. As outward indications of inward feelings and thoughts, gestures and postures are universal in human experience as means of communication and probably preceded the development of speech in the history of human culture.

Nor is this form of communication limited to human beings and human societies. It exists among animals and is found among them in various stages of development. The lifted lip of a dog, the stamp of a horse's hoof, and the mating dance of a demoiselle crane may be regarded as progressive stages in the development of gesture significance. The lifted lip of a dog—the prelude to snapping—is basically an act that has been halted halfway to completion and so has become a signal suggesting the act. The stamp of a horse's hoof is an act that has become largely a symbol and therefore a signal. And the mating dance of cranes is an act that has become still further stylized and is, in fact, a ritual. Such gesture-signals among animals may even indicate status and have prestige significance, as shown by the "peck order" in the hen-house society of domesticated fowl.[1]

In human societies, there is an even greater variety and range in the transformation of acts into signals. The shaken fist is an incompleted blow

[1] E. R. Hall, *The Silent Language* (1959), pp. 46–47.

and threatens or announces the possible completion of the act. Many such signals of incompleted acts, which are recognizably linked to the action from which they derive, serve the function of communication and are found in great variety in all human cultures. An equally great number of gestures and postures, whose origins in action are now lost or forgotten, are used as signals to warn, summon, command, or inform. They have meaning because the members of the culture within which they are found have assigned meanings to them and because, between users and observers, those meanings have a common acceptance. Still other gestures and postures have been stylized and combined in rituals of great complexity. Such rituals are interwoven into the fabric of social behavior on many levels, from the most elementary satisfaction of physical needs, such as hunger and thirst, through the entire gamut of social activity, to the most esoteric activities of the human mind and spirit. In acknowledging status and assigning prestige, gestures and postures often have more meaning and greater power of expression than words. For example, no word or phrase in any language would appear to be sufficiently abject to displace the full-length body prostration as the most complete acknowledgment of a difference in status.

Although, as a form of communication, gestures and postures are comparable to words, there is a difference with regard to universality. The number of sounds that have universally recognized meaning—that is, that are understood by everyone regardless of the language he speaks—is extremely small if, indeed, any exist. There are, however, quite a number of gestures and postures whose meanings are sufficiently basic to be universally understood. Thus men instinctively resort to the use of gestures, or sign language, when they have no common spoken language. The universally understood gestures and postures, supplemented by improvisations, become at times surprisingly effective substitutes for speech.

A further step in the use of sign language—the arbitrary assignment of meanings to gestures and postures—when accepted by both user and observer, may equal in clarity as well as emphasis, and in some instances surpass, speech as a form of communication. When meanings have not been mutually accepted, however, much confusion may result. A gesture that may be highly complimentary in the context of one culture may be an insult in the context of another. In the West a fist fight may start because someone has stuck out his tongue. Among the Tibetans, the protruding tongue accompanies the spreading of the hands, palms outward, in the most respectful form of greeting.

Action is the natural response of the Tibetan to the exigencies of any situation. The teachings of contemplation and tales of meditative lamas to the contrary, the Tibetan—even the lama—has a bias in favor of energetic action. In real life he is not a passive figure, lost in contemplation like a saint on a painted scroll. He is a man who battles with vim and explosive energy against the rigors of his environment and the exigencies of a habit of life that demands action as the price of survival. The members of the clergy share this bias. The monk, riding with a revolving prayer wheel in his hand and ceaselessly muttering prayers, goes into action as fast or faster than anyone else in a caravan when a load is spilled by a wayward pack animal. With a minimum of delay, he lifts a heavy load to the saddle or pulls a packrope tight, matching muscle and effort with his fellows, though his breath comes in gasps—with no time for praying—for the air is very thin.

RELATIONSHIP OF SALUTATION TO OTHER OBSERVANCES

The Tibetan drive and compulsion to act finds relief and expression, to a satisfying degree, in the performance of the two distinctively *Lus Las* ("body work"), or activity, religious observances. Of these salutation is the first and, in the Tibetan system of evaluation, the more important. It has, however, significant conceptual and functional links with all the other religious observances postulated in chapter iii and a brief discussion of these links will contribute to a description and definition of the observance itself.

More than any of the other observances it may, as has been already shown, become an attitude. Thus it is, in some degree, the physical analogue of the mental attitude of faith (*Dad Pa*). This is particularly true in those manifestations of *PHyag* which reflect reverence, the so-called *Gus Pai rNam aGyur* ("the manner-change of reverence"). In addition to the symbiotic and analogous relationship of salutation and faith, Tibetan religious exhortation and teaching has linked the two in a motivation-implementation relationship. It is repeatedly stressed that *PHyag*, or action, has no value unless it originates from and is matched by *Dad Pa*, or belief.

The logical link between salutation and the expression of verbalized religion (*CHos aDon*) is that of a basic similarity of function—to communicate, with an emphasis on repetition as an end in itself. As a means of communication, however, salutation does not have the uniquely high status of speech, which is linked both with the *CHos* ("doctrine") of *dKon mCHog gSum* ("Rare-Perfect Three")—in essence, the word of the Buddha—and with the concept of personal existence as manifest in body, mind, and speech. That the emphasis on repetition as an end in itself is very much the same for both observances is aptly illustrated by the use of the rosary to keep both records of the number of repetitions. Unlike the performance of *CHos aDon,* however, the Tibetan has found no acceptable means whereby he may buy the services of others to perform salutations for him, nor has he been able to introduce into the observance mechanical means of multiplication such as the prayer wheel.

The relationship of salutation to offering is both general—the performance of any observance is considered an offering—and somewhat special—an offering may be reflected or expressed by an entire series of intricate gestures of the two hands, either as an accompaniment to an offering or as a substitute.

The resemblance between the physical act of salutation and the physical act of circumambulation is so obvious and close that the two observances are frequently bracketed in Tibetan stories and histories.[2] *Mi La Ras Pa,* the twelfth-century mystic, links them in the authoritative injunction: *PHyag Dang bsKor Ba Byed Pa* ("Do salutations and circumambulations").[3] Both of them are, in a special sense, *Lus Las* ("body work"). Both offer the Tibetan something to do; they satisfy the need for action, in what may resemble calesthenics, and the demands of religion and the compulsions of the spirit. Of the two, salutation is considered the more important and efficacious.

TERMINOLOGY OF THE OBSERVANCE

The Tibetan word for "salutation" (*PHyag*) is a homonym of the word for "hand" (*PHyag*). "Hand" is probably the primary meaning, and "salutation" is one of several derived meanings. Thus the Tibetan formulation of the concept of salutation is linked to universal sign language for greeting, which depends, to a large extent, on the use of the hand—the handshake, the salute, and applause.

In Tibetan behavior patterns, apart from salutation, the hands and fingers are used for numbering and expressing levels of evaluation. In common with the Chinese—this may indeed be an instance of the borrowing of cultural traits—the numbers one to nine may be expressed with the fingers of one hand. Thus, using the decimal principle, any number, no matter how large, may be signalled with the fingers of one hand. The

[2] G.-Ch. Toussaint, *Le dict de Padma* (1933), pp. 149, 210, 369, 432; *dPal lDan Bla Ma Dam Pa rJe bTSun Blo bZang Ye SHes Kyi gSung Las gSang Bai rNam THar bZHugs So* [a Tibetan play], f. 21 *b.*

[3] H. A. Jaschke, *A Tibetan-English Dictionary* (1949), p. 24.

numbers one to five are signalled by the corresponding number of fingers; six, by holding up the thumb and little finger while keeping the other fingers bent; seven, by holding together the extended thumb, index, and middle fingers; eight, by spreading the thumb and index finger in a V sign; and nine, by the crooked index finger. The system is extensively used in trading, particularly for livestock, to make unmistakably clear the prices asked and offered. It is frequently used to keep the exchange of prices confidential. Hands joined up a long sleeve or under a coat flap, the two principals may argue vehemently without letting bystanders know what prices are sucessively asked, offered, or refused.

Value or relative excellence is also indicated by the fingers, ranging from most excellent and the height of regard—the thumb—to the worst and the depth of disdain—the little finger. For indicating various levels between these two extremes, there are no words—or possibly only long paragraphs of descriptive exposition or mathematical formulations of percentages, which are as neatly precise as the levels represented by the fingers between the thumb and little finger. Even uncertainty that cannot be put into words may be shown by flicking two fingers back and forth in vacillation leaving the viewer to make his own decision as to which is meant. A rather amusing gesture, which also uses the fingers, is that which designates a stingy man: clenching the fist and then licking it at the thumb and little finger sides—a graphic representation of one who clenches what he can get and even licks off what might leak out.

Linear measurements are also related to the hand: *Sor Mo* or *Sor* ("width of finger"); *mDZub* ("span between digit finger and thumb"); *THo* ("span between middle finger and thumb"); and *aDom Ba* ("fathom —distance between the two hands with arms spread").

Another meaning of *PHyag* is "to sweep," an obviously secondary or derived meaning. In religious discussion and elaboration, this meaning is adduced, particularly when combined with *aTSHal* ("wish"), to give prostration an esoteric significance as a rite of cleansing or purification.

With little semantic strain, however, *PHyag* does duty very well for the concept of salutation. Combined with *rGya* ("token"), or *PHyag rGya* ("hand-token of salutation"), it is the term for all the many complicated hand gestures, which may include other postures, that are part of Tibetan religious ritual. Combined with *aTSHal* ("wish"), or *PHyag aTSHal* ("salutation wish"), it is the term for the forms of prostration, both complete and incomplete, which constitute the core of the observance. Used alone *PHyag* also refers, either specifically or by inference, to an entire series of gestures, actions, and body attitudes which have both religious and social significance and which are subsumed in Tibetan as the *Gus Pai rNam aGyur* ("the manner-change of reverence"), or the attitudes of reverence.

CONFORMITY TO CRITERIA

The observance of salutation conforms to each of the criteria postulated in chapter iii. In the Tibetan frame of reference, it is a universal behavior pattern. Every Tibetan has participated in its gestures, postures, and exercises, which are the physical expression of worship. This does not mean that every Tibetan has performed all the gestures and assumed all the postures subsumed by *PHyag* but that he has at least participated in the minimal form of the observance.

Salutation consists of observable phenomena. Indeed, of all the Tibetan universals of religious observance, it is the one that is performed with the express purpose of being observed, for only then does it communicate. And even if done for its own sake, without thought of communication, it cannot be hidden. It has been observed by everyone who has had any firsthand contact with Tibetans in their own cultural setting. Deep hollows and grooves worn by hands and knees in the stone slabs and wooden planking before or within shrines are irrefutable evidence of the frequency and volume of this observance.[4]

It is religious in nature and purpose and is recognized and defined as such by the Tibetans. Many of the gestures and postures, it is true, have secular origins; and some of them are now used equally to express religious reverence and social or status reverence; but there are others that are reserved for religious purposes alone. Those that are now used for social purposes are mostly in the *Gus Pai rNam aGyur* ("the manner-change of reverence") category; those classified as *PHyag aTSHal* ("salutation wish"), or prostrations, though in general reserved for the purposes of religion, may, in instances of urgent need, be diverted to the purpose of placating secular authorities; but the numerous *PHyag rGya* ("salutation-token[s]") are strictly reserved for religious ritual. The most modern Tibetan dictionary defines *PHyag* and *PHyag aTSHal* as "making salutation to the Rare-Perfect Three,"[5] thus relating their function exclusively

---

[4] T. J. Norbu, *Tibet Is My Country* (1961), pp. 95–96. Few of those who have passed by shrines and their approaches have recorded the tell-tale marks left by millions of prostrations, which I have seen at every shrine that I have visited. Norbu's description was quoted to the other Tibetan scholars, who said in effect, "Why, of course, the marks which worshippers make when performing salutations are everywhere."

[5] dGe bSHes CHos Grags, *brTSams Pai brDa Dag Ming TSHig gSal Ba bZHugs So* (1957), p. 390.

to the highest concept in Buddhism, which in many respects occupies the place of God.

Lastly, the observance of *PHyag* has clearly delimited conceptual identity and unity. Although it has, as has been shown, close links with the other observances, in particular with circumambulation, and almost invariably is combined with one or more of them, it stands alone as the expression of mental attitudes and status relationships by gestures and postures.

PRE-BUDDHIST AND BUDDHIST HISTORY OF THE OBSERVANCE

The concept of salutation embodied in the word *PHyag* ("hand") existed in Tibet prior to the introduction of Buddhism. In the context of pre-Buddhist belief and behavior, however, the observance did not necessarily have the same significance and function it has now. The earliest known records of Tibetan history are made up principally of matter-of-fact and brief chronological entries, scraps of administrative and business trivia, emotion-charged prosody that often dramatically throws light on historical events, and the minute descriptions of burial rites. These records, in the main, are singularly devoid of any traces of Buddhist influence but reveal many instances of intrigue, conquest, and aggrandizement and exercise of royal power. In the records, the term *PHyag aTSHal,* or prostration, appears in two contexts: (1) when homage is offered to Tibetan kings, whether from conquered rivals to signalize surrender, from the leaders of subject peoples as they paid tribute or renewed their allegiance, or from Chinese diplomatic envoys, who, though they came from the Chinese emperor himself, were obliged to render the same homage;[6] and (2) during royal burial rites, which are unmistakably non-Buddhist in character. In the latter context, *PHyag aTSHal* signalizes the beginning of the elaborate rites and then is repeated again and again at every stage throughout the ceremony.[7] From the descriptions of early and obviously non-Buddhist funeral ceremonies, it seems clear that salutation and prostration were religious in nature and purpose.

In the first context—the offering of homage—prostration would appear to have an exclusively, or predominantly, political significance and secular function. There is much evidence, however, that the early Tibetan kings, who claimed descent from heaven and the power and right to re-

[6] J. Bacot, *Documents de Touen Houang* (1946), pp. 33, 39, 41, 45, 46, 48–50.

[7] M. Lalou, "Rituel Bon-po des funerailles royales," *Journal Asiatique,* T–CCXL–3 (1952), pp. 343–48.

turn there and were the reputed possessors of *aPHrul* ("manifestation magic"), sometimes called *aPHrul Rin Po CHe* ("great value magic"), exercised a religious as well as secular power.[8] For them, royal power was as much a function of their status as demigods, or manifestations of divinity, as it was of the exercise of secular leadership. The swearing and renewing of allegiance was a promise addressed equally to the king and to heaven and the gods. The kings exacted both worship and allegiance from those over whom they exercised control, and thus it seems clear that in pre-Buddhist times the performance of *PHyal aTSHal,* or prostration, was, if not predominantly, at least equally a religious observance.

As a religious observance salutation appeared in the very earliest stages of the development of Buddhism as a natural outgrowth of folkways and observances already in existence and not as a practice unique to the new teaching. In the story of the Buddha himself, we find such phrases as "approached with clasped hands," "paid reverence to the feet," "fell at the feet," "stretched out clasped hands," "with his cloak over his shoulder and one knee on the ground clasped hands," and "clasped his feet and put them on her head" to described postures and acts of reverence.[9] All these were quite obviously customary in the culture of that time.

The first appearance of these gestures and postures in Buddhism was in their function as symbols intended to communicate. Brahma himself, having become convinced, "entreated the Buddha with folded hands";[10] Sunanda, when vanquished in a musical competition, became full of faith and "made his salutations";[11] and the five ascetics who had previously agreed not to rise to show their rejection of the Buddha's new way, were so moved by his approach that they arose to greet him,[12] and that spontaneous gesture—stronger than any words—was their confession of faith. In each instance—with or without words—salutation communicated.

By the time Buddhism was established in Tibet, a process that had occurred in stages, from about A.D. 400 to about A.D. 800, the observance of salutation had undergone considerable change. That change may best be understood by brief reference to a similar change (described in a previous chapter) that took place in the expression of verbalized religion, which was also primarily concerned with the use of symbols in a system

[8] J. Bacot, *op. cit.*, pp. 85–86.

[9] E. J. Thomas, *The Life of the Buddha* (1931), pp. 39–40, 42, 100.

[10] E. Obermiller, *History of Buddhism* (1932), Part II, p. 41.

[11] *Ibid.*, p. 59.   [12] E. J. Thomas, *op. cit.*, p. 84.

of communication. The function of the verbalization of religion had at first been to maintain a continually verified and corrected oral tradition and to express such avowals as the "three refuge formulas" and similar confessions of faith. Then the idea gained acceptance that the words in themselves had power and were of value. From that point on, the expression of verbalized religion developed along two lines: (1) if words, both in meaning and in sound, had power in themselves, power was exerted by utterance and could be used for subjugating and controlling spirit beings; and (2) since words had value in themselves, the repetitious utterance of them could be utilized to achieve religious goals and could aid in the amassing of merit.

The changes in the development of the observance of salutation were along analogous lines. Gestures and postures were gradually assumed to have power and value in themselves. Because of their power, they gave added force to evocations, adjurations, and imprecations in thaumaturgic practice. And because they had value in themselves, their performance, and the multiplication of that performance, became a method whereby their value could be realized by the participants.

At the time of the final and most effective official introduction of Buddhism of the tantric school into Tibet, by Padma Sambhava in the eighth century, this development along the two lines of power and value, but with special emphasis upon the first, was already far advanced. Descriptions of the great thaumaturge's progress and activities in Tibet picture vividly the gestures and postures that were an important part of his effort. The theme of the *Padma Thang Yig* (*Le dict de Padma*) is characterized as the *gesture* of Padma.[13] One of his eight names is the lord who dances,[14] and it is said that the yoga method is practiced by taking full power in the *hand*.[15]

The gestures of his hands were the most important: he seized the muzzle of the great white yak, bound him, enchained him, and beat him; by describing with his finger a circle around the female spirit of the snow, he threw her into a lake of boiling water;[16] he opened his hands, and his enemies died; a flame of fire shot from his finger and burnt the robe of the king; he threw rocks at the feet of statues, and they moved and obediently followed him; and he traced a circle with his finger, and the sky turned red.[17] All of these are the manifestations of *PHyag* ("hand"), or salutation, which he used to further his mission.

[13] G.-Ch. Toussaint, *op. cit.*, "Argument Liminaire" (in Preface).
[14] *Ibid.*, p. 18.   [16] *Ibid.*, pp. 244-45.
[15] *Ibid.*, p. 327.   [17] *Ibid.*, pp. 340-41.

In the course of his mission, he and his various assistants were the objects of salutation by those impressed by, or converted to, his teaching. They are said to have greeted him with joined hands; to have knelt; to have prostrated themselves *comme un mur qui tombe* or *comme roulant à terre;* and to have danced to meet him, "the lord who dances." And there was a *KHa aGro Ma* ("sky-goer female") who learned *a souhait l'union qui sauve* (which probably means ritual sexual intercourse). Such were the gestures and postures offered as confessions of faith and in worship.[18]

It is, however, the successive conflicts concerning salutation between the Tibetan king of that time, *KHri Srong lDe bTSan,* and Padma Sambhava that are of particular significance, for they throw light on the transferral of certain forms of salutation from secular to religious uses and on the political changes of which that transferral was the portent. The tale is told in some detail. The king, who with great earnestness had invited Padma Sambhava to effect the conversion of Tibet to Buddhism, debated with himself, when preparing for their meeting, whether he should make salutation. He decided that since he was king and accustomed to receiving homage he should wait for the salutation to originate from the great Teacher. Padma Sambhava, in the meantime, had had a similar debate with himself and had decided that since he was the emanation of supernatural power and was bringing religion, rather than tribute and homage he should let the king make salutation. The meeting thus became a dramatic impasse, which the Teacher broke by moving his hands and letting fire shoot from his finger to scorch the robe of the king, whereupon the king and his courtiers bowed down and rolled on the ground; afterward the king confessed that he had been wrong and was told to create stupas, in which Padma placed treasures, as an act of penance.[19]

At a later period of their association, the king had second thoughts about the advisability of his concession and tried to reassert his preeminence over the same issue. Calling himself the most high chief of all the black heads and claiming to be able to dispatch the beasts with spirit manes [cavalry?], he declared that he felt the Teacher should make salutation to him. But the thaumaturge answered that since he was lord of all yoga, the essence of the body of knowledge, and since the king had requested power from him the king should make salutation. He then summoned the lightning, threw rocks at the feet of the guardian gods to exact their obedience, and by drawing a circle with his finger, turned the sky

18 *Ibid.,* pp. 183, 185, 249, 255, 302.
19 *Ibid.,* pp. 249–55.

red. With carefuly stated reluctance, the king conceded again and made salutation, voicing the fear, however, that by this act he was placing in jeopardy what was due him as a descendant of kings. The writer of the chronicle then makes the comment that every reader must make his own judgment of the case. The narrative includes a cryptic statement to the effect that the king, in making salutation, let fall his crown.[20] This may mean, of course, merely that his helmet fell off.

The real significance of these incidents in the conflict between the religious and the secular, in which religion appears to have emerged as victor, is quite clear. They reveal a head-on confrontation of two power systems engaged in a fight for eventual control of Tibet. The conflict continued, in varying degrees of intensity, for centuries. Indeed, in some form or other, it has continued down into the present. But history has recorded the over-all outcome as a victory of the religious interests and a steady gain in ascendency of religious power over secular power. The victory of the thaumaturge and mystic over the king in the matter of salutation is symbolic of all the changes that took place. In the process of change, many of the traditional gestures and postures of respect that had functioned both as worship and as recognition of power and prestige, were appropriated exclusively to the uses of religion. Others continued to be used as a respectful acknowledgment of differences in status and power. In the latter role, they appear in social intercourse, political activities, and even trade relationships.

CATEGORIES OF THE OBSERVANCE

The heritage of the past from which the Tibetan draws the postures and gestures that constitute his present system of salutation is made up of universal symbols of communication common to all mankind; the practices of greeting and homage current in ancient Tibetan society; pre-Buddhist religious observances; and Buddhist importations of both the earlier and the later tantric schools. As now practiced, the forms of salutation fall into three categories: (1) the somewhat general *Gus Pai rNam aGyur* ("the manner-change[s] of reverence"), or attitudes of reverence, which are utilized for both religious and secular purposes; (2) the forms of *PHyag aTSHal*, or prostration, which are, with few exceptions, limited to religious purposes; and (3) the very numerous *PHyag rGya*, or ritual gestures and postures, which are used exclusively in religious rituals of varying complexity.

[20] *Ibid.*, pp. 309, 339–41.

The Attitudes of Reverence

The *Gus Pai rNam aGyur,* or attitudes of reverence, may in fact be either attitudes or gestures, for when a gesture is arrested in time and fixed in space it becomes an attitude: removing one's hat, for example, is a gesture that becomes an attitude when the one who made it continues to stand or sit with head bared. These attitudes and gestures are numerous and interwoven with much complexity in the web of Tibetan behavior patterns. Sometimes they are conditioned by the situation, the same gesture having different meanings in different situations; and frequently they reflect avoidances and nuances in interpersonal relationships that cannot be expressed in words. With few exceptions, they appear in both secular and religious use, the emphasis varying with the individual. A complete listing of them, which is far beyond the scope of this book, would probably constitute a cultural inventory of such magnitude that ethos and configuration might appear. The principal ones, however, will be listed and briefly described.

As confirmation of their close relationship to *PHyag* ("hand"), although that word is not a part of their name, most of them involve the use of the hands either alone or as aids to gestures and postures. The simplest hand gesture, and one of which the Tibetans appear scarcely conscious, is the raising of the right hand to the level of the head to accompany greeting or ejaculations of wonder and surprise. When, for example, *AH* ("hail") is sounded alone with no ritual involvement and unaccompanied by this simple gesture, it has, in general, no religious significance; but when the hand goes up, the gesture of reverence makes the utterance of *AH* religious in nature. *AH* then no longer means "hail," the word with which one greets kinsfolk (e.g., *AH KHu* ["hail uncle"], *AH Ma* ["hail mother"], and so on), but has become, to quote a dictionary definition, "a mystic Sanskrit syllable"[21] and a part of the expression of verbalized religion.

A hand gesture may also accompany the pouring of tea into the bowl of an honored guest. The hand which is not holding the kettle is held palm upward while the tea is poured. The gesture becomes part of a religious observance when it accompanies the pouring of water into offering bowls.

Both hands are used in a gesture of greeting: the palms are joined, fingers pointing upward, and held against the chest. The gesture becomes exclusively religious when care is taken to keep the hands hollowed so that only the finger tips, sides of the thumbs, and base of the hand at the

[21] H. A. Jaschke, *op. cit.,* p. 603.

wrist have contact. This form of the gesture, called the *Me Tog aBu* ("flower bud"), is also the first stage of all the *PHyag aTSHal*, or prostrations, which constitute a separate category. It is possible that, as a greeting, this gesture is an Indic importation, for Eastern Tibetans sometimes use the clasped hands of the Chinese gesture in the same circumstances. Borrowing of gestures goes on constantly, and modern Tibetans are learning to shake—or rather hold—hands.

In another form of greeting, both hands are used, with the palms turned upward, either alone or in combination with other gestures. This is equally a secular greeting and, when meeting lamas and other clergy, a religious gesture. The presentation to a friend or in greeting of the *KHa bDag* ("mouth tie"), or scarf, with gifts or by itself, using both hands, is a secular social gesture; when presented to a lama or image as an offering, it becomes religious. Passing a bowl of tea with both hands—if just one is used, it is an insult—is also a social gesture; but when a bowl of pure water is so presented as one of the eight offerings, the gesture becomes a religious one.

One or both hands are used to aid or facilitate a number of other gestures or attitudes. As a religious gesture a cloth mask is worn over the mouth; in an emergency, any bit of cloth or the edge of a garment held in the teeth may do. Lacking any of these, a hand may be held over the mouth. Hands are also used in removing hats, by both men and women, and whenever the queue is worn wrapped around the head as in Eastern Tibet, it is taken down to hang free in a similar gesture. This is a Chinese practice and may well be an instance of the borrowing of a culture trait.

In this context, the handling of weapons is a somewhat complicated one. Guns, which are usually carried slung on the back, are brought around to a position across the chest when on horseback or are taken off and carried when on foot as a gesture of reverence toward religious persons or objects. But the same gesture is also merely good manners when entering a house or tent. The sword is generally worn by laymen tucked into the girdle at the front of the body and is almost as universal as that necessary part of apparel. In greeting religious persons or on approaching a religious object, the sword is removed—still in the sheath—and carried in the hand. This, too, is good manners when entering a house or tent.

All of the gestures thus far mentioned are used equally as secular forms of greeting and as expressions of religious reverence; but the ceremonial covering of the upper body, especially the breasts of women, is one gesture that, by the manner in which it is performed, appears to draw a line between secular and religious reverence. Among the common folk of Tibet—peasants and herders alike—the women engage in strenuous work with the torso exposed; the arms are withdrawn from the sleeves of the outer cloak, and the sleeves are wrapped around the body. When greeting guests or others—even those to whom secular reverence is due—these women leave their breasts uncovered with no embarrassment or even apparent self-consciousness. But if they meet clerics or have any occasion to approach a shrine, they either pull up their outer garments or at least raise one of the sleeves carefully to cover their breasts. The same woman who is stripped to the waist as she goes around in the hot sun doing her chores pulls up her cloak in order to be fully covered, in the same hot sun, when she goes through the strenuous routine of a hundred full prostrations before a shrine or sacred object.

Attitudes and gestures of reverence expressed by the body are the following: dismounting from a horse, dropping to the knees, rising to the feet, and bending the body into a stooping posture or bowing the head. All of these are universal and might easily be taken to be unambiguous. In the context of Tibetan patterns of behavior, however, some of them are conditioned by the situations in which they occur and thus are ambiguous. Dismounting from a horse is seemingly unambiguous as a gesture of reverence, but as a simple action—the implications of which are in the back of every Tibetan's mind—it might be the prelude to the throwing of stones or gunfire. Rising to the feet and its reverse, the taking of a seat, are also situation-conditioned gestures or attitudes, which have differing significance, depending on the situation. To leave one's seat and remain standing is, in general, an obvious gesture of reverence; and the reverse is at best a discourtesy and at worst an insult. As religious forms of salutation, this remains unfailingly true. However, in Tibet, whenever there is a situation of disagreement and tension, rising to one's feet may be almost as provocative as laying hands on a weapon; deliberately taking a seat, on the other hand, while others stand or move becomes, not a discourtesy, but a conciliatory gesture—an offer of argument and negotiation instead of violence. It takes iron nerve to take one's seat in such circumstances, but I have seen it work, with disputatious bullies spoiling for a fight as well as with charging dogs.

Maintaining a stooping posture and remaining on one's knees are also used as both religious and secular acts and attitudes of reverence. The two, however, have a much more frequent incidence, and wider and more general base of participation, as expressions of religious reverence. This is especially true in those regions farthest from the tightly, and more harshly, ruled peoples of Central Tibet. Indeed, in eastern and northeastern Tibet, kneeling, although compatible with a man's self-esteem as a religious gesture, is quite unacceptable as a secular gesture and only occurs at the breaking point from great need or terror.

Among the many gestures and attitudes of reverence, there is one that is distinctively and even grotesquely Tibetan: the protrusion of the tongue as far as it will go to indicate admiration and reverence. How grotesque this may seem is revealed in the recorded reactions—not altogether felicitous in many instances—of many Westerners. An eighth-century Chinese account says: *Quand ils saluent, ils touchent la terre de leur deux mains et font l'aboiement du chien. . . ."* The detail concerning the "barking like dogs" probably referred to the combination of the tongue gesture and the utterance of *Lags So!*—the Tibetan assent and homage honorific.[22] Only inferentially does this tongue gesture become religious.

Finally, the touching of heads and the holding of hands when meeting constitute a class of observance that mark the point where *Gus Pai rNam aGyur*, or attitude of reverence, may also function as simple *dGaa Bai rHan aGyur* ("the manner-change of liking"), or attitude of affection. The touching of heads as part of the bow of greeting is mostly seen among the clergy but also takes place between members of the laity. A sort of friendly taking and holding of hands also occurs. This is an indigenous gesture and not the shaking of hands acquired from the West. Both of these observances may be nothing more than expressions of affection, having nothing to do with reverence. Indeed, holding hands is also part of flirting between the sexes.

Forms and Objects of Prostration

In the category of *PHyag aTSHal*, or prostration, there are only three standard and generally accepted forms or variations, although individuals may occasionally improvise variations of detail. In the order of their increasing "depth" or effectiveness and worth, the three are known as *Yan Log gSum TSHogs* ("threefold members"), or three-point prostration, *Yan Log lNGa TSHogs* ("fivefold members"), or five-point prostration, and *Yan Log brGyad TSHogs* ("eightfold members") or eight-point prostration.

The first of these is not universally or even widely in use. It consists

[22] P. Pelliot, *Histoire ancienne de Tibet* (1962), p. 3. The correlation of this ascription of "barking like a dog"—a strongly pejorative and typically Chinese view—and the tongue gesture receives additional support from Dezhung Rinpoche. Without any self-consciousness, he explained that it was a most natural way to express friendliness and liking, for dogs showed their tongues and licked to show affection—a good index of the Tibetan attitude toward dogs.

of cupping the hands in the "lotus-bud" gesture; then placing the palms of the hands on a conveniently located ledge or shelf; and finally bringing the forehead down to touch the ledge between the hands, after which the upright posture is resumed. This is, in effect, the minimal observance of prostration; the two hands and the forehead having touched, it is three-point. The second consists of cupping the hands in the lotus-bud gesture; going down on the knees; placing both hands on the ground; touching the forehead to the ground between the hands; and then resuming the upright posture. The two palms, the two knees, and the forehead having touched, it is five-point. The third and most highly regarded form of prostration, or eight-point, consists of cupping the hands; going down on the knees; placing the palms of both hands forward on the ground; pushing them as far ahead as possible in order to bring the entire body flat on the ground, making certain that the two knees, the stomach, the chest, the mouth, the forehead, and the two hands have touched.

In the execution of each of these three forms of prostration, it is the hands which lead, with the body and all motion following, emphasizing again the basic relationship between hands and salutation. *PHYag* ("salutation") is derived from and is but an extension of *PHyag* ("hand"). It is these three forms of prostration that, in basic form, significance, and universality, constitute the core of the observance of salutation in Tibetan behavior patterns.

The gestures and attitudes of the two categories previously mentioned are peripheral in importance. The attitudes of reverence have a certain base of universal practice but are expressions of social behavior—courtesy and avoidance—as well as expressions of religious reverence. They are conditioned by the situation and cannot be repeated merely for the sake of repetition. The ritual gestures and posturing of *PHyag rGya*, on the other hand, are exclusively religious in nature but lack universality in Tibetan behavior patterns. They are the activities of the specialists and adepts and are not performed by the average Tibetan. As the component parts or accompaniment of ritual, moreover, they offer the possibility of repetition only if the entire routine of the ritual is repeated. As the core observance, *PHyag aTSHal*, or prostration, is both devoted to religion and universally practiced with much repetition. This is the form that is emphasized in the often repeated asseveration that punctuates much praying: *SHa Kya THub Pa Dang dKon mCHog gSum La PHyag aTSHal Lo* ("I make salutation to Gotama the Buddha and the Rare-Perfect Three").

It is in the meticulous persistence with which this observance is repeated and the use of the rosary to record the totals that it becomes a close analogue of the observance of *CHos aDon,* the expression of verbal-ized religion. Of the three degrees of prostration, the relatively easy three-point one is least used. It requires the special facility of a ledge or coun-ter and is, moreover, considered the shirker's way out. The most compli-cated, or eight-point, form is reserved for particular forms of penance or is addressed toward religious persons or objects of very special sanctity and importance. The form which is in most general use, and of which the greatest totals of repetition are recorded, is the five-point—knees, hands, and forehead. When the best part of the day is devoted to this form of salutation, two thousand prostrations constitute an average stint. Those who put in extra long hours and are tirelessly energetic can rack up a total of five thousand in a single day. Individual accumulations within a lifetime—all carefully recorded—may run into the millions.

Prostrations are always centered on an object. They are not simply acts but salutations to a person or object. They are intended to communi-cate specifically and directly and are not vague broadcasts, although at-tention often wanders and shifts from object to manner. In general, the object has material, or phenomenal, existence, but the Tibetan concept of existence also permits the projected, or noumenal, to be the focus of the performance. Thus, prostrations are made to the following: images and graphic representations; persons, as individuals or in assembly; the Bud-dhist scriptures and religious writings; shrines, which may range from the great structures of a monastery complex to a personal charm box placed on a piece of turf; offerings, either presented or displayed; topo-graphical features such as mountains, lakes, springs, caves, and trees; and noumenal conceptualizations which are the realization of *sGom* ("medi-tation").

Images, either three dimensional, in relief, or graphically repre-sented, are the most frequent objects of this form of the observance. The *sKu aDraa* ("bodylike"), or image, is an already prepared point of focus, needing no mental or psychic effort of projection or conceptualization. It is the Buddha, saint, god or demon being addressed who receives the sal-utation, although the physical form of the act points toward the image. Hollows and grooves are worn in the stone slabs and wooden planks be-fore these images by the knees and palms of those who may spend a full day performing five thousand prostrations in order that virtue may be amassed and the sins of the body expiated by the work of the body. Large and small, in gold, silver, brass, stone, wood, and clay, and traced on pa-per, silk, and stone, there are millions of religious images in Tibet. Most of them are collected in the *lHa KHang* ("god-house[s]") of religious establishments such as monasteries, hermitages, and village or familial chapels. Many, however, are in the possession of individuals and so are immediately available at any time or place.

The intensity of object-directed salutation and the ratio of its performance to that of circumambulation are aptly illustrated in the direct account of religious observance by one Tibetan woman: "In one day of the time I spent at the monastery I made 2,000 *PHyag aTSHal Yan Log INGa TSHogs*, or five-point prostrations, before the *lHa KHang* ("god-house") and accomplished 300 circumambulations—it was a small building."[23]

Persons, as individuals or in assembly, may and do become the objects of this rite. For example, salutation may be directed toward emanation-body lamas, because they partake of the Buddhahood. Not only may they receive this expression of homage when alive but their mummies or, if they are cremated, their funeral pyres may become the focus of the rite. Diviners and sorcerers—even those who are not clerics—frequently become the objects of the rite, particularly when they are in the state of seizure and as *lHa Pa* ("god one[s]") are regarded as directly representing deity.

Individual *Grwa Ba*, or monks, are not entitled to receive such homage, except when they are performing religious rituals of offering or expressing the verbalization of religion, at which times prostrations may be made to them. When they are congregated in either large or small assemblies, however—four monks or more constitute an assembly—they become a proper object of the rite, for they then are the *dKon mCHog dGe aDun* ("rare-perfect virtuous assembly"), or Community, the third entity of the Buddhist Triad.

The sacred writings are the record, and thus the most concrete manifestation, of *CHos* ("religion"), which as "the law" is the second entity of the Triad. As shown in chapter iv, they have acquired very high and holy status. Thus, whenever they are carried in a procession or are exhibited, prostrations are made to them. The knowledge that some portion of them is within a shrine or container of any kind is sufficient to make it an object worthy of the rite. Touching the forehead with a book, or touching a book with the forehead, is a variant development of a reverent gesture which, in the special context of honoring the book, sometimes does duty for the rite of prostration.

Next to images, shrines are the most frequent objects of prostration.

---

[23] Personal communication from Dalmo La. This was part of a detailed description of what she did when she went on pilgrimage.

Such shrines vary in size from the largest and most elaborate *CHos rTen* ("religion base[s]"), or stupas, of the great monastery complexes and the *Jo KHang* ("lord house") of Lhasa, which is the holiest shrine of Tibetan Buddhism,[24] down to the single inscription carved on a stone slab in a stone pile, topped by one clay image, and the even smaller *Gau* ("charm box"), which most Tibetans possess and wear suspended on the chest, slung under the arm, or carried on the back. These charm boxes may be extremely ornate, of gold and silver, and may house relics, scraps of writing, or pills made and blessed by emanation-body lamas. They may also be, however, the merest amulets, preferably sewn within red leather packets or wrapped in cloth and suspended from the neck by a leather thong. In the latter case, they are called *Srung aKHor* ("protection wheel"), but their function is the same as that of the charm box. Whenever any one of them is set up—on a block of sod, a mound of earth, a stone, or a block of wood—it becomes a shrine at which prostrations may be made.

Prostrations to offerings that are displayed as a part of the ritual of offering or to such visual offerings as arrow-offerings to mountain gods, mountain-pass cairns, butter friezes, and so on, do occur, but the appropriateness of such homage is questionable. Many of the clergy discourage such practice and insist that *PHyag aTSHal* should only be directed toward the Rare-Perfect Three, or "Jewel Triad," in all its manifestations and toward the gods. The prostrations of those who are officiating at offerings are considered to be directed toward the deity who is the recipient rather than to the offering itself. The stages of any religious observance are not in themselves the proper objects of the homage of prostration.

Topographical features such as mountains, lakes, caves, springs, unusual cliff and rock formations, and even trees, because of their association with the great mountain gods, serpent spirits, earth-owners, and other autochthonous deities of Tibet, constitute focuses for the rite. Of these deities, the mountain gods are those of greatest repute. Those associated with such mountains as gNYan CHen THang lHa ("Great-Argali-Expanse God"), gNYan Po gYu rTSe ("the Argali Turquoise Peak"), and the AH Mes rMa Ma CHen ("Hail Ancient One, Great Peacock") are well-known representatives of the many mountain gods that perch on the numerous mountain peaks of Tibet. The *Klu* ("serpent spirits") are primarily associated with bodies of water, lakes and springs, which are the gateways of their watery realm; and the *Sa bDag* ("soil-owners") are associ-

[24] L. A. Waddell, *The Buddhism of Tibet* (1895), pp. 300–304; P. Landon, *The Opening of Tibet* (1906), pp. 383–94.

ated with unusual rock and cliff formations and caves. Caves, however, more frequently owe their importance to having been the abodes of famous hermits and saints. Prostrations at these topographical features are a concomitant of the rite of circumambulation. That is, the primary reason for visiting the great mountains, for example, is to perform the rite of circumambulation, and the performance of salutation by prostrations is interspersed throughout the course of this primary activity. This qualification also holds good for most of the performances of the rite before shrines. Tibetans, in general, do not make journeys to the topographical features to perform salutations to them but primarily to circumambulate them; when there, however, they mix prostrations with circumambulation.

The making of salutations to noumenal conceptualizations resulting from *sGom* ("meditation") theoretically offers an unlimited number of possibilities; all the manifestations of the Buddhahood and all the gods and demons can, by meditative practice, be evoked into a noumenal existence in any convenient place. In practice, such conceptualization is generally related to the four points of the compass. It is said that when one faces toward the east in the "field of manifest delight," the Buddha *rDo rJe Sems dPaa* ("lord stone"—i.e., diamond—"hero mind") may be evoked by meditation to become the object of salutations; when one faces south in the "glorious field," the Buddha *Rin CHen aByung gNas* ("from whence the precious") may be evoked; when one faces west in the "realm of peace," the Buddha *mGon Po Od dPag Med* ("lord of unmeasured light") may be evoked; and finally, when one faces northward where "excellent deeds are completed," the Buddha *Don Yod Grub Pa* ("cause-possessing realization") may be evoked.[25]

PHyag aTSHal, or salutation by prostration, in the overwhelming majority of instances, is religious in intent. When directed toward all the persons and objects that have been enumerated, it is exclusively religious. It is not part of an over-all pattern of behavior that may be equally secular or religious in intent. But on somewhat rare occasions, when great urgency or overwhelming terror raises a secular need to the level of religious desire, prostration may be performed toward secular authorities. It is then known as *aJig rTen PHyag aTSHal* ("worldly prostration"). But, as in the matter of genuflection, prostration is not made willingly for secular purposes, nor is it recalled with pride or recorded, as it is when it is *CHos PHyag aTSHal,* or "religious prostration."

The minimal observance of both *Gus Pai rHam aGyur,* the attitude

---

25 L. A. Waddell, *op. cit.*, pp. 130, 347, 350, 351. Waddell lists five possibilities: the four directions plus the center. My Tibetan collaborators listed only four.

of reverence, and *PHyag aTSHal,* prostration, is universal. Every Tibetan has made some gesture or assumed some attitude of reverence toward the phenomenal aspects of religion and, by intention, toward the noumenal essence of religion. Every Tibetan has also performed some, if not all, of the forms of prostration toward religious objects with religious intent. Thus, both of these categories of salutation are universals of behavior in the Tibetan context.

The Symbolic Gestures and Postures

The ritual gestures and postures in the category of *PHyag rGya* ("hand-token salutation") differ from the salutations of the first two categories in a number of particulars. First, their performance, like the verbalization of a charm or sutra, is reserved for the experts and mainly occurs in the course of the rituals of offering and during verbalization of religion. Second, they are never employed in any secular context or for any secular purpose but only occur in religious rituals. Furthermore, although they resemble the gestures and attitudes of reverence—in that they are frequently conditioned by the situation in which they occur and, of themselves, offer no possibility of repetition for the sake of repetition— they are often repeated, as the rituals of which they constitute a part are repeated, and to this degree resemble the repetitious performance of prostration. The category for which *PHyag aGya* has been used as the over-all classificatory term is made up of three subcategories: (1) *PHyag rGya* ("hand-token salutation"), *PHyag rGya CHen Po* ("the great hand-token salutation"), and (3) *Las Kyi PHyag rGya* ("the hand-token salutation of the deed").

In the subcategory *PHyag rGya,* there are more than a thousand different hand gestures. There are, for example, corresponding hand gestures for each of the many different kinds of offerings and many others that are integral parts of numerous rituals—supplication, imprecation, exorcism, and so on. The gestures involve the precise positioning of the hands and fingers and are normally performed when the participant is seated in any of the postures in which the clergy traditionally sit.[26] When

---

[26] *Ibid.,* pp. 141, 147, 335, 336, 349. The citations from Waddell's book give examples of the kind and number of gestures and postures found in Tibetan iconography in which the hands play the most important part. The gestures and postures shown in such books as *Tibetan Painted Scrolls,* by G. Tucci, and *Tibetan Iconography,* by A. Gordon, are only a part of the hand gestures—"over a thousand"—spoken of by my Tibetan colleagues. Dezhung Rinpoche gave some remarkable demonstrations of both still and moving gestures synchronized with the intoning of spells. Only motion-picture photography with sound effects could make a satisfactory record of their variety, grace, and rhythm.

making offerings, the participant may be standing; and in iconography, Buddhas are sometimes represented as standing while exhibiting the hand gestures. Generally, however, whenever the gestures are executed from a kneeling, standing, or moving position, they are considered to have become part of dance and dramatic routines. While primarily religious—in origin, at least—the latter activities have become, in some instances, secular in nature and purpose.

The *PHyag rGya* are most closely linked with the expression of verbalized religion, for many of them are designed to mirror, in sign language, the content of what is being expressed verbally. With the rhythmic chant of verbalization, the hands move in a synchronized rhythm, forming a symbolic visual accompaniment of much grace.

The *PHyag rGya* that correspond to the many forms of offering may be used with the presentation of the offering or as an esoteric substitute for the offering. For example, the following gestures may accompany or be substituted for the eight offerings "to accomplish drawing-near": (1) the fee offering—the two hands closed into fists, backs downward, with the thumbs inside the pointer fingers and the middle finger on each hand pointing straight out to touch the tip of the other middle finger; (2) the cooling-feet offering—the same as number one but with the backs of the hands upward; (3) the flower offering—hands closed into fists side by side, backs downward and the thumb of each hand inside the fingers of each hand; (4) the burnt-incense offering—the same as number three but with the backs of the hands upward; (5) the butter-fire offering—hands closed into fists, palms facing, with thumbs up (this gesture is identical with the secular gesture for excellence or highest appreciation); (6) the scented-water offering—hands open, palms downward, with the fingers pointing straight forward; (7) the face-food offering—the same as number six but with palms upward; and (8) the music offering—hands closed into fists, with thumbs inside fingers but with the two pointer fingers straight and the tips touching.

The second subcategory, *PHyag rGya Chen Po*, is the form of *PHyag rGya* based on meditation. By meditation and psychic effort, a noumenal, or conceptualized, salutation is substituted, presumably on a higher level, for the act of salutation having phenomenal existence. In the tantric tradition, such exercises are for the adepts alone, and their performance— although unverifiable by nature—is a part of legend and story.

Las Kyi PHyag rGya ("the hand-token salutation of the deed")— "deed" may also refer to Karma—is the term which subsumes all the effort and exercises leading to and including ritual sexual union, which appears in Tibetan iconography in the *Yab-Yum* ("father-mother") representations. Meditation is, of course, a most important part of this ritual and leads, in the tantric tradition, to final realization. It, too, is only for the adept, and its existence is more a matter of legend and story than trustworthy attestation. Leaders of the tantric school, however, such as Padma Sambhava, Marpa, and Milaraspa may be cited as examples.

THE FUNCTIONAL ROLE OF SALUTATION

The performance of salutation, which is a strictly religious effort in the great majority of its manifestations and is so judged by the Tibetans, is somewhat more difficult to evaluate in terms of contributions to the individual and to the culture of the society than the observance of offering. It lends itself less easily to quantitative measurement, for it has nothing to do with material possessions and can only be tabulated as units of effort. None of the effort is harnessed in any way to production, except, in a metaphysical context, production of unmeasured and immeasurable virtue. Yet contributions do exist and are related both to the individual and to his culture and society. In varying degrees, the provenance of the contributions of salutation is shared with one or more of the other religious observances. In each instance of sharing, however, the observance of salutation places its own distinctive stamp on its portion of the contribution, and in one instance, the contribution is uniquely its own.

The Function of Salutation in Relation to the Individual Tibetan

In common with the observances of the verbalization of religion and the making of offerings, the observance of salutation gives the individual Tibetan assurance that with each prostration or attitude of reverence he is being involved in the processes of religion and that as the prostrations and attitudes are repeated and tallied the lords or powers of religion have cause to view him with favor and extend their blessing. Furthermore, the gesture itself, by its intrinsic power, has operated on his behalf. The degree to which this has been accomplished is somewhat less than in the case of the other two observances. Gestures are neither quite as powerful as verbalized religion nor as well sanctioned by sacred history. They cannot operate indirectly by sponsorship, and they cannot be multiplied. Nor do they have the fruitful associations and promises of offerings.

The observance also has a very direct and personal application. The Tibetan feels that the pains and ills of his body are being met by that same body and that the sins of the body are likewise being expiated by his effort. These satisfactions, moreover, are psychologically and physiologically real. Fears, frustrations, tensions, and problems are being resolved by action. There is an opportunity to pit muscle, wind, and stamina against impending disaster. One can act, not sit and wait, and the results of action are real.

In common with the other religious observances, salutation establishes patterns of behavior that are identification and recognition signs for the members of the group. But the degree to which salutations operate in this way is less than in the other observances. Salutations are not as continuous in time, and thus as easily noted, as the expression of verbalized religion; nor do they have the impact value of offering. Much of the binding power of joint effort is also lacking. The performance is largely a personal matter: the participant is alone or too occupied to notice others, who are equally occupied and have neither time nor strength to look his way. He is preoccupied with his shortness of breath, his cramping muscles, and the tally he makes on the beads of his rosary.

The direct contribution to the physical well-being and health of the individual—as distinct from the reduction of tension—is a function of this observance that is not shared by the two activity observances thus far investigated. Stated in simple terms, *PHyag aTSHal*, or prostration—the aspect of salutation that is universal in the Tibetan context—is a moderately rigorous series of limbering and conditioning exercises involving the limbs and the trunk of the body. These exercises are in general little practiced by the young—and presumably the most vigorous—nor at times when other activity is at its height. They are, however, diligently practiced by those who have leisure and special motivation and at seasons when there is the least demand on everyone for physical activity. Thus, the older Tibetans, who, with increasing years, begin to think more and more of amassing virtue and who have already transferred to the younger generation the management of affairs; the wealthy, who have more leisure; and the members of the clergy, who have been released from worldly and material responsibilities, are the ones who put most effort and gain the most from this exercise, which can be quite strenuous. (Let anyone who doubts this perform one hundred prostrations without pause and he will be convinced.)

These members of the Tibetan population are the ones who most need exercise. The wealthy and the clergy are frequently sedentary in their habits to a very considerable degree; the food they eat is costive, and many have elimination troubles. The aged take on, more and more, the habit of sitting in the sun or by the fire. For all of them, the compulsion to perform salutations at any and all shrines, intensified by the knowledge that others are also making prostrations, sets them to bending, kneeling, and stretching. They work hard, motivated not by the desire, of doubtful worth, to take off a few pounds but by the sanctions and rewards of religion, for they use the body, which has been the vehicle of most of their sins, as the instrument for canceling out some of those sins. Thus, the contribution that salutation—diligently practiced—makes to physical and mental health is a real one.

The Function of Salutation in Relation to the Culture and Society

In common with the other religious observances, salutation provides a culture-wide pattern for the use of time that might otherwise be empty or conducive to boredom. Thus, in the sense of being a positive addition, this observance enriches the culture and is a stabilizing factor in society.

The observance makes two other, more specific contributions. One of these owes its existence solely to the observance of salutation; the other, to the observance of salutation and the other observances, in particular, circumambulation. The former affects the arts and Tibetan forms of politeness and manual habits; and the latter, by its power to attract individual Tibetans to religious, trade, and cultural centers, exerts a strong unifying influence on the society as a whole.

As a religious observance salutation emphasizes the functional value of gestures and postures, giving to the hands a special role. This emphasis exerts considerable influence on the art of design and on drama. In sculpture and painting, much attention is given to the lines and proportions of the hands, because the gestures, in addition to being graceful, have crucial significance in the total representation. The gesturing hands, rather than the face, often constitute the real focus toward which attention is drawn. The obvious importance of manual gestures leads first to mimicry and then carries over into their employment in religious drama and dance. From there, it is but a step to their use, with all the improvisations that stem from the action of the play, in secular drama and the recital of epics and ballads, thus diffusing them throughout the folklore of a people.

Everyone who hears these dramas and epics sees, too, with heightened receptiveness, the graceful gestures, which, as an embellishment of action, tempt each observer to mimic their pattern. That mimicry appears in the play of children, in the gestures of hospitality, as an accompaniment to oratory, and in the proliferation of graceful forms of politeness so marked in Tibetan social usage. Perhaps, it has also contributed to the often remarked grace of movement of the hands and fingers, possessed by so many Tibetans.

I have known nomadic women, who milked cows, tended fires, and spread cow dung to dry for fuel, and whose unwashed hands and wrists were incrusted with the traces of these chores, but who, when they offered a bowl of tea to a guest or even assayed employment of an unfamiliar fork or spoon, made each movement with sure grace and with faultless line of wrist, hand, and finger.

The function which the observance of salutations shares with the other religious observances, but particularly with circumambulation, is the establishment of factors of strong centripal attraction that draw the widely scattered people of Tibet to centers where a commonality of culture and behavior patterns may be sensed and strengthened. The population is distributed thinly over vast areas—the peasants in their individual farmhouses, hamlets, and villages, and the nomads not only scattered but always on the move. Cities, as centers where the people may gather, do not exist. Lhasa, which most closely approaches the status of a city, is not a true city but a somewhat unique aggregation of ecclesiastical and governmental dignitaries—including the nobility—and their retinues, a large population of monks, and a trading community, which together form a permanent nucleus around which a large floating population of pilgrims swarms.

The other large centers of trade in Tibet are located, almost without exception, in the immediate vicinity of monasteries and are frequently known by the names of the latter. The town so-called, or community of traders, is an outgrowth, or enlargement, of the original settlement of the *mTHaa Ba* ("edge one[s]") around the monastery. The *mTHaa Ba* lived as close to the monastery as permitted for protection and to supply the needs of the monks. They naturally traded with the worshipers who came because of religious motivation but who found trade an additional incentive and convenience. Eventually, such a community becomes a center of trade in its own right. It is, in effect, a market town but never a true city. In many instances the *PHo Brang* ("palace"), *mKHar* ("tower"), or *rDZongs* ("fort") of the local feudal lord is cheek by jowl with the monastery, which may have been built under his patronage. Much of the administration of government, whether by feudal lords, appointed officials, or the authorities of the monastic hierarchy, proceeds from this center, which has a threefold character and reason for being—religious, commercial, and political.

All of the religious observances play some role in attracting the widely scattered and conspicuously foot-loose people of Tibet from their isolated villages and encampments to these centers. The observance of salutation, however, by being distinctively object-directed, plays a special role in focusing religious activity on a place and localizing religious observance. All the visible manifestations of *dKon mCHog gSum* ("Rare-Perfect Three")—emanation-body lamas and images of the Buddhahood, the complete written record of the doctrine, and the congregated monks of the community—are within the monastery, to be found and worshiped by salutation. To that point in space, the ones who would make salutation must come. Thus drawn, like iron filings to a magnet, the people of Tibet are brought to these centers to make salutation and stay for the length of time that is necessary. While there, in a common purpose, they come to sense the oneness of their habits and viewpoints and the focus of their desires and aspirations; and they realize themselves to be one people— the *Bod KHa Ba* ("the Tibet part one[s]"). Nor do they neglect the opportunities of a market that is synchronized with their gathering. In this manner, the observance of salutation becomes one of the factors—and an important one—contributing to the homogeneity of Tibetan culture, to the strong societal self-consciousness of the Tibetans, and to the surprising solidarity of their society.

CHAPTER EIGHT

THE PERFORMANCE OF

BSKOR BA:

CIRCUMAMBULATION

The observances considered thus far, although gathered under the heading "Tibetan universals of religious observance," have a broader frame of reference than Tibet. They are all demonstrably part of universal human experience and practice. But the performance of *bsKor Ba* ("circumambulation") appears to be more restricted although it is evident that one aspect of this practice has a very wide distribution among many cultures as a form of religious observance. However, it cannot be shown that, as a consciously formalized rite, it is found in all human societies.

The making of a circuit, for one purpose or another, appears in many histories and in the mythology and folklore of many peoples. The children of Israel ceremoniously circled the walls of Jericho a stated number of times. The fairies of the English greensward dance in a ring, and the Maypole festival follows the same pattern. American Indian dances, in common with most African or any other tribal dances, make a circle around a fixed and significant center. Moslem pilgrims in Mecca circle the Kaaba seven times, but in a counterclockwise direction.[1] There are instances of it in Grecian, Roman, and Egyptian practices, and its persistence in Celtic tradition is of particular interest. The modern Gaels characterize the relative merits of clockwise versus counterclockwise circling as follows: *deisul,* the clockwise circuit, is lucky and propitious; and *widdershins,* the counterclockwise circuit, is unlucky and portends evil.[2]

PRE-BUDDHIST AND BUDDHIST HISTORY AND DOCTRINE

It is not at all certain that circumambulation—as a rite performed for its own sake and possessing a special religious significance—existed in Ti-

---

[1] W. Simpson, *The Buddhist Praying Wheel* (1896), pp. 123–32.

[2] *Ibid.,* pp. 29, 31, 61, 79, 89; L. A. Waddell, *The Buddhism of Tibet* (1895), p. 287, n. 7.

bet prior to the introduction of Buddhism. A somewhat similar practice is mentioned as a part of funeral rites that appear to be completely non-Buddhist in character. But the specific terminology that is now used to specify circumambulation is not employed, and the details of the description—"the horsemen go around three times" and "the women made three turn-abouts"—suggest that the making of a circuit and the turning about were somewhat incidental, arising out of the exigencies of the funeral ceremony, and were not the rite of circumambulation as now known and performed.[3]

Nor does the existence of both the concept and the practice of *Bon bsKor* ("Bon circuit"), also called *gYon bsKor* ("left [or counterclockwise] circuit"), which is, in effect, a kind of defiant denial of the *CHos bsKor* ("religion circuit"), also called *gYas bsKor* ("right circuit"), prove that there was formal circumambulation in Tibet prior to the introduction of Buddhism. In accordance with what has been pointed out in chapter ii, this could very well be a purposeful perversion of the Buddhist rite, which developed at a comparatively late date, following the triumph of Buddhism.

The presumption is very strong that circumambulation, defined as "going around an object keeping the right side toward it," came into Tibet with Buddhism. But it existed in India, with much the same ritual significance, long prior to the life of the Buddha and the beginnings of his doctrine. Krishnu and his followers are said to have "circumambulate[d] the mountain to the right."[4] There is considerable evidence that the clockwise rite of circumambulation was brought into India by the Aryans, and the earliest context in which it has been noted suggests that it originated in ideas and practices related to sun worship and the course of the sun as observed in the northern hemisphere.[5]

In early Buddhism, the Buddha was the object of the rite,[6] the performance of which was also ascribed to him. After he had met the five ascetics, but before he began to preach to them, and as a preliminary to turning the wheel of the doctrine, he circumambulated the three seats of the previous Buddhas and then sat in the fourth seat.[7] When the five hundred disciples moved around the bier of the Buddha, it burst into flame. And when Ananda was called to account by the assembly for his care of

[3] M. Lalou, "Rituel Bon-po des funerailles royales," *Journal Asiatique*, T–CCXL–3 (1952), p. 344.

[4] W. Simpson, *op. cit.*, p. 83.

[5] *Ibid.*, pp. 87–103.

[6] E. Obermiller, *The History of Buddhism* (1932), Part II, p. 14.

[7] *Ibid.*, p. 45.

the Buddha, he circumambulated the pulpit prior to mounting it to make his defense.[8] Thus, there is much evidence to show that, from the very beginning of Buddhism, the circumambulation rite was established by precept and example as an important act of worship.

By the time Padma Sambhava and his disciples and helpers carried out the third and most effective introduction of Buddhism into Tibet in the eighth century, circumambulation was an important and integral part of the Tantric Buddhism which they propagated. In numerous references, the act is bracketed with salutation as the sign of submission, homage, and faith.[9] Two centuries later, Milaraspa refers to the making of salutation and circumambulation in the phrase *PHyag Dang bsKor Ba Byed Pa* ("to do salutation and circumambulation").[10] By that time circumambulation had acquired significance, not only as a gesture signifying homage, but also as an act that had the power to create virtue and thus that was of equal importance with offering and the expression of verbalized religion. It had become a religious tour de force by which one could effect a short cut toward eventual liberation. When consecrating the temple of *bSam Yas*, Padma Sambhava is reported to have said that those who make the ritual circumambulation around it "even though they were butchers will be reborn into a heavenly state."[11]

PREDISPOSITION AND ITS REFLECTION IN TERMINOLOGY

Certain traits of the Tibetan character—for example, the primal urge to get up and get going—would seem to predispose the Tibetans toward the acceptance of *bsKor Ba*. They put some stress in their thinking, as evidenced in their language, on mobility—the simple act of going. As a people, they are remarkably foot-loose—wanderers who range widely and who are not at all parochial. Nomadism, the necessity to trade, and the urge to go on pilgrimage may be cited as factors that foster this mobility. For whatever cause, however, the fact remains that they move easily and daringly from place to place, and region to region, and accept the hardships of travel with equanimity.

The concept of "going" has become of great importance throughout the Tibetan language. A living being is a *aGro Ba* ("go one") or, in the aggregate, *aGro Ba Rigs Drug* ("six classes of goers"). Buddha is called

[8] W. W. Rockhill, *The Life of the Buddha* (1907), p. 156.

[9] G.-Ch. Toussaint, *Le dict de Padma* (1933), pp. 68, 149, 199, 210, 220, 226, 246, 264, 284.

[10] H. A. Jaschke, *A Tibetan-English Dictionary* (1949), p. 24.

[11] G.-Ch. Toussant, *op. cit.*, p. 257.

aGro Bai Bla Ma ("high one of the goers"), and Avalokitesvara is known as *aGro Bai mGon Po* ("lord of the goers"). Man is variously called *aGro Ba Rin CHen* ("great-value goer"), *aGro mCHog* ("perfect goer"), or *Langs aGro* ("erect goer"). Animals are *Dud aGro* ("stooping goer"); birds are *PHur aGro* ("flying goer"); frogs are *mCHong aGro* ("jumping goer"); fish are *rKyal aGro* ("swimming goer"); worms are *NYal aGro* ("lying-down goer"); and snakes are *lTo aGro* ("belly goer"). The fairies, or dakini, of the sky, about whom the Tibetans learned from the Hindus, are not characterized as living in the sky but, in accordance with one of their attributes, as *mKHaa aGro Ma* ("sky-going females"). If the concepts imbedded in the verbal symbols with which he communicates at present are valid as indexes, then, in the conceptual world of the Tibetan, *being* is evidenced by *going*. Thus, even if circumambulation as a special rite did not exist in Tibet prior to the importation of Buddhism, the importance assigned to going in the thinking of Tibetans might predispose them to accept with enthusiasm and zealously practice this new rite whereby one might get up and go and walk toward liberation.

We may also go to the Tibetan language for a preliminary understanding of the meaning of *bsKor Ba* ("to go in a circuit"), which is the Tibetan term denoting ritual circumambulation. Unlike the terms *CHos aDon* ("express verbalized religion") and *mCHod Pa* ("offering"), which have an exclusively religious connotation, *bsKor Ba,* in its several forms as noun, adjective, and verb and in many combinations, is frequently used in entirely secular contexts. Thus, in terminology, as well as in being an activity observance, *bsKor Ba* somewhat resembles *PHyag* ("salutation"), the observance analyzed in the preceding chapter. In its meaning "circuit," *bsKor Ba* is both noun and verb and can be translated "circuit," "circle," "to besiege," and "to go round about." The following combinations, used in secular contexts, are illustrative of its meanings: *bsKor Lam* ("circuit path"), a round-about way or detour, *mGo bsKor* ("head circuit"), to deceive, *Sa bsKor* ("place circuit"), a by-way, and *Ru bsKor* ("tent circuit"), an encampment.

bsKor Ba is a cognate of such words as *KHor* ("flow around"), *KHor Ba* ("to spin" or "to totter"), *Kor* ("round"), and *aKHor* ("turn about"), the last more commonly appearing as *aKHor Ba* ("cycle" or "entourage") and *aKHor Lo* ("wheel"). It is closely linked semantically with *aKHor Lo,* and the two words exhibit a morphological change similar to the change that is evident in a number of pairs of Tibetan words, of which the pair *sPrul* ("emanation") and *aPHrul* ("magic") is a good example. In addition to the meanings already indicated for *bsKor Ba* and *aKHor*

Ba, the former functions as the transitive form of the verb "turn" and the latter as the intransitive form. Thus *bsKor* is the verb used when one turns a wheel; and *aKHor,* when a wheel turns. The morphological difference is reflected in an interesting phonetic distinction in some dialects —principally in the more archaic forms of those of Amdo and Khams. *bsKor* is pronounced with an expirate preceding the "k," as "hkor"; and *aKHor* is pronounced—allowing for the nasalization of the lower-case "a"—with the expirate following the "k," as "ngkhor." The shifting of the expirate is a tricky phonetic distinction, and Tibetans themselves sometimes have slips of the tongue; but they do not confuse the two words either semantically or phonetically.

It should be noted that whenever *aKHor* is combined with some of the words with which *bsKor* is combined, the meanings are quite different. *aKHor Lam* ("turn-around path") means return path, whereas *bsKor Lam* ("circuit path"), in a secular context, means a round-about way or detour. *mGo aKHor* ("head turn-around") means dizziness, whereas *mGo bsKor* ("head circuit") means to deceive. *aKHor* has an additional basic importance in such compounds as *aKHor Lo* ("wheel"), which may have either religious or secular meanings, and in the latter context appears in many compounds relating to *aKHor Lo Can Po* ("the wheel-having one"), or machinery.

The term *bsKor Ba* ("to go in a circuit"), as the definitive term for ritual circumambulation is our main concern. In most dialects the "b" of *Ba* disappears and the word is pronounced "hkora." When written, it may also appear as *bsKor Ra.*[12] In its exclusively religious context, it is a verbal noun and requires the addition of such verbs as *Bya* ("do") and *aGro* ("go"). The combinations *bsKor Lam* ("circuit path"), *PHyi bsKor* ("outer circuit"), *Bar bsKor* ("between circuit"), and *Nang bsKor* ("inside circuit") have also acquired specific religious meanings designating different circumambulation paths.

Although in its verbal forms, *bsKor* is ambiguous in meaning, since it may be either secular or religious, as a noun requiring verbs of performance—*bsKor Ba*—it is unambiguously religious and means circumambulation.

CONFORMITY TO CRITERIA

Circumambulation conforms to the four criteria postulated in chapter iii for judging the universality of an observance within the context of Tibetan life and behavior patterns. All Tibetans, at some time or other,

---

[12] gZHon Nu dPal, *Deb THer sNGon Po,* Book III, f. 7 *a.*

have circumambulated. The occasions, objects, and frequency of performance of the rite vary for every individual, but the obligation to perform it is accepted by every Tibetan, and with considerable enthusiasm by many. Lamas, doctors of religion, hermits of renowned sanctity, monks, rebel monks, nobles, peasants, herdsmen, tradesmen, bandits, and criminals of every category rub shoulders, figuratively and actually, in the performance of what is for them a universal observance. It is the most egalitarian of all the observances—the same path and the same manner of walk for all, from the highest and most learned to the lowest and most ignorant.

It is an observable phenomenon throughout Tibet and particularly at all the places that are the destinations of pilgrimages. Of all the Tibetan universals of religious observances, it is the one that could be most easily made the object of statistical analysis, expressed, perhaps, in terms of man-miles. Though it may be performed anywhere, general acceptance and habit have fixed on the monasteries, with their cloisters, image houses, and shrines, as the preferred centers. It is not performed only to be seen and in that respect differs from *PHyag* ("salutation"), which employs visible gestures to communicate attitudes and aspirations. But it is practiced in conformity with what is conceived to be a cosmic pattern of motion and that aspect is obviously meant to be seen.

It is religious in nature and intent. The act of walking itself and the galleries, paths, and mountain trails along which it takes place have been appropriated for a religious purpose: the accumulation of *dGe Ba* ("virtue") to further progress toward *THar Ba* ("liberation"). The secular meanings of these terms which designate the purposes of circumambulation been pre-empted by religious meanings, and thus the terms have become consecrated to religion. Any intention which is less than the religious one of gaining virtue renders the performance invalid.

The rite has conceptual unity. Although often combined with other observances, it is not an aggregate of acts and rites itself. Indeed, more than any of the other Tibetan universals of religious observance, it has a basic simplicity. It may be performed around a multiplicity of objects, yet there are only two, or at most four, ways in which it is done.[13] There are

---

[13] Walking and walking interspersed with prostrations are the usual ways of performing circumambulation. Somewhat rarely, short circuits are performed on the knees (De Riencourt, *Lost World* [1949], p. 127; and one instance noted by the author), but this is not the normal manner of performance. A Tibetan once told me he had done circumambulation by creeping on his belly, but other Tibetans argue that such action is not in character—a human being is a *Langs aGro Ba* ("erect goer") not a *lTo aGro Ba* ("belly goer"), that is, a snake.

no great refinements and gradations of forms of the observance as in the case of the expression of verbalized religion and even salutation, in which some of the forms are reserved exclusively for the initiates.

GOALS AND MANNER OF PERFORMANCE

The promises and exhortations in the religious records and the instructions that have accumulated throughout the centuries have established in the minds of Tibetans, of all classes, the assurance that the rite of circumambulation is not simply a religio-physical exercise that aids and strengthens his spiritual health—in somewhat the same manner that it strengthens his legs and gives him a good appetite—but a productive activity that creates a specific amount of virtue, which is added to whatever accumulation of virtue he may already have. This religious "walk-around," therefore, becomes for him what might be called an assembly-line activity that efficiently and with absolute certainty produces virtue at each operation. The virtue thus produced is instrumental in furthering the progress of the individual toward liberation, conceived either as an immediate entrance into the fabled western heaven or as a favorable rebirth in the long round of rebirths on the path to Nirvana.

The observance is also of benefit to all sentient beings, through the compassion, *sNYing rJe* ("lord heart"), of the *Byang CHub Sems dPaa* ("Purged Permeated Hero Mind"), commonly termed Bodhisattva, which is cited as a reason for its observance, particularly when it is performed by an emanation-body lama. In the semantics of the Tibetan language, *sDig Pa* ("sin") also carries the connotation of suffering, so *dGe Be* ("virtue") also carries the connotation of well-being or bliss. Thus the Tibetan walker on the circumambulation path believes quite simply that, in addition to religious virtue, he is gaining health, happiness, and success in mundane matters, such as bountiful crops, profits in trade, and the well-being of his livestock. In fact, the advice of the clergy or the results of divination may frequently assure him that some particular problem—whether it is the pains of rheumatism or indigestion or the chances of a far-ranging trade venture that is hazardous at best—will be solved by sufficient performance of the rite.

If a Tibetan wished to increase the efficiency of the observance, he could do so in only two ways: by refining the manner of performance or by repeating the performance. Except by combining circumambulation with other religious observances, there is little that could be done to refine or add to the manner of performance. Personal effort being essential, riding or being carried—except for the sick or the very young—cuts the result in half. The animal or individual carrying the person performing circumambulation receives the other half of the benefits accruing from the observance. Thus the most efficient performance is for the one on the *bsKor Ba* path to make progress under his own power if at all possible.

Circumambulation is invariably combined with some form of verbalization of religion, and it thus becomes an integral part of that observance. All those who walk the circuit mutter prayers, most commonly the six-syllable formula. Such vocalization may be combined with a vow of silence, covering all speech but prayers; but if there is no vow of silence, praying does not preclude conversation. The Tibetans are very skilful at interspersing prayers in discourse of entirely different and secular content. Verbalization entails the use of the rosary to keep a count of both the prayers and the circuits completed. Prayer wheels are often used on the *bsKor Ba* path. Frequently, much, or a large portion, of the circuit is along porches and galleries where rows of large prayer wheels have been installed with conveniently protruding handles by which they may be set spinning on behalf of the one who walks; and where there are no prayer wheels, many carry small personal ones, which they keep spinning by a twist of the wrist.

A special combination of circumambulation and the verbalization of religion occurs when the members of a community form a procession to carry the volumes of the Buddhist sacred writings around a monastery or shrine in order to gain a general blessing or advantage for the community, such as the breaking of a drought, the stamping out of an epidemic, or success in some community enterprise.

The Tibetan may also combine circumambulation with salutation. This can be done by making salutation at the beginning and end of each circuit or at points along the way, wherever there is an image, symbolic structure, shrine, or any other object meriting veneration. A most effective combination of circumambulation and salutation is the performance of the rite of circumambulation by a series of linked prostrations. As each full prostration is completed, the participant gets up and places his toes on the mark that his fingers made when he was lying full length on the ground, and then repeats the process until the end of the circuit has been reached. There, if his stint is not completed and sufficient daylight remains, he starts the entire process over again. Both for those who go on foot and for those who make their way like measuring worms, one basic rule holds good: nothing has been gained if the full circuit has not been completed.

In the latter combination, circumambulation, although, as *CHos Las* ("religion-work"), held to be inferior to salutation, dominates the manner of performance. Both function within the context of a spatial relationship to a center: an idol, a shrine, and so on. Salutation is toward, and circumambulation is around, that center. In the combination, however, salutation is not made toward the center but along the path that goes around the center. This manner of observance reflects the practical preference of the Tibetans for circumambulation over salutation. Very frankly, they much prefer a walk in the open to strenuous and monotonous exercises in a dark shrine.

The performance of circumambulation may also be combined with offering. This combination may take the form of simply adding a stone to a cairn; placing a symbolic arrow offering into the sheaf or stack of arrows already marking the place where a mountain god is worshiped; or lighting a butter lamp before a shrine or image. It may also involve the presentation of considerable wealth or special ceremonial offerings to the monasteries and temples.

One thing more needs to be said about the manner in which circumambulation is performed. The participant must actually or symbolically be unarmed. When circumambulation has been adequately prepared, so that weapons may be cached in a safe place, arms are not carried by the participants. Even when enemies are using the same path, they need not fear because the truce of the circumambulation path will not be broken. When a circuit has been begun in a somewhat incidental manner and a worshiper is wearing or carrying weapons, he will remove his sword in its sheath from his girdle and his gun, if there is one, and carry them in his hand to express symbolic disarmament—in the same manner used when approaching to make salutation. Weapons are discarded, however, at the earliest opportunity and placed in safekeeping.

Conforming to the trend clearly exemplified in both the verbalization of religion and salutation, repetition—and thus the accumulation of virtue —is of basic importance. In the first observance, by the employment of the techniques of printing and devices powered by wind and water as well as by man, the Tibetan has found it possible to use multiplication as a factor in accumulating a total. No way has been found to multiply the performance of circumambulation, but by zealous and tireless repetition, a most impressive total may be gained by every individual by addition, and a total of astronomical proportions by the population as a whole.

The rite of circumambulation has one other aspect that sets it apart from all the other religious observances: it affords the Tibetan the opportunity to express his rather special sense of identification and commonality with animals. He believes that they are like him in kind and that they, too, are caught in the round of existence in which, in whatever way possible, the accumulation of virtue is desirable. Circumambulation is the only religious observance into which the Tibetan can bring his valued livestock as direct participants, for they cannot be taught or forced to perform any of the other religious observances. But any of the *rKang bZHi* ("four-footed") can go along the *bsKor Ba* path and gain virtue; and so the Tibetan, who wants to bring a blessing to his favorite horse or even goat—especially when the animal is getting old—leads it in circumambulation. Sometimes, too, entire herds are driven around the circuit to create protection against, or the healing of, cattle disease.

To one who has lived among the Tibetans for an extended period of time, in intimate and daily contact with their manner of living, a strange discrepancy appears between the reality of some aspects of Tibetan behavior patterns and what has been written about them by travelers and observers. Nowhere is this discrepancy more striking than in accounts of the circumambulation rite. Practically everyone who has written about Tibet refers to the rite and mentions that there are places and paths for the performance of it. But such reference is generally casual in nature— an incidental part of the description of Tibetan crowds or worshipers. Frequently, many pages are devoted to the description of incidental aspects of Tibetan life or to certain intricacies of religious ritual, but circumambulation is only briefly mentioned and dropped. It is as though the travelers saw movement but never realized how ceaseless and universal it was and how, in the crowds, the same faces would recur again and again as the circuits were made.

It is no play on words to state that the rite is a pivotal activity in Tibetan society. In Tibetan folktales and traditions, gods, demons, sprites, and superhuman beings of every class perform it at appropriate occasions; birds, beasts, and reptiles also follow the same circuit.[14] The concept permeates Tibetan thinking; and the pattern of motion has a cosmic universality. To illustrate, when the Tibetan picks up his bowl of tea and tsamba and uses his fingers to mix the whole, he carefully spins the bowl clockwise in his left hand in conformity to a cosmic and pious pattern of motion.

[14] G.-Ch. Toussaint, *op. cit.*, pp. 68, 199, 210, 226; G. N. Roerich, *The Blue Annals* (1949), p. 134; J. Bacot, *Trois mystères tibétains* (1921), pp. 100, 109-10; *dPal lDan Bla Ma Dam Pa eJe bTSun Blo bZang Ye SHes Kyis gSung Las gSang Bai rNam THar bZHugs So*, ff. 15 *b*, 16 *a*.

CLASSES OF FOCUSES

Thus, the manner in which circumambulation may be performed is limited, but the focuses around which it may take place are extremely numerous. The following annotated list is representative rather than exhaustive, but it should help to place the observance in its proper perspective and to add to an understanding of the importance of the rite in Tibetan religious practice and patterns of behavior. The objects of the rite fall roughly into the following categories: persons, images, offerings, religious structures, topographical features, and noumenal projections achieved by meditation.

Persons

The observance may be performed around any emanation-body lama, no matter where he is or what he is doing. He is, per se, a proper object of the rite, for he represents, in varying degrees of tenuousness, the Buddhahood. If he is engaged in religious ritual, that is an additional reason for making him the center of circumambulation. The funeral pyre, the remains, or the mummy of a lama are also preferred objects of the rite.

Monks, on the other hand, are circumambulated only when they are engaged in various religious rituals or when they are gathered into an assembly. In the latter case, they become representative of the community entity of the Triad. That individual monks are no longer considered valid objects of the rite is attributed to the current general degeneracy of the monkish community and consequent loss of general esteem. Originally, it is held, the robe of the monk entitled him to salutations and circumambulations.

To illustrate this, the following story is told. *Kun dGaa sNYing Po*, a famous layman of the Sakya line, worldling though he might be, was always on the lookout for objects and occasions for the performance of *CHos Las* ("religion-work"). One day he came upon a pile of monastic robes beside a stream where the monks—young and old—were bathing. The robes suggested the occasion for religious observance but by themselves were not enough; and the naked monks splashing in the stream could not very well be saluted and reverenced. So he begged them to put on their robes so he could make properly directed salutations and circumambulations.[15]

Images

Any image, of the millions in Tibet, may be the object around which circumambulation is performed. The holiest of all is *Jo Bo* ("the lord"),

[15] Personal communication from Dezhung Rinpoche.

the image of the Buddha reputedly brought to Tibet by the Chinese bride of *Srong bTSan sGam Po,* which is housed in the *Jo KHang,* the religious heart of Lhasa itself.[16] Another famous image is the 150-feet-high Buddha housed in a seven-story temple in Shigatze.[17] But throughout Tibet, there are images of every sort and every size—from the giant ones of plaster, stone, bronze, and precious metals, down to the tiny relief images pressed out of clay that are stacked and heaped in the *lHa KHang* ("god-house[s]") of the monasteries and in every household shrine. At some time or other, each one of this incalculable number may become the object of circumambulation.

Scriptures

A volume or any collection of sacred writings may become the proper object of circumambulation. A man who has a single prayer manual may set it up in any place and it becomes a shrine; and members of the clergy may stack their books on a stand or even on a chest within their rooms and vary their verbalization of religion or other routine by performing circumambulation around the stack.

Offerings

Any offering displayed ceremonially, whether mandala, the broken-up offering, incense, or the frequent, almost daily, offering of lighted juniper boughs, which are burnt in the evening on the little stove altars on cloister roofs and on house tops or on makeshift sod and stone altars at campsites, may be the object around which circumambulation is performed.

The burning of juniper boughs on a temporary altar at a campsite may also be the occasion for an aberrant and frankly heterodox rite. A group of Tibetan hunters with whom I once went on an extended hunt after important big game built a stone or sod altar at each campsite and made a *bSangs sBud* ("burn scent") offering of juniper boughs sprinkled with tea, salt, butter, tsamba, and bits of whatever other provisions, such as flour or rice, were available. As the fragrant smoke rose toward the darkening sky or was swept away by the wind, the members of the party, carrying their guns at the trail, circumambulated the altar, shouting unabashed appeals to the mountain gods for success in such terms as "many killed—fat ones—a male with wide antlers," and so on. The prayers were interspersed with the wild and ringing *ku-hu-u-u,* the Tibetan yell of exultation that equally marks a horse race, the excitement of a mounted

16 P. Landon, *The Opening of Tibet* (1906), pp. 390–92.

17 A. Winnington, *Tibet* (1957), p. 157.

charge, or the annual burning of the *gTor Ma* ("broken-up offering"). Most paradoxically, the six-syllable formula was mixed with such verbalization, and rosaries were carried and used.

Circumambulation is also performed around accumulated offerings that have become permanent monuments. Examples of such shrines are the cairns, called *rDo mCHod* ("stone offering") or *rDo sPungs* ("stone heap"), which mark mountain passes and which grow to great size since each passer-by makes his offering by adding a stone to the pile. After the offering is made, circumambulation is performed at least once, and maybe many times, before the worshiper goes on. Additions are made in a similar manner either at set times throughout the year or when community disaster or some special need sends horsemen or mountain climbers to the tops of the mountains, where the stacks or sheaves of great symbolic arrows mark the shrines of local mountain gods. Circumambulation, following the placing of the arrows in the stack, is a certain and inevitable part of the ceremony.

Religious Structures

Before discussing chortens and monasteries, the classic and obvious examples of religious structures around which circumambulation is performed, familial and parochial structures should be mentioned. With few exceptions, every Tibetan carries with him the requisites for the creation of a personal religious structure. The *Gau* ("charm box"), which he wears on his chest or shoulder or attached to his girdle, is potentially a shrine. It may be set up on a rock or a block of sod, thus becoming a religious monument around which its owner may circumambulate.

A very wealthy family may have a separate building as a chapel. A family of lesser wealth may have a special room set apart for the same purpose. Among the nomads, a chief or a very wealthy man may have a beehive-shaped Mongolian yurt of white felt—as distinct from the flat-roofed living tent made from black yak-hair cloth—which is set up at each camp as the family chapel and devoted exclusively to religious uses. All of these are the objects of repeated circumambulation, not only by the members of the family but by neighbors and guests. In the case of a special room in a building, doors and passageways are arranged to make possible an easily accessible circumambulation path.

In most villages, there is a communal *Ma Ni lHa KHang* ("mani god-house") that serves as a chapel for the members of the village community and around which they circumambulate whenever they gather to worship and make offerings and whenever they have spare time and feel like taking a walk with the certainty of accruing virtue as a result.

mCHod rTen ("offering base"), or stupas, together with *Ma Ni gDong* (*"mani* face"), or the so-called prayer dykes, are solid structures (although the stupas, characteristically, are tombs and contain receptacles for relics or other sacred objects) that serve no other purpose than as objects of worship—in particular, of salutation and circumambulation. They are most frequently, but not exclusively, located near or sometimes within monastery limits. The stupa, which has developed a very distinctively Tibetan architectural form, is an importation from India. The *Ma Ni gDong*, or prayer wall or dyke, on the other hand, may have grown out of a very early pre-Buddhist practice of stone worship, which has been fused with the Buddhist practice of writing or engraving the formula *OHm Ma Ni Padme Hum* as often and as durably as possible. Around these two types of structures, whether at or near lamaseries, at some special spot beside a lake, in a valley mouth, at a bridge or ford, or on some mountain top, the Tibetans circumambulate tirelessly, halting their journeyings to perform the act or making special visits to such spots for the purpose.

The most frequent objects of circumambulation, however, are religious structures such as monasteries and their component buildings. Around every monastery there is a *PHyi bsKor* ("outer circuit"), a path which includes all buildings and monuments of the monastery. Such a circuit may be several miles in length and is always clearly marked; it is known to all who come as the *bsKor Lam* ("circuit path"). In fact, it marks the formal limits of the monastery, within which the special regulations of monastic life are in force. It is seldom—even approximately—circular in outline but conforms roughly to the ground plan of the complex of structures that make up the monastery, modified further by such topographical factors as steep slopes, ravines, gullies, and the points at which crossings may be made over rivulets. The most famous of the outer circuits is the six-mile long *Gling bsKor* ("area circuit") around Lhasa.[18] But this circuit, since it includes not only the shrines, temples, and monastic institutions but all of Lhasa, including residence and business areas, is not a true monastery *PHyi bsKor* ("outer circuit").

Within the outer circuit of each monastery, there are a number of circuits, varying with the size and special characteristics of the monastery. Each of these is around some shrine or special building, such as the various *lHa KHang* ("god-house[s]"); the *mGon KHang* ("lord building"),

[18] L. A. Waddell, *Lhasa and Its Mysteries* (1905), p. 375.

where the *sPyan gZigs* ("eye-viewed") offerings are on exhibition; the general or special *aDu KHang* ("assembly building"); and the stupas and *Ma Ni gDong* monuments that are included within the monastery complex. Some of these circuits have been assigned a special value for various reasons. The rabbit-warren-like tunnel leading through the maze of buildings that crowd around the relatively small *Jo KHang* in Lhasa is a circuit around the most sacred structure of Tibetan Buddhism—a building of even greater value than the mighty wonder of the Potala, red and white against the unearthly clarity of the Tibetan sky—and *bsKor Ba* around it is correspondingly efficacious.

A small circuit in the monastery of *rTSe dBus* in Amdo also has a special significance, although of another kind, and is much in vogue. At the fifth level of the nine-story building housing a great image of one manifestation of the Buddhahood, there is a narrow scaffoldlike gallery on the *outside* of the building, unguarded by rails and with only precarious handholds for safety. This circumambulation path attracts many. Quite frequently, there are accidents, sometimes fatal ones, but the value of the circuit seems enhanced by the danger. Similarly enhanced are some of the circumambulation paths around hermitages and monasteries built on peaks and into the sides of cliffs, which are marked only by chains and handholds.

Each person who performs circumambulation along one of these small circuits has one or more reasons for his choice of a path. Frequently, divination or clerical advice may have designated some special circuit as especially efficacious for his particular need. Or a particular shrine may have been chosen because the deity is believed to have some special interest in or relation to either the worshiper or his special need. Or again, a special circuit may be chosen because the particular length will make possible the daily stint of circumambulation that has been prescribed or selected as a goal.

Topographical Features

Natural features of the landscape that may be circumambulated include trees, springs, caves, lakes, and mountains. Performance of the rite around natural objects, which in all sizes and every degree of significance constantly meet the Tibetan's eye and challenge his attention in all activities of his predominantly outdoor life, links his religious and conceptual world with his land and the features of that land that he enjoys and venerates with an almost childlike intensity. In ordinary life, he picnics beside a spring or by a great tree, he takes refuge in caves, he camps by lakes, and he sees—with wonder and yet a keen sense of their beauty—the ever-visible great mountains, rocky or snow-crowned, near or far, against the sky. In circumambulating these natural features, he links, in a religious observance, the worlds of the seen and the unseen.

Trees and springs, but especially trees, are borderline cases as topographic objects of circumambulation. When trees are circumambulated, it is difficult to separate the shrine or altar that is generally in the grove or at the foot of the tree from the tree as the center around which the rite is performed. A spring, *CHu Mig* ("water eye") or *CHu mGo* ("water head"), on the other hand, because it is closely related to the underworld of the powerful mysterious *Klu* or nagas, is in itself an object of veneration and circumambulation.

Caves, too, are objects of veneration and circumambulation. Some of them have become shrines because hermits or famed religious leaders lived in them at one time or another. If they are occupied, they are in effect—because of their function—components of a monastery complex and as such suitable for circumambulation. Those that are no longer occupied are shrines in the narrow sense of the word. The cave of the *sTag TSHang* ("Tiger Den") of the *Gur Du* monastery in Amdo near the upper knee of the Yellow River is a good example of such a shrine. According to legend, it was the first dwelling of the hermit who founded the monastery about two hundred and fifty years ago. The opening to the cave is so low that one must almost crawl to enter, but inside, it becomes a vaulted room, roughly circular in shape and approximately thirty feet in diameter. There is nothing within the cave but a few inscriptions on the wall. At the entrance, however, there is a stone altar on which incense and juniper boughs may be burned, and *KHa bTag* ("felicity scarves") may be hung over the entrance as offerings. Circumambulation may take place either around the entrance, involving a climb around the bit of cliff in which it is set, or, preferably, by walking or performing a series of linked prostrations clockwise around the edge of the vault.

Some caves are venerated because they are striking and awe-inspiring geologic phenomena whose extended galleries, passages, and underground rivers suggest access to the underworld of the nagas. In such caves, a path leading through the rooms and galleries and conforming roughly to the principle of a clockwise circuit will be plotted and recognized as a circumambulation path. Near the *Brag dKar* ("white cliff") monastery in Amdo, there is such a cave, and performance of the circuit takes over an hour, with the aid of both torches and a monk guide. When I made the circuit with a party of Tibetans, I discovered at one point that we were standing on the bank of a pool of unknown size. Somewhat surreptitiously I slipped off my Tibetan cloak—we were all barefoot as a precaution against slipping—and was in the water and swimming before the guide realized what I was doing. Once he recovered from his fears for me—and possibly for himself, though no actual sacrilege was involved —he was most anxious that I explore all sides of the pool to ascertain whether it would be possible to plot a circumambulation path around the underground lake and thus add another circumambulation attraction to the *Brag dKar* cave.

The lakes in Tibet, which are considered sacred and from which, therefore, blessing emanates, range from tiny unmarked glacial tarns high up in the mountains to such great inland seas as the Koko Nor, or blue lake, whose circuit measures 168 miles.[19] I have ridden high up in the mountains with hunters or travelers who would make a detour to reach a small, round greenish-blue pool, the last trace of a glacier, that was not more than fifty yards in diameter and unmarked by path, altar, or the crudest stone shrine; yet it was the object of circumambulation duly and decorously performed by the members of the party. On the other hand, the circuit around the Koko Nor is reported to take many days. The principal lakes around which circumambulation takes place are the *mTSHo sNGon Bo* ("Blue Lake"), the *gNam mTSHo* ("Sky Lake"), and the most sacred of all, the *mTSHo Mo Ma PHam* ("Undefeated-Female Lake"), so-called because of a tradition that it was there that a Bon magician failed to defeat Milaraspa.[20] It is the reputed source of the Brahmaputra, the Indus, and the Sutlej rivers.

To be an object of circumambulation, any lake, large or small, must have a *gNas* ("an abiding"), or something holy, in residence. This may be either a god or daemon or one of the "gift-revelation" treasures—ritual objects—or special prophecies that are reputed to have been hidden, mostly by Padma Sambhava, all over Tibet.

Among the topographical features, however, it is the mountains of Tibet that are the preferred objects of circumambulation, possibly because they relate most closely to the mountain gods—the ancient and most noteworthy of the original gods of Tibet. In circumambulating the mountains, these gods are worshiped by a Buddhist observance.

The great and austerely beautiful mountains of Tibet are natural shrines, true objects of wonder, and around any mountain of consequence

---

[19] G. Sandberg, *Tibet and the Tibetans* (1906), p. 39.

[20] Personal opinion of Dezhung Rinpoche. He considers himself in a very special sense a follower of Mi La and is steeped in lore concerning that poet-saint.

there is a circumambulation path. In some instances veneration of a mountain appears to be very closely linked with one of the ancient deities known variously as *AH Mes* ("hail ancient"), *gNYan* ("argali"), *mGul lHa* ("hunting god"), *lHa CHen* ("great god"), *Sa bDag* ("soil-owner"), and so on. In other instances, the original god seems to have been displaced by a Buddhist and tantric importation; in the process, the god has lost prominence and the mountain itself, as a symbol, has gained importance. The two most famous mountains in Tibet around which circumambulation is in vogue illustrate this phenomenon well.

The great snow mountain known as *AH Mes rMa CHen* ("hail ancient one, great peacock"), within the upper knee of the *rMa CHu* ("peacock water"), or Yellow River, in Amdo, is the abode of the mountain god variously called *rMa CHen sPom Ra* ("*sPom Ra* Great Peacock") or *rMa rGyal Po CHen Po sPom Ra* ("*sPom Ra* Great King Peacock"). In the Gesar epic, this god is the ruling regional deity to whom Gesar addresses his invocations and under whose protection he places himself when he is making the momentous and fiercely exultant change from the petty life of a farmer, with narrow fields in a deep valley, to the raiding, roving, freer life of the nomad, in a land where pastures are wide and opportunity promises much of substance and prestige. There is a legend that Gesar's sword, originally given him by the mountain god, is still hidden somewhere in the mountain; not only has it been a protective and stimulating influence that has fostered the freedom and turbulence of the *mGo Log* tribes, but it will be ready for Gesar's use when he returns to re-establish Tibetan hegemony. Around the circumambulation path that encircles the mountain, thousands of Tibetans make the seven-day-long walk, especially in the year of the horse—the sign-year of the nomad—which is a particularly propitious year for worshiping this mountain's god, who has persisted from times long prior to the arrival of Buddhism and tantric importations.[21]

Circumambulation around the other famous Tibetan mountain, *Ti Se Gangs* (Mount Kailas), has associations that are somewhat different from the foregoing. The mountain is consecrated to *bDe mCHog* (Samvara or Heruka), who is not an autochthonous mountain god but a more recent tantric importation and contributes little to making the mountain as a shrine. It gains its sacred character as the legendary scene of Milaraspa's dramatic victory over the Bon wizard and because of proximity to a lake

[21] J. F. Rock, *The Amnye Ma Chhen Range and Adjacent Regions* (1956), pp. 107–8; R. A. Stein, *L'épopée tibétaine de Gésar* (1956), pp. 65, 72, 76, 91, 135, 218; R. Nebesky-Wojkowitz, *Oracles and Demons of Tibet* (1956), pp. 95, 160, 202, 209–13; 221, 304, 323, 406, 543.

holy to Buddhists and Hindus alike. Moreover, the mountain itself, a regular pyramid, is of singular beauty. It has been called the mandala mountain. In form, it is a natural and gigantic stupa of rock and glacial snow, resembling to a great extent a sublimated realization of a *Byin rTen* ("bounty base") for the bestowing of blessing on those who worship by circumambulation. The long circuit over a particularly rocky trail requires two days. There is also a higher circumambulation path, which, although it is so dangerous that there are frequent fatal accidents, is much traveled nevertheless.[22]

Meditation Conceptualizations

Finally, some mention must be made of a form of circumambulation for which one creates, through meditation and conceptualization, a mental projection of deity, which takes form on the right. Walking in any direction then becomes circumambulation around that conceptualization. This form is known as *PHrag Pa gYas La sGom sKor Ba* ("meditate-to-the-right-shoulder circumambulation"). Placed on the right, *sPyan Ras gZigs* or any other of the special bodhisattvas become the object of the rite as the adept walks on.

CHARACTER OF PERFORMANCE

Circumambulation around these different classes of objects can be divided into three categories on the basis of length of circuit: short circuits around individual shrines and structures; circuits of medium length, such as those around monastery complexes of a few hundred yards to several miles, like the six-mile outer circuit of Lhasa; and circuits around topographical features, which may be scores of miles in length and require journeys of several days' duration. For each of these, the mode and mood in which circumambulation is performed are of significance in relation to the function of the observance.

Those who circle individual shrines and structures seem to be in a constant hurry; they move rapidly and intently again and again around the short circuit, stopping only to prostrate themselves or to add a pebble to the pebble heap, which is frequently the manner in which a record is kept of the number of circuits. They seem to scurry along, entirely preoccupied with the task, paying no attention to their fellows, and speaking to no one. In a sense, each one is isolated within an individual apperception and performance of the rite to the exclusion of all else.

[22] S. Hedin, *Trans-Himalaya* (1909), Vol. II, p. 189, and Vol. III, p. 84; E. Kawaguchi, *Three Years in Tibet* (1909), p. 93; I. Desideri, *An Account of Tibet* (1712–27), p. 143.

The longer walk along the outer circumambulation path is equally strenuous, for there may be steep ascents and difficult defiles to negotiate, but the pace, although not a stroll, is not rushed. Completion of the circuit is somewhat far away in both space and time. There is opportunity to notice one's fellows and to stop with them to catch one's breath at the top of a climb. By moving faster or more slowly, one overtakes or is overtaken by others; and as the group moves along, conversation, adroitly punctuated by habitual verbalization of religion, is not out of order. If so desired, one may rest—still spinning a prayer wheel industriously—and talk with others who are resting, before again taking up the long walk into the wind or with the sun in one's face. The mood of such performance is relaxed and assured, for the longer outside circuit encircles all the objects of worship of the place and is known to be of the greatest efficacy.

The even longer walk for the observance of religion around a lake or mountain has still other characteristics and moods that accompany its performance. Some of the character of a journey is imposed. The techniques of travel in the wilderness, in which the Tibetans excel, come into play. Camps must be made and campfires built. At least rudimentary shelter, even if no more than a carefully arranged great felt raincoat, must be provided. A minimal formal or informal organization of those who find themselves companions on speaking terms must be set up. The basic travel and camp unit is called the "kettle," to indicate that the members of the group use one kettle and sit around one fire. Co-operation in the tasks of setting up kettle stones, finding fuel, and bringing water, and most important, in the collective presentation of offerings by burning juniper boughs and incense at each campsite creates group consciousness and cohesiveness. Thus while the goal—completion of the circuit—is never forgotten, days and nights of association and the co-operative sharing of chores, set amidst the uncertainties of weather and trail conditions, make this form of circumambulation something of an adventure, both in space and in human relations. The over-all mood, although firmly religious and reverential, mirrors the influence of these factors.

When consideration and analysis of circumambulation as a Tibetan universal of religious observance is shifted from descriptions of origin, doctrinal position, history, and present forms of the phenomenon to an analysis of its function in Tibetan society and culture, it becomes apparent that the rite to which functional roles are attributed is a construct and not exactly like any one of the three forms described in this section. However, this construct most resembles the performance of circumambulation along the outer path around a monastery complex, which in many aspects is the mean form of the observance and, in terms of man-miles, the optimum form: the largest number of Tibetans spending the greatest amount of time in walking the greatest distance.

FUNCTION OF THE OBSERVANCE

When circumambulation, which is the last of the observances that are unequivocally religious, is examined to determine its function, it becomes apparent that a number of its functional roles are also roles, in varying degrees, of the other activity observances. Several functions that it has in common with other observances will be examined first.

In common with the others, but in particular with the observance of salutation, circumambulation makes the benefits and goals of religious aspiration attainable merely by *doing* something. It has been noted how, in each of the other activity observances, certain aspects of behavior, which are universal in human experience and culture, have, nevertheless, in Tibet a certain distinctive emphasis that predisposes the Tibetans to accept and rely on the particular observances. The same holds good for the observance of circumambulation. All men walk, although some neglect it almost to the point of atrophy of the power. The Tibetan, too—especially the nomad—has found that much sitting in a saddle bows the legs and saps their vigor. He is adverse to walking for the sake of walking, but in theory he would have to agree that *going* is evidence of *being*.

There is a certain aptness and significance in the fact that the Tibetan, who defines himself as a human being in terms of *Langs aGro* ("erect goer"), *aGro Ba Rin CHen* ("the precious going one"), or *aGro mCHog* ("perfect goer") and yet is disinclined to walk, should make circumambulation one of the universals of his religious observance. In it, he has found motivation strong enough to bring activity into line with conceptualization. He will then walk against the wind, the drag of an uphill slope, or a feeling of fatigue, which in itself is proof of effort well put forth, with a sense of making progress, walking upright like a man, toward the far, mystic goals of religious aspiration. At the same time, he gains hope of happiness and a foretaste of health along the way.

Because he believes that the observance of circumambulation promises virtue and blessing, the Tibetan receives benefits of fulfilment and satisfaction similar to the benefits he receives from the other religious observances. Those benefits are solely religious in concept, but, to the extent that his world view and culture are strongly religious, they are real to him as an individual and are diffused throughout his society and culture.

In common with the other religious observances, circumambulation plays a part in creating a pattern of behavior, under certain circumstances and stimuli, that is culture-wide. Thus the Tibetan is associated with his fellows in what is essentially a group activity, performed either with the members of his own group or in the knowledge that they have engaged in, are engaged in, or will engage in the same activity. He responds to the stimuli of such association and partakes of its satisfactions. To the extent that he feels he is participating in a common endeavor, he is given a sense of oneness with his fellows, for they all, the Dalai Lama not excepted, walk the *bsKor Ba* path. This pattern of behavior gives him sure criteria for recognizing his fellows. He may even predict with fair accuracy where, when, and how they will spend a portion of their time, for he himself responds to the same needs, occasions, and stimuli.

Circumambulation, because of the special characteristics of the rite— a pleasantly demanding walk with friendly company in the out-of-doors —functions as a form of psychosomatic therapy to reduce tensions and repair the ravages of frustration. The Tibetans have considerable need for such therapy. For many reasons, of which extreme altitudes may not be the least, many Tibetans exhibit signs of nervous tension and strain. The fractured political structure, the unequal and at times arbitrary operation of control devices resulting from mixed or competing systems of ecclesiastical and tribal law, and the wide prevalence of the feud system with its violence, menace, and uncertainty contribute to a widespread sense of insecurity, which directly reveals itself in a high incidence of stomach ulcers and aggravated insomnia.[23] To mitigate all this, circumambulation, the safe walk where weapons are not carried and no danger may intrude, functions therapeutically to reduce tensions and alleviate their effects.

As a minor, though by no means negligible, aspect of a purely physiological value, circumambulation provides physical exercise for those who need it when it is needed. A considerable number of Tibetans, either because of the season or because of their occupation, are sedentary in their habits to a marked degree. The nomad, for example, throughout much of

[23] Without exception, everyone who has done any extensive traveling in Tibet has experienced attack and/or robbery or the menace of it, and has seen victims of such an attack or the culprits. The list is long: Hedin, Tucci, Huc, Futterer, Bailey, Bacot, Migot, Filchner, Taffel, Bonvalot, d'Ollone, Kawaguchi, David-Neel, Kaulback, Handbury-Tracy, Patterson, Rijnhart, Harrer, and many others. A number have been killed or disappeared. Travel and life are, in general, equally unsafe for Tibetans. Madame David-Neel sums it up flatly: "People live in a constant sense of insecurity in a large part of Tibet" (*My Journey to Lhasa*, p. 141). In the summer of 1931, I traveled with an English doctor among Tibetan tribes for over two months. Among the many hundreds of Tibetans who came to him for treatment, he was amazed to note a disproportionately large number with either stomach ulcers or insomnia.

the year, lives a life of extreme movement and effort that is at times explosive in intensity. But winter for him is a season of much food and little to do except sit by the fire and eat. He and most of the members of his family live in a state of what might be called semihibernation. When he does move, it is on horseback, which, as horsemen know, is a direct aggravation of the elimination troubles he suffers from his costive diet. During such periods of leisure, the performance of circumambulation takes him to a monastery for many days, which are spent in long walks in the open —as truly health-giving as a daily eighteen holes of golf. In fact, the performance of the rite is often the only inducement that will get many a saddle-bound nomad to walk. The monks, too, especially the higher ecclesiastics, are more occupationally sedentary in habit than the most deskbound bank president, but the duty of circumambulation also sets them to walking, to the great benefit of their digestive systems and appetites

The observance of circumambulation shares this role to a considerable degree with the observance of salutation. Indeed, in many respects, the roles of the two observances overlap, and what may be said about one as physical exercise may be said about the other. There are, nevertheless, significant differences between them. As has been shown, the observance of salutation functions to establish a center—a point in space toward which prostrations are made—and thus brings the Tibetans to that point. Circumambulation also operates to localize religious observance, but it introduces in addition factors of time and social contact that are lacking, or less marked, in the performance of salutation. Although both performances are equally subject to quantitative evaluation, the performance of circumambulation is less concentrated, and the accumulation of a worthwhile number of circuits to be tallied on the beads requires a longer period of time. Observance of the rite thus requires a considerable amount of time—extending to many days—spent in the locale for the accomplishment of any predetermined number of circuits.

Because the Tibetan, in his "religion work," is influenced to some extent by pleasure, he finds circumambulation much more pleasant than the making of prostrations. The latter observance is hard, monotonous work in a dark interior or at the entrance to a shrine that may be in the frosty shadow of a mid-winter day when it is pleasantly sunny elsewhere or in the hot sun of summer when shade and cool breezes are just around the corner. Circumambulation, on the other hand, is a pleasant walk in the open in weather to which he is accustomed, with sky, sun, mountains, and —in spring or summer—flowers in view. The additional factor of ample and pleasurable social contact is not only a gain in itself but an inducement to prolong the time allotted to circumambulation. It is the most social of all the religious observances, affording the greatest opportunity for contact and conversation. Even when no talking is done, the mere observation of one's fellows—who they are, what they wear, how they look, and so on—is pleasurable social involvement, helping to make easy the choice of circumambulation as a way in which to employ one's time with profit.[24]

The close symbiotic relationship between the monastery, as a religious center, and the so-called town, as trading center, has already been discussed in chapter vii. The centripetal attraction that the observance of salutation exerts to bring Tibetans together at these bifunctional centers is strengthened, and its results are *lengthened* in time, by the observance of circumambulation. In order to circumambulate the monastery in whole or in part and also to haunt the market and stalls of the trade center, the Tibetan—half pilgrim–half trader—will spend days, even many days, at such centers. From that practice flows a number of consequences of considerable importance.

The long sojourn necessitates the establishment of certain interpersonal relationships, which are either strictly commercial or of a socioeconomic nature and in which prestige, patronage, and mutual obligation and responsibility are mixed in varying proportions. The links of this latter relationship, reaching to distant communities, are both enduring and strong.

In the first instance, some person in the greater community of the center, either a monk or a member of the lay community of the town, provides quarters or a place to camp within the walls, thus giving some degree of protection to the pilgrims. For this, rent is paid; and thus some of the wealth of the distant village or encampment community flows into the greater community of the monastery. Many members of the central community derive considerable income from this practice and plan their dwellings and enclosures accordingly.

In the second instance, which is the one most in vogue because of prestige factors and long-term advantages, lodging or camp space—with minimal provision of water and fuel—is made available, but no fixed immediate remuneration is expected or received. Gifts, token or real, are exchanged, and a complex of interlocking responsibilities and duties, accompanied by the appropriate attitudes, is built up between the pilgrim and the permanent resident. Nor is this arrangement limited to those who

[24] The pleasurable aspects—sunshine, companionship, and the vistas and events—of the observance are almost invariably mentioned and even stressed by Tibetans when they talk about *bsKor Ba:* that pleasant walk which is such a welcome duty.

are already acquaintances. It is easily, even eagerly, extended to strangers who are introduced by, or who only give as references, mutual acquaintances. Having worshipers staying in one's dwelling confers prestige; additional guests who are brought in from the *bsKor Ba* path and introduced are welcome. Thus the vast web of acquaintanceship and responsibility is spun long and wide, and occasions for meeting and co-operating multiply.

The extended sojourn gives much opportunity for intercommunity contact, contact between those who would normally be complete strangers to each other. All meet repeatedly on neutral ground and in an activity that has a high degree of social approval. Traders who may have come from the farthest limits of the land of "all who speak the Tibetan language"[25] and who are detained for business reasons occupy their spare time and mitigate boredom by performing circumambulation. Pilgrims who may recently have returned from Lhasa and beyond—as far, indeed, as the holy places of India—may be on the same path. The news and speech of far places is heard, and in the effort to communicate, linguistic adjustments are made. In common with pilgrimage and the contacts it affords, the doing of *bsKor Ba* promotes a rough standardization of language usage and places a check on the rate of dialectal change.

Personal and familial enemies or members of tribes that are at war or have long-time feuds meet unarmed; for traditionally, the circumambulation path is a sanctuary. They meet in leisurely fashion and in a mood that is relatively relaxed and even pacific. Many of the first moves toward *détente,* peace talks, and truces take place on that path. Thus the performance of *bsKor Ba* makes its contribution to such public order as exists.

Finally, if intellectual ferment can be linked to the Grecian tradition and habit of meeting and discussing "some new thing," then the rudiments of the same stimulation, which comes from the hearing and telling of news, awakened curiosity, and frequent lively debate, may be said to exist on the public circumambulation circuit. The influence of such stimulation has a part in the Tibetan's intellectual life. The nomad, peasant, trader, or monk, who would normally be exposed only fleetingly to such influences, is constrained to a longer and more effective exposure by the characteristics of the observance of circumambulation. Thus the performance of the rite has a role, limited but certain, in making the average Tibetan—even when he is illiterate—intelligent, articulate, and the possessor of a surprisingly sophisticated poise.

25 G. Tucci, *Tibetan Painted Scrolls* (1949), p. 10.

CHAPTER NINE

MO:

DIVINATION

The position of *Mo* ("divination") among the religious observances of the Tibetan people is an extremely controversial one. *Mo* has been included in this study, therefore, not because it has an unchallenged right to be categorized as a religious practice, but rather for the negative reason that its exclusion would be most difficult. Its position, which is as controversial as the identification—or at least, relationship—of magic and religion, is the subject of argument by anthropologists and sociologists and is debated with equal heat by Tibetan scholars.

Nor does it conform unequivocally to all four of the criteria previously postulated for judging religious observances. Yet as a widespread quasi-religious practice, which in some aspects has links with religious dogma, the other religious observances, and the clergy, it cannot be omitted. Its position is anomalous but important, because it has certain distinctive characteristics possessed by none of the religious observances that have been examined thus far. It demands consideration and analysis if only for its special and unique functional roles in Tibetan culture and society.

Quite apart from its practice in Tibet, divination has an extremely wide incidence, if not complete universality, in human belief and behavior patterns. It is certainly not an exclusively Tibetan cultural or behavioral phenomenon, for it is well documented in many of the recorded histories of mankind. It has permeated folkways the world over and has persisted, not only in cultures called primitive, but in highly developed civilizations, whose people continue to flip coins, draw lots, read tea leaves, consult the stars, refrain from walking under ladders, avoid the number thirteen, and shudder at black cats crossing their paths. Moreover, in the attention which it focuses on the significance of signs, divination has undergone an interesting metamorphosis, emerging as respectably scientific in the work of the weather forecaster, the economic and market expert, and the business consultant. Every doctor who makes a prognosis practices divination of a sort. The exact line between what is scientific and what is unscientific can be none too clearly drawn and is subject to change: witness the scientific research in the field of supersensory perception.

The many forms of prediction are all manifestations of an effort to extend comprehension; and they are all founded on the premise that the universe is an ordered whole and that the law of causality is one aspect of that order. The primitive diviner, the weather forecaster, and the doctor all seek to know today what will be, or happen, tomorrow, and to communicate that knowledge to their clientele.

If it were assumed that events are not subject to the rules of a universal order but are capriciously accidental, there could be no divination, no forecast, and no prognosis. Thus, the existence of divination is a confession of faith in an ordered universe. The practice of divination is also a tacit admission that man does not know all the rules, although he believes that they are knowable. The Tibetan *rTSis Pa* ("numberer"), although dealing primarily with astrology, holds that numbers are a key to knowledge, and he manipulates them in calculations. In method and function he is, in a sense, a distant relative of the modern mathematician-physicist. Thus, as a background to scrutinizing divination in the Tibetan context, we are obliged to concede that it approaches universality in the larger frame of reference of the experience of mankind.

Prior to ascribing universality to the observance in Tibet, a functional definition of divination and some discussion of the Tibetan way of thinking and the frame of reference within which divination is accepted will help place the observance in perspective. *Mo* and functionally related observances can be defined as attempts to project perception or comprehension from the point in time of the "now," or present, into the time field of the future and, similarly, to project perception into space beyond the limits reached by normal sense perception. Frequently, these two efforts are combined. For example, the question "Will I be in danger tomorrow?" is answered by projection of perception into the time field of the future. The question "Is the road safe?" is answered by projection of perception into space. But the question "Will I meet danger on the road tomorrow?" can only be answered by projection of perception into both time and space.

This definition—with which all four of the Tibetan scholars at the University of Washington were in complete agreement—pinpoints the essential function of *Mo*. By it, such other magical practices as those that aim at healing, guarding, or doing harm, which are often confused with divination, are excluded from consideration. Not only are they ruled out by this definition of divination but also by their lack of universality in Tibetan practice. It must be mentioned, however, that, with regard to healing, answers gained through divination frequently contain advice and prescribe particular avoidances, actions, and remedies.

The nature of existence and time in the Tibetan conceptual frame of reference has favored the development of divination, as thus defined, and the extension of its role in Tibetan life. In a frame of reference in which existence is equally regarded as absolute, relative, and imaginary, facts and events take on a variability and fluidity in reference to both time and space. Time itself has a very distinctive quality of undifferentiated wholeness, transcending a breakdown into past, present, and future. This quality is mirrored in the formula "We two father-son [or any other combination of number and relationship] are of many rebirths," which, with numerous elaborations and variations, appears in Tibetan legends and tales. The relationship so predicated is often referred to in equally specific terms as having existed ten thousand years ago, as existing in the historical present of the particular tale, and as foreordained to exist in another rebirth ten thousand years in the future.[1]

Time in Tibetan thinking is measured by the recurrence of events, relationships, and attitudes in the past, present, and future; time becomes a modal device for linking those events, relationships, and attitudes. Rebirth brings a return in time—occasionally even the memory and habits of the past accompany such a return—and a repetition of a round of life that is conditioned by the modes of an earlier life and in turn conditions the manner of a future life. The past, present, and future thus tend to blend into one undifferentiated whole. It then becomes logical to assume that what is known of the past by recall or recorded history and of the present by observation and perception can also be known of the future by divination. Guiseppe Tucci, speaking of this phenomenon from the viewpoint of a believer, expresses something of the same idea in the following fragment: ". . . to escape time's limitations and look from the glittering heights of the eternal present down upon the passing show of things past and future."[2]

Space as a factor hindering perception presents even less difficulty than time. It is, of course, a natural continuum, and the projection of per-

---

[1] dPal lDan Bla Ma rJe bTSun Blo bZang Ye SHes Kyi gSung Las gSang Bai rNam THar bZHugs So, ff. 2 a, 21 b, 24 a-b, 28 a, 34 a, 42 a.

[2] G. Tucci, *To Lhasa and Beyond* (1956), p. 28.

ception across that continuum is a problem only of means. The distinction between normal and supranormal kinds of means is of no significance to the Tibetan. What can be seen with poor eyesight at one hundred paces may be seen with good eyesight at half a mile and with the aid of binoculars at two miles. "Why," said one Tibetan scholar, "should it not be possible to see the same at twenty or two hundred miles, by the aid of divination, which calls into action strengthened and great powers? If one has succeeded in meditation, he has vultures' eyes and can see the distance of eighteen days' journey."[3]

In the Tibetan conceptual frame of reference, the close link between omens and causation further strengthens the rationalization of divination. The same term, *rTen aBrel* ("base-connection"), is used to designate both omen and dependent causation. The latter is an important doctrinal concept that postulates twelve links or stages in the chain of causation in the achievement of liberation; thus *rTen aBrel* is a pivotal religious concept. In this context, it is held to be much the same as, although comprehended within, *rGyu aBras* ("cause-fruit"), or cause and effect. The former is a folk term and colloquial to the extent that the flight of a water ouzel under a bridge is hailed as a *rTen aBrel,* or omen, that the passerby may cross the bridge without fear. In the context of omens, it is equated with *brTags* ("mark") and used interchangeably in all discussion of the interpretation of signs.

The paradox that is posed by the assignment of such disparate meanings to the same term is resolved to some extent by defining omen as *PHyii rTen aBrel* ("outer base-connection") and dependent causation as *Nang Gi rTen aBrel* ("inner base-connection"). Between these two—outer and inner—there is another *aBrel* ("connection"): omens lead into dependent causation, and dependent causation produces omens. Whenever omens are observed and interpreted, the twelve-link chain of dependent causation comes into play. For example, when a bowl of *ZHo* ("yoghurt") is given to anyone, it is a very good *PHyii rTen aBrel* ("outer base-connection"), or omen; but when the one who receives it takes it as a good omen, he thereby brings it into *Nang Gi rTen aBrel* ("inner base-connection"), or the dependent causation chain of his life, at the point of *TSHor Ba* ("sensation"). At some later point in the twelve stages of causation, this may produce other omens.[4]

[3] Direct quote from a personal communication by Dezhung Rinpoche.

[4] A. L. Basham, "Theravada Buddhism," in *Sources of Indian Tradition* (1958), pp. 102–5; E. J. Thomas, *The Sources of Buddhist Thought* (1933), pp. 58–70. The books cited in this note were consulted for differing nuances that have appeared in dis-

HISTORY OF DIVINATION IN TIBET
AND CONFORMITY TO CRITERIA

It is certain that divination was practiced in Tibet prior to the official introduction of Buddhism in the seventh century, particularly those forms which are now narrowly defined as *Mo* by the Tibetans and which are considered either definitely non-religious (non-Buddhist) or at best questionable. The earliest records, which show no, or at most, only a trace of, Buddhist influence, make many references to the practice of *Mo* and link it with the pre-Buddhistic Bon; and ancient divination manuals that are thought to be translations or close parallels of Turkish shamanistic formulas have been found.[5] Chinese records of the eighth century connect worship of the original "wild sheep" gods of the Tibetan mountains with belief in seers and witches.[6] The interpretation of dreams, the assignment of meaning to omens, and the function of prophecy, which are all a part of early Buddhism and directly linked with the Buddha himself, were brought to Tibet either as new importations or as teachings and practices that confirmed and reinforced earlier indigenous practices.

As thus defined and placed in the conceptual world of the Tibetans, the universality of divination in the Tibetan pattern of behavior is unquestionable. Waddell stigmatizes it as the mark of a fear- and superstition-ridden existence.[7] Tucci (see footnote 2 above) describes recourse to it as a valuable immersion—though in his case admittedly unsuccessful—in a deep sea of primal folk wisdom that he feels may be more truly wise than Western science. In humorous anecdote, Madame David-Neel gives the details of its practice, also from the viewpoint of an outsider, and interprets it as a form of sympathetic helpfulness toward a folk confronted with the need, although strangely fearful of the hazards, of decision-making.[8] Thus these and many other observers furnish ample evidence of the universality of *Mo* in the Tibetan context. Accepted and practiced in some way by every Tibetan, it has a part in influencing or

cussions of the twelve-link chain of dependent causation. They are not sources in the accepted sense, for my discussion of dependent causes and omens was formulated after careful review of the results of several hours of discussion with Dezhung Rinpoche. The argument is entirely his, the condensation mine. Leon Hurwitz offered much helpful comment.

[5] F. W. Thomas, *Ancient Folk-Literature from Northeastern Tibet* (1957), pp. 113–57.

[6] P. Pelliot, *Histoire ancienne du Tibet* (1961), p. 3.

[7] L. A. Waddell, *The Buddhism of Tibet* (1895), p. 450.

[8] A. David-Neel, *Voyage d'une parisienne à Lhasa* (1926), pp. 55–58.

guiding his decisions and plans. Not all Tibetans I have known have equal faith in its value—their comments are very frequently tinged with skepticism and are sometimes disparaging and even denunciatory—but everyone I have consulted has stated flatly that every Tibetan must have had repeated recourse to divination throughout his life, either as practitioner, client, or both.

Divination is also an observable phenomenon (the second criterion postulated), or rather a collection of observable phenomena that differ in form but have one common objective. The throwing of dice, the counting of beads, the manipulation of numbers, the writing of horoscopes, and the frenetic utterance of those in seizures and states of trance may all be seen and heard by any firsthand observer of the Tibetan patterns of behavior. The existence of divination may also be established by any inquiry into the process of decision-making. The simplest question of trade, such as "Will you sell this sheep now?" is frequently met with the answer *Mo aDebs dGos Gi* ("must sow divination"); and to the question "Why are you doing this?" the answer, in a great number of instances, will be *Mo bDab Ni Mo aTHig sTe Yod Gi* ("divination having been sown, divination dropped—exactly").

The third criterion requires that the observance be religious in nature and intent. The cultural anthropologists' uncertainty as to whether magic is religion and their continuing debate concerning the relationship of the two are not compellingly important in this context. What is of importance is the equal uncertainty and contradictions of qualified Tibetan opinion. There is complete unanimity about the other religious observances (*CHos Las*), which are held to be unquestionably religious in nature and generally religious in intent; but there is wide divergence of opinion about divination. One qualified dialectician of the Yellow, or dominant, sect insists that *Mo* cannot be considered to be within *CHos* ("religion") unless *CHos* is defined as universal natural law, within which every action or system finds its place.[9] Several members of the older, Sakya sect, although somewhat less categorical in divorcing *Mo* from *CHos* are not in complete agreement among themselves. All of them point out that *Mo* is neither *enjoined* nor *prohibited* by the "word of the Buddha." One of them maintains that in nature and value *Mo* is a mixture of the religious and the worldly.[10] Another comments that *Mo* might be called religious, since it, too, is founded and operates on faith, the basis of all the other religious observances.[11] The most learned of the Sakya theologians argues that it

9 Personal communication from T. J. Norbu, brother of the Dalai Lama.

10 Personal communication from Dachen Rinpoche.

11 Personal communication from Trinlay Rinpoche.

cannot be a *CHos Las* ("religion-work") because all the true works of religion are not only observances in themselves but may be presented as
offerings and *Mo* is not acceptable as an offering. He then volunteered his
own analysis of *Mo: CHos Ma Red Bod KHa Ba Gi dPe TSHul KHo Na
Red* ("Not religion—just the custom-manner of the Tibetans").[12]

Among the Tibetan scholars, however, there was greater unanimity
of opinion that *Mo* is ambivalent in intent; those who have recourse to
divination are not motivated by a desire to accumulate merit, nor can it
directly contribute to that end. It can be directed toward worldly as well
as religious purposes. In fact, in the majority of instances, it is invoked for
help in mundane circumstances, often for questionable results, such as
success in a robbing raid or an elopement with another man's wife. The
almost infinite variety of requests will be touched on later. Occasionally,
however, it is directly concerned with religious matters both in purpose
and in effect. For example, a man may inquire about his future in the
afterworld and his rebirth, and the answer he receives may stimulate religious observance. Or again, the answer may be concerned with whether
and when to go on pilgrimage, and even more frequently, it may suggest
religious observance as a condition of success in a worldly venture. The
one who resorts to divination to determine whether a trade venture will
be successful will probably be told that prayers, offerings, and salutations
should be observed as a valuable adjunct of all other effort. Thus *Mo*, although it is quasi-religious and of doubtful status, may stimulate religious
zeal and increase the quantitative and qualitative performance of religious duties, thereby contributing to the religious observances.

Although all of the religious observances recognized as *CHos Las*
have some links (more or less tenuous) with divination, the expression of
verbalized religion and the making of offerings are most closely interwoven in its practice. Prayers are breathed on the beads before they are
counted and on the dice before they are thrown; the utterance of formulas is an inseparable prelude to purposely induced states of trance or
seizure; and no interpretation is given without a prior invocation or the
utterance of a spell. Offerings, too, are a part of divination, both as thinly
disguised payment for services to the member of the clergy who has been
asked to divine and in the symbolic presentations that are an important
part of certain divination ceremonies. By these and similar links, the close
association of divination with forms of religious observance is strengthened.

One of the difficulties of defining *Mo* is that the Tibetan word has a

[12] Personal communication from Dezhung Rinpoche.

more restricted meaning than the English word "divination." A number of forms that would obviously fall within the meaning of the English word "divination" are categorized differently in Tibetan terminology. Some of the Tibetan categories not included in *Mo* have respectable religious antecedents and are recognized as being, in varying degrees, authentically religious. And all of them are recognized as having the same functional role as *Mo*—to look into the future—and thus as being essentially alike. These categories and their forms and relationships will be analyzed later in some detail.

Mo also does not conform—or at best, conforms only imperfectly—to the fourth criterion of conceptual unity. It is not an easily defined simplistic action like circumambulation, nor does it resemble the expression of verbalized religion, the many diverse forms of which are all traceable to the basic principles of verbalization. Like the latter, however, divination is an effort in communication, but an effort that is an extremely complex process, involving both verbal and non-verbal means. Only rarely, as when an oracle is consulted, is it limited to verbal means alone. In the typical process, a question is formulated verbally; the question is submitted by non-verbal means of great diversity; an answer is received and comprehended from signs; and that answer is finally verbalized for transmission to the one who asked the question.

The non-verbal links in the process of communication are extremely diverse: dice are thrown and the numbers are counted; pebbles are scattered and the pattern of their distribution is studied; stones are skipped and the spacing and number of the skips are noted; butter lamps are lit and the color, shape, duration, and smoke of the flame are watched; and the scapulae of sheep are heated over fire and the resulting cracks are traced. These are only a few examples showing the wide range of diversity. As phenomena, the means of divination are so unlike in form that only their unitary purpose brings them into a single classification. Only in their common objective can the disparate practices of the observance of divination be said to manifest conceptual unity.

TERMINOLOGY AND CATEGORIES OF DIVINATION

The Tibetan word *Mo* has a more particularized meaning in relation to the entire field of divination practices than the general terms used for the other Tibetan religious observances. In Tibetan terminology, *Pra PHab* ("lot fall"), for example, is not comprehended within the meaning of *Mo*. Strictly speaking, *Mo* designates a certain class of observances within the general field of divination by which Tibetans seek to look into the future and extend the limits of their spatial perception. In a somewhat arbitrary manner, which, however, is justified on the basis of function, it is used here to subsume all the practices of the observance. Within the category of *Mo*, the various subcategories of practices are specifically linked with it in terminology, for example, *SHo Mo* ("dice divination"), *mDaa Mo* ("arrow divination"), *lHam sGrog Mo* ("boot-strap divination"), and so on. These subcategories will be enumerated and described.

The cognate categories of somewhat similar observances are *Pra PHab* ("lot fall"), or the casting of lots; *brTags ZHu* ("request for examination"), which has a number of subcategories; and *lHa Babs* ("god-fallen-on"), or the oracle of the god-possessed. They are not specifically related to *Mo* in terminology, but their function is so similar to that of *Mo* that my Tibetan collaborators, although stating that they are not divination, discuss them from the point of view of function as forms of divination. The rationalization as formulated in Tibetan is, *Ha Lam Mo Red* ("are pretty nearly divination").[13]

The word *Mo* has none of the diversity of meaning, association, or usage of the terms designating the other, unequivocally religious observances. It has only one homophone: *Mo*, the female suffix. In conversation the latter syllable is occasionally used alone, in a somewhat facetious or slightly pejorative sense, for "woman." Combined with particles denoting persons, *Mo* appears as *Mo Pa* ("male diviner"), *Mo Ma* ("female diviner"), and *Mo mKHan* ("divination specialist").

The verbs generally used with *Mo* are *lTa* ("look"), *aDebs* ("sow"), *rGyab* ("strike"), and *aBab* ("fall on"). The first of these, *lTa*, refers most specifically to the motive and act of divining. *aDebs*, which is the verb employed in the vast majority of instances, refers to the underlying principle of the observance. *aDebs* is also the word most frequently used with *sMon Lam* ("wish-way"), or wish-prayer; and in both cases, it relates the observance to the natural logic of cause and effect: seed and fruit, and seedtime and harvest. For *sMon Lam*, the fruition is the wish granted: for *Mo*, the fruition is the knowledge revealed. *rGyab* ("strike") and *aBab* ("fall on") have a somewhat more limited significance. They refer to special aspects of divination techniques: *rGyab* ("strike"), to the act of throwing the dice; and *aBab* ("fall on"), to the way the dice fall. The latter word also has another connotation with regard to those who go into trances and seizures; they are commonly called *lHa Pa* ("god one[s]"), but for the occasion of the seizure, they are called *lHa Babs* ("god-fallen-on"). When the result of divination is confirmed by subsequent events, it

[13] *Ibid.*

is called *gSal Po* ("the clear one"), or the *Mo* ("divination") is said to *aTHig Gi* ("fall in a drop")—that is, forecast and event are matched like drops.

DIVINATION IN DOCTRINE AND TIBETAN HISTORY

Divination itself has no acknowledged position in early Buddhist doctrine comparable to the positions occupied by the religious observances thus far investigated. Lacking either prescription or proscription by the Buddha, or in the great mass of didactical utterance ascribed to him, its practice cannot be said to be either obedience or disobedience to the "word of the Buddha." Buddhism officially refused to note its existence. It was not prohibited, and it was not formally permitted; it was ignored. Like the hero of Sartor Resartus, it lay in the "center of indifference," and there, by dint of continued practice, the pressure of need, and the gradual accumulation of historical precedent and sanction, it achieved the status of the tacitly permitted.

In the pre-Buddhist religious system, or systems, of Tibet, on the other hand, divination occupied a much stronger, and fully sanctioned, position. It was an important part of religious practice and ritual. By means of oracle bones, colored cords, the internal organs of animals, and the close observation of omens, the future was revealed. It was the magic by which treasures and mines were discovered and shamans, in states of frenzy, foretold future events.[14]

Since Buddhism would not prohibit divination, it was obliged to come to terms with it as an indigenous practice, and the result was universal recourse to divination by Tibetans and the assignment of a quasi-religious status to it. Cognate forms that had Buddhist doctrinal sanction were the drawing of lots, the interpretation of dreams, the evaluation of face and body marks, and appeals to the clairvoyant wisdom of those who had gained that power through meditation. The sanction of these forms contributed to the general acceptability of and faith in the observance.

Two developments in Tibetan history further strengthened the position of divination. The first was the development of a tradition of including prophecy within historical records and related literature. Many, if not all, of these "prophecies" were, in reality, *ex post facto* accounts of religious and political developments ascribed by the writers to speakers of early times. Moreover, the content of the prophecies was not always lim-

---

14 G. Tucci, *Tibetan Painted Scrolls* (1949), pp. 715–17; R. Nebesky-Wojkowitz, *Oracles and Demons of Tibet* (1956), p. 428; S. C. Das, "Contributions on Tibet," *JASB*, 1881, pp. 187–98; H. Hoffmann, *The Religions of Tibet* (1961), p. 105; M. Lalou, *Les religions du Tibet* (1957), p. 78.

ited to the historically known. They were often combined with certain stock Buddhist eschatological doctrines—chief among them the progressive degeneracy of human life and culture that will mark the end of the present kalpa, or age of the Buddha. By linking the religious prophecy to the "prophecy" that is known to have been fulfilled an apparent validity was given to the whole.[15]

The prophecy tradition was strengthened by the device of the "hidden treasures," whereby doctrinal utterances are reputed to have been hidden in the earth, or some other place, and are then "discovered" or "revealed" at appropriate times. The close functional link between this form of religiously sanctioned prophecy and divination has served to enhance the status and religious authority of the humble and more mundane soothsayer.[16]

The second development in Tibetan history that greatly encouraged acceptance of the observance was the employment of various forms of divination in the selection of the *sPrul sKu* ("emanation-body") lamas, chief of whom are the Dalai Lama and the Panchen Lama. One of the unique developments in the Tibetan religio-political system was the manner in which the problem of an orderly, non-violent leadership succession or transference of power was solved. With the final victory—following the reforms instituted by *TSong KHa Pa*—of the principle of celibacy, which had been placed in question by some of the practices of the older sects, hereditary succession was no longer feasible in the politically dominant Yellow sect, and the designation of a successor became a matter of decision—individual, collective, or non-personal. By introducing clairvoyance and various forms of divination into the process of nomination, the final choice took on a non-personal character and acquired the additional sanction of very special authority. As a manifestation of the express will of the Buddhahood, it was not subject to debate, and there could be no disagreement. The loyalty of the Tibetans toward the sixth Dalai Lama is a striking example of this acceptance. He was known to all as a most unmonkish profligate and also as the writer of some very beautiful love songs. The Chinese intervened in Tibetan politics to declare that he was not the true Dalai Lama and eventually arranged his death. But for all of this, he is deeply revered by the Tibetans, and he never lost his place in the line of

[15] F. W. Thomas, *Tibetan Texts and Documents* (1935), Part I, pp. 1–257; E. Obermiller, *History of Buddhism* (1932), Part II, pp. 4–5, 108–22; A. L. Basham, *op. cit.*, pp. 140–41; *dPal lDan Bla Ma rJe bTSun . . .* , ff. 41 *b*–42 *b*.

[16] G. Tucci, *op. cit.*, pp. 109–14; H. Hoffmann, *op. cit.*, pp. 74, 175, 176; G.-Ch. Toussaint, *Le dict de Padma* (1933), pp. 220–29; L. A. Waddell, *op. cit.*, pp. 57, 58, 165.

the Dalai Lamas. Prophecies or specific instructions based on clairvoyance, the pronouncements of the state oracle, and visions seen in the waters of the sacred lake *CHos aKHor rGyal mTSHo,* which are aids to the selection of a Dalai Lama, brought the observance of divination into a very high level of Tibetan religious administration; and in fact, utterances of the oracle influenced statecraft. Their use by the religious hierarchy constituted strong endorsement of divination.[17]

Although according to Tibetan doctrinal purists divination may not be a part of religion, it certainly nestles closely, even comfortably, under the wing of religion, though its employment in the great majority of instances is directed toward the solution of mundane problems.

SUBCATEGORIES OF DIVINATION

Even in the restricted Tibetan sense, *Mo* is not a single observance but a category embracing different forms, or subcategories. The list which follows cannot be said to show all the subcategories performed by all Tibetans in all parts of Tibet. Unquestionably, there are many local practices that have not been included. Thus it is only a representative list and does not pretend to be exhaustive. It is, however, the total I was able to elicit from the four Tibetan scholars available to me for consultation.

1. *aPHreng Mo* ("rosary divination") is probably the most frequently practiced form, both because the means are immediately available—everyone has a rosary and is generally always wearing it—and because the use of the rosary links it with the verbalization of religion. By association with that most important of the religious observances, it is believed to acquire enhanced validity. The technique is a simple one. The rosary is taken and rubbed between the two hands; raised to touch the forehead while prayers are said; and then one strand is stretched between both hands. At random a bead is grasped by the thumb and finger tips of each hand; with these beads as starting point, the beads are counted off by threes, as the hands move toward each other. From one to six beads will remain at the end of the process, since zero is not permitted. Odd numbers are *Yag Po* ("the good one"), or favorable; and the even numbers are *sDug Po* ("the evil one"), or unfavorable.

2. *SHo Mo* ("dice divination") is probably the next most frequently used form. Every lama who practices divination—and there are few who do not—has divination dice. There are either three, with the usual spots, or

[17] M. Lalou, *op. cit.,* p. 6; R. Nebesky-Wojkowitz, *op. cit.,* pp. 449–54; Li Tieh-tseng, *Tibet* (1960), pp. 176, 179, 181; T. J. Norbu, *Tibet Is My Country* (1960), pp. 130–32; A. Winnington, *Tibet* (1957), p. 94.

Mig ("eye[s]"), which are thrown together, or a single die having the letters *Na, Ma, Ya, Ra, Sa,* and *AH* of the Tibetan alphabet marked on the six faces. Special dice not used for gaming are preferred; and they should be of rosewood, sandalwood, or ivory, in that order of preference. They may be thrown by hand but more frequently are thrown from a box, first being raised to the mouth as a prayer is breathed upon them.[18]

Basically, this is a mechanical operation; yet there are many complicated systems for evaluating the numbers which turn up. For example, the lama who has been asked to divine by this method may pose his own special formulation of the problem in a series of questions progressively based on the answers which appear. Thus there remains considerable latitude for the injection of subjective opinion and interpretation into the process.

3. *mDaa Mo* ("arrow divination") involves the use of two arrows, like archery arrows in every respect—length, feathering, and so on—except that they have no metal points. One in each hand, the diviner holds them lightly, flat on the table, with the unfeathered ends pointing toward each other. After an intensive recital of spells and meditation, the two arrows will rise and lean toward each other until the two ends touch, after which they will fall forward (favorable) or backward (unfavorable). This form is also known as *Ge Sar Mo* ("Gesar divination"). It is rarely used but is considered of great authority and true efficacy—*sTobs CHen* ("great power").

4. *lHam sGrog Mo* ("boot-strap divination") is a quick technique, using means always available, and is quite common in some parts of the country, notably Khams, but little known elsewhere. The strap that binds the top of the boot just below the knee is taken off, prayed over, and stretched between the two hands, which then move toward each other, taking positions on the strap measured by units of finger breadth or finger joint. The space remaining between the two hands is then estimated according to the same units, and again odd numbers are good omens and even numbers evil. In method, this form corresponds to rosary divination but may have an older folk origin.

5. *Sog Mo* ("scapula divination") is accomplished by roasting the fresh scapula of an animal—generally a sheep—over a fire or in hot ashes

[18] L. A. Waddell, *op. cit.*, pp. 470–71; T. J. Norbu, *op. cit.*, p. 93. The die with the letters of the alphabet on the six faces, which was described by the Tibetan scholars, is different from the two sets cited by Waddell. Norbu tells of another kind, a die marked with the six letters of the six-syllable formula, which, although used to play a game, could obviously have been used—and indeed certainly was used—in divination. Evidently there are several different kinds in use.

until cracks appear; answers or signs are then deduced from the pattern of the cracks. This is done to a muttered barrage of formulas and spells. In general, cracks which run in parallel lines are favorable; and those which cross and form a web suggest, at least, complications and tend to be unfavorable. The use of this form of divination is much practiced by hunters and is frequently resorted to during the butchering season in the late fall. It involves the violation of a strong and widespread taboo prohibiting the scorching of any part of a butchered animal—meat, fat, hide, hair, horns, or hooves—in the belief that such action may arouse the anger of various *Sa bDag* ("earth-owners") or *Klu* ("serpent spirits").

6. *rNGa Mo* ("drum divination") is performed by placing a pinch or small handful of grain, either barley or rice, on a drum head and vibrating the tympanum with the hands, to the accompaniment of spells, until the grains shift into patterns on its surface. These patterns are then interpreted. It is apparent that this form of divination relies to a great extent on the presumptive clairvoyance of the diviner, who is allowed considerable latitude in determining when the patterns are finally formed and what they may mean. It unquestionably derives from early pre-Buddhist shamanistic practices in which the drum was of prime importance.

7. *rDo Mo* ("stone divination") is performed by taking a handful of stones—the number, sizes, color, and so on, are immaterial—blowing prayers upon them, and throwing them on the ground. Their pattern of distribution is then the basis for interpretation. There are manuals that give detailed instruction with regard to both this and the following, closely related form of divination. Much, however, is left to the psychic perception or imagination of the one who looks to the stones for guidance for himself or on the behalf of others.

8. *rDeu Mo* ("pebble divination") differs from the preceding practice in being more formalized. The number and color of the pebbles are specified: there must be fifteen whites ones and fifteen black ones. After a suitable amount of praying, they are thrown upon a board that is marked into a grid by intersecting lines. Each square and the number of pebbles that falls into it have prescribed significance. Also important is whether the pebbles are all black, all white, or in varying proportions of the two. The answers gained by this form are generally more involved—and packed with qualifying conditions—than those from stone divination. The pebbles, marked board, and instruction manual are all essential operating equipment for this form of *Mo*.

9. *mTSHo Mo* ("lake divination"), also called *CHab Mo* ("water divination"), is performed by skipping stones. The elements of chance in-

volved in finding a suitable stone, in the relative dexterity of the thrower, and in water surface conditions, impact angle, and velocity make this seemingly simple version of the "toss-up" a complicated problem of possibilities. The search for a stone and the throw are accompanied by prayer. The answer that emerges is based on the number and spacing of the skips, with some consideration being given to the manner of flight. The general rule that odd numbers are favorable and even numbers unfavorable holds good, although determination of the count may not be entirely unequivocal. The spacing of the skips and manner of flight require special knowledge of omens, intuition, or imagination and create the occasion for subjective opinion or calculated advice.

10. *dPe Mo* ("book divination") is a characteristic Tibetan form of the observance; yet it is familiar in many cultures. A volume of religious writings—the scriptures themselves, commentary, a prayer manual, or the biography of a saint—is taken in both hands and raised to the head to the accompaniment of prayers; it is then opened at random, and a spot picked out, without looking, by a finger tip. The nearest word is then examined as to number of letters, their esoteric significance, and so on. The meaning, or meanings, of the word; the sentence or the phrases to which it belongs; and even its association with recognized axioms and epigrams may be considered. This form of divination has great prestige and is reputedly very dependable.

11. *Mar Me Mo* ("butter-fire—or butter-lamp—divination") is a form of divination for which careful preparations are required. The cotton wick must be made and the butter selected and packed into the bowl of the lamp; prayers and spells mark each stage of preparation. After the lamp has been lighted, the shape, height, color, and fluctuations of the flame must be noted. The color and volume of the smoke are important signs, as is the length of time the lamp burns in comparison with other lamps of the same size. All the various indications can be put together into formulations that are authoritative and much valued only by those who have experience and special knowledge.

12. *SHa Mo* ("flesh divination") involves the use of the internal organs and the flesh and blood of animals that either have been killed for the purpose or have died. Since it is based on killing, it is considered a heretical practice; and none of the Tibetans who supplied most of the information concerning the other forms of divination would admit to any personal knowledge of the techniques of the rite. All agreed, however, that it was practiced by the Bon Po or by some of the *sNGags Pa* ("sorcerer") sects. Some of the signs are common knowledge with hunters and

with those Tibetans who do the butchering of animals, and are valued by them as auguries.

13. *rTSis Mo* ("number divination"), the form by which horoscopes are made, is the most complicated of the practices through which knowledge of the future is sought. Most of the factors upon which a horoscope is based have been borrowed from the Chinese but some owe their provenance to Indian sources. The calendar of the twelve animals, five elements, and sixty-year cycle is the basis of a very complicated calculation. In the calendar, the animals and the elements all differ in nature and, in combination, produce patterns of antagonism and agreement of great complexity. The days of the week, linked with the planets and the sun and moon, also exert special influence. Years are characterized alternately as male and female; and in the basic rhythm of existence, there is an alternating expansion and contraction of the active and passive principles. The four seasons have their special characteristics, and the influences of the "eight trigrams" and the nine *sMe Ba*, which are the numerals one to nine and which, arranged in a quadratic combination, relate to what are called the "lunar mansions," must be considered. "Backward reckoning," the factors of the "sky-seizing rope," the hanging dagger, the favorable or unfavorable character of each day of the lunar month, and even the special significance of each hour of the day further complicate the calculation. By juggling all these factors, in accordance with rules of similar complexity, birth, marriage, annual, and life horoscopes of infinite variety are prepared which not only name the threatening dangers but suggest various ways of avoiding them and of adequately protecting one's self by judicious and more frequent religious observance.[19]

14. *Glu Mo* ("song divination"), or as it is sometimes called, *mGur Mo* ("hymn divination"), combines singing with forecasting. Although it often turns into hilarious social entertainment, it is taken very seriously as a kind of divination that, depending on the reputation of the practitioner, may be very efficacious. The songs sung may be standard, well-known ones or new ones created calypso style either by combining lines from well-known verses and songs or, depending on the versifying skill of the performer, by an extemporaneous tour de force. It is mostly done by

[19] L. A. Waddell, *op. cit.*, pp. 450–75. Of those who have written about various aspects of divination, Waddell describes and illustrates the making of horoscopes in greatest detail. Nothing given by my Tibetan collaborators and incorporated into my text is at variance with Waddell's more detailed account. This is also true of his account of the use of stones in divination; on the other hand, the Tibetans insisted that they had never known playing cards to be used for divination, as described by Waddell. They claim that playing cards are used only for gaming but admit that any set of cards with numbers on them could be used for divination.

women. Some personal belonging of each member of the group—nine is a preferred number—is collected, without letting the singer identify the owners; then, as each object is held up, she sings a verse of her song. The owner of the object claims his property, and his verse, which is identified as a divination utterance, foretells tendencies and possible happenings in his life.

In the exhibition staged at a party in our home, two of the nine verses were identified as quotes or paraphrases from the love songs of the sixth Dalai Lama; and all were either somewhat ambiguous or, if pointed, metaphorical in style. There was much merriment, but the feeling that it wasn't all just play was quite marked. The singer—the wife of the Sakya lama—enjoyed very much some of the tabs she pinned on her friends but took it all seriously, nevertheless, and was very happy when some particularly felicitous saying fell to the lot of an obvious favorite.[20]

COGNATE OBSERVANCES

The principal practices that are clearly related to *Mo*, because of a similarity of objective and motive, are *Pra PHab* ("lot fall"), or the casting of lots; the entire system of the interpretation of situations and omens and the giving of advice, through the exercise of clairvoyance, the many forms of which are somewhat loosely categorized as *brTags ZHu* ("request for examination of marks"); and the oracle of the possessed, variously called *lHa Pa* ("god one"), *lHa Babs* ("god-fallen-on"), or *lHa aDZin* ("god-seized").

With the exception of the last practice, these cognate observances are more closely linked with religion—in fact, are given unequivocal religious status—than are the various forms of *Mo* previously discussed. Recourse

[20] This listing makes no pretension to being a complete record of all the forms of *Mo* that are found throughout Tibet. It stands as an enumeration made by four Tibetan scholars—one of whom has special competence in the field—in response to questioning. Their memories were not jogged by references to the personal observations or second-hand experiences of any of the writers listed below. Some of the observances listed in the references do not appear in my text, but there are also some that have not been previously listed, for example, *Ge Sar Mo* ("Gesar divination"), about which Nebesky-Wojkowitz (*op. cit.*, p. 462) could secure no details. I have briefly described what is said to be *Ge Sar Mo* under the heading of *mDaa Mo* ("arrow divination").

R. Nebesky-Wojkowitz, *op. cit.*, pp. 455–66; H. Hoffmann, *Quellen zur Geschichte der tibetischen Bon Religion* (1950), pp. 192–97; L. A. Waddell, *op. cit.*, pp. 465–74; B. Laufer, "Bird Divination among the Tibetans," *T'oung Pao*, XV (1901), 1–110; W. W. Rockhill, "Tibet, a Geographical, Ethnographical, and Historical Sketch Derived from Chinese Sources," *JRAS*, 1891, pp. 186–291, esp. p. 235; J. Bacot, "La table des presages signific par l'éclair," *Journal Asiatique*, 1913, pp. 445–49; A. David-Neel, *op. cit.*, pp. 55–58 ff.; A. David-Neel, *Le lama au cinq sagesses* (1939), pp. 1 ff.; G. Tucci, *To Lhasa and Beyond* (1956), pp. 19–30.

to lots, for example, was prescribed in the very earliest Buddhist practice. The exercise of prescience, clairvoyance, and perceptive powers involving the interpretation of signs and dreams was also a fully authenticated and authorized part of early Buddhist practice and was linked with the Buddha himself.[21] The oracle of the possessed was not a part of early Buddhist tradition, but at present, its manifestation in Tibet is attended with such respect—as a direct communication from the deity—reinforced indirectly by the use of the state oracle, that its religious status is no longer challenged, although deprecating voices are occasionally raised.

The casting of lots mainly takes the form of ceremonies leading to seeing and recognizing signs and scenes in a mirror or inducing a state of mind wherein signs and scenes are seen in the surface of a lake. Such vision may mark the high point of a lama's effort and his career, and it may also come to the most unlearned, of whom some women have become famous for their gift. This is the observance that is frequently employed to *Bar CHad Sel Ba* ("cleanse away the intervening obstruction").

The category known as *brTags ZHu*, or request for examination, subsumes a number of subcategories, which, in the frequency of their observance, are a close second to *Mo* ("divination"). They differ from *Mo*, however, in two important respects: their more unequivocal religious status and the fact that the phenomena for which examination is requested are self-originating. Whether mark or sign, omen or dream, the object of *brTags ZHu* has not been induced but is *Rang Byung* ("self-originating"). Or there may be no object at all, as in prophecy.

1. The first of the subcategories consists in the utterance of those who have *mNGon SHes* ("clairvoyant perception"). This may take the form of *Lung sTon* ("prophecy display"), as so often recorded in the religiously interpreted histories of Tibet. It may be in the form of advice in response to supplication and the expression of need. It may take the form of a pronouncement that has not been solicited: guidance concerning doctrine, religious administration, or closely linked political and even economic affairs. Clairvoyant utterance is primarily an attribute of the *Byang CHub Sems dPaa*, or Bodhisattva. However, it is agreed that not all *sPrul sKu* ("emanation-body") lamas have that attribute and that there are some monks who, through meditation, have acquired it. It follows only upon successful *sGom*, or meditation.

2. The second of the subcategories is called *brTags bsGril ZHu* ("re-

---

[21] E. J. Thomas, *The Life of the Buddha* (1931), pp. 32, 110, 114, 120, 213, 214; E. Obermiller, *op. cit.*, pp. 10, 14, 27, 29, 34, 57, 58; G. N. Roerich, *The Blue Annals* (1949), pp. 17–18, 25–27.

quest for the examination of wrapped-up signs"). Advice is sought by writing out the details of the problem or question on narrow strips of paper, with a different course of action on each one. Generally, only two are written and are labeled good or bad, positive or negative. The strips of paper are then rolled up—sometimes each is enclosed in a ball of dough—and the rolled paper or balls of dough are mixed up in a box or by hand, with appropriate charms and prayers. Afterward one is selected and opened to determine the answer. Although in form this is similar to casting lots, it is not included within that category.

3. The third of the subcategories is the interpretation of *brTags* ("signs") or *rTen aBrel* ("base-connection[s]"), or omens. This practice is fully authorized in both the spell and the sutra portions of the Buddhist scriptures. Animals, birds, plants, colors, and natural phenomena may be signs of either good or evil. Many specific objects are listed in books on the significance of marks, others are commonly known, and still others are known only to those who have gained clairvoyance.

Classification of these objects as good or bad omens is often, but not unfailingly, in accord with their natural character as demonstrably good or evil. Thus all weapons, tattered and soiled clothing, tattered and defaced books, and broken utensils are evil, and all objects used in worship, books in good condition, and new clothes are good; on the other hand, corpses are good omens and wedding processions are evil omens. Of foodstuffs, *ZHo* ("yoghurt"), *Ma rMos Lo Tog* ("unsown"—or wild—"produce of the year")—this name is now applied to maize but, as its name implies, was originally given to the first magically produced food of mankind—and *Gro Ma* ("potentilla tubers") are particularly favorable omens. All birds of prey—because they kill—are evil omens. Ravens, too, are evil, except when they eat the broken-up offerings; then they become good and are called *lHai Bya* ("birds of the god"). Vultures, geese, ruddy sheldrakes, cranes, ram chukars, eared pheasants, and water ouzels are good omens. There is an odd inconsistency in the classification of partridges, for the ram chukar (also known as snow fowl), which is a variety of partridge, is such a good sign it is also called "the god bird," whereas the steppe partridge is hated and feared and is called "the famine bird" and an omen of robber attack. Among the wild animals, the kiang, stags (except for the short period in summer when their antlers are in the velvet and thus are medicine), blue sheep, orongo antelopes, musk deer, hares, marmots, wild pigs, and monkeys are evil omens; but argali, wild yak, and serou are good omens. Here again there is an odd inconsistency: the argali, or Asiatic bighorn sheep, are considered good and the blue sheep evil. Among the beasts of prey, brown bears, black bears, lynx, jackals, fox, and badgers are evil omens, whereas tigers, leopards, snow leopards, and wolves are good. Since the latter prey on livestock, they are actually hated in everyday life, but as omens they are hailed as belonging to the goddess. Otters have a seasonal variation as omens, for which, unlike the changing status of stags, there is no explanation. Seen in the spring and summer, they are a very bad omen, but seen in the fall and winter, they are considered a good omen. Of the domesticated animals, donkeys, mules, bulls, sheep, and goats are evil; horses, yak (male and female), cows, yak-cow hybrids (male and female), and dogs are good. Of the colors, black, red, and blue are evil; white, yellow, and green are good. Only white and blue waters, however, are good, whereas red, yellow, and muddy waters are evil. Of cliffs or rock formations, the white ones belong to the gods and are good; the gNYan ("argali") dwell in multicolored ones, which are good; black ones belong to the devils and are evil; red ones belong to the fearful harelipped red bTSan ("goblins") and are evil; blue ones belong to the serpent spirits and, depending on the context, may be either good or evil.

4. The fourth of the subcategories consists of the Rlung brDa ("wind signs"). Interpretation is based on the manner of a person's breathing—force, tempo, whether through the mouth or nostrils, and so on—and the power of retention. It does not occur apart from the practice of meditation, and only rarely.

5. The fifth subcategory is Dud brDa ("smoke signs"). The color, volume, and drift—direction, height, and spread—of the smoke all have significance. The most elaborate interpretations are based on the patterns that may be discerned when the smoke has spread almost to the point of disappearing against the sky. It is only the smoke from bSang ("scent") offerings (burning juniper boughs, fragrant herbs, and so on) that has value. The lore of this practice is not widely known but belongs to those who are recognized as specialists. From the appearance of the smoke, Marpa characterized a bSang ("scent") offering of burning juniper boughs as empty because no grain had been scattered on the fire.[22]

6. The sixth of the subcategories is TSHig brTags ("phrase mark"), sometimes also known as TSHig brDa ("phrase sign"). It involves finding metasemantic significance in the phonetic and/or semantic accordance of words or phrases in uttered discourse. It comes into play most frequently when two people exchange greetings or become involved in a series of

---

[22] *Mi Lai rNam THar* [biography of <u>Mi La</u>] (gTSang Ding Ri edition), Vol. *Ka*, f. 56 *b*.

specific questions and answers at first meeting. The relative ease with which phonetic parallelisms may be achieved in Tibetan discourse and the marked tendency to use such echo effects in proverbs, verse, and the measured, sententious style into which formal Tibetan conversation frequently turns create numerous opportunities for finding phonetic accordance. Semantic accordance, on the other hand, is often obvious and even banal—in particular when it is linked with enumeration of objects and punning—but for the Tibetan looking for "phrase signs" it is accepted as satisfyingly significant, as is well illustrated in the following example.

A member of the clergy met a somewhat suspicious looking character at a fork in the trail. With some internal uneasiness, he sought to reassure himself by engaging him in conversation, for talking may often forestall unpleasantness. He also wished to find out which of the branching trails would take him to his destination. Beginning with the name of the spot and running throughout the various answers and statements of the suspicious one, the word *bKra SHis* ("benediction" or "good fortune") appeared like a persistent echo. Finally, the monk asked, "What is your name?" "My name is <u>*bKra SHis TSHe Ring*</u>," was the answer, and the monk could not hide his relief. "Now all is well, and good fortune for both you and me. The name of this place and all your words are marked with *bKra SHis*, and even your name is in agreement." A historic example of the significance of signs in words is also found in the account of the first meeting of Marpa and Mila.[23]

7. *sKad brTags* ("speech mark"), the seventh subcategory, somewhat resembles the sixth category since it is concerned with utterance. It involves, however, the utterance of animals and birds and the ascription of clairvoyant wisdom, in certain cases and to a certain degree, to them. It is widely held that dogs and horses are able to see the *lHa Ma Yin* ("non-god one[s]") and *aDre* ("goblin[s]"), which cannot be seen by human beings. "Speech marks" are found in the cries and utterances of living creatures, of which the most frequently cited are the raven, crow, magpie, owl, and dog, possibly because they are noticeably given to utterance. A certain amount of clairvoyant perception is involved in each instance.

Of the birds, the *PHo Rog* ("raven"), called *lHa Bya* ("god bird") and *gTor Bya* ("scatter bird"), is the most important and an especially favorable omen when he eats the scattered offerings. Both the time of day or night and the point of the compass toward which his beak is directed

[23] This is one of the stories told by Dezhung Rinpoche to illustrate "phrase-mark" divination. He also cited the meeting of Mila and Marpa (*Mi Lai rNam THar*, Vol. *Ka*, f. 33 *a*).

when he croaks have great significance. No significance is attached to the direction in which crows and magpies point their beaks when uttering cries, but the time of day is important. If their cries are heard in the three periods of the morning from daybreak to noon, the meanings are respectively: beer and meat, the hearing of news, and guests from afar. Any such cries in the afternoon or night are inauspicious. The howling, *KHyi NGu* ("dog weeping"), of a dog is interpreted as a favorable or unfavorable sign depending on the hour of the day and the auspices of the different days.[24]

The "laughter" of the owl is an omen of evil. The story is told that shortly before the death of the thirteenth Dalai Lama he was informed that an owl had twice lighted on the roof of the *gNas CHung* oracle "and had spoken 'ha ha.'" The Dalai Lama's answer was "All right, the time is come."[25]

8. The eighth subcategory of signs includes such phenomena as *Mig sGul* ("eye move"), the involuntary twitching of the eyelids; *rNa mCHog Ur Ur* ("roaring or humming in the ears"); and *sBrid Pa* ("sneezing"). The twitching eyelid is interpreted in a somewhat complicated manner according to which eye twitches and at what time. Humming in the ears and sneezing are interpreted according to the time of day in much the same manner as the calls of crows and magpies. In fact, the signs in this subcategory are associated in Tibetan writings and manuals with those of the preceding category.

9. The ninth and last of the subcategories is that of the *rMi Lam brTags* ("dream mark" or "sign"). Of all the categories of divination, that of dreams is invested with the greatest degree of religious authority. It appears and functions with crucial significance in the life story and mission of the Buddha; and it has the explicit authority of the "word of the Buddha."[26] According to Dezhung Rinpoche, it is the most trustworthy of all the observances and gives the most exact answers. Daytime dreams are of questionable value, although at times one of them will produce sig-

---

24 For this subcategory Dezhung Rinpoche cited the following: *Vaidurya dKar Poi Glegs Bam Pod gNYis*, by Sangs Gyas Gya mTSHo, Vol. II, ff. 334 *b*, 335 *a-b*, 336 *a*, 337 *a*; and *dGra lHa rTa THugs* [not available for folio citation]. Laufer, in "Bird Divination among the Tibetans" (see footnote 20 above), has treated in great detail the significance given to the calls of the raven. Tibetan manuals listing the significance of these signs were formerly on sale in the Lhasa market and extensively used.

25 *rNam THar Rin CHen PHreng Ba* [biography of the thirteenth Dalai Lama], Vol II, f. 316 *a*.

26 It is said that dreams are in accordance with "the word of The Buddha" because they are cited in the *mDo* ("sutra") division of the Tibetan Buddhist scriptures. *The Tibetan Tripitika* (Peking edition, Tokyo-Kyoto printing), Vol. 26 (*mDo Ku*), ff. 110 *a*– 115 *b*; Vol. 37 (*mDo Zu*), f. 281 *a-b*; Vol. 39 (*mDo SHu*), f. 28 *a-b*.

nificant omens. The good and evil character assigned to objects in the other categories holds good when they appear in dreams. Indeed, it is possible that particular characterizations have been assigned because of the way objects have been interpreted in dreams by persons of recognized authority. The classification of the dog as good, for example, may have resulted from the interpretation of a dream of Ras CHung's by Mila, which is often cited as an argument for that goodness. Ras CHung, the disciple of Mila, dreamed that he was a lion surrounded by dogs; and Mila said, "You are truly like a lion in strength, and the dogs around you are the sign of the *mKHaa aGro Ma* ("sky-going female[s]") who gather to you."[27]

The validity of dreams varies in accordance with the period of the night in which they were dreamed. Those of the period from nine to midnight are merely recollections of the events and cares of the day and of little value. Those from midnight until three in the morning are not reliable, for they are the *lHai CHo aPHrul* ("trickery of the god"). Those from three until morning, and even naps after first awakening, are the ones that have the most meaning. But a dream to be fully trustworthy must also be clear "like the tracing of lines on the mind."

The third category of cognate observances—those practices that are divination in function but not in name—consists of the utterances of the "possessed" ones of Tibet. They are known as *lHa Pa* ("god one[s]"), sometimes also called *lHa KHa* ("god mouth"); when they have been "possessed" and produce significant utterances, they are known as *lHa Babs* ("god-fallen-on"), *lHa aDZin* ("god-seized"), or *lHa SHon* ("god-ridden"). The *lHa Pa* may be lamas and other members of the clergy or laymen, either men or women. The seizures may be sought and induced, or they may come unsought, in which case they are often feared; the latter may be known as *aDre aDZin* ("goblin seizure"). The physical aspects of the seizures—sweating, convulsions, and an access of supernormal strength—and the links which this phenomenon has with the early shamanistic religion of Tibet have been discussed in chapter ii. Neither they nor other functional aspects such as exorcism and healing are germane to a discussion of the divination function of the phenomenon. What is pertinent to this function is the substitution of identity which occurs during a seizure—the personality of the medium gives place to the personality of the god. The possessed one loses his character as an intermediary. Like a good interpreter, he speaks in the first person, with the voice—often hoarse

[27] Personal communication from Dezhung Rinpoche. The story of Ras CHung's dream is found in *CHag Med Ri CHos,* Vol. I (not available for folio citation).

and strange—of the god. His own antecedents and characteristics no longer relate to the authority with which he speaks and his function. With particular reference to the processes of communication, he has become the god himself. His hearing is the hearing of the god; and his speech is the speech of the god.

While inhaling and exhaling in great gasps like a swimmer doing a fast crawl, the seized ones are able to speak. In general, what they say is understood, although interpretation and clarification sometimes take place. The utterance is accepted as a message from deity, part of a complete cycle of communication in verbal symbols; signs and omens, with all their accompanying mystification, are not involved. The cycle begins when one asks a question of deity, proffering in one's hand a gift or cup of liquor. The request goes to the ear of the god, is heard, and then from the mouth of the god the answer comes back, thus completing the cycle. The advice, reassurance, prognosis of sickness, or prophecy contained in the answer is accepted as coming from the sublime level of divine knowledge and wisdom. Speech has fulfilled its highest possible function: two-way communication between deity and man.

The phenomenon of oracular utterance has no doctrinal Buddhist endorsement, but rituals, semireligious in character, play a part in inducing some of the seizures. Many Tibetan religious authorities speak disparagingly of them and question the genuineness of many of the "god ones." The oracle is often derided and mocked. Such mockery, however, is never quite free from persistent half-belief, for oracular utterance, by its nature, assumes divine authority. It has had an assured and great part in Tibetan statecraft and policymaking, both ancient and modern. Influenced by such precedents, by the awesome nature of direct communication with deity, and by the pressure to know something of the future, Tibetans of all classes gather whenever and wherever such seizures take place. There they proffer their gifts and pose the questions for which they seek answers from deity. The spoken word from the *lHa KHa* ("god mouth") is, by its nature, the highest form of divination.[28]

28 The material relating to the *lHa Pa* ("god one[s]") is largely derived from personal firsthand observation of the phenomenon. Much of it is well known, for Tucci, Waddell, Nebesky-Wojkowitz, Schafer, and others have described various aspects of it (see chapter ii, footnote 27). My Tibetan collaborators have also described it, giving many interesting details. Another young Tibetan who is at the University of Washington at present as a language informant has several times most realistically presented a take-off on seizures at strictly Tibetan gatherings in my home. He himself is generally one of the most outspoken critics of the observance of *Mo* ("divination"); yet, when he had finished mimicking a *lHa aDZin* ("god-seized one"), his face straightened out and he said, "But there are true ones."

The categories and subcategories of *Mo* and the cognate observances outlined in this chapter represent the devices available to those who seek advice or knowledge of the future. Although recourse to some form of divination, in its more inclusive sense, is unquestionably universal in Tibet, this does not mean that each Tibetan has had recourse to all these different forms. Recourse to divination is selective, influenced by personal preference or the forms that are available. Thus most frequently, he resorts to the simpler procedures: counting off the beads of his rosary by threes; measuring his bootstrap; and throwing the dice. The last, however, generally requires recourse to a *Mo mKHan* ("divination specialist"), who has the proper dice and can throw them to the accompaniment of the appropriate prayers and charms.

Although the average Tibetan is thus somewhat narrowly limited in the forms of divination he may employ, his application of the principle of divination to the affairs of life approaches universality. Problems or questions relating to all aspects of life are referred to the observance: his diurnal and seasonal routines; the uncertainties of health and sickness that beset him; his familial and social decisions and problems concerning births, marriages, deaths, and social contacts; his need to know the developments that will follow upon crisis and disaster; the planning and staging of movements and journeyings; and many other matters, from such small details as which horse to saddle for the day's ride to the great final question of how much nearer to Nirvana he will be after death. To each of these and similar problems he seeks answers by divination.

A lively and recurrent skepticism is oddly mixed with the near universality of the practice. Even in such a simple matter as searching for a runaway horse, when successive forecasts and suggested directions have proved barren of result, the owner of the horse may vociferously damn all *Mo mKHan* ("diviner specialists") as liars and frauds, never letting up, however, in the attempt to find a true forecast. When a forecast which conforms to subsequent events as "one drop to another drop" is found, the diviner who made it will be hailed as the only one who has *Mo gSal Po* ("the clear divinations"). In subsequent situations when guidance is needed, he will be sought out, and thus his reputation will be well advertised.

Not only does divination share with the expression of verbalized religion an involvement with the processes of communication, but it also resembles the latter in the manner of its practice, which may be either direct, by personal participation, or indirect, by enlisting the services of a professional practitioner. In direct personal participation, the individual either counts his beads, throws the dice, or looks for signs, and depends on his own understanding to make the right moves and correct evaluations. In indirect participation, he enlists professional understanding on his own behalf by securing the services of one known as a divination specialist.

In the great majority of instances, the specialists are emanation-body lamas, although old men and women of the laity are sometimes known for their special aptitude and are sought out to perform certain kinds of divination. Not all lamas are especially eager to engage in the practice, but few, if any, refuse their services. Some lamas accept all clients, but others, of greater ethical sensitivity, operate on a selective basis, refusing to practice divination with regard to such matters as plans for a robbing expedition, a cattle raid, or a seduction and/or elopement.[29] But it is generally assumed, by both the specialists and their clients, that a lama cannot, in good part, refuse to practice divination for the one who, with a gift or just a scarf of greeting as a token in his hands, requests such service.

This enforced participation leads, moreover, to the very natural ambition to be known as successful rather than unsuccessful. Considerations not only of material profit but of enhancement of status and the satisfaction that comes from being sought out and courted for advice and pronouncements exert pressure on each lama to acquire skill in divination and knowledge of all signs and indications. His reputation depends on his forecasts' being clear and true.

Many considerations contribute to the self-satisfaction of the lama diviner who has the reputation of being an able and successful divination specialist. He is conscious of answering an urgent need: he helps, consoles, and guides those in perplexity and uncertainty. He often feels that it is his answer that makes the difference between recovery from sickness and death, success or failure in business ventures, and peace or possible violence. In a somewhat unique manner, he has his finger on the pulse of community life and has a special awareness of events and developments. No one asks a question—most often explaining in detail the causes and many ramifications of the problem—without unconsciously giving as

29 There were much discussion and some disagreement among all four lama collaborators as to what was permissible or proper and what was not. They cited lamas who would divine even for projects of violence and killing, as in the case of blood-feud reprisals, and others who would divine only when the proposed action could be shown to lead to increased religious observance. But it was generally agreed that a lama was under considerable pressure, both from his own sense of obligation and from public opinion, to divine for anyone who requested it. This is in agreement with Madame David-Neel's experience (see footnote 8).

much, and perhaps more, information than he seeks. In the exchange of question and answer, the divination specialist maintains his unique observation vantage point and accumulates knowledge of affairs and men. The specialist finds himself with unusual levers of power and strings of influence in his hands. He can manipulate public opinion and guide the development of political, religious, and economic interests. He can set opposing factions against each other, in direct confrontation and tests of strength, or he can bring about agreement between them. As his exercise of power increases, that increase is matched by ever larger contributions to his own wealth. It is well worthwhile to become a famous and sought-after *Mo mKHan*.

THE FUNCTION OF DIVINATION

To arrive at an analysis of the function of divination in Tibetan society and culture it is necessary to categorize the various forms of divination in a manner different from that of the Tibetan taxonomic system used thus far. In this different classification, the forms may be said to fall under three headings: (1) the mechanical, (2) the interpretive, and (3) the subjective. These categories are not tightly exclusive. There is a very strong tendency for the distinctions between them to become blurred, and there are many borderline cases. Most of the mechanical forms require interpretation to a greater or lesser degree; and the line between the interpretive and the subjective is not altogther clear and often shifts. The counting of the beads, with the resulting remainders of odd or even numbers which have fixed values as either good or evil, is the closest to being purely mechanical; and the throwing of the dice is predominantly mechanical, although the factor of ESP may furnish ground for argument. Unsolicited prophecy and clairvoyant pronouncements are closest to being purely subjective, that is, unaffected by the influence of a specific question or the posing of a problem. Other predominantly subjective forms of divination are the utterances of the possessed and the identification of persons and scenes in lakes or mirrors. In the former, however, questions prompt the utterance, and in the latter, some kind of interpretation is being sought. Between the two extremes of mechanical and subjective divination, most of the practices involve a considerable amount of interpretation. And interpretive divining itself either is dependent on data produced by mechanical processes or is an adjunct of subjective pronouncements, as when the confused utterances of an oracle must be explained.

In examining the functional role of divination in Tibetan culture and society, most attention should be focused on the element of interpretation.

The lama practitioners of divination are well aware that interpretation makes up the greatest part of the service they render their clients. They are called on to interpret the combinations resulting from the fall of the dice; the results of the horoscope; the pattern of smoke in the air; the lines in the fire-scorched scapula; the letters or word spotted on the page of a book; and even—as sometimes happens—the unclear utterance of a god-possessed one. Interpretation is largely based on fixed values and meanings which have been assigned, in the lore of divination, to animals, birds, objects, numbers, colors, and so on, but there is much opportunity for the exercise of personal bias. Even when the values are unequivocally prescribed, the formulation of the question and the matching of successive answers and questions may afford opportunity for the injection, in the final answer, of personal knowledge and opinion. Even those lamas who have complete faith in the validity of the way the dice fall, or in the steps by which the complicated results of the horoscope finally emerge, admit that many of the answers they give—arising presumably from fixed indications and values—are in fact opinions and conclusions they have extrapolated from their own wide experience and the extra information to which they have access. Their answers are slanted by their own intuition, and why, they might say, should not an emanation-body lama be touched with inspiration and know more than most men? At best, a diviner may give expert advice, and at worst, an educated guess. The lama who traveled with Madame David-Neel on her journey to Lhasa discussed quite frankly with her the answers he felt would be the best advice for the sick and injured, and in practice framed his divination answers in accordance with those sympathetically rational considerations.[30] The lama diviner himself is most satisfied when the omens and signs corroborate the answer he has based on his own opinion and knowledge—"assurance made doubly sure."

Given these facts and their frame of reference, the observance of divination may be shown to have the following functional roles in the society: (1) it fills and answers to a deeply felt need for information and guidance in the making of personal and communal decisions; (2) it operates to create, in effect, research centers where data relating to many as-

[30] A. David-Neel, *op. cit.*, pp. 55 ff. Madame David-Neel describes with much candor how her lama companion, when called on to divine for Yellow pilgrims and others, gave carefully calculated advice, based partly on his knowledge of road conditions and partly on what he considered would be beneficial rest and treatment of sickness or injuries. All four of the lama collaborators at the University of Washington admitted to having given similar advice based on similar motives when called upon to divine.

pects of Tibetan life are collated and processed for indications of trends and possible developments; and (3) it has resulted in the establishment of an effective mechanism for influencing public opinion and for setting trends. These trends may point toward preservation of the status quo, but are more likely to lead to change and even the initiation of radical innovation.[31]

The need of the average Tibetan for information on which to base decisions and plans is great and real. Media such as newspapers and radio for the collection and dissemination of news and basic data are non-existent. The Tibetan's first question to the passerby or anyone met on the trail or in gathering places is "What new is there to be said?" But the news he gets in this way is factually poor and mostly rumour. There are no weather forecasts, market reports, adequate and up-to-date maps of regions to which he will travel, nor are there highway police to keep him informed that the mountain trail has been blocked by a slide or that a stream is temporarily turbulent. Thus, beyond his own weather nose, he has no way of knowing about approaching storms that may menace fields and livestock. He has no up-to-date market quotations—the world price level for wool that he finally hears by word of mouth is at best three months old—and in the meantime he must buy and sell, unsure whether it will be for a profit or a loss. The exigencies of his life continually press him for decisions; yet he realizes that he knows few of the facts or developments on which decisions should be made. In his uncertainty, he seeks to shift the responsibility of decision-making by recourse to divination. His own final decision may or may not be in accordance with the answer given by divination, but if it is not, he has at least been stimulated to re-

[31] The three functional roles of divination postulated here, with the elaboration that is given in the pages that follow, were presented to the Tibetan collaborators simply as the conclusions of an outsider who had thought over the phenomena we had discussed together and had come up with strange ideas. They were not asked to endorse those ideas but were purposely incited to discuss them. This they did with some wonder at the odd secular frame of reference and yet with a certain irreverent gusto and considerable variety of opinion. They denied none of the conclusions and even told stories in support of the three functional roles. The consensus of their collective argument was, however, that, although the conclusions probably were true, it was an odd way of thinking. They also argued, at least inferentially, that other factors entered into the matter of *Mo*. The most sophisticated and skeptical Tibetan remembered one vision in the surface of a holy lake that could not be explained, and the others told stories reflecting deep credence in dreams, omens, and horoscopes. One of them, the most scholarly, then told me to drop all other matters and devote one long book to the things he could tell about dreams and omens. In deference to their opinions and to my own strong consciousness that not nearly enough is known about these matters, I enter a disclaimer to any pretension that these three functional roles, important though they may be, are the complete explanation of how divination operates in Tibetan society.

view the situation and, quite possibly, has found data in his own or his fellows' knowledge to warrant his choice. If, as is more likely to be the case, his decision is in accordance with the results of divination, he may then move on to action with the added assurance and confidence that can mean the difference between success and failure. Such behavior very soon becomes a pattern and hardens into habit.

The research centers that the observance of divination could be said to have brought into being are not formally organized and staffed. Yet each successful divination specialist is, in his person and with the assistance of whatever retinue or associates he may have, just such a research institute. He is in a most advantageous position to collect data on a wide variety of subjects, for the sources of data gather around him. Every query put to him is, in itself, information of a sort, and it is frequently accompanied by explanations and elaborations that are highly informative. By the very imperatives of his function, his mind and curiosity are stimulated to seek and analyze data.

For some specialists I have known, these processes of fact-finding and analysis were carried on with a clear realization of what was taking place and a consciousness, too, that the results would quite likely appear in some subsequent interpretation of omens and indications. I have heard divination experts probe their clients and visitors for all categories of information in a manner that would do justice to the collection and organization of data that takes place in any scientific survey. For other practitioners, however, given the same stimulation and opportunity, the research and analysis that took place was largely internalized or a function of the subconscious. The results, however, were still the results of research. For example, in the course of doing extensive first aid and amateur medical work, I noticed, during the early period of my stay in a community, that in answer to the question, "Why have you come?" advice gained from divination was never cited as a reason. After a certain length of time, which would have permitted careful evaluation of the significant, if at times spotty, successes of my treatments, the same question produced the following answer with recurring and marked frequency: "Because the lama sowed divination and the answer was good. He told me to come to you." My efforts had, indeed, been the subject of fact-finding, research, and some analysis: the reputation of a divination specialist (*Mo mKHan*) was being built upon them. Once, in a bantering way, I was told this by a *Mo mKHan*, and the symbiotic relationship between an amateur doctor and the interpreter of omens continued with a certain amount of mutual respect.

That divination has resulted in the creation of a mechanism for influencing and pressuring public opinion is a conclusion that follows naturally from the considerations and experience previously stated. One historical event attests to this: The Tibetan troops whose fanatical bravery so impressed British officers in the British Expeditionary Force in 1904 had been informed by divination that they were invulnerable and that the British would be defeated.[32]

Succesive prognostications slanted in a certain way can build up trends in public opinion which eventually find expression in action. Sometimes the trend is toward a stubborn maintenance of the status quo in attitudes and behavior. More frequently, for reasons which are given below, it may point toward change, at times even radical change.

The Chinese Communists who occupied Tibet and Lhasa were not liked. But in time, although they and all their works were hated, an increasing number of divination answers advised recourse to the doctors of the Chinese hospital, which resulted in an increasing number of patients applying there for treatment.[33] This was no doubt a partial confirmation of a popular trend which, based on the hard facts of a percentage of cures, had already begun to take place. Divination, however, was aware of and responsive to the trend and by endorsement strengthened it, as against a possible conservative attempt to boycott the Chinese.

On the other hand, I have heard about an innovation that took place as a result of oracular divination in a district of Amdo, which involved the violation of two very strong taboos and was in fact a radical change in deeply based behavior patterns. During an epidemic of rinderpest, a famous lama <u>Mo mKHan,</u> in response to a community request for advice, directed that some of the stricken cattle should have their throats cut and that their blood should be allowed to flow into the source of the stream from which the herds drank. Thereafter, many of the cattle had light cases of the disease, but losses from death were greatly reduced. Cutting the throats of animals instead of strangling them and the great offense committed against the *Klu* by polluting the water source with blood were radical innovations which would have been unacceptable in traditional patterns of behavior, for they violate strong taboos that have their origins in religious belief. In this case, however, divination, through the daring experimentation of someone who had probably heard distorted accounts of the phenomena of virus dilution and the practice of immunization, became the agent of radical and unthought-of change.

[32] F. Younghusband, *India and Tibet* (1910), pp. 125, 315; L. A. Waddell, *Lhasa and Its Mysteries* (1906), pp. 160–73, 254, 269, 274.

[33] A. Winnington, *op. cit.*, p. 209.

From the very first uncertainties that impel a man to seek answers by divination, through the dilemmas that confront the diviner and the motivations that push him to seek renown and financial gain, the entire process is slanted toward innovation and change, or at least experimentation. The completely routine solution to a problem is known without divination. It is the possibility of shifting action from that which is completely routine to something new that creates the initial uncertainty, and that uncertainty leads to the decision to ask for divination. The man who asks for a divination answer is already seeking something outside the commonplace answer that he knows without divination. At this point, the diviner is confronted with a dilemma. Within the context of what he knows or thinks he knows, he may give a safe commonplace solution or he may suggest something that is more or less an innovation. But commonplace answers are so obvious that they make divination seem no longer necessary. The reputations of famous divination experts are not built on saying what everyone knows. Within the limits of the probabilities in the case, the urge is toward tentative experimentation, or even radical innovation, as shown in the instances that have been cited.

It is not intended that this somewhat matter-of-fact discussion of the more commonplace or explicable aspects of divination should be taken as a denial of the possibility that some aspects of Tibetan divination are manifestations of intuitive or psychic powers or are affected by esoteric links with supersensory perception, thought transference, and other, as yet unexplained, phenomena. Strange things do sometimes occur. Not every aspect of divination lends itself to easy explanation and rationalization; but, to prevent any too facile credence, it should be noted that, although all Tibetans have had experience of divination in one form or another, there exists a growing skepticism concerning it. If it can be called a form of primitive science, or a pseudo science, then it is this aspect that is first vulnerable to the impact of scientific knowledge. And if, as a quasi-religious observance, it seeks a place among the religious observances of the Tibetans, it becomes the point at which denial and disbelief first make their attack on faith and belief. But whichever it is, and whatever its nature, there is no doubt that it is under attack by a growing skepticism, which has some of its roots in the streak of irrepressible irreverence that most Tibetans possess but which is fostered and stimulated by the impact of modernism. Nevertheless, the observance is not likely to disappear completely or soon from the behavior patterns and practices of the Tibetans.

CHAPTER TEN

A TIBETAN EVERYMAN

AND HIS *CHOS LAS:*

RELIGIOUS WORK

The subject of this chapter is a construct. This Tibetan Everyman is not a true life figure; yet he is a figure true to life. A narrative of his activities throughout a period of a number of days' duration has been put together in an attempt to reflect the sum of the roles of religious observances in the life of a representative of his society and culture. Although the ordering of the pattern is mine, every detail of the mosaic is a fragment of real life, taken from incidents and scenes I witnessed and from the discussions, explanations, and narratives I heard from hundreds of Tibetans during my more than eight years among them. To that extent I vouch for its validity as an example and illustration.

Rather than being a completely anonymous figure, the Tibetan Everyman bears the name of *rDo rJe Rin CHen* ("lord stone of great value"), or Precious Thunderbolt. It is one of the commonest Tibetan names and in its meanings reflects certain values and an awareness of the thunderbolt or adamantine doctrine of the "Diamond Sutra." The one who bears this name, rich in religious meanings, is a nomad who lives in the *aBrog* ("wilderness"), that range of upland meadows, grassy plains, and mountain slopes above the limits of agriculture and below the snow line of the highest plateau and mountains. As a nomad, he depends upon his herds—yak, yak-cow hybrids, sheep, and horses—for subsistence and for the supply of the necessary equipment and trappings of his way of life. He lives in an average-sized encampment made up of some twenty tents.

He is in his mid-forties, that time of life somewhat before the moment when, obedient to the Buddhist ideal of withdrawal, he will turn over management of the affairs of his family to his son and spend more and more time in *CHos Las* ("religion-work"). Yet it is a time when the teachings of his faith concerning the need for *CHos Las,* which he accepts with deep devotion, are beginning to take on greater urgency than during his somewhat reckless youth. In those days, he prayed but infrequently, at odd moments during pauses in activity; now the day begins with prayer —*OHm Ma Ni Padme Hum*—even before he takes his early tea.

Then there are the display offerings, which must be freshly arranged or replenished. These are set out on a chest that serves as an altar in front of a *THang KHa* ("image scroll"), which is hung in the upper right-hand corner of the tent and draped with votive scarves, testifying to often repeated gestures of reverence. The entire arrangement makes a chapel of the upper right-hand corner of the tent, which is kept free of other objects. The special offering bowls are made of silver; very early in the history of the fortunes of the tent, wealth was set aside for this purpose.

The beauty and the value of these bowls, which are devoted to religious purposes, give *rDo rJe Rin CHen* both esthetic and pious satisfaction as he polishes them and fills them with clean water, grain, dried fruit, and whatever other delicacies the tent possesses, in order to make as many as possible of the prescribed eight "drawing-near" offerings. The "fire offering"—wicks set into little bowls filled with butter—must be lit, after which he takes out a stick of fine incense which has been brought from China, where the best incense is made, lights it, waves its smoke before the scroll and over the other offerings, and then sets it in a holder.

Throughout the entire process, his murmured repetition of the six-syllable prayer, with which he began the day, has never ceased. As he turns back to the fireside, he takes with him one of the books of sacred writings—*CHos* ("religion") itself—that are neatly stacked beside the offerings on the altar. While waiting for his early tea, he turns the pages, chanting in deep, solemn tones the words and phrases of prayer and doctrine. He is minimally literate, but even when the more difficult words of esoteric import mean nothing to him, he can sound them out. As a matter of fact, he knows the entire book by heart, but the gesture of turning the pages covered with letters, which in themselves are sacred and have special power, brings him added assurance that his expression of religion has an increased efficacy. As he waits for his early tea, he is not only filling segments of idleness with activity but doing something supremely worthwhile; and he is building a defense against the troubles—and perhaps the dangers—of the day.

When his tea is ready, the book is reverently wrapped and put away. His prayers change to a grace, as, with his forefinger, he flips drops of buttered tea as offerings to hearth gods, soil-owners, and the serpent spirits of the waters. Then he can settle comfortably to the enjoyment of his meal and the coziness of his fireside within his wintertime tent, and discuss family and tent affairs with his wife. Discussion or thinking about these problems continues long after he has finished his tea. But talk does not interfere with further verbalization of religion, for he has taken the prayer wheel from its place beside the family shrine, and a simple twist of the wrist is sufficient to keep the cylinder of prayers spinning and efficacious, with only a faint whine and hum as an accompaniment, not interruption, to words and thoughts.

There is no crisis in the affairs of the tent to occasion too great worry. By the standards of his nomadic community, he is well off—more than a thousand sheep, a couple hundred yak and hybrid cattle, and a horse herd of several score. No one in the family is seriously ill. Yet *rDo rJe Rin CHen* is conscious of worry, foreboding, and dissatisfaction with life. Perhaps it is the time of the year rather than his particular time of life, for it is the season when the fag end of winter has as yet no promise of spring. The once lush green grass is dead, yellow, and scant; and the sun-eaten patches of snow are stained by the dust storms which sweep over the encampment with driving fury throughout the latter half of every day. The herds barely move, depending more on stored-up reserves of strength than on the winter-killed bits of hay for survival. Thus there is little effort needed to herd and guard them, although watching them often consists of a sad survey of losses and anticipated losses.

There is also little general movement in the land of tents; few visitors come and go. The isolation of each small group of tents is at its height. The tent, on the other hand, is snugly warm with its well-tended fire, for it is stretched tightly over the low sod walls of the winter encampment. If fresh milk, for whitening the tea, is scarce, fuel—the droppings of the herds—is abundant and dry. There is little to do except sit by the fire and eat, although the food no longer tastes as it did when intense activity and long rides produced a hunger that made every mouthful savory and good. The meat, too—butchered months ago and frozen and drying—though in great quantity, is no longer well flavored. Maybe that is why digestive processes are slowed, and nausea and pain sometimes disturb his sleep.

He senses matters such as these only vaguely; yet two problems at least are clear and distinct in his mind and press for solutions. One is of grave importance; and one a potential nuisance, affecting, however, the economic profit or loss of the tent. Unable either to solve or rid himself of them, he prays and counts the beads of his rosary as he continues to sit by the fire, while the wind begins to rise outside and shake the tent roof.

The fact that his tribe is in a state of siege and countersiege because of a feud with the nearest tribe is the problem of grave importance. Such a state of affairs is easily endured when distance separates tribes but is intolerable when tribes are near neighbors. Then a constant watch must be kept to forestall, if possible, raids on the herds, attacks against individuals or small groups moving outside the tribal territory or caught off guard, and the setting of fires in the dry grass of the winter range.

In this particular feud *rDo rJe Rin CHen* has a special personal worry, since he played an effective part in reacting to the initial incident —a raid on one of the horse herds of the tribe. He is credited with shooting one of the two raiders who were killed. His fellow tribesmen praise his action, and the praise of one's fellows is pleasant; but he himself, remembering what he saw through the sights of his rifle and the feeling of the sure squeeze of his trigger finger, remembers, too, similar actions of his own wild youth, which he has now given up, along with raiding for excitement and booty and seducing other men's wives.

The "time after life" is getting near, and one must think of virtue and retribution. Although in the final settlement of the affair—whenever that may come about—the payment of life indemnity will be a tribal matter, yet, until that settlement does take place, he is uncomfortably aware that he would be the prime target of any reprisal. Even after settlement, the religious guilt, in contrast to the approval of his fellows, will always stay with him. Such thoughts, dark and unpleasant, give added intensity to his praying. The beads slip through his fingers, *OHm Ma Ni Padme Hum.*

The somewhat minor, though nagging, cause for worry is a matter of miscalculation in trade. During the summer's wool shearing and trading, by holding out for special prices, he failed to sell his wool. Shortly thereafter, the feud, and its state of siege, reduced the amount of movement for trade throughout the tribe, and he now has a dozen bales of wool stacked in his tent. He must either dispose of them before the tribe starts moving camps in the spring or arrange for their storage. Prior to the spring and summer movement, the extra equipment of the tent, including the bulky winter clothing, is customarily left in the quarters of the younger son, who is a monk—an offering to religion of life itself, made long before—and lives in the nearby monastery. Storing many bales of wool, however, would be more difficult. Then there is the problem of the extra young mares of his horse herd. The herd has reached the maximum size he and his son can conveniently handle, and it would be wisest to trade a few of the young mares for the silver the horse-buyers pay. With the money, he could buy some yak cows, who not only produce young but give milk, supply hair for cloth and ropes, and, if necessary, meat and hides. Thinking of these matters, his praying falters, and he suspends his counting of prayers to use the beads to rack up sums concerning numbers, quantities, and prices. The totals he gets clarify but do not solve his problems.

Consideration of these problems with his wife and in thoughts that turn uneasily in his own mind results in a number of tentative half-formed plans; and again he changes the use of the beads. He rubs them together, prays over them, and, stretching them between his hands, counts them by threes from both ends, noting the number left. An odd number would be favorable, an even number unfavorable. It is the simplest and most convenient form of divination, to which, in uncertainty or lacking sufficient knowledge of facts, he refers the problems of life.

Of all the tentative plans, only one reaches a point of decision, possibly because of a continuing clamor of trumpet and drum from a neighboring tent. There a number of monks and an emanation-body lama are performing a day-long chanting service of prayers and incantations. The beads having revealed a favorable omen for this idea, he decides to invite monks and lama to his tent for a similar service. The chanting the monks do, turning the pages of the many sacred books they carry, is much more efficacious than his own efforts and well worth hiring. An emanation-body lama, moreover, is a source of blessing and may become a point of contact with clairvoyant wisdom.

The lama and his assistants are invited or retained for the morrow, and the rest of the day is spent in preparation of special food for the occasion. In this, _rDo rJe Rin CHen_ takes charge, for he is the expert of the family in preparing special dishes. Furthermore, he feels he is doing something toward solving his problems. During moments of concentration, when cutting meat or shaping meat-stuffed dumplings, he even forgets to pray.

The day-long service of incantation, which is an impressive combination of the exercise of thaumaturgic power and festive good-fellowship, is centered around the making and offering of _gTor Ma_ ("broken-up offerings"). These consist of an array of symbolic figures made with considerable artistry of butter and _TSam Ba_ ("parched barley flour") dough, in which, by the power of verbalized religion, misfortune and bad luck have been enclosed. When the figures are broken up and disposed of, the misfortune and bad luck are also put out of the way.

Late in the afternoon, the climax of the service comes when all the figures, which were formed to the accompaniment of prayers and finger and hand gestures, are broken apart. With shouted incantations, the fragments are thrown some distance from the tent. There is relief and rejoicing when, almost immediately, several ravens appear and snap up the pieces. The instantaneous coming of the "birds of the gods" is the very best of omens, so good, in fact, that rDo rJe Rin CHen is encouraged to talk of his troubles and half-formed plans to the lama and to ask him to divine for him. Not only does the lama possess special divination dice and divination manuals, but it may even be that he is one of those who possess clairvoyant wisdom.

The process of divination is a lengthy one. The dice are prayed over, breathed upon, and thrown many times. There is recourse to book divination. One of the volumes of scripture in the lama's possession is opened at random, and with one of the special salutation gestures, his finger spots a phrase that turns out to have concealed meanings. He ponders all the answers, integrating them into a coherent pattern by the force of his meditation. The meanings are clarified, possibly by clairvoyance, but certainly by the knowledge and understanding that have come to him as he travels widely and sees and hears much, for when men ask him for advice they also tell him many things.

The advice that the lama gives with an air of authority is thus based on many factors of chance, knowledge, judgment, and whatever psychic resource men may draw upon when they seek to telescope time and make a forecast. rDo rJe Rin CHen accepts the advice as the best possible guidance. He has not always accepted the answers of divination, for in his experience they have not always been accurate. He, too, has had his moments of disillusion when he broadly cursed all "lying diviners." This time, however, he feels he has faith, and faith makes forecasts come true.

The advice is both general and specific. In general, it re-emphasizes the importance of all CHos Las ("religion-works") for the betterment of life in the here and now and for the improvement of prospects in the afterlife. Specifically, the advice points out that, of these works, salutations and circumambulations are most advantageously performed at the nearest monastery, where the resources of religion are centralized. At the monastery, it is suggested that it would be worthwhile to spend some days —even many days—expressing religion and sowing supplication, making offerings, and performing salutations and circumambulations. And further, that all of these are good, but that two—salutation and circumambulation—are directed specifically toward the images, shrines, and buildings of the monastery. They should be performed in good round numbers: salutations by the thousands before shrines and images; and circumambulations by the hundreds, if around individual buildings, and by the scores, if along the outer circuit of the monastery.

Some additional details are stressed. Before going on the pilgrimage, the chief of the tribe should be consulted. The start should be made on the earliest definitely auspicious day. Among the observances, special attention should be given to circumambulation, with particular attention to the outer and longer circuit. And it might also be well to think of sponsoring a *Mang Ja* ("much tea"), or day-long subsidized chanting service by the assembled monks.

For all his services—chanting, vicarious offering, benediction, and advice by divination—the lama receives ample acknowledgment and due respect, expressed in gifts of butter, whole carcasses of sheep, and some choice lambskins that will do well for next winter's new robe. Both parties are made to feel that there has been a fair and equitable exchange of value. *rDo rJe Rin CHen*'s decision is now quickly made, and his wife gives her, by no means inconsiderable, endorsement.

She, too, has internal aches and pains at times. Life is dull, especially since her favorite milk cows ceased giving milk; and she has not seen her younger son for many months. At the monastery there are always people to meet and incidents and events worth watching, if no more than the coming and going of those on multifarious errands. She, too, will count her beads, make salutations, and walk with zest along the circumambulation path.

On the earliest auspicious day, they start off; by the simple fact of being in motion, *rDo rJe Rin CHen* feels that the beginning is good. He has consulted with the chief of the tribe, who has said that his going is a good thing. The chief then went on to talk about the feud in a roundabout manner; and as a result of the talk, *rDo rJe Rin CHen* feels that any exploratory probing he can do on his own will not be taken amiss. The venture begins to take on enough importance to prod him into thinking of sponsoring a day-long service by the monks. The thought keeps coming back to him, but he puts off a final decision; he will wait and see how matters go.

The party is a large one, for the lama, too, is traveling homeward on the same day. *rDo rJe Rin CHen*'s older son and a number of the men of the tribe—several, indeed, from the encampment of the chief—are riding as escorts. They will bring the horses back to the camp since it will be difficult to find grazing or forage in the vicinity of the monastery. In addition to the mounts for himself and his wife, there are a number of pack horses carrying supplies of fuel and food for them, and for their monk son at the monastery.

They move away from the encampment with rising elation, and at the pass, which is the halfway point in the day's ride to the monastery—and dangerously closer to the territory of the tribe with which they are feud-ing—*rDo rJe Rin CHen* dismounts to place a pebble on the cairn that marks the spot. He makes one circle on foot around it as he prays and then joins in the shout, *lHa rGyal Lo* ("god wins"), feeling satisfaction that what he is engaged in should put him on the winning side.

When the riders cross the last, pass, the monastery is in view. At the sight, they pull their horses to a halt to doff their hats and pray. It is something splendidly different from the low black tents which are their homes, and different, too, from the earth-colored houses of the farming people. The cloisters of the monks are white, and from their midst, rise the variegated outlines of the red "god-houses" and chanting halls, whose roofs are crowned with gilded pinnacles and emblems. There is harmony of line between the man-made sloping walls and terraced roofs of the buildings and the slopes and crest of the hill against which they are set. There is also an assertion of man's ability and need to raise something toward the sky, in accordance with a cosmic pattern and executed with the artistry and craftsmanship of his culture. Little of this is consciously sensed by the riders. They only feel it is good to see the *dGon Pa* ("the solitary"), with its attendant *mCHod rTen* ("offering base[s]"), or stu-pas, ranged like sentinels or sign posts. They are content that they have arrived at the destination toward which they were drawn—a shrine of their faith, which is also a monument of a people's culture.

Upon their arrival, the monk son helps his father find quarters—a tiny, separate hut which has, however, a neat serviceable fireplace and a door which can be locked—in the *mTHa Ba* ("the edge"). The build-ings of "the edge" are indeed located on the edge of the monastery; and the community of "the edge," since it serves the monastery and the ac-tivities that are attracted to it, has a peripheral function that is often of great importance.

The nucleus of this aggregate of buildings, huts, and small pens is made up of shops and storehouses of Tibetan and Chinese traders, to-gether with the workshops of blacksmiths, silversmiths, carpenters, and leatherworkers. From this nucleus, the huts, sheds, and cattle pens of the hangers-on of both the market and the monastery, extend in a sprawling pattern. The hangers-on keep a few milk cows and horses as a subsistence base but no cattle or sheep; nor, since the monastery is above the limits of agriculture, do they grow crops. They have, however, a few fenced-in plots of turnips. The latter, when dried out and frozen, are much in demand by visiting nomads because of their sweetness. The people of "the edge" also cater to the needs of those who gather at the monastery by letting rooms or separate huts for income. They supply labor for monastery undertakings; and amongst them may be found informers, middlemen, professional guides, and escorts, as well as thieves and men whose profession is violence of some sort. From the womenfolk of this community, temporary wives are available whenever desired. Because the people of "the edge" are ambivalent in loyalty and are naturally better informed on trade news and current prices than the nomads, the latter regard them with some misgivings; yet they admit their many forms of usefulness.

Because of their usefulness, *rDo rJe Rin CHen* is quite content that the matter of paying rent is not put on a strictly commercial basis. Scarves and gifts are exchanged, with his gift to his host being of much greater value than his host's gift to him. The formal host-guest relationship thus established will involve sponsorship and future friend-to-friend dealing. He assumes that his son is well advised in the choice of an obliging houselord and that the new friend is a good one, or at least good enough for his purposes. It is well understood, although not stated in words, that if there are jobs he wants done or commissions he wishes to give he will give the houselord first option to make himself useful or to derive benefit. It is also understood that, when he finally leaves, his gift on parting will be proportioned in value to the length of his stay and that, if the houselord should ever come among the tents or to his tribe, adequate sponsorship will be extended. One can never have too many friends in too many places. Many friends, even those of different kinds and capabilities, in many places are an important part of the pattern of successful living.

The first two or three days of their stay are taken up with making preliminary offerings at all the shrines where butter lamps may be set or replenished and with the presentation of gifts to the various emanation-body lamas of the monastery, receiving their blessing in return. The visible tokens of these benedictions, called *Sruug mDud* ("protective knots"), are the small scarves of bright colors that are draped around their necks as they receive the blessing. At each stage in this round of preliminaries, the matter of sponsoring a chanting service—the *Mang Ja* ("much tea") —becomes slightly more real in his mind but not a firm decision.

Once the rounds have been completed and offerings have been made to all the gods and persons to whom they are due, his wife and he get down to the work and routine of salutations and circumambulations. These religion-works have a unique spatial context—prostration is performed toward objects in space, and circumambulation around objects in, and areas of, space. As such, they relate in a particular way to the monastery as an aggregate of shrines and other objects of veneration. There are many of these, but inevitably, for a variety of reasons, one of the shrines becomes preferred to the others; and there rDo rJe Rin CHen and his wife concentrate their efforts to accomplish a daily stint apiece of one thousand "eightfold salutations." This is a modest goal, for there are strong and enthusiastic worshipers who have been known to complete three thousand in a single day.

The "eightfold salutation" is not a simple or trifling gesture. Beginning from an erect standing position, the palms are joined at the forehead in the "lotus-bud" gesture; then, as the worshiper goes to his knees, the hands are placed on the ground; and finally, his hands are extended as far as his arms will stretch and his body is flat on the ground. Knees, stomach, chest, mouth, forehead, and extended hands—eight contacts in all—touch the ground, after which he returns to the upright position. One salutation has been completed, to be tallied on the beads.

rDo rJe Rin CHen, bending, lowering his weight, stretching every limb and muscle, and then raising his weight, soon finds himself sensing his muscles and beginning to breathe hard. He is newly conscious of his body as he works and stretches; and this too is fitting. It is the way—Lus Kyi CHos Las ("religion-work of body") in which he may best make payment—short of the pains of the eighteen hells—for the sins of his body. There are accounts, such as the death of a man, or that pert and willing servant girl of the previous summer, which need canceling. He is conscious, too, of a history of prostrations by numberless others before him. Believing as he believes and standing where he stands, they, too, bowed and stretched as he does, leaving in the planks of the floor smooth hollows and grooves which fit his knees and arms and even the pressure of his finger tips. Not for months, since the season of moving camp, packing loads, shearing wool, and breaking-in colts, has he so stirred himself.

At the end, still gasping his prayers, he is glad to turn to the bsKor Ba ("circumambulation") path, which at certain points follows galleries lined with prayer wheels, which he may turn as he walks by. It is good to walk into the wind and sunshine, in the company of those who follow the long clockwise circuit around the whole of the monastery. Since the lama had divined that circumambulation would be of particular importance, he thus has good authority for spending much time on that more pleasurable path.

Like all who walk that path, he is unarmed, having only his rosary and prayer wheel. He feels at once defenseless and yet well defended, for the path is safe ground, where he may occasionally meet tribal foes without fear or even embarrassment, as they too circumambulate. Some of them are, in fact, personal friends, and on the path they can meet and talk with each other without considering the feud; or if they do consider it, they may sound each other out on the state of public opinion in each tribe and explore various possibilities of settlement. Other members of the enemy tribe, whom he does not know personally, may be truly hostile because men have been killed; still they constitute no menace, for, though they may pass without greeting, they walk the same road in the same direction and say the same prayers.

Many others also pass, and in the half-sensed comradeship of movement in a common activity, they greet each other and talk as they walk together or rest at points along the steeper slope. *rDo rJe Rin CHen* hears gossip, news of places near and far, the trends of trade, the areas where cattle disease has broken out, and the shifting prices of products he buys and sells. Thus one day he hears of a caravan of tea traders who are coming to the region to trade tea for wool. Following that chance remark, he is finally able to conclude arrangements with the advance agent of the caravan to buy tea with his wool, which they will pick up when they pass through his tribe. Merchants in the trading post are persuaded to accept the promise of bales of tea as credit against which he may draw the supplies of foodstuffs for which he now has an urgent need.

At some point in time during the days filled with the making of salutations and circumambulations, the decision has been made to sponsor a *Mang Ja* ("much tea"). He will make one great effort to cap all his own religion-work with the most complete expression of verbalized religion possible—the chanting of the scriptures. For one day, all the monks of the monastery will pray on his behalf.

Implementing the decision leaves him, for several days, with scant time for other activities. His monk son and the houselord of his quarters are also commissioned and kept busy helping him in all that must be done. Supplies must be assembled for the making of enough rice, meat, and cheese stew for a meal for four hundred monks. Each of the four hundred, moreover, must also receive three pounds of *TSam Ba* ("parched barley flour"), one pound of butter, and one pound of tea. On the day of the service, tea must be served all day long. The credit from his wool is but a fraction of the total cost, but he has also found a buyer for his mares, and he has been able to borrow on next year's crop of wool.

On the day of the service, he is very busy overseeing the distribution of the portions and the serving of food and tea. He does many sums on his beads having to do with tsamba, butter, and tea; but he also makes other calculations on his beads concerning the possible number of pages scanned and their contents intoned by four hundred monks in a single day. The prayers he would never be able to say are being said expertly, with special authority and unction, and multiplied four hundred fold.

The impressiveness of the chanting service in the assembly hall affords him great satisfaction. The emanation-body lamas of the monastery, in so far as they represent the Buddahood—the first entity of the Rare-Perfect Three—sit in the incense smoke and flare from the butter lamps to receive adoration and dispense benediction. The monks, as members of the Community—the third entity of the Rare-Perfect Three—led by the choir leader and to the accompaniment of the music of horns, clarinets, cymbals, and drums, murmur a chorus much like rumbling thunder. Their chanting is the expression, or verbalization, of religion itself—the second entity of the Rare-Perfect Three. Deeply wondering, he murmurs, *dKon mCHog mKHyen* ("Rare-Perfect knows"), and is content.

Other satisfactions, too, come to *rDo rJe Rin CHen*. He is conscious that in each greeting or gesture of courtesy from the monastery officials— the urgency with which he is asked to drink tea or pressed to have a seat— there is a regard and an ascription of status that was previously lacking. Even his monk son moves among his fellow monks with a touch of newly gained or enhanced importance.

The day following the *Mang Ja* ("much tea") he and his wife are back performing prostrations at the shrines and walking the circumambulation path. His horseman's legs no longer cramp and tire. He, who has never walked when he could ride, begins to find walking pleasant in itself. Acquaintances whom he meets extend their congratulations on the celebration of the "much tea," and from the others, who only stare, he senses some additional respect that did not exist before.

The first day back on the path also brings something of an adventure in communication. Throughout the many days he had previously spent in circumambulation, he had talked with or overheard others who spoke in many dialects, which, as always, gave quick and sure identification of the regions from which they had come. Some from not far away—down in the nearest deep valley—had very strange-sounding speech; yet because he had heard them on many occasions—they were practically neighbors—he could understand them. A ragged Golok pilgrim, on the other hand, weather-beaten and oddly intent in all he did, had sounded harshly all the letters that in other dialects are silent or half-silent; but half-remembered spelling had helped him make identification of what was meant. Quite to his surprise a wanderer—refugee or whatever he might be—from faraway western Tibet had said his prayers and formed his words almost as though he were a neighbor. The breadth of the land where all speak Tibetan is indeed very great.

On this particular day, however, as he rests at mid-point in his walk, he speaks with a Tibetan from Central Tibet, speaks but diffidently, however, because the man is the member of an official delegation that is stopping for a few days at the "great house" of the principal lama of the monastery. In boredom or in piety, this man had wandered, prayer wheel in hand, onto the common path. His speech is the strangest *rDo rJe Rin CHen* has ever heard, yet it must be Tibetan, for the stranger comes from the center of Tibetan society and culture, Lhasa itself, to which *rDo rJe Rin CHen* himself hopes to go on pilgrimage some day. So he listens again, straining for comprehension, and with the second hearing, he suddenly recalls the time he went with a grain-buying caravan and dickered with the farmers of *Co Ni*, who claim their ancestors came from Lhasa eighteen generations ago. He begins to understand, and the prayers that he and the stranger have in common, although pronounced somewhat differently, are also helpful keys to understanding. With this base of understanding, he presses the conversation, for he would learn more about Lhasa, where the Precious Victorious One lives, and about the trails and stages that lead to that holy place. Again he thinks of the wideness of the land where all speak Tibetan.

Spring begins to show in lengthening days and the faintest hint of green on the slopes that face toward the sun. It is getting near the time when the camps must move, and there are preparations that must be made; yet *rDo rJe Rin CHen* and his wife linger. The days are pleasant and the benefits that come from religion-work are freshly real. Interest and zest have come into life; they sleep well at night, and food is savory once more.

Then one day, before he has quite made up his mind when to leave, he is called to the audience room of the abbot of the monastery, and there finds himself, without any warning, seated in company with a number of persons from the enemy tribe. Some are personal friends and some are not, but this is not the circumambulation path and all face toward him impassively. As he is the only one present from his own tribe, he feels uncomfortably alone in the gravity of the confrontation.

Tea and food are served ceremoniously, but it is evident that something is afoot and talk must follow. Remembering his own conversation with the chief of his tribe, he suddenly feels weighted with tribal responsibility. Quite obviously, the monastery authorities are contemplating "descent as mediators" into the feud situation, and the two tribes are being sounded out for trends of feeling and opinion.

While he awaits his turn to speak, his fingers are busied with the beads in his lap, and nervousness and tension find some release. It is reassuring to mutter prayers, instead of clearing his throat, and the faint murmur is in no sense a discourtesy, even while the abbot is making the opening speech. The abbot himself prays in a sibilant whisper as he listens, with the close intentness of one who takes the pulse of the sick, to the speeches made in reply from both sides. The meeting breaks up after much circumlocutory oratory that has been cautiously vague and yet has touched tentatively on specifics, but not before the abbot has made it clear that he—with all the power and influence of the monastery behind him—is "tying the affair," thus imposing a truce for fifteen days.

After that meeting, it is more than time to return to his tribe. It only remains for him to consult the lama whose divination answers have been true to fact like one drop to another and to ask him to divine for an auspicious day. When that day is known, he sends word back to the home encampment for horses and an escort. The proper and sufficient gift and a pressing invitation to visit with the tribe "when the grass is long, the flowers thick, and fresh butter is plentiful" are proffered to the houselord, who is so responsive that he in turn offers to arm, mount, and escort them to the first pass—a friend who knows his responsibilities and the right gestures.

On the right day—as divined by the lama—*rDo rJe Rin CHen* and his wife, renewed in health and spirits, turn their backs on the monastery and face toward home. The interlude is ended but for them *CHos Las* ("religion-works")—the verbalization of religion, supplication, offerings, salutations, and circumambulations—have worked the believed-in wonders. The boredom of their lives is lifted; their health is much improved; their worries are diminished; some of their problems have been solved; and belief in the power and protection of their faith is stronger than ever before. They are not alone in that faith and its observances. All those who have worshiped and "worked" with them are their fellows, even those Tibetans from faraway. This segment of time and activity from the life of *rDo rJe Rin CHen*—the Tibetan Everyman—ends as it began with those universal words of power on his lips, *OHm Ma Ni Padme Hum!*

BIBLIOGRAPHY

I. GENERAL SOURCES

BACOT, J. *Dans les marches tibétaines: Autour de Dokerla, novembre 1906–janvier 1908.* Paris: Plon, 1909.

——. *Grammaire du tibétain littéraire.* Paris: Librairie d' Amérique et d'Orient, 1946.

——. *Grammaire du tibétain littéraire: Index morphologique.* Paris: Librairie d'Amérique et d'Orient, 1948.

——. *Le poète tibétain Milarepa.* Paris: Éditions Bossard, 1925.

——. *Les slokas grammaticaux de Thonmi Sambhota.* Paris: Librairie Orientaliste, Paul Geuthner, 1928.

——. *Tibet revoltée: Vers Nepemako, la terre promise des Tibétains.* Paris: Hachette, 1912.

——. *Trois mystères tibétains.* Paris: Éditions Bossard, 1921.

——. *La vie de Marpa le "traducteur."* Paris: Librairie Orientaliste, Paul Geuthner, 1937.

BACOT, J., THOMAS, F. W., and TOUSSAINT, G.-CH. *Documents de Touen-houang relatifs à l'histoire du Tibet.* Paris: Librairie Orientaliste, Paul Geuthner, 1940–46.

BAILEY, F. M. *No Passport for Tibet.* London: Rupert Hart-Davis, 1957.

BASHAM, A. L. "Jainism and Buddhism," in *Sources of Indian Tradition,* ed. WM. THEODORE DE BARY, JR. *et al.* New York: Columbia University Press, 1958.

BELL, SIR CHARLES. *The People of Tibet.* Oxford: Clarendon Press, 1928.

——. *Portrait of the Dalai Lama.* London: Collins, 1946.

——. *The Religion of Tibet.* Oxford: Clarendon Press, 1931.

——. *Tibet, Past and Present.* Oxford: Clarendon Press, 1924.

BERNARD, L. L. "Attitudes: Social," *Encyclopedia of the Social Sciences,* ed. EDWIN R. A. SELIGMAN (New York: Macmillan Co., 1950), II, 305–6.

BERNARD, THEO. *Penthouse of the Gods: A Pilgrimage into the Heart of Tibet and the Sacred City of Lhasa.* New York: Charles Scribner's Sons, 1939.

BLOOMFIELD, LEONARD. *Language.* New York: Henry Holt & Co., 1933.

BODMER, FREDERICK. *The Loom of Language.* Edited by L. HOGBEN. New York: W. W. Norton & Co., 1944.

BONVALOT, GABRIEL. *L'Asie inconnue, à travers le Tibet et la Chine.* Paris: E. Flammarion, 1896.

BOWER, H. *Diary of a Journey across Tibet.* London: Rivington, Percival & Co., 1894.

BRAM, JOSEPH. *Language and Society.* New York: Random House, 1955.

BUSHELL, S. W. "The Early History of Tibet from Chinese Sources," *Journal of the Royal Asiatic Society,* N.S. XII (1880), 435–541.

CAMMANN, SCHUYLER. *Trade through the Himalayas.* Princeton, N.J.: Princeton University Press, 1951.

CARRASCO, PEDRO. *Land and Polity in Tibet.* Seattle: University of Washington Press, 1959.

CARTER, T. F. *The Invention of Printing in China.* Revised by L. CARRINGTON GOODRICH. New York: Ronald Press Co., 1955.

CHANG, KUN. "Chinese Records of the Early History of Tibet." Unpublished manuscript submitted to the Inner Asia Colloquium, University of Washington. It uses as sources *T'ung Chien, Ts'e Fu Yuan Kuei, Hsin T'ang Shu, Chiu T'ang Shu, T'ung Tien,* and *T'ang Hui Yao.*

CHAPMAN, F. SPENCER. *Lhasa, the Holy City.* Introduction by SIR CHARLES BELL. London: Readers Union, 1940.

CLARK, LEONARD. *The Marching Wind.* New York: Funk & Wagnalls Co., 1954.

COMBE, G. A. *A Tibetan on Tibet.* London: T. Fisher Unwin, 1926.

COSMA DE KOROS, A. *Tibetan Studies.* A collection of his contributions to the *Journal of the Asiatic Society of Bengal.* Edited by E. DENISON Ross. Calcutta: Baptist Mission Press, 1912.

CUTTING, SUYDAM. *The Fire Ox and Other Years.* New York: Charles Scribner's Sons, 1940.

DAINELLI, GIOTTO. *Buddhists and Glaciers of Western Tibet.* New York: E. P. Dutton & Co., 1934.

DAS, SARAT CHANDRA. "Contributions on Tibet," *Journal of the Asiatic Society of Bengal,* 1881, No. 2, pp. 187–251.

———. "Contributions on Tibet," *Journal of the Asiatic Society of Bengal,* 1882, No. 1, pp. 1–75.

———. *Journey to Lhasa and Central Tibet.* Edited by W. W. Rockhill. London: J. Murray, 1902.

———. *A Tibetan-English Dictionary with Sanskrit Synonyms.* Calcutta: Bengal Secretariat Book Depot, 1902.

DAVID-NEEL, A. "Le bouc émissaire des Thibétains," *Mercure,* 1924, pp. 649–60.

———. *Buddhism: Its Doctrines and Its Methods.* London: John Lane, 1939.

———. *Initiations lamaiques.* Paris: Adyar, 1947.

———. *My Journey to Lhasa.* New York: Harper, 1927.

———. *Mystiques et magiciens du Thibet.* Paris: Plon, 1930.

———. *Au pays des brigands-gentilhommes, Grand Thibet.* Paris: Plon, 1933.

———. *La vie surhumaine de Guesar de ling.* Paris: Adyar, 1931.

——. *Voyage d'une parisienne à Lhassa.* Paris: Plon, 1926.

——. (trans.). *Le lama aux cinq sagesses.* From the Tibetan by Lama Yongden. Paris: Plon, 1933.

DAWSON, C. H. *The Mongol Mission.* New York: Sheed & Ward, 1955.

——. *Debar Gazette* (Gangtok, Sikkim), No. 1, February 2, 1958.

DEMIEVILLE, PAUL. *Le concile de Lhasa.* Paris: Imprimerie Nationale de France, 1952.

DESIDERI, IPPOLITO. *An Account of Tibet (1712–1727).* Edited by FILIPPO DE FILIPPI. London: G. Routledge & Sons, 1937.

D'OLLONE, H. M. G. *Les derniers barbares.* Paris: P. Lafitte & Cie, 1911.

DOUGLAS, WILLIAM O. *Beyond the High Himalayas.* Garden City, N.Y.: Doubleday & Co., 1953.

DUNCAN, MARION H. *Harvest Festival Dramas of Tibet.* Hongkong: Published by author, 1955.

DURKHEIM, É. *Les formes élémentaires de la vie religieuse.* Paris: F. Alcan, 1912.

——. "Religion and Society," *Theories of Society.* I, 677. New York: Free Press of Glencoe, Inc., 1961.

DUTT, N. *Early Monastic Buddhism.* Calcutta: Calcutta Oriental Book Agency, 1960.

EDGAR, J. H. *The Marches of the Mantse.* London: Morgan & Scott, 1908.

EKVALL, ROBERT B. *Cultural Relations on the Kansu-Tibetan Border.* Chicago: University of Chicago Press, 1939.

——. "Five Universals of Tibetan Religious Observance," *Orien,* VI (1953), No. 2, 334–43.

——. "Some Aspects of Divination in Tibetan Society," *Ethnology,* II (1963), No. 1, 31–39.

——. "Three Categories of Inmates within Tibetan Monasteries: Status and Function," *Central Asiatic Journal,* V (1960), No. 3, 206–20.

——. "The Tibetan Self-image," *Pacific Affairs,* XXXIII (1961), No. 4, 375–82.

——. *Tibetan Skylines.* New York: Farrar, Straus & Young, 1952.

ELIADE, MIRCEA. *Mythes, rêves, et mystères.* Paris: Gallimard, 1957.

——. *Traité d'histoire des religions.* Paris: Payot, 1953.

EVANS-WENTZ, W. Y. *The Tibetan Book of the Dead.* Preface by SIR JOHN WOODROFFE. London: Oxford University Press, 1927.

FERRARI, ALFONSA. *Mk'yen brtse's guide to the holy places of central Tibet.* Edited by LUCIANO PETECH, with the collaboration of HUGH RICHARDSON. Rome: Istituto Italiano per il Medio ed Estremo Oriente, 1958.

FILCHNER, WILHELM. *Kumbum Dschamba Ling, das Kloster des hunderttausend Bilder Maitreyas.* Leipzig: F. A. Brockhaus, 1933.

——. *Das Ratsel des Matschu.* Berlin: E. S. Mittler und Sohn, 1930.

FLEMING, PETER. *Bayonets to Lhasa.* London: Rupert Hart-Davis, 1961.

FRANCKE, A. H. *Antiquities of Indian Tibet*. Calcutta: Superintendent of Government Printing, 1914–26.

——. *A Lower Ladakhi Version of the Kesar Sage*. Introduction by SUNITI KUMAR CHATTERJI. Calcutta. Bibliotheca Indica, Vol. XXXII (1904), No. 168. Reprinted in 1941.

——. *A History of Western Tibet*. London: S. W. Partridge, 1907.

FUTTERER, KARL. *Geographische Skizze nordost Tibet*. Gotha: J. Perthes, 1903.

GETTY, A. *The Gods of Northern Buddhism*. Oxford: Clarendon Press, 1928.

GORDON, ANTOINETTE K. *The Iconography of Tibetan Lamaism*. New York: Columbia University Press, 1939.

——. *The Hundred Thousand Songs: Selections from Milarepa, Poet-Saint of Tibet*. Rutland, Vt.: Charles E. Tuttle Co., 1961.

——. *Tibetan Religious Art*. New York: Columbia University Press, 1952.

GORE, FRANCIS. *Trente ans aux portes du Thibet interdit*. Hong Kong: Maison de Nazareth, 1939.

GRAHAM, DAVID CROCKETT. *The Customs and Religion of the Ch'iang*. Washington, D.C.: Smithsonian Institution, 1958.

GREENBERG, J. H. "Historical Linguistics and Unwritten Languages," in *Anthropology Today*, ed. A. L. KROEBER (Chicago: University of Chicago Press, 1953), pp. 265–86.

GRENARD, FERNAND. *Tibet: The Country and Its Inhabitants*. London: Hutchinson & Co., 1904.

GROUSSET, RENÉ. *L'empire des steppes*. Paris: Payot, 1941.

——. *Histoire de la Chine*. Paris: Arthème Fayard, 1942.

GUIBAUT, ANDRE. *Tibetan Venture*. Translated by LORD SUDLEY. London: J. Murray, 1947.

HALL, EDWARD T. *The Silent Language*. Garden City, N.Y.: Doubleday & Co., 1959.

HALLOWELL, A. IRVING. "Culture, Personality, and Society," in *Anthropology Today*, ed. A. L. KROEBER (Chicago: University of Chicago Press, 1953), pp. 597–620.

HANDBURY-TRACY, JOHN. *Black River of Tibet*. London: F. Muller, 1938.

HANNAH, HERBERT BRUCE. *Grammar of the Tibetan Language*. Calcutta: Baptist Mission Press, 1912.

HARRER, HEINRICH. *Seven Years in Tibet*. New York: E. P. Dutton & Co., 1954.

HARRIS, SELLIG S. *Structural Linguistics*. Chicago: University of Chicago Press, 1951.

HEDIN, SVEN. *Central Asia towards the Holy City of Lhasa*. New York: Charles Scribner's Sons, 1903.

——. *Trans-Himalaya*. 3 vols. London: Macmillan & Co., 1910.

HERMANNS, MATHIAS. *Mythen und Mysterien, Magie und Religion der Tibeter.* Cologne: B. Pick, 1956.

——. *Die Nomaden von Tibet.* Vienna: Verlag Herold, 1949.

HERSKOWITZ, M. J. *The Economic Life of Primitive Peoples.* New York: Alfred A. Knopf, Inc., 1940.

HOFFMANN, HELMUT. *Quellen zur Geschichte der tibetischen Bon-Religion.* Wiesbaden: F. Steiner, 1950.

——. *The Religions of Tibet.* Translated by EDWARD FITZGERALD. London: George Allen & Unwin, Ltd., 1961.

HOJER, HARRY. "The Relation of Language to Culture," in *Anthropology Today,* ed. A. L. KROEBER (Chicago: University of Chicago Press, 1953), pp. 554–73.

HOLDICH, SIR THOMAS. *Tibet, the Mysterious.* London: Alston Rivers, 1908.

HUC, M. *Travels in Tartary, Thibet and China.* Translated by W. HAZLITT. 2 vols. London: National Illustrated Library, 1879.

HUMMEL, S. *Elements der tibetischen Kunst.* Leipzig: O. Harrassowitz, 1949.

——. *Geschichte der tibetischen Kunst.* Leipzig: O. Harrassowitz, 1953.

HUTHEESING, RAJA (ed.). *Tibet Fights for Freedom.* With a Foreword by the DALAI LAMA. Published for the Indian Committee for Cultural Freedom. Bombay: Orient Longmans, Ltd., 1960.

JASCHKE, H. A. *Tibetan-English Dictionary.* London: Lowe and Brydon, 1949. (Reprint of 1881 edition.)

——. *Tibetan Grammar.* With a supplement of readings and vocabulary, by JOHN L. MISH. New York: Fred Ungar Pub. Co., 1954.

KAULBACK, RONALD. *Salween.* New York: Harcourt, Brace & Co., 1939.

KAWAGUCHI, EKAI. *Three Years in Tibet.* Madras: Theosophical Pub. Co., 1909.

KEESING, F. M. *Cultural Anthropology.* New York: Rinehart & Co., 1958.

KING, RIN-CHEN. *We Tibetans.* London: Seeley, Service & Co., 1926.

KOERBER, H. N. VON. *Morphology of the Tibetan Language.* Los Angeles–San Francisco: Sutton House, 1935.

LALOU, MARCELLE. *Les religions du Tibet.* Paris: Presses Universitaires de France, 1957.

——. "Rituel Bon-po des funerailles royales," *Journal Asiatique,* T–CCXL–3 (1952), pp. 339–61.

LANDON, PERCEVAL. *The Opening of Tibet.* With an Introduction by COLONEL YOUNGHUSBAND. New York: Doubleday, Page & Co., 1905.

LAUFER, BERTHOLD. "Bird Divination among the Tibetans, with a Study of Phonology of the Ninth Century," *T'oung Pao,* XV (1914), 1–110.

——. *Loan Words in Tibetan.* Leiden: E. J. Brill, 1918.

——. "Origin of Tibetan Writing," *American Oriental Society Journal,* XXXVIII (1918), 34–46.

LAUFER, BERTHOLD. *The Si-Hia Language*. Leiden: E. J. Brill, 1916.

LESSING, FERDINAND. *Yung-ho-kung, and Iconography of the Lamaist Mythology and Cult*. In collaboration with GORTA MONTELL. Stockholm: Goteborg Elanders, 1942.

LI, AN-CHE. "Bon: The Magico-Religious Belief of the Tibetan-Speaking Peoples," *Southwestern Journal of Anthropology*, IV (1948), 31–42.

———. "Dege: A Study of Tibetan Population," *Southwestern Journal of Anthropology*, III (1947), 279–94.

LI TIEH-TSENG. *Tibet, Today and Yesterday*. New York: Bookman Assoc., 1960.

MA, HO-T'IEN. "Kan Ch'ing Tsang pien ch'u k'ao Ch'a chi." 3 vols. (in manuscript form). Shanghai: n.p., 1947. Translated for the Human Relations Area Files by LINCOLN WONG.

MACDONALD, DAVID. *The Land of the Lama*. London: Seeley, Service & Co., 1929.

———. *Twenty Years in Tibet*. Philadelphia: J. B. Lippincott Co., 1932.

MALINOWSKI, B. *Argonauts of the Western Pacific*. With a Preface by SIR JAMES GEORGE FRAZER. New York: E. P. Dutton & Co., 1922.

———. *Magic, Science and Religion, and Other Essays*. With an Introduction by ROBERT REDFIELD (1948). Garden City, N.Y.: Doubleday & Co., 1954.

MARAINI, FOSCO. *Tibet secret*. Translated from Italian to French by JULIETTE BERTRAND. Paris: B. Arthaud, 1954.

MARKHAM, C. R. *Narratives of the Mission of George Bogle to Tibet, and of the Journey of Thomas Manning to Lhasa*. London: Trubner & Co., 1876.

MARTINET, ANDRE. "Structural Linguistics," in *Anthropology Today*, ed. A. L. KROEBER (Chicago: University of Chicago Press, 1953), pp. 574–86.

MATHEWS, R. H. *Chinese-English Dictionary* (New American edition). Cambridge, Mass., Harvard University Press, 1950.

MAUSS, MARCEL. *The Gift*. Translated by IAN CUNNISON, with an Introduction by E. E. EVANS-PRITCHARD. Glencoe, Ill.: Free Press of Glencoe, Ill., 1954.

MIGOT, ANDRE. *Tibetan Marches*. Translated from French with an Introduction by PETER FLEMING. New York: E. P. Dutton & Co., 1955.

MILLER, ROBERT J. *Monasteries and Culture Change in Inner Mongolia*. Wiesbaden: O. Harrassowitz, 1959.

MONGE, CARLOS. "Biological Basis of Human Behavior," in *Anthropology Today*, ed. A. L. KROEBER (Chicago: University of Chicago Press, 1953), pp. 127–44.

MORAES, FRANK. *The Revolt in Tibet*. New York: Macmillan Co., 1960.

NEBESKY-WOJKOWITZ, R. *Oracles and Demons of Tibet*. The Hague: Mouton, 1956.

NORBU, T. J. *Tibet Is My Country* (*As told to Heinrich Harrer*). Translated from the German by EDWARD FITZGERALD. London: Rupert Hart-Davis, 1960.

NOYES, ALFRED. *Tales of the Mermaid Tavern.* New York: Frederick A. Stokes Co., 1913.

OBERMILLER, E. (trans.) *History of Buddhism.* In two parts. Translated from the Tibetan text of Bu sTon. Heidelberg: O. Harrassowitz, 1931.

PALLIS, MARCO. *Peaks and Lamas.* New York: Alfred A. Knopf, Inc., 1940.

PASCALLIS, C. *La collection tibétaine.* Hanoi: École Française d'Extrême Orient, 1935.

PATTERSON, GEORGE N. *Tibetan Journey.* London: Faber & Faber, 1954.

——. *Tibet in Revolt.* London: Faber & Faber, 1960.

PELLIOT, PAUL. *Histoire ancienne du Tibet.* Paris: Librairie d'Amérique et d'Orient Adrien-Maisonneuve, 1961.

PEMBA, TSEWANG Y. *Young Days in Tibet.* London: Jonathan Cape, 1957.

PETECH, LUCIANO. *China and Tibet in the Early Eighteenth Century.* Leiden: E. J. Brill, 1950.

PRANAVANDA, SWAMI. *Kailas-Manasarowar.* With a Foreword by PANDIT JAWAHARLAL NEHRU. Calcutta: S. P. League, 1949.

PRZHEVALSKII, N. M. *Mongolia, the Tangut Country and Solitudes of Northern Tibet.* London: S. Low, Marston, Searle and Rivington, 1876.

RAWLING, C. G. *The Great Plateau.* London: Arnold, 1905.

RICHARDSON, H. E. *A Short History of Tibet.* New York: E. P. Dutton & Co., 1962.

RIENCOURT, A. DE. *Roof of the World.* New York: Rinehart & Co., 1950.

RIJNHART, SUSIE. *With the Tibetans in Tent and Temple.* New York: F. H. Revell Co., 1901 (2d. ed., 1911).

ROCK, J. F. *The Amnye Ma-Chhen Range and Adjacent Regions.* Rome: Istituto Italiano per il Medio ed Estremo Oriente, 1956.

ROCKHILL, W. W. *Diary of a Journey through Mongolia and Tibet, 1891 and 1892.* Washington, D.C.: Smithsonian Institution, 1894.

——. *Land of the Lamas.* New York: Century Co., 1891.

——. *The Life of the Buddha.* London: Paul, Trench, Trubner & Co., 1907.

——. *Notes on the Ethnology of Tibet.* (Smithsonian Institution, No. 2, pp. 665–747.) Washington: Government Printing Office, 1895.

ROERICH, G. N. *The Blue Annals.* Calcutta: Royal Asiatic Society of Bengal, 1949 (Part I), 1953 (Part II). See also *Deb THer sNGon Po* under Tibetan sources.

——. *Le parler de l'Amdo.* Rome: Istituto Italiano per il Medio ed Estremo Oriente, 1958.

——. *Trails to Innermost Asia.* New Haven, Conn.: Yale University Press, 1931.

ROERICH, G. N., and TSE-TRUNG LOPSANG PHUNTSHOK. *Textbook of Collo-*

quial Tibetan. Calcutta: Government of West Bengal, Education Department, Education Bureau, 1957.

ROERICH, N. K. *Altai-Himalaya.* New York: Frederick A. Stokes, 1929.

SANDBERG, G. *The Exploration of Tibet.* Calcutta: Thacker, Spink & Co., 1904.

——. *Tibet and the Tibetans.* London: Society for Promoting Christian Knowledge, 1906.

SAPIR, EDWARD. *Culture, Language, and Personality.* Edited by DAVID G. MANDELBAUM. Berkeley, University of California Press, 1956.

——. *Language.* New York: Harcourt, Brace & World, 1957.

SCHAFER, E. *Fest der weissen Schleier.* Brunswick: Vieweg-Verlag, 1952.

——. *Unbekanntes Tibet.* Berlin: P. Parey, 1937.

SCHLAGINTWEIT, E. *Le bouddhisme au Tibet.* Translated by LIDE MILLOUE. Paris: E. Leroux, 1881.

SCHMID, TONI. *The Cotton-clad Mila: The Tibetan Poet-Saint's Life in Pictures.* Stockholm: Statens Etnografiska Museum, 1952.

SEN, CHANAKYA. *Tibet Disappears.* New York: Asia Publishing House, 1960.

SHELTON, F. B. *Shelton of Tibet.* New York: George H. Doran Co., 1923.

SHEN, TSUNG-LIEN, and LIU, SHEN-CHI. *Tibet and the Tibetans.* Stanford, Calif.: Stanford University Press, 1953.

SIMON, WALTER. *Tibetisch-chinesische Wortlgleichungen.* Berlin: Verlag von Walter de Gruyter & Co., 1930.

SIMPSON, W. W. *The Buddhist Praying Wheel.* London: Macmillan & Co., 1896.

SNELLGROVE, DAVID. *Buddhist Himalaya.* Oxford: Bruno Cassirer, 1957.

SPIRO, MELFORD E. "A Typology of Functional Analysis," *Explorations,* I (1953), 84–95.

STEIN, R. A. *La civilisation tibétaine.* Paris: Dunod, 1962.

——. *L'épopée tibétain de Gésar dans sa version lamalque de Ling.* Paris: Presses Universitaires de France, 1956.

——. *Recherches sur l'épopée et le barde au Tibet.* Paris: Presses Universitaires de France, 1959.

——. *Les tribus anciennes des marches sino-tibétaines.* Paris: Imprimerie Nationale de France, 1959.

STUBEL, HANS. *Mewu Fantzu, a Tibetan Tribe.* New Haven, Conn.: Yale University Press, 1958.

STURTEVANT, EDGAR HOWARD. *An Introduction to Linguistic Science.* New Haven, Conn.: Yale University Press, 1960.

TAFEL, ALBERT. *Meine Tibetreise.* 2 vols. Stuttgart: Union Deutsche Verlagsgesellschaft, 1914.

TEICHMAN, ERIC. *Travels of a Consular Officer in Eastern Tibet.* Cambridge: Cambridge University Press, 1922.

THOMAS, E. J. *The History of Buddhist Thought*. New York: A. A. Knopf, Inc., 1933.

———. *The Life of the Buddha*. London: Kasar, Paul, Trench, Trubner & Co., 1931.

THOMAS, F. W. *Ancient Folk-Literature from Northeastern Tibet*. Berlin: Akademie-Verlag, 1957.

———. *Tibetan Literary Texts and Documents concerning Chinese Turkestan*. 3 vols. London: Royal Asiatic Society, Oriental Translation Fund, 1935–55.

THOMAS, LOWELL, JR. *Out of This World*. New York: Greystone Press, 1950.

———. *The Silent War in Tibet*. Garden City, N.Y.: Doubleday & Co., 1959.

TOUSSAINT, GUSTAVE CHARLES. *Le dict de Padma*. (Translation of *Padma THang Yig*.) Paris: E. Leroux, 1933.

TUCCI, G. *Preliminary Report on Two Scientific Expeditions in Nepal*. Rome: Istituto Italiano per il Medio ed Estremo Oriente, 1956.

———. *The Theory and Practice of the Mandala*. Translated by ALAN HOUGHTON BRODRICK. London: Rider & Co., 1961.

———. *Tibetan Painted Scrolls*. 2 vols. Rome: La Libreria dello Stato, 1949.

———. *To Lhasa and Beyond*. Rome: Istituto Poligrafico dello Stato, 1956.

———. *The Tombs of the Tibetan Kings*. Rome: Istituto Italiano per il Medio ed Estremo Oriente, 1950.

TURNER, S. *An Account of an Embassy to the Court of the Teshoo Lama*. London: C. W. Nichol, 1800.

URAY, G. "The Four Horns of Tibet according to the Royal Annals," *Acta Orient Hungar*, X (1960), No. 1, 31–57.

WADDELL, L. AUSTINE. *The Buddhism of Tibet, or Lamaism*. London: W. H. Allen & Co., 1895.

———. *Lhasa and Its Mysteries: With a Record of the Expedition of 1903–1904*. London: J. Murray, 1905.

WARD, F. K. *Plant Hunter in Tibet*. London: J. Cape, 1934.

WESSELS, C. *Early Jesuit Travellers in Central Asia 1607–1721*. The Hague: M. Nijoff, 1924.

WHORF, BENJAMIN LEE. *Language, Thought, and Reality*. Edited by JOHN B. CARROLL, with a Foreword by STUART CHASE. Boston: Massachusetts Institute of Technology, 1959.

WINNINGTON, ALAN. *Tibet*. New York: International Publishers, Inc., 1957.

WYLIE, TURRELL V. *The Geography of Tibet according to the 'Dzam-ling rgyas-bshad*. Rome: Istituto Italiano per il Medio ed Estremo Oriente, 1963.

YOUNGHUSBAND, SIR FRANCIS. *India and Tibet*. London: J. Murray, 1910.

II. TIBETAN SOURCES (ordered according to Tibetan alphabet)

Kun dGaa rDo rJe. *Deb THer dMar Po.* (1346). Edited by C. Tharchin and the Namgyal Institute of Tibetology, 1961.

dGe SHes CHos Kyi Grags Pa. *brTSams Pai brDa Dag Ming TSHig gSal Ba bZHugs So: Tsang Wen Tz'u Tien.* (Tibetan–Tibetan–Chinese Dictionary.) Peking. Ming Tsu Ch'uh Pan Ch'u, 1957.

CHag Med Ri CHos.

Blo bZang rGya mTSHo (Fifth Dalai Lama). *Bod Kyi Deb THer dPyid Kyi rGyal Moi Glu dByangs.* Printed in 1643.

gZHon Nu dPal. *Deb THer sNGon Po.* Translated by G. N. Roerich as *Blue Annals* (see Sec. I of Bibliography). The *Yangs Pa Can* edition, written in 1476–78, was the Tibetan text consulted.

SHes Rab Od Zer. *Padma Yi THang Yig.* Discovery attributed to O rGyan Gling Pa in 1352; revised by SHes Rab Od Zer (1518–84); translated by Gustave Charles Toussaint as *Le dict de Padma* (Paris, 1933).

Sangs rGyas rGya mTSHo. *Vaidurya dKar Po.* Vol. II. 1669–87.

Sum Pa mKHan Po. *dPag bSam lJon bZang.* Part III, containing the *Reu Mig*—chronological tables of Tibetan history—was written in 1748. Edited by Lokesh Chandra. New Delhi: International Academy of Indian Culture, 1959.

bSod Nams rGyal mTSHan. *rGyal Rab gSal Bai Me Long.* 1508.

Gesar sGrung. Printed in Gling, Eastern Tibet; date and authorship not known. (Complete Tibetan text in R. A. Stein's *L'épopée tibétaine de Gésar,* which is an abridged translation.)

dGra lHa rTa THugs.

rJe bTSun Mi La Ras Pai rNam THar rGyas Par PHye Ba mGur aBum bZHugs So. Biography and one hundred thousand songs of the reverend Mi La Ras Pa; compiled in the thirteenth century. Multiple authorship.

rNam THar Rin CHen PHreng Ba. Biography of the 13th Dalai Lama.

dPal lDan Bla Ma Dam Pa eJe bTSun Blo bZang Ye SHes Kyi gSung Las gSang Bai rNam THar bZHugs So. (Being the Spoken Secret Biography of the Glorious Lama the Holy Reverend Blo bZang Ye SHes.) Date attribution, 1674. Translated by Robert B. Ekvall and T. J. Norbu. Unpublished.

The Tibetan Tripitaka. Edited by Daisetz T. Suzuki. Peking edition (Tokyo-Kyoto printing): Tibetan Tripitaka Research Institute, 1957.

INDEX

Adoration (*Mos*), 62
Afterlife, 33, 39; in Bon religion, 19, 30, 38; in Buddhism, 29–30
Agriculturalists, 3, 4, 153
Agriculture, 35, 75
AH, 115–16, 118, 210
AH KHu dKon mChog, 101
AH Mes rMa CHen, 243
All Buddhists; *see* Within-ones (*Nang Ba*)
Almsgiving, 77, 162–63
Alphabet, considered sacred, 105–6
Altitude, 7–8
Amdo, 95
Ananda, 227–28
Anatomy, 82–83
Ancestors: in Tibetan society, 85; worship of, 33, 34, 37, 38
Animals: treatment of, 72–77 *passim*; worship of, 25, 32–33, 39
Arrow divination (*mDaa Mo*), 263
Arts, 11–12, 40, 112; architecture, 188–89; painting, 189, 223; sculpture, 189, 223; *see also* Dance; Drama; Iconography
Astrology; *see* Numberer (*rTsis Pa*)
Atisha, 110
Attitudes of reverence (*Gus Pai rNam aGyur*), 209, 210–13; universal, 218–19; *see also* Salutation
Authority center (*sDe Pa gZHung*); *see* Tibet, government of
Avalokitesvara, 112, 116, 117

Bacot, J., 44, 64
Balti (people), 94
Barter; *see* Trade
Beads, uses of, 146, 147–48
Bell, on rosary, 118
Between state (*Bar Do*), 38
Blood, shedding of, 75–76
Bodhisattvas, 47, 73, 268
Body work (*Lus Las*), 102, 150, 201, 202
Bon, in compound words, 16
Bon Po, 17–18, 23, 26, 28, 265
Bon religion, 16–30, 50; afterlife in, 19; and Buddhism, 18, 21, 22, 23, 24, 29, 30, 58; circumambulation in, 227; dualism in, 19, 25; founder of, 19, 20, 21,

22; heaven in, 19; historical development of, 21; pantheon of, 25; ritual of, 22, 23
Book of the Dead, Tibetan, 38
Book divination (*dPe Mo*), 265
Books, 129; as status symbol, 125–26
Boot-strap divination (*lHam sGrog Mo*), 263
Bounty master (*Byin bDag*), 137
Bowl, begging, 162, 163, 171
Brag dKar monastery, 241–42
Broken-up offerings (*gTor Ma*), 28–29, 41, 163, 164–65, 174
Buddha, the, 63, 64, 65, 161, 162, 163, 227
Buddhism, Mahayana, 5, 14, 47, 110
Buddhism, Tantric, 5, 13, 26, 110, 228
Buddhism, Theravada (Hinayana), 47
Buddhism, Tibetan, 5, 13, 14, 15, 18, 22, 23, 26, 27–28, 29, 44, 47, 54, 110; and Bon religion, 18, 21, 22, 23, 24, 29, 30, 58; called *mani* by Chinese, 117; cosmology of, 77–78, 96; development of, 111; introduction of, into Tibet, 110–11, 113, 206, 207–9, 228, 255; scriptures and commentaries of, 42, 127, 128, 129, 216, 237; suppression of blood-feud and sacrifice by, 74–75
Burial practices, 73–74, 85
Buriats, 35
Bu sTon, 64, 65
Burnt-incense (*bDug sPos*) offering, 158, 167–68, 220
Butchering, 75–76
Butter-fire divination (*Mar Me Mo*), 265
Butter-fire (*Mar Me*) offering, 158, 168, 220
Butter images, 158, 175, 190

Cairns, 173–74
Caves, as objects of circumambulation, 241–42
Ceremony; *see* Ritual, religious
Chapels, as objects of circumambulation, 238–39
Charm box (*Gau*), 217; as object of circumambulation, 238; as object of prostration, 217

NOTE.—Tibetan words are alphabetized according to the initial phonetically effective consonant; for example, *aJam dPral* and *Jo KHang* are both listed under "J." Tibetan proper nouns are in italics and underscored, as in the text.